THE
MIXED COURTS OF EGYPT

PUBLISHED ON THE FUND ESTABLISHED IN MEMORY
OF GANSON GOODYEAR DEPEW

NUBAR PASHA
FOUNDER OF THE MIXED COURTS

THE MIXED COURTS
OF EGYPT

BY

JASPER YEATES BRINTON

JUSTICE OF THE COURT OF APPEALS
MIXED COURTS OF EGYPT

NEW HAVEN
YALE UNIVERSITY PRESS
LONDON · HUMPHREY MILFORD · OXFORD UNIVERSITY PRESS

TO MY WIFE

"I HAVE often taken occasion to remark that next to the Church, the Mixed Courts are the most successful international institution in history."

Farewell address of SIR MAURICE AMOS, *Judicial Adviser to the Egyptian Government, Alexandria, March 25, 1925* (*trans.*)

"THE Mixed Courts have opened more than one perspective in the law of nations. By the exercise of their legislative functions in the interests of many nationalities, they were the forerunners of the Assemblies of Geneva. By the collectivity of their judicial work they foretold the success of the World Court at the Hague."

Address of THEODORE HEYLIGERS, *Judge of the District Court, Alexandria, before the Academy of International Law. The Hague, 1928 (trans.)*

CONTENTS

XIV. The Administrative Machine 239

XV. The Bar and Legal Education 253

XVI. The Mixed Courts and Other Judicial Institutions   276

XVII. Lawmaking for Foreigners and the Legislative Functions of the Mixed Courts   299

XVIII. Reforming the Reform   330

Conclusion   349

Appendix   353

ILLUSTRATIONS

PREFACE

THE visitor to Egypt disembarking at the Port of
Alexandria and entering the city through the
winding streets of the native quarter will suddenly find opening before him the city's principal
square. His attention will at once be attracted to a large
and handsome structure which commands the scene.
Above its columned portals are inscribed in French,
Arabic, and Italian, the words *Palace of Justice;* and
above these words, in Arabic characters, the legend
"Justice is the Foundation of the State." Entering the
building, he will find himself beneath the lofty dome of a
great rotunda at whose farther end branching marble
stairways lead to the upper stories. Facing him on the
principal landing is a marble tablet, which explains that
in this hall was celebrated, on the twenty-sixth day of
February, 1926, the Fiftieth Anniversary of the Mixed
Courts of Egypt. To most visitors this phrase imports
little. Should he ask, therefore, to be told, in a word,
what is the position occupied by these courts in the
Egyptian world, the reply could be made as follows.
"The Mixed Courts of Egypt are the dominating judicial institution of the country. They correspond broadly
to the federal judicial system in the United States. All
litigation which involves a foreign party or a foreign
interest (except suits between persons of the same nationality—'family disputes' as they are regarded in
the international world of Egypt), comes before them.
As the activities of the one hundred and fifty thousand
foreigners in Egypt largely control the commercial life
of the fourteen million inhabitants, there is practically
no litigation of any large or general importance which

is not attracted to their jurisdiction. With a personnel of seventy judges (two-thirds of whom are foreigners selected from the principal countries of the world), and fourteen hundred employees, the courts have an annual output of some forty thousand written opinions. The annual budget, including the revenue from the offices for the recording of deeds, which are part of their system, shows a net credit balance of nearly $5,000,000. Their employees are scattered throughout the length of Egypt. No law can be passed affecting foreigners without the approval of the Mixed Courts. They are the rock upon which commercial credit is founded. They guarantee to foreigners as complete a protection of legal rights as exists in any country in the world. The Egyptian Government is subject to their jurisdiction and their judgments. On the one hand they are part of the judicial system of the Egyptian state; on the other, they are under the protection of a dozen foreign nations. Founded seven years before the British occupation of Egypt, their existence is altogether independent of the existing political *régime*. They have survived intact the many political changes which have rolled over the country since their creation. They have rendered justice alike in the name of Khedive, Sultan, and King. They have resisted every attempt to transform their essential features. Fifty years of labor finds their prestige undimmed. Changes in the political relations of the country, so far from seeking to restrict their authority, invariably contemplate an extension of their powers. There is every likelihood that the near future will witness a material enlargement of their usefulness.''

It is the purpose of this volume to sketch briefly the origins of the institution thus summarized, to tell the story of its founding, to follow its history throughout half a century, and then to give a description of the judicial machine actually at work, with summary of the principal problems connected with its probable future activities.

The field of inquiry is indeed a broad one. Apart from those phases which are of special interest to students of international organization, we have before us the spectacle of a fully equipped French judicial system working under high pressure. At every turn we encounter features which bring into sharp relief the characteristic differences between the world's two foremost judicial systems—the Latin and the Anglo-Saxon. Scarcely any topic of law or judicial administration has not been discussed (and often very elaborately) at some period of the history of the courts. The material is limitless. The difficulty is to know what features to select for review and comment. Nor is it less difficult to reconcile accuracy of detail with those somewhat broad outlines to which the treatment of each topic must be limited. The vocabulary, too, is a stumblingblock. French is the language of the courts but the literal rendering of French legal terms into English is almost always misleading and the constant use of French words is not adapted to a work of this character. An effort has thus been made to employ as far as possible the English term or phrase, however different in form, which is the nearest equivalent in meaning, and also to indicate the exact French term. This has the advantage of bringing before the reader something of the current daily vocabulary of the courts as expressed in those traditional legal phrases which are familiar throughout the world wherever the *Code Napoleon* has extended its sway.

In the matter of references and footnotes—this volume consists in considerable part of the assembling and arrangement of a mass of facts based on documentary sources. A large proportion of these sources are the or-

ganic laws and codes of the courts and the reported decisions. These sources are not likely to be readily accessible to the readers for whom this work is primarily
intended. On the other hand, those few who may have occasion to consult these sources will be readily able,
through the medium of available indexes, to locate the
particular text upon which the statement in the text is
based. To have inserted in the notes the particular reference for each statement of fact when based merely on
one of these authorities would have been a needless en-
cumbrance. The notes, therefore, have been confined to
self-explanatory quotations or observations which may
illustrate the text, or to indications of sources less
easily identified than those mentioned. For the rest, reference is made to the summary of source material to be
found in the Appendix.

One word of warning. In a work of such brief com-
pass it has been impossible to discuss many points of
detail where improvements in the system are needed.
The system has its shortcomings. These are largely the
defects of its own virtues—the result of that stability
and that rigidity—too great perhaps—which has enabled it to stand unshaken amid many storms. While
reforms have been plentiful, others are needed, and the
reader must not gain the impression that in the eyes of
the writer all is *couleur de rose*. But on the other hand,
were not the subject, in the writer's opinion, one fitted
to command the profound admiration of any student of
legal institutions, this work would not have been undertaken.

On the continent the Mixed Courts of Egypt are
widely known. Their place is on a par with the foremost European legal institutions. In America (and to a
lesser extent in England) they are scarcely more than a
name, so much so, indeed, that a Secretary of State, in

presenting a member of the courts to a gathering of his American judicial brethren, observed that, if most of his listeners had perhaps never heard of the Mixed Courts, he himself might have been in hardly better situation had it not been for a chance incident which brought them for the moment into official notice. Yet the United States played a large part in the founding of the institution and has been continuously represented on its benches. At times it has been one of its most effective champions. For this reason alone it is fitting that a record of the history of these courts and a description of their working should be presented to the American public by an American who has enjoyed the privilege of being a toiler at this unique judicial machine.

But there is another reason which may well entitle these courts to a share of public interest. The half century of quiet achievement recently completed has a meaning which is not without special value today. The Mixed Courts of Egypt stand, above all, for the essential solidarity of justice the world over. They are a witness to the power of the science of the Law to bind her servants into a common loyalty strong enough to triumph over all considerations of national partisanship and international jealousies. Their example may well give courage to all who are laboring to advance the cause of justice among nations.

J. Y. B.

Alexandria, Egypt,
    March 4, 1930.

ADDENDUM

DURING the recent treaty negotiations between England and Egypt which broke down (May, 1930) over the question of the Sudan, the representatives of the two nations accepted, practically unchanged, all of the various proposals of the 1929 negotiations relating to the Capitulations and the Mixed Courts, and which have been referred to at various points throughout this work. See Judicial Advisers p. 56; Legislative Reforms p. 328; Extension of Jurisdiction of Mixed Courts, etc., p. 341 and pp. 347–348.

CHAPTER I

ORIGIN OF THE MIXED COURTS

A FEW years ago, on the site of the ancient Egyptian city of Philadelphia, there was discovered a papyrus which bore on its back the copy of a letter addressed by the Roman Emperor Claudius to his people of Alexandria. The letter deals with many topics, —birthday honors, the erection of golden statues, the request of the Alexandrians for a senate,—but its final paragraph is reserved for an expression of imperial indignation over the feuds "or rather," says the Emperor, "if the truth must be told, the war" between the Alexandrians and the Jews. In turn the Emperor addresses himself to each of the contending factions, and to the Alexandrians gives this stern but fatherly admonition. "Wherefore I conjure you yet once again that you show yourselves forbearing and kindly towards the Jews and permit them to observe their customs as in the time of the Divine Augustus, which customs I also, after hearing both sides, have solemnly confirmed."

In such documents as these, and they are legion, we see reflected the remoter origins of that remarkable *régime* of special privileges for foreigners which came to extend itself throughout the entire Ottoman Empire, and whose manifold abuses eventually led in Egypt to the founding of the Mixed Courts.

The story of this *régime* of the Capitulations is one of the most fascinating chapters in the history of the Near East. It leads back to the very dawn of the Christian era and introduces some of the most stirring characters and events which history has to record. The story is long and complicated, often baffling in its details, and replete with problems on which scholars have sharply differed. Even to sketch its outlines would fall outside the scope of the present volume which is concerned rather with a living institution,—the Mixed Courts of Egypt— formed by treaty agreement in 1875, and standing upon a footing quite independent of the traditional capitulatory *régime* which, in large part, it replaced. But some idea of the origin of the early capitulatory *régime* is essential to an understanding of the place occupied by the Mixed Courts today. Certain portions of the earlier system were not affected by the Reform of 1875. Some of the historic capitulatory privileges still exist and are under the protection of the Mixed Courts themselves, who are on occasion called upon to turn to the pages of history to interpret these ancient but still living rights.

The special privileges enjoyed by foreigners in the Ottoman Empire are commonly taken as having their origin in the formal concessions or Capitulations—so called from the many separate headings or *capitula* of the lengthy and pompous documents which contained them—granted to western nations by the Ottoman rulers after the capture of Constantinople in 1453. Usage, however, had long before this accepted many of these privileges, and even under the Greek Empire the Turks themselves in Constantinople had enjoyed the right to the administration of their Moslem law.

In Egypt, too, an independent capitulatory *régime* had long established itself. Rameses the Great first opened the door of Egypt to strangers. It has never since been closed.[1] On the invitation of this enlightened

---

[1] Compare the public declaration of the present Egyptian Prime Minister, Nahas Pasha: ''We want strangers to feel that they are more free and at home in our country than they are in their own.'' *Journal of Mixed Courts*, June 11–12, 1928.

monarch a foreign merchant colony established itself in the land. They were accorded large immunities. In the times of the Ptolemies the Jews enjoyed a large measure of self-government, and the Egyptians themselves, under this foreign rule, were allowed to bring their civil disputes before native judges, thus giving rise to a double system of law and legal administration: Egyptian and Greek.[2] But these were matters of custom and not of treaty. Formal definition of immunities came with the advent of the Italian trader. As early as 1154 we have record of a commercial treaty between Egypt and Pisa which embodies a grant of special privileges to Pisa merchants, which closely foreshadow the later Capitulations. Soon after, in 1171, Saladin the Great became master of Egypt. In spite of the unfriendly part which the Pisans had played in encouraging the project of the rival king of Jerusalem, the magnanimous conqueror, some fifteen years before he retook Jerusalem from the Crusaders, extended the privileges of the Pisans in a document which is entitled to hold first place among Egyptian Capitulations. It opens thus: "In the name of God, the Merciful and Compassionate. This is a copy of the convention which the King of Babylon,[3] Saladin, made with the Commonwealth of Pisa through the instrumentality of Aldebrand sent to him by the Consuls as Ambassador. . . ."

The document is an interesting one. It is for the most part in the form of a record of a series of prayers and complaints by the Pisans, followed by orders of redress by the Egyptian ruler. On his part it accords liberal privileges and protection to the merchants of Pisa, specifying *inter alia* the duties to which their merchan-

[2] See Bevan, *A History of Egypt under the Ptolemaic Dynasty* (London, 1927), pp. 113, 159.

[3] The original name of Cairo, so called from the Roman fortress near the Old City.

dise shall be subject and according a large measure of religious and civil self-government: "As to the church that belonged to them and that we gave them, they shall have it as they had it before:—they may observe their law even as the precepts of God and their laws ordain."

In matters of litigation, which concerns us more particularly, their privileges were even larger. "I have also given orders to my Bajuli, both in the past and for the future that they cannot occupy themselves with any litigation or matter between the merchants without their consent, nor institute actions against the merchants so as to delay them; it being my firm will that they are to be treated with the greatest justice, now and hereafter." The treaty, however, while in form a grant of privilege, was not without its "consideration." In return the Pisans bound themselves "to faithfully and diligently keep in safety all our Kingdom" and to give no aid or comfort to its enemies. In witness whereof the agreements were drawn up and read before the Ambassador "who guaranteed them by a thorough oath before the archbishop and priest—Mark, Patriarch of Alexandria and of Babylon and of Nubia and of Saba, and Michel, Bishop of Barbacana and Homodeus, Priest and Prior of Cairo."

In 1290 we have the record of a treaty with Genoa in which appears the first expression of a principle whose existence was responsible for the founding of the Mixed Courts. "If a Sarrazin (Egyptian)," the document reads, "or a Christian of a foreign state, has a litigation with a Genoese, the consul shall decide the case." This is indeed nothing else than a consecration of the famous maxim, destined to play such a capital rôle in later Egyptian legal history: "The plaintiff must seek his remedy in the defendant's court:" *Actor sequitur forum rei.* But other and later Capitulations are silent on this point, or contain provisions to the contrary, and we shall see that only in comparatively recent times was the revival of this principle brought about. Thus, in 1488, a Capitulation was granted to the Florentines by Kâït Bey, the ruler whose beautiful tomb is by many considered the finest flower of Arabic art in Cairo. While confirming the right of the consul to judge in matters arising between Florentines, this Capitulation provided that Mohammedans should not institute actions against Florentines except in the special court of the President of the Custom House; and that if the action should not be satisfactorily terminated there, "resort should be had to the Sublime Porte of the Sultan, that justice may be rendered to whom it may be due."

In 1517 the Turkish Sultan Selim I stormed Cairo; and Egypt became a Turkish Pashalic. The new ruler immediately confirmed the Capitulations which the French and Venetians had enjoyed under the Mamelukes, and his successor, Soliman II, in 1528 renewed this confirmation in a Capitulation addressed to the French and Catalians. This is the last Capitulation which was applied solely to Egypt. Thereafter Egypt, as part of the Ottoman Empire, fell within the scope of the concessions accorded to foreign Powers by the rulers of Constantinople, and we enter the domain of the Ottoman Capitulations.

The most important of the early Turkish Capitulations was that granted to Francis I of France in 1535. This was the prototype of the long series of capitulatory agreements entered into with the principal Powers of Europe and with the United States, extending down to the middle of the last century.

The question of the exact extent to which, as a result of these engagements, foreigners were exempt from the jurisdiction of the Turkish courts, gave rise to much controversy, and its answer varied largely at different periods and as regards different Powers.

In spite of the outward form of "gracious concession" in which many of these Capitulations were clothed,[4] it is reasonably clear that the earliest concessions represented nothing more or less than a good business transaction in the mutual interest of the parties involved, in other words, were simply a means of securing to Turkey the trade and other benefits resulting from the presence in the country of large bodies of industrious and intelligent people, in exchange for a protection and a right of self-government which had the advantage of relieving the Turkish state from complicated administrative burdens. Certainly the Capitulations were very far from being privileges wrung from unwilling eastern religious rulers. Founded on mutual interest they were above everything else the expression of a practical working agreement dominated by a factor of controlling importance, namely, the essentially religious conception of the early idea of sovereignty as distinguished from the later and western conception of sovereignty as coexistent with territorial control. The law of the Koran was a law for the faithful alone. It was but natural to accord to those of alien religious faiths, whether subjects of the Sultan or foreigners, the privilege—conceived also as to the obligation—of being judged by their own laws and customs.

The principal privileges guaranteed by the Capitula-

[4] Compare, for instance, the preamble of the British Capitulations of 1675, Hertslet, II, 346 ff., also *100 British and Foreign State Papers*, 575: "The Sultan Mohammed. May He Live Forever. Let everything be performed according to these Capitulations. Contrary to them let nothing be done. *The Command* given under the sublime and lofty Signet (which imparts sublimity to every place) and the Imperial and Noble Cypher, whose glory is renowned throughout all the world, given by the Emperor and Conqueror of the Earth, with the assistance of the Omnipotent and by the special grace of God, Is This:—" There followed seventy-five numbered articles or *capitula*.

tions were the exemption of foreigners from arbitrary taxation, their freedom from searches in their homes without the consent or presence of their consuls, and, that which more particularly concerns our present inquiry, their right to enjoy very large immunities from the jurisdiction of the Turkish law courts. These latter immunities may be summarized as follows: To the consuls was reserved jurisdiction over all disputes between foreigners of the same or different nationality. Consuls also exercised jurisdiction over criminal offenses, not involving natives, as well as in all questions of personal status, involving marriage and divorce, testamentary succession, guardian and ward and kindred questions. On the other hand civil and commercial litigation between foreigners and natives was, in the later stages of the system, tried either before special commercial tribunals composed of three Turkish judges and two foreigners, or before the ordinary Turkish courts, but always in the presence of a consular dragoman, who exercised a very material control over the proceedings.

Such, substantially, was the system as it existed in Turkey at the beginning of the War. It was a system whose definition depended essentially on the attitude— on the power to resist, or to enforce—of the various parties concerned. Jealous of foreign influence, the Turk resisted and, in the end, at a heavy price, gained his point. The Capitulations disappeared. Abolished in fact at the opening of the World War, the suppression of the Capitulations was finally recognized by the Powers in the Treaty of Lausanne.[5]

---

[5] July 24, 1923. Art. 28. *A.J.I.L.*, Vol. XVIII, January, 1924. Off. Docs., p. 12. British Treaty Series, No. 16, 1923. The unratified treaty with the United States, of August 6, 1923, also declares the Capitulations "completely abolished." (See for text, Presidential Message Executive Z, Sixty-eighth Congress, first session.)

The rulers of Egypt, however, pursued a different policy. The creator of modern Egypt, the Albanian adventurer Mohammed Ali, born in the same year as Napoleon and by 1807 master of Egypt by right of conquest, had other views as to the value of European civilization. He appreciated in a manner other than the Turk the necessity of European coöperation in the completion of his many imposing projects for the internal development of his country. He encouraged Europeans to come as travelers to Egypt, invited French savants to join his sons in their expedition to the Sudan, and made it his settled policy to attract European enterprise by every means in his power. This meant according strangers the amplest measure of protection. But protection spelled privilege, and the appetite for privilege grew with what it fed on. Prompted largely by reasons of practical necessity and convenience, little by little the consuls assumed jurisdiction in all cases, civil or criminal, which involved their nationals. It was the liberal, the overliberal, application of the Latin maxim to which reference has been made, that the suitor must follow his opponent into the latter's court. It was an expansion of consular jurisdiction unsupported in the Capitulations and based purely on usage. Usage, however, is the strongest of all sanctions which the law may acquire in Mohammedan countries, and usage itself soon became established beyond all danger of attack. But this development was accompanied by another consequence of far-reaching character. The consul's jurisdiction was necessarily confined to the enforcement of the laws of his own country, except in so far as those laws expressly called for the application, in special cases, of the foreign law. Therefore, foreigners were subject only to their own laws, as such laws were interpreted by their own consuls. Thus, the laws of the country where they resided, being unenforceable in any forum against them, became for them practically non-existent, and the consequence was the establishment of a complete immunity from the jurisdiction of local courts and the application of local laws.[6]

The evils which resulted from a system of some fifteen sovereign consular jurisdictions, functioning at the same time, can be readily imagined. The administration of justice in Egypt fell into what was aptly termed a state of judicial chaos. When parties contracted, they were ignorant of the jurisdiction before which they might be obliged to plead. Whenever a possibility of litigation arose each party endeavored to get his hands on whatever property there might be involved, so as to provoke the suit before his own consul. Suit had to be brought in as many different forums as there were defendants. A foreigner of different nationality could not be brought into the principal cause. Appeals from consular decisions were generally not heard in Egypt. The situation was intolerable.

Before the founding of the Mixed Courts efforts at relief had been undertaken at Constantinople. As early as 1820 there had been organized, by virtue of a verbal diplomatic agreement entered into between the representatives of France, England, Austria, and Russia, a system of mixed commissions for the trial of cases involving foreigners of different nationalities. These were composed of three members, two chosen by the legation

[6] Cf. the following extract from an opinion of the Court of Appeals of the Mixed Courts rendered in 1890: "In Turkey, contrary to the practice which long usage has sanctioned in Egypt, the maxim 'actor sequitur forum rei' has no application, that is, in the sense that Ottoman subjects must sue foreigners before their several consulates. On the contrary, in their litigation with Ottomans, foreign subjects, whether plaintiffs or defendants fall within the jurisdiction of the Courts of the Empire, with the single guarantee of the presence of the dragoman of their consulate" (trans.) (Bulletin, II, 159).

of the defendant and the third by that of the plaintiff. They continued to function in Turkey until 1864, when they came to an end as a result of a decision of the French Court of Appeals, sitting at Aix, holding that they were based on no legal authority, and that submission to their jurisdiction was therefore purely voluntary. Meanwhile, as a result of reforms undertaken in Turkey in 1839, the jurisdiction which had long been reserved under the Capitulations to the Imperial Turkish Divan, in cases between foreigners and Turks, was conferred upon a sort of mixed commercial court composed of Turkish and foreign merchants freely chosen by the parties. The two systems continued to exist contemporaneously and were theoretically at least applicable to Egypt. In 1847–48 the latter system was reorganized under a decree, elaborated with the coöperation of the foreign ministers, which set in motion a veritable Turkish mixed court composed of fourteen merchants, half of them Turks and half of them foreigners, sitting under the presidency of the Turkish Minister of Commerce or his representative. In 1856, by virtue of the celebrated reform known under the name of the charter in which it was embodied—the Hatti Humayoun, these courts were reorganized and an attempt was made to extend them to Egypt, but without much success. As the American consul-general remarks, the Egyptian Pasha, Said, "shrugged his shoulders" and submitted the proposal to the foreign consuls-general. They in turn refused to countenance the innovation and without their support the plan fell through. "Imagine," writes the consul, in a dispatch to his government under date of May 1, 1856,[7] "a Tribunal composed of several Mos-

[7] *The Khedives of Egypt*, by Edwin de Leon (London, 1877), p. 300. The same writer attributes the authorship of this early project to Nubar Pasha, the founder of the Mixed Courts. Writing in 1877 he observes:

lems, two Christian Armenians, two Latin and two
Greek Christians (every native Christian sect here bitterly hating the other) and add two Jewish rabbis, and
you would have a most 'striking' illustration of 'the
happy family' in the museums, composed of the most
uncongenial animals possibly to be found.''

As history shows, however, the fears of the consul
and his colleagues were not justified.

In 1860 a new effort was made to introduce a revised
system of mixed courts based on that of Constantinople, for handling claims against the Government and
the members of the royal family. But this plan again
aroused diplomatic opposition. The American consul-
general officially reported his objections to the Secretary of State: The High Court of Appeal was to be Constantinople ''where the laws, usages, customs, currency
and language are as widely dissimilar from those of
Egypt, as those of England would be from those of Austria, and where neither judge, jury nor witnesses would
be accessible''; the law was to be that of the Code Napoleon; ''When the Mediterranean shall really have become a 'French lake' either by conquest or treaty, it
will be time to adopt the French code as the supreme
law of the Levant; but until then we prefer the common
law''; the judges were to be selected from five great
Powers only, ''giving those 'five' effectively a protectorate over Egypt, and all foreigners therein''; these
judges were to be offered a ''bribe'' to protract, instead
of to hasten judgment,—as each judge was to receive
five pounds for every sitting; large advance deposits

''More than twenty years ago, in the reign of Said, he (Nubar) sought
to persuade the Consuls General to divest themselves of their judicial
powers, by consenting to some such scheme. But neither the country nor the
time was ripe for it; and year after year, with dogged patience and inexhaustible resource, under different administrations, he persevered until
his efforts were crowned with success.''

too were required, thus calculated to make the court "the resort of rich speculators." Finally, urged the consul-general, "the creation of such tribunal is utterly uncalled for. The Egyptian Government exercises authority over the princes who are Egyptian subjects, as well as over the rest of the natives; and arbitration, the simplest and most honest mode of settling controversies, is always open to them, should their Government feel any delicacy on their behalf; while as relates to the Egyptian Government itself, I must bear testimony, after several years experience, to its good faith in the fulfillment of all *bona fide* contracts or obligations."[8]

According to the author of this report "the scheme was dropped," but it appears to have been revived in a form which eliminated part of the objections above recorded, for in 1861 there was promulgated an order of the president of the Egyptian cabinet for the reorganization of the Mixed Courts of Alexandria and Cairo. Under the new system the judges were elected annually by an assembly of the foreign "notables," or leading citizens, whose membership was designated by the consulates. Each trial court was composed of five members, two foreigners and two natives, under the presidency of an Egyptian. Two courts of appeal of nine members each were established in Cairo and Alexandria, being composed of the existing and local court with the addition of four lay judges or "assessors." Appeals from the Cairo court were heard by the Alexandria court and *vice versa*. The law followed was the customs of the country, the Ottoman Code of Commerce, and a specially prepared short code of procedure. When these were found to be inadequate, resort was had to

8 The consulate of Sweden and Norway presented also an elaborate criticism of the project, but declared itself as being in principle favorably disposed. See *Livre d'Or*, p. 421.

the French Civil Code as far as it could be applied to commercial cases.

The courts, thus organized, modified, in a measure, the existing system under which full jurisdiction had been assumed by consuls in all matters touching foreigners. The innovation gave little satisfaction. These courts were effective only in cases where the Egyptian party litigant was defendant. The Egyptian element was found to preponderate; the "judges" were for the most part without legal qualifications,[9] the courts lacked every attribute necessary to impose authority where the privilege of the consul in matters of jurisdiction still reigned supreme whenever an attempt was made to exercise it. The situation called for sterner and larger measures of relief, and it was left for "the one great statesman whom Egypt has produced since the days of Joseph," Nubar Pasha, the Armenian Foreign Minister of the Khedive Ismail, to propose the remedy and, what was hardly less than a miracle, to carry it into execution.

The opening gun in Nubar Pasha's campaign was an elaborate report presented to his sovereign in 1867. It became the basis of the long negotiations which followed. This report is a diplomatic masterpiece, sound in reasoning, eloquent in expression, scathing in its denunciation of existing evils, unanswerable in its appeal to fundamental principles, prophetic in its foresight of the dangers to be avoided, and adroit to the highest degree in its appeal to the self-interest of those upon

9 Compare the observation of a contemporaneous Italian writer, D. Gatteschi, that "an arsenal guard was appointed as President, then an inspector of railways, and lastly an admiral." See Scott, p. 203. See also *Bulletin de l'Institute Egyptien*, No. 9 (1866), p. 85. See also the criticisms contained in the report of the French Commission of 1867, Borelli Bey, p. xxxviii. For the best review of these early courts see report of an address by M. F. Gilly before the Egyptian Institute in 1864, published in the *Bulletin* cited above.

whose consent the success of the new program would entirely depend.

"The jurisdiction which determines the relations between Europeans and the Government of Egypt and the inhabitants of the country," he complains, "is no longer based on the Capitulations. *The Capitulations exist only in name.* They have been replaced by an arbitrary law of custom, varying with the character of each new diplomatic chief,—a law based upon precedents frequently abusive, which has been permitted to take root in Egypt through force of circumstances and constant pressure and a desire to make easy the lot of the foreigner. It leaves the Government powerless in its relation to such foreigners and the people without any security that even-handed justice will be done. Such a state of affairs violates the Capitulations in both letter and spirit; it impedes the country in the development of its resources; it prevents it from putting its true riches at the service of European enterprise and capital; it destroys its progress and brings moral and material ruin in its train."

No feature of the proposals advanced by Nubar was more skilful than that by which he contrived always to emphasize the desire of the Khedive to accord the fullest measure of guaranty for the protection of the rights of foreigners. While adroitly suppressing a large portion of the old system of Capitulations, he managed always to emphasize the fact that Egypt was giving in exchange something of far greater value. "The phrase which Your Highness has pronounced," Nubar adroitly writes to his master, "is enough for my purpose. 'Let us give guarantees that are even superfluous.'"

With this insinuating introduction to his program, Nubar outlines with admirable skill a plan for the establishment of a system of Mixed Courts which should exercise commercial and civil jurisdiction in all cases arising between foreigners and natives, as well as a general criminal jurisdiction in all cases involving foreigners alone. On the independence of the judiciary he laid greatest emphasis. To his success in securing it is due more than anything else the success of the institution of which he is the founder. Above all, declares he, justice must be independent of the Government. The separation of powers is imperative. "The principle is the complete separation of justice from the administration. Justice must emanate from the Government. It must not depend upon it. It should no more depend upon the Government than upon the consulates." The guaranty of this independence Nubar found in the participation of the foreign judge,—the extension, as he expressed it, into the administration of justice of a principle which had been in fact recognized by Egypt in her army and railway, her engineering, and many other services,—namely, the introduction of a foreign element which would serve to mold and educate the native. "That which has been done in the material order must be done in the moral order."

Guided by these principles Nubar found the germ of his new proposal in the scheme of the Mixed Courts of Commerce of Constantinople which, as we have seen, had been extended with such poor results to Egypt.[10] "The Tribunal of Commerce sitting at Alexandria," he

[10] It may be remarked that the new Mixed Courts, when finally organized in Egypt resembled their Turkish prototypes principally in name. As the present author observed in 1924, "In all that concerns jurisprudence, jurisdiction, authority and in general the essential tests of a real judicial system, the differences were unfortunately more marked than the resemblances." "Notes on Turkish Reform." Sixty-eighth Congress, second session, *Senate Committee Print*, p. 35. See also, same author's "Notes on Law Reforms in Turkey," 1925. Sixty-ninth Congress, first session, *Senate Committee Print*, p. 2; also his article on "Turkey's New System of Laws and Courts," *Current History*, January, 1927.

observes, "is not, properly speaking, a Tribunal. It differs from that of Constantinople. It is rather a jury. In point of fact it has already been abandoned. But the basis of the institution is good and deserves to be retained." Taking this principle as a basis, he proposed to establish a complete new system of Mixed Courts whose membership should be evenly divided between Europeans and Egyptians. A Court of Appeals should be established at Alexandria, to be composed of three natives and three foreigners. As to the law to be applied in these new courts, Nubar proposed the adoption of the French Commercial Code, which had theretofore been generally applied in Egypt. For civil affairs he proposed the adoption of a special code to be framed by a committee of foreign jurists, charged with the duty of reconciling the provisions of the Napoleonic Code with the existing Egyptian law. To the same commission should be committed the duty of revision of the criminal law.

The designation of the new institution, the "Mixed Courts," was taken ready-made from history. The term conveys a somewhat uncertain meaning to the English reader. In what sense "Mixed"? Why not "International"?

When, under the provisions of the French Capitulations of 1740, the earlier capitulatory practices were crystallized through withdrawing from the Turkish courts cases involving foreigners and committing them to the special jurisdiction and protection of the Imperial Turkish Divan, there was, of course, no question of establishing an international tribunal. Nor would it have occurred to the jurists or diplomats of those days to characterize as international the litigation thus specially provided for. Any such suggestion would have been in contradiction to historical facts. The Ottoman

Porte was not called upon to establish within its domains an "international court," and the litigation thus provided for was not between nations; it was in no sense "international." But the adoption of a convenient French phrase to describe it was the natural result of its existence; and the words *mixte* and *procès mixtes* gradually came into use, as relating primarily to the mixture of nationality represented in the controversy. After the reforms of 1839, the tribunal itself assumed a "mixed" character through the formation of a "mixed" commission of merchants for the solution of "mixed" litigation. Thus the word took on a double significance. But here again there was no thought of an international institution. Finally the jurisdiction over such cases passed to purely national commercial courts, with certain foreign elements added to the bench—courts which, so far as such litigation is concerned, were said to function "as mixed courts," although the decrees and circulars defining such jurisdiction do not commonly employ such a term in their text.[11]

The use of the phrase thus adopted in Turkey was extended naturally throughout Egypt. Long before the Mixed Courts of today were established this term was an accepted one—although of none too good a reputation. It was but natural that it should have been seized upon by Nubar Pasha, as it expressed an idea which undoubtedly was fundamental to his conception of the institution he was seeking to found, namely, of a *national* institution, drawing the source and fountain of its authority from the sovereignty of the state, even though the exercise of this sovereignty required an international consent to make it effective.

In this sense then the designation "Mixed Courts"

[11] See, for instance, Circular of May, 1872, published in Young, I, 246, and in Aristarchi Bey, II, 427.

must be understood, as contrasted with those "international" courts whose source of authority is, properly speaking, not a national but a group sovereignty. The Mixed Courts are national courts, functioning under conditions fixed by international agreements for the trial not of international but of "mixed" causes.[12] They exist elsewhere, in a variety of forms, both as relates to their jurisdiction, their composition, and the measure of international control, direct or indirect, to which they may be subject. In some instances their "mixed" composition is a measure of guarantee voluntarily adopted by the sovereign, without any special international agreement.[13] But in every case they represent the na-

[12] This question of the proper qualification of the Mixed Courts has given rise to many different answers at various periods in their history. Compare, for instance, the observation of the American representative in the Commission of 1869, "The Court will always be an Egyptian Court," with the observation of his successor on the Commission of 1880 who saw in the Mixed Courts, "an international rather than an Egyptian institution." Compare, also, the observation of Mr. Brunyate in his note to Lord Cromer's report for 1904: "The Tribunals, though established with the concurrence of the Powers, were intended to be Egyptian Tribunals, and it is probable that they would never have come to be regarded as International Tribunals in the sense now current, if their establishment had not almost exactly synchronized with the utter collapse of autonomous Egyptian Government," and the observation of a prior judicial adviser (Sir Malcolm McIlwraith): "Though technically and officially a purely Egyptian forum, it is in reality an international judicature of a highly distinguished character." Lecture on "Legal War Work in Egypt" before Grotius Society, reported in *Egyptian Gazette,* December 6, 8, and 9, 1918. Again, Lord Milner, "They might nominally be the Courts of the Khedive, who appointed their foreign members, although on the proposal of the Powers. But they were in reality foreign courts deriving their authority from outside, and they have not hesitated to exercise that authority against the Native government whenever they thought it right to do so." *England in Egypt,* Chap. IV. See also observations of Henri Lamba, *De l'Evolution de la Condition Juridique des Européens en Egypte* (Paris, 1896), p. 96.

[13] See, for instance, the mixed courts of New Hebrides (of which the Count d'Andino, of the Court of Appeals, Alexandria, was formerly a member); the mixed courts created under the mandates for Irak, Syria and the Liban, and Palestine; the mixed courts in French Indo-China, Morocco, and Siam (and which latter are occasionally but erroneously referred to as "international" courts, e.g., Eldon R. James, "Juris-

tional sovereignty. They are not in the proper sense "international courts" and no such characterization would have been accepted by Nubar nor insisted upon by the Powers with whom he was negotiating.

Such, then, in brief outline, was the solution by which Nubar Pasha proposed to rid Egypt of the most grievous plagues which had ever affected her body politic. In the next chapter we will follow the progress of the campaign which followed. Judged alike by the sustained generalship with which it was conducted, by the heavy odds to which it was opposed, by the success which finally crowned it, and by the witness which fifty years of the enjoyment of its fruits bears to the prophetic wisdom of its leader, Nubar's struggle is entitled to be ranked among the foremost diplomatic achievements of modern history.

diction over Foreigners in Siam," *A.J.I.L.*, October, 1922, p. 585; also Francis B. Sayre, "The Passing of Extraterritoriality in Siam," *A.J.I.L.*, January, 1928, p. 70. "This so-called 'Siamese International Court' was not in fact international at all," p. 76). With these it is interesting to compare the so-called "International Mixed Court at Shanghai" (see title used by Professor Hudson, *A.J.I.L.*, July, 1927, p. 451) and "The International Mixed Court of Tangier" (same author, *A.J.I.L.*, August, 1927, p. 231). The latter is expressly defined in the instrument creating it as "an international jurisdiction," designed to "replace the existing consular jurisdictions" (*op. cit.*, p. 233. See also Supp., *A.J.I.L.*, October, 1929, p. 273). As such, both it and the Chinese mixed courts, in the light of the distinction presented above, may properly be considered in the category of "international" rather than of "mixed."

CHAPTER II

THE DIPLOMATIC BATTLE

THE report of Nubar Pasha, which has been sketched in the preceding chapter, was transmitted to the Powers and immediately encountered potent opposition on the part of France, whose dominating influence in Egypt was emphasized at the moment by the large French interests involved in the construction of the Suez Canal. The rights of French citizens in Egypt were too well safeguarded by the network of the Capitulations to be lightly risked in a new experiment. But on the other hand, the traditional friendship between France and Egypt demanded conciliatory measures. So the proposals were referred by the French Government to a commission which included several of her most distinguished citizens, and in due season an elaborate report appeared, minimizing the shortcomings of the existing *régime* in Egypt, criticizing most of the features of the proposed solution, and suggesting a program of halfway measures. Vigorously reaffirming the necessity of maintaining intact the jurisdiction of the Consular Courts in controversies between citizens of the same nationality, or of different foreign nationalities, the report conceded a transfer of very limited jurisdiction to the proposed courts in cases where the defendant was an Egyptian, as well as in a few other special cases. These courts, the report insisted, must contain always a majority of European judges, to be named by the Khedive upon the nomination of the several foreign Governments.

In an effort to bring about a compromise, Nubar

conceded the European majority, but held firm as to the right of the Egyptian Government to control the selection of judges. As to the other differences no compromise seemed possible.

The situation would have discouraged a less valiant spirit. For Nubar it was an invitation to display his remarkable diplomatic resourcefulness. His nimble mind at once perceived in the approaching ceremonies of the opening of the Suez Canal an occasion that would readily lend itself to a furtherance of his project through the medium of an international commission to be contemporaneously convened to discuss judicial reform.

The story of the negotiations which led to the assembling of this commission forms one of the most picturesque chapters in the history of the Mixed Courts. It was a period of engrossing diplomatic interest, replete with historic sidelights and human touches, enlivened by the opening of the Suez Canal, and interrupted by the Franco-Prussian War. In turn the stage moves from Cairo to Constantinople, from Constantinople to Paris, from Paris to London, and so through the capitals of Europe.[1]

In Paris lay the first stumblingblock. It was here that Nubar encountered the most obstinate objections. The French Foreign Office had little confidence in the practical working of the new scheme.

[1] This story has long lain hidden in the correspondence exchanged between the Khedive Ismail and his Prime Minister, much of which is preserved in the royal archives at Cairo. Permission to examine these archives was graciously accorded by the present King, the son of the Khedive Ismail, on the occasion of the recent Semi-Centennial of the Mixed Courts. This phase of the history of the courts formed the subject of the admirable address delivered on that occasion by Procureur-General of the Mixed Courts, Baron Firmin Van den Bosch (*Livre d'Or*, p. 481), and which has been freely consulted in the preparation of this chapter.

The Viceroy's plan [said the Marquis de Moustier, the French Minister], resembles a magnificent clock. All the world admires it, but when it is necessary to wind it up they will wind it backwards and in the place of the clock which you already have,—a poor one it is true, but one which still keeps time after a fashion,—you will have a handsome case with a broken spring (*trans.*).

The stubbornness of the French resistance moved the Khedive to assume the aggressive and to consider forcing the hands of the Powers by actually establishing a Mixed Court and engaging for its magistracy competent judges from some of the smaller Powers, as, for instance, Belgium, Switzerland, and other European countries. He mentioned his plan to Nubar, assuring him that if such a step were taken most of the foreign Powers would not only withhold their objections but would soon seek of their own accord to bring their judicial affairs before the new tribunal. But the scheme was a last resort. The Khedive realized the full importance of convoking a commission, if it were by any means possible. Leaving the problem of French opposition to later development, Nubar was ordered to make the circuit of the foreign courts, beginning with London. There he lobbied in the corridors of Parliament, endeavoring to have the question brought before the House of Commons. Failing to find the member on whom he counted for aid, he seeks him out at the race course. Later he visits Manchester, where he hopes to find support, the question of the new courts being necessarily closely related to the security of the cotton trade. With great difficulty he gets together a group of commercial and political personages committed to support his appeal to parliament. "Never," writes he to his royal master, "did a hen work as hard to gather together her little chickens as I have labored to bring the ideas of these

gentlemen into harmony with mine." At the same
time he conducts a press campaign. The *Times,* the
Standard, and the *Morning Post* publish articles from
his pen. He interviews Lord Stanley, the British Foreign Minister, and his efforts are successful. England
agrees to participate in an international commission
which should accept, as a *minimum,* the French proposal. Nubar returns to Paris and writes home in great
enthusiasm. To his political adversaries who criticize
the methods of his campaign he replies that it has cost
him the utmost labor and persuasion, "but not a brass
farthing." At this juncture he receives word from the
Khedive to proceed immediately to Berlin. An exchange
of views in Egypt between the German consul-general
and the Egyptian ruler has led the latter to conclude
that a visit to Bismarck is imperative and will probably
have a successful issue. With a letter of introduction
from the Khedive in his pocket Nubar seeks out the Iron
Chancellor and supports his oral persuasions with an
admirable written argument. The next day he is informed that the German Government is prepared to
participate in the deliberations of the proposed commission. In the fashion of the times, and as an interesting
token of the understanding reached, Germany offers the
Viceroy a new Krupp cannon, it being explained to
Nubar that it is one of the type which was recently
tested at Antwerp and that no armor plate can resist it.

German support thus gained and the telegraphic con-
gratulations of his master received, Nubar proceeds
without loss of time to Italy, stopping at Marseilles
only long enough to secure the adoption by the chamber
of commerce of a resolution favoring his program. He
proceeds to Florence and is captivated with the cordial
welcome which he receives from the Italian Premier

Menabrea. Expressing sympathy with Nubar's plan, the Premier asks time to reflect. A few days later, in the depths of a box at the performance of a play, "to which," writes Nubar, "neither he nor I paid the slightest attention," momentous topics are discussed—projects which both statesmen realize may entail far-reaching possibilities. Before the curtain fell the support of Italy is assured.

Encouraged by this success Nubar asks his master if he shall not direct his steps to Vienna. But the Khedive, who is at the moment in Constantinople, is himself "working" the Austrian problem, as well as that of Russia and America, through the intervention of the several ambassadors at the Sublime Porte. Let Nubar concentrate on Paris, where he may find support in the friendly advances of the Khedive who has sent one of his sons to complete his studies at the French capital. Such a flattering tribute to the Latin civilization could not fail to have its effect on Napoleon and his Queen. The suggestion was fruitful. To the friendly aid of the beautiful Empress Nubar owes the important support of the creator of the Suez Canal.

I saw the Person in question [writes Ferdinand de Lesseps to Nubar on November 9, 1868], before my departure from Paris for Biarritz. At Her suggestion I am urging on the Ministry of Foreign Affairs, in the name of my company, that the question of judicial reforms shall be immediately submitted to a new Commission (*trans.*).

Possibly Nubar's success contributes to the political discomfiture of the French Foreign Minister who has resisted his project. At any rate the minister's removal by the Emperor is referred to by Nubar as "the downfall of this enemy of our country." It leads him to assure the Khedive that the question would soon receive a fa-

vorable solution. Ismail loses no time in showing his satisfaction with the turn of events by instructing Nubar to
use the good offices of the French Government to commission the great French sculptor Jacquemart to design a statue of Mohammed Ali to be placed in the central square of Alexandria, where it stands today, facing
the Palace of the Mixed Courts.

Before resuming negotiations with the new French
minister, Nubar makes a flying visit to Egypt. While
there he has an interview with the young Prince Napoleon, who engages in a violent attack on Egyptian in-
trigue and corruption. But Nubar takes the words from
his mouth. "All the world agrees that our country is ill!
Why refuse us the examination necessary to diagnose
our disease? When the evil is understood the remedy
can be applied." The Prince demands that the examination be public. Nubar replies that above everything else
it *must* be public, and that it is precisely the secret remedies which Europe seeks to administer to Egypt that
have aroused the indignation of the Khedive. The interview ends by the promise of the Prince to give his support to the request for assembling of the commission.

Another incident may be mentioned. One of Nubar's
trusted supporters in France, a personal friend of the
Emperor, suggests that as it was the Empress herself
who could best persuade the Minister of Foreign Affairs
with respect to the question in hand it would be an excellent plan if Nubar could convey the Khedive's desire
to ascertain whether Her Highness intended to visit
Egypt at the opening of the canal, and if so, to express
his intention to prepare a reception worthy of so great
and gracious a sovereign. The Khedive loses no time in
approving the suggestion of his minister. The Empress
receives Nubar's invitation with her proverbial gra-
ciousness—and accepts. And so there slips into the his-

tory of the Great Reform in Egypt a page which fore-
tells a story of royal hospitality and official pageantry
unsurpassed in its generation. And with it, success
crowns Nubar's efforts. On April 28, 1869, he writes,
"Twenty months have been required to bring France
to consent to abolish treaties of centuries' duration, but
what are twenty months as compared with the grandeur
of the work we have in hand? History alone can answer."

Thus was brought about the convening in Cairo in
October, 1869, under the presidency of Nubar himself,
of an international commission attended by the representatives of Austria, Germany, England, Italy, Russia, France, and the United States. The scope of the
powers of the commission had given rise to considerable
anxiety on the part of the Khedive. Impatient to secure
results and distrustful of the support of France, the
Khedive was anxious that full powers should be granted
the commission to decide upon a plan of reform. Nubar, however, reassures his sovereign that it is not only
wise that the French report should be taken as a basis
of discussion, but that it is essential in the interests of
Egypt that the decisions of the commission should be
merely advisory. Tactfully reminding the Khedive that
it would be most imprudent to place his arms, that is to
say his rights, at the disposition of his adversaries, he
adds, "It is for the Commissioners to deliberate, but it
is for the Powers and for Your Highness to make the
final decision."

At an early period in these negotiations, Nubar presented on behalf of his Government a revised and elaborate plan, broader far in its outlines than that which he
had previously advanced. Freely conceding the European majority in the new courts, he sought to bring
within their jurisdiction *all* the inhabitants of Egypt—

native as well as European—and including the Egyptian Government itself. In addition to relieving Egypt from what he termed the existing "judicial Babel," the effects of which have already been described, Nubar had in mind, as Lord Cromer points out, two vital purposes. One was to protect the Egyptian Government against raids upon the treasury by unscrupulous adventurers supported by their diplomatic representatives—in a word, to substitute law for diplomacy. The other was to protect the people themselves against the despotism of their rulers by effecting a complete separation between justice and the state, and by giving to every inhabitant of Egypt the protection of a judicial system the integrity and independence of which should be guaranteed, as far as human provision could accomplish such an end. His proposals therefore extended the jurisdiction of the new courts not only to all judicial controversies between foreigners and Egyptians and between Europeans of different nationalities (with the exception of matters relating to personal status), but also to suits involving commercial litigation arising between Egyptians themselves, as well as to all non-commercial litigation between Egyptians which the parties might agree to submit to the courts. More radical still were his proposals in the field of criminal law. The jurisdiction of the new courts was to include all criminal offenses whether committed by Europeans or by Egyptians—the more serious offenses (felonies and misdemeanors) to be tried before a jury composed of an equal number of Europeans and Egyptians.[2]

The remarkable character of these proposals strikes

[2] The breadth of Nubar's proposals has not always been properly appreciated. See, for instance, the incorrect statement in the *Encyclopaedia Britannica*, 13th ed., XIX, 834, "Nubar made no attempt to get rid of the criminal jurisdiction exercised by the consular representatives of the foreign powers."

one with admiration for the vision of the man who framed them. In an effort to establish in Egypt the principle of territorial sovereignty, under which justice should be rendered to all the dwellers of Egypt in the name of the Egyptian ruler, Nubar was willing to bring Egyptians themselves within the jurisdiction of a system of courts in which a majority of the judges should be always Europeans. The result would have been the closing of the Consular Courts to all but a very limited and, from the Egyptian point of view, relatively innocuous, class of cases—those relating to suits between foreigners of the same nationality and those questions of personal status. The criminal jurisdiction which Nubar sought to abolish represented the most vital expression of the Capitulations in Egypt. His plan would thus have gone far to "abolish the Capitulations." But the plan was ahead of the times. Twenty years later it would have been almost certain of success. In 1869 the European colonies in Egypt viewed it with fatal suspicion. Indeed it is no small part of the credit due to Nubar Pasha and his master, the Khedive, that they found their efforts opposed, almost solidly, by those very foreign communities who were later to prove the principal beneficiaries of the new system. In 1875 the principal foreign colony in Egypt was that of the Greeks, numbering about 35,000. The French followed with half this number; the Italians had 14,000; the Austrians and the English were about equally divided at 6,000 each, the Germans, curiously enough, being in much smaller number than the Austrians—scarcely over a 1,000; then there were some 500 Persians, 200 Dutch, 150 Spaniards, slightly over 100 each of Russians and of Belgians. A miscellaneous group of 40 Swedes, Danes, Portuguese, Swiss, Americans, and subjects of other Powers completed the total of 80,000 foreigners, a solid little army sheltered behind the bulwark of the Capitulations.

Curiously enough in the very disparity of numbers was found a reason for the support eventually given to the reform by some of the smaller nations, who, having little practical interest one way or another in the proposed change, saw in it, nevertheless, a means of increasing their own scanty colonies and, as a consequence, their influence in Egypt by contributing judges to the new courts.

Such considerations, however, did not move the larger colonies who bombarded their own governments with petitions and memorials protesting against the plans which were under way.

The native members of the new Courts [complained the French citizens of Alexandria, in a petition to the National Assembly at Versailles], will never have that independence towards their own Government which is necessary for the administration of justice, and the European judges themselves, selected from many different nations, and thus prevented from forming a homogeneous magistracy, will not be free from those pernicious influences which are so powerful in Egypt. We therefore dare hope that the Assembly of Versailles will not abandon the traditional policy of France in the Orient by permitting the disappearance of those laws and customs on the strength of which have been created and developed many prosperous institutions whose future is menaced by the projects of the Government (*trans.*).

The English colony was no less eloquent in its defense of the existing British Consular Courts. They besought their government not to allow them to be deprived of the benefit of resort to an impartial and independent judge guided in his decisions by the principles of English commercial law, by placing them at the mercy of a new court in which they could have no confidence.

Even more brusque were the views of the Italian
colony, which claimed that the proposed reform ''could
produce no other effect than the irremediable ruin of
all foreign colonies, in leaving them unarmed at the
mercy of the most reckless caprice and despotism and
in thus reducing foreign subjects to the miserable plane
of the native population.'' The Italian petition, bearing
a thousand signatures, was accompanied by a separate
petition of the Italian lawyers of Alexandria, who insisted that the new project, if it were put into execution,
would have an effect exactly the contrary of that which
it was desired to produce. Curiously enough these members of the Italian bar invoked, with doubtful logic, precisely the very argument which the Khedive and his
Prime Minister had presented in favor of the reform,
in pointing out the existence of many cases against the
Egyptian Government which had been for a long time
pending, without receiving any just solution. With far
wiser vision Nubar invoked the necessity of a system
which should represent the joint efforts of Egypt and
the Powers precisely in order to bring about a just and
fearless disposition of this very mass of vexatious controversies.

In measuring the efforts expended by Ismail to realize the success of this commission, it is interesting to
learn that the pen of the novelist was employed to support that of the diplomat. Through the good offices of
Nubar, the French novelist, Edmond About, who was
reputed to be the grandson of Voltaire, was invited to
Egypt and widely received. The result was the publication in the *Revue des Deux Mondes* during the sittings
of the commission, of a story of Egyptian life under the
title ''Ahmed le Fellah.'' For this tale the author was
paid by Egypt the then princely sum of twenty-five
thousand francs. In the pages of this tale the hero, a

simple tiller of the soil, finds occasion to denounce, in the language of a statesman, the existing *régime* in Egypt.

By diplomatic agreements, which usage, abuse and the law of the stronger have singularly distorted, every European who sets foot in Egypt is his own master. He brings with him the laws of his own country, not to respect them but to authorize him to disobey our own. He recognizes neither the Government, its officials nor the judges of Egypt. He knows but his own consul. Remember then that there are nearly twenty consulates in our poor country of Egypt—nearly twenty states within our state. Consider then that one hundred times a day a quarrel, a scandal, a scratch of the knife, can arouse a conflict between the sovereign law of our Khedive and the pretended law of our visitors (*trans.*).

These observations of a hero of fiction recall an even more trenchant contemporary summary of the situation, to be found in one of Nubar's own letters:

You wish to know my opinion of consular justice in Egypt. It is as just and as honorable as the justice of Heaven. The consulate of Greece represents in Egypt the court of the archangel Gabriel. The archangel Michael is represented by the consulate of Italy. St. Paul in person has installed himself at the British consulate, and St. Peter, his keys in his hand, administers justice at the consulate of France. Pray, what loftier conception may one have of Justice! But there is just one drawback to all this. It is that each one of these archangels and these saints is his own law and his private system of procedure. Thus it comes about that since the poor devil who embarks on a judicial enterprise never knows by what court he is to be judged, he is never able to assure himself in advance that he is obeying the laws. He is summoned before St. Peter, when he thought the case belonged to St. Paul. He is troubled. He is confounded. His case is just. He is in the right. But this is of no avail. The Saints have sent him to the Devil (*trans.*).

But Nubar's proposals encountered more formidable obstacles than the protests of the foreign colonies. The French commissioners were strictly bound by their instructions. On their demand the proposal to extend the jurisdiction over questions involving only Egyptian subjects was swept aside. On two points only did Nubar gain his ground. The international commission agreed to include in the jurisdiction of the new courts disputes between foreigners of different nationalities and conceded to these courts the right to enforce judgments against foreigners without resort to consular assistance. In penal matters the commission proposed to open the doors to offenses of all descriptions committed by foreigners—but, as a condition precedent to this extension, stipulated for the preparation of a body of penal legislation which should afford effective guarantees.

This proposal alarmed the French Government and a new French commission was at once organized to consider and report. Its report denied the propriety of conferring on the new courts jurisdiction over suits involving foreigners of different nationalities, and disapproved equally the proposed extension of criminal jurisdiction over foreigners. In fact it substantially reasserted the conclusions of the earlier commission. These proposals Nubar declined to accept, and the fate of the reform again hung in the balance when the intervention of the French premier, who was a friend both of Nubar and of the Khedive Ismail, led to the adoption of a compromise which brought the long negotiations to a sudden and welcome termination. It was agreed that criminal jurisdiction should remain limited to violations of police ordinances, but that civil jurisdiction should be extended to controversies between foreigners of different nationalities. The experiment was to be for a five-year period, at the end of which the Powers might elect to revert to the former *status quo*.[3]

In this form the proposals were approved by various foreign Powers and were about to be submitted to the French parliament when the Franco-Prussian War broke out. The two years' interruption which ensued brought to the front a new element of difficulty, in a display of restlessness on the part of the Turkish Government over the independent character of the negotiations carried on directly between Egypt and the Powers. This, the Turkish Government feared, was calculated to prove a step in the final emancipation of Egypt from the last remnants of Turkish suzerainty. After the disastrous ending of the war the reassurances given by France upon this point proved hardly satisfying, and to judge from Nubar's own expressions, it required the Khedive's utmost tact to dissipate the misgivings of the Ottoman Porte. Replying to the observations of the Porte on this delicate topic, the Khedive, observes Nubar, allayed the fears of his titular sovereign by the use of "one of those phrases to which the Turkish language lends itself so admirably, and which has the appearance of promising without contracting and of saying something when it says nothing."

In the presence of these misgivings, Nubar undertook the delicate task of securing from the Porte an enlargement of the powers of self-government which had in the past been conceded to Egypt by successive de-

[3] "It was Germany who prevented the entire withdrawal of the scheme, which therefore had to go on; it was France who saw her opportunity of changing the whole nature of it so as to suit her own interests. France insisted, so France's interests only were considered. Other European Powers claimed, of course, similar concessions and the same were nominally granted; but because France stuck out to the last, and gave Cherif most trouble, France got pretty well all she wanted. The courts and the codes became practically French." *Khedives and Pashas*, *Anon* (London: Sampson Low, 1884), p. 171.

crees. In June, 1873, he was able to secure from the
Turkish Sultan the concession of a firman authorizing
the Khedive to make special agreements with the Powers regarding customs and commerce, and including
also the promulgation of police measures affecting foreigners.

The continual vigilance of the Turkish ruler is apparent in that negotiations were transferred from Egypt
to Constantinople, although, on his part, the Khedive
was unremitting in his efforts to secure the favorable
support of foreign representatives stationed in Egypt.
The Khedive was particularly insistent on the unity of
the reform and the importance of securing for the new
courts a general criminal jurisdiction. Thus in September, 1872, he writes to Nubar at Constantinople,

I have seen here nearly all the foreign agents and have discussed the matter with them at length, giving them clearly to
understand that it was by my express order that you have submitted to the Powers the plan for complete jurisdiction. I have
explained that your idea had been to get the civil courts under
way first, but that for me this combination appeared but a lame
one and that I considered the coexistence of civil and criminal
jurisdiction a practical necessity (*trans.*).

To this the Khedive went so far as to add that, rather
than abandon his claims to criminal jurisdiction without which he believed that the civil courts could have but
little authority, he preferred to allow matters to remain
as they were. Encouraged by his master, Nubar val-
iantly renewed the fight, hoping that the recent defeat
of France might lead her to adopt a more liberal attitude toward his plan. He even went so far as to hint that
the inclusion of penal jurisdiction was the cornerstone
of the building and that its rejection might lead to the
crumbling of the walls that had so long been under con-

struction. But the opposition of France proved more than formidable. On the larger question of general criminal jurisdiction she stood obdurate. And while she was willing to admit that offenses directed against judges and officers of justice should be judged by the Mixed Courts, she insisted that even these should be limited to cases where the offenses should be committed within the judicial precincts. Before this claim Ismail raised vigorous protest. How could Egypt assume responsibility for the execution of judgments if it was not in a position to impose immediate punishment for all crimes affecting the execution of those judgments, whether within a courthouse or outside it? He adds with emphasis: "I see here a question of vital importance to the existence of the Courts."

The Khedive spared no effort to secure support for his contention. He wrote personally to the King of Italy and exercised his powers of persuasion in many other directions. In one direction, however, he found himself helpless. Nubar inquired of him if there was no way of moving Austria to give her support. The Khedive replied that this was impossible. "The Consul General of Austria is a charming man, but it is quite impossible to talk with him upon affairs of State."

On the Bosphorus Nubar was equally tireless. "From morning to night," he wrote, "I am splitting my head in an effort to find a compromise between these points of view." And at last the compromise was found. Once more seeking the friendly offices of Ferdinand de Lesseps Nubar submitted directly to the French Government the Khedive's proposition to give to the new courts, forthwith, jurisdiction over all crimes and misdemeanors committed against judges and officers of justice, and to convene immediately a new international commission for the purpose of defining these crimes and

of fixing their penalties. To this end, as also to approve
the new codes of civil and commercial law, a second international commission was assembled at Constantinople in January, 1873. Its labors were quickly and well
accomplished. In February of the same year Nubar was
able to submit to the Powers the proposed charter of the
new courts as well as the six codes which were to form
the basis of their judicial labors.

The Charter thus submitted to the Powers was in
form a statute (known as the Règlement d'Organisation
Judiciaire), but in essence a treaty and has been so
characterized by the highest courts of Egypt.[4] It outlines a system of courts which should have jurisdiction
over foreigners. Its acceptance by the several Powers
implied the subjection of their citizens to the new jurisdiction and the consequent suppression, to that extent,
of the jurisdiction of the consular courts. It contained
also a stipulation fixing the duration of the new system
at a trial period of five years, with a declaration of the
right of the Powers to withdraw from the arrangement
after the expiration of that period.[5] While the Charter
itself was not actually signed on behalf of the Powers,
by whom it was accepted in the course of diplomatic negotiations, its character as a binding international obligation, valid until formally terminated, and not subject
to amendment except by the consent of all the Powers,
has never been contested.

Subject to the necessary parliamentary or other rati-

[4] "This statute must be regarded as rather of the nature of a treaty
than as a law emanating solely from the will of the legislator." Court of
Appeals, Native Courts, December 10, 1901. Also to same effect Court of
Appeals, Mixed Courts, *Bulletin*, IV (May 25, 1892), 294; XXXIV
(March 8, 1922), 227.

[5] By the Franco-Egyptian convention of November 10, 1874, France
reserved the right to withdraw at any time within five years, if not satisfied with the operation of the new system. The benefit of this and other
reservations in the same document was later separately extended to various of the other Powers, including Great Britain and Germany.

fications, which were speedily forthcoming,[6] England
the United States, Germany, Austria, and Italy signi-
fied immediately their willingness to accept the new
plan. Some of the smaller Powers, however, showed a
disposition to be recalcitrant and their objections were
only overcome by a display of firmness on the part of
Ismail and Nubar. Thus we read in the newspapers of
the day that, at a diplomatic reception held in the early
part of 1874, the Khedive, relying on Nubar's assurances of the consent of the Powers, made a short address in which he stated that the reform could practically be considered as an accomplished fact; that the
Powers had given their consent, and that the new courts
would shortly begin functioning without opposition.
Some of the consuls ventured to express their surprise
at this announcement, and observed to the Khedive that
their governments had not only not given their consent
but had not even been consulted. The Khedive, who had
relied upon the assurances of his Prime Minister that
everything was in order, was somewhat disturbed by
these objections, but a short time later the Prime Minister himself received the recalcitrant representatives
and with considerable show of anger assured them that
the success of the plan could no longer be allowed to remain a matter of doubt, and that those Powers who did
not wish to join with the new project would have to accept the consequences.

France, however, still held back, and even after the
support of her foreign office had been secured, in November, 1874, difficulty was experienced in securing the
approval of the French Parliament. The parliamentary
commission appointed to study the project and which

6 The final agreement between England and Egypt was signed July
31, 1875, and England suspended consular jurisdiction by Orders in Council, February 5, 1876. For American ratification see Appendix H.

conducted an extensive investigation, was almost unanimously opposed to the plan. The fate of the reform hung in the balance, but once again the situation was saved by a master stroke. Ismail determined to create a *fait accompli* to which the French parliament would be compelled to yield. Encouraged by the support of the remaining Powers, the Khedive, on June 28, 1875, inaugurated the new courts in the absence, and in anticipation, of French approval. The stroke was successful. Unable to resist the logic of events and faced by the prospect of the creation of a judicial system before which Frenchmen might be sued, regardless of the consent of their country, the French parliament, before the end of the year, gave its belated approval to the new *régime,* but not until after having exacted a number of special conditions and reservations, the benefit of which was subsequently extended to the other Powers. By the irony of fate, however, the founder of the courts was not present on this occasion. He had become the victim of his own creation, just as, later on, his royal master was to share a similar fate. Alarmed at the possibilities hidden in the clause which gave the new courts jurisdiction over the royal estates, the Khedive had quarreled with his minister and had dismissed him.[7]

The ceremonies of inauguration were conducted with a dignity and upon a scale worthy of a great historic occasion and in the presence of the most distinguished assembly that could be gathered in Egypt. The newly appointed judges were received in state by the Khedive,

[7] "With immense labor he overcame all difficulties, and the new Courts were about to be formed, when Ismail, taking fright at a clause which made the government itself subject to the tribunals, backed out, dismissed Nubar and recalled Cherif." *Khedives and Pashas, Anon* (London: Sampson Low, 1884), p. 171. But in *The Story of the Khedivate* by Edward Dicey (1903), p. 144, it is stated that the cause of Nubar's removal was the suspicion of Ismail as to his "Minister's relations with the existing British financial mission."

who was attended by the royal princes and the principal members of the royal household. The remarks of the Khedive were prophetic and deserve recording:

Gentlemen: With the approval of my August Sovereign, His Majesty the Sultan, and the gracious coöperation of the Powers, permit me today to inaugurate the Judicial Reform of Egypt and to establish her new Courts. I am happy to see around me the distinguished judges to whom I now confide, in complete confidence, the task of administering justice. All interests will find complete security in your enlightened conscience and your decisions will obtain respect and obedience on the part of all. This day, gentlemen, will mark the commencement of a new era of civilization in the history of Egypt. God helping us, the future of our great work is assured (*trans.*).

Following this address the judges, through the Minister of Justice, expressed their appreciation of confidence which had marked their selection. Thereafter in turn the several consuls were given special audience in order to receive the Khedive's personal thanks for the contribution which their respective countries had made to carrying out the reform, with an expression of his hopes that these same Powers would continue the support needed for carrying to a successful conclusion the work so auspiciously inaugurated.

Thus ended triumphantly the long and costly battle for judicial reform in Egypt—the crowning of an achievement which, in the words of Lord Milner, had earned for Nubar Pasha "the lasting gratitude of Egypt and the respect of the civilized world."[8] How well the institution, which was thus set up, has stood the test of time, the reader may judge from the chapters which follow.

[8] The cost of the campaign to Egypt has been roughly estimated at two and a half billion gold francs, or practically the equivalent of the Egyptian debt of that period. Leo Pangalo, "L'Age Héroïque," *Livre d'Or*, p. 71.

CHAPTER III

FIFTY YEARS

THE fourteen capitulatory Powers which gave adherence to the *régime* of the Mixed Courts were Germany, Austria, Belgium, Denmark, Spain, United States, France, Great Britain, Greece, Italy, Norway, Holland, Portugal, and Russia. Of these, Germany and Austria have since surrendered their capitulatory rights by the treaties of Versailles and St. Germain, and Russia has, temporarily at least, lost hers by the rupture of diplomatic relations following the Russian revolution and the closing of her consulates, the existence of which is a condition of the exercise of capitulatory rights. None of these Powers therefore continues to enjoy a legal right to be represented in the Mixed Courts. The Russian judges, however, still retain their places, and following the signing of a treaty with Egypt in 1925 which restored to Germany, in large measure, the exercise of her former capitulatory privileges, a judge from Germany was named to one of the foreign appointments reserved to the free discretion of the Egyptian Government. On the other hand, through the dissolution of the political union between Norway and Sweden the latter has been added as an independent member of this international judicial family.[1]

[1] By its treaty with Turkey in 1858, Brazil acquired what have sometimes been spoken of as capitulatory rights. See Brown, *Foreigners in Turkey*, p. 41. Milner, *England in Egypt*, 13th ed., chap. ix, p. 45, note. However, that country, which had no subjects and no interests in Egypt, took no part in the founding of the Mixed Courts and has never been represented on their benches. Indeed it is curious to note that, in 1873, Nubar assured the Powers that no Chinese, Japanese, or Brazilian judges would be named to the Mixed Courts. See *Livre d'Or*, p. 494. In an opin-

GIOVANNI GIACCONE

(ITALY)

1881–94

DR. ALOYSE LAPENNA

(AUSTRIA)

1875–81

MAURICE BELLET

(FRANCE)

1894–1902

EARLY PRESIDENTS OF THE COURT OF APPEALS

The Charter of the courts, as accepted by the Powers, fixed a trial period of five years. After that time, "if experience has not confirmed the practical usefulness of the judicial reform," the Powers were to be at liberty to return to the old order of things or to discuss new arrangements. But resort to these alternatives was unnecessary. The "practical usefulness" sufficiently manifested itself. After the expiration of the trial period a long series of decrees successively renewed the life of the courts for periods varying from six months to five years, until October 31, 1921, on which date, following extensive negotiations with the Powers, the Egyptian Government was able to publish a decree prolonging the powers of the courts "for an indefinite period," the date of their expiration to be "fixed by decree published in the *Official Journal* at least one year in advance of such date." Such a proviso, assented to by the Powers, would on its face seem to place the question of the abolition of the *régime* in the hands of the Egyptian Government.[2] Some of the Powers, however,

ion rendered in 1882, the Court of Appeals expressed the view that Brazil had never been entitled to the privilege of consular jurisdiction (R.O., 1882, p. 93). As contrasted with the position of Brazil, Roumania, by the Treaty of Berlin (1878) was guaranteed for her nationals in the Ottoman Empire the same rights as other European subjects. This included "consular protection." In 1906, when Brazil established diplomatic and consular representation in Egypt, she secured the tacit acquiescence of the Egyptian Government to the opening of consular courts, which are now functioning.

[2] Under the former system of periodical renewals the question of the right of Egypt to terminate the *régime* had been open to discussion. See, for instance, the observations of Lord Cromer in his *Annual Report for 1898*, p. 29: "Some difference of opinion exists as to whether the Egyptian Government has or has not the right to denounce the Conventions under which the Tribunals exist. It has been contended that the arrangement, though bilateral in form, is really unilateral in favor of the Powers, in the sense that the Powers alone have the right to withdraw at their option, Egypt, on her side, having tacitly renounced such right. Without entering into the various arguments which may be adduced in connection with this point, it will be sufficient in this place, if I state briefly that the view of the Egyptian Government, which is supported by many eminent

took the precaution to reserve specifically a right to
withdraw from the *régime* upon a year's notice. The
United States reserved the right "to withdraw its adherence to the arrangement at any time after one
year," but later coupled this reservation with the declaration that in the absence of any such modifications in
the existing arrangements "as would render it doubtful whether American citizens could obtain in the Mixed
Courts the same impartial justice now administered in
those courts," it would not withdraw without having
given notice of its intention at least one year in advance.
This reservation was made in contemplation of a pending proposal, which had not received the approval of
the American Government, looking to the radical reorganization of the Mixed Courts.

As to certain other Powers which made no such reservation the question of their right to withdraw has
been considered arguable, but when it is recalled that
the result of withdrawal would merely be to reinstate
as far as that Power was concerned an old and intolerable order of things, it would hardly seem likely that the
question will ever become one of practical importance.

From time to time the interesting question has presented itself as to the effect of the failure of one of the
capitulatory Powers to renew its adhesion to the Mixed
Courts in time for such adhesion to become effective
before the termination of the then current period.[3]
While the indefinite renewal of the life of the courts in
1921 precludes the possibility of the question arising in
precisely the same way in the future, the question is im-

jurists in England and elsewhere, is that Egypt has the right to withdraw
at will from the Mixed Tribunals. It is greatly to be hoped that no question will arise of exercising that right.''

[3] ''A few years since, when some of the Powers were dilatory in giving
their adhesion to the extension of the Courts—for every five years there is
a formal renewal—something like a panic occurred among the commercial
community.'' See Penfield, *Present Day Egypt* (1899), p. 115.

portant as bearing on the effect of the possible future withdrawal of any one or other of the Powers.

Delays of the character referred to have occurred four times in the history of the court: In 1890, a few days delay in the case of Greece; in 1916 in the case of Italy; in 1920 in the case of Holland,[4] and finally, in 1921, a week's delay in the case of the United States. These delays have raised a double question as to the status of the judges representing the country in question, and as to the position of its litigants before the Mixed Courts. The short delay in the case of Greece aroused no special comment. In the case of Italy in 1916, however, the situation was made the subject of considerable discussion, and the Court of Appeals, accepting a suggestion of the Government, decided, without expressing an opinion on the question of principle, that under all the circumstances it would be desirable for the Italian judges to temporarily refrain from exercising both their judicial and administrative functions. It also decided that the trial of cases concerning Italians should be postponed till a later date, but that the clerical and administrative services of the courts should continue to be placed at their disposition.

On the merits of the question it would seem clear that the status of the judges, once they have been named and commissioned by the Egyptian Government, cannot be affected by the actions of their own several governments. The courts are Egyptian courts. The judges, by the express provisions of the Charter of the courts, are irremovable from office. Their appointments once made are irrespective of political relations with the countries

---

[4] At that moment Holland, by virtue of the death of the two Dutch judges, was not represented in the Mixed Courts. It was not until the assurance was given that two new Dutch judges should be promptly appointed, that her adhesion was forthcoming. See Heyligers, *Recueil des Cours, Académie de Droit International* (1927), II, 52.

from which they come. There is no doubt that they would always be respected by the Egyptian Government.

On the second branch of the question, touching the rights of foreign litigants who are citizens or subjects of a country which is, temporarily at least, no longer party to the system, the problem is more delicate. It has been the subject of conflicting decisions in the District Courts and has never been definitely determined by the Court of Appeals. On the one hand it has been held that the unilateral action of Italy in delaying her renewal could not affect the vested rights of the subjects of other foreign countries or of Egyptian subjects, and that during the period of delay Italians might therefore be sued in the Mixed Courts, although they might not invoke the jurisdiction of the courts as plaintiffs. But a contrary view was taken by another District Court which held that temporary delay of Holland in renewing her adhesion to the *régime* was to be considered as an election on her part, accepted by the Egyptian Government, to return to the former system. For this reason the court declined to assume jurisdiction in a case where a Hollander had been sued.

The delicate question here presented would not arise in cases between Egyptian subjects and subjects of a foreign Power. Here there could be no question of the vested right of a third foreign nation. Two nations only would be interested, and, as between them, the situation, by mutual consent, would be considered as having been restored to the old order of things. The jurisdiction of the Mixed Courts would therefore no longer exist and the *régime* of the Consular Courts would resume its full effect. A similar conclusion would presumably follow in the case of a suit brought against another foreigner by the subject of a Power whose adherence had lapsed. The right to resort to the Mixed Courts is a privilege based on adherence to the system. Where such adherence has lapsed or been withdrawn the privilege would fall with it.

Such questions, however, while interesting, are more theoretical than practical. If, from time to time, one or other of the member Powers has been slow in renewing its adherence, the strong common interest of the Powers in maintaining the courts gives little ground to antici-pate individual defections in the future.

From the outset the Mixed Courts were a success. The judicial posts were considered attractive and the foreign Powers nominated for them sufficient jurists of the first rank to give standing and character to the in-stitution.[5] They responded immediately to the pressing needs of the community. So encouraging indeed was the experiment that scarcely two years after they had opened their doors the Khedive Ismail invited his Min-ister of Justice to prepare a plan for the further exten-sion of the jurisdiction of the courts, to be submitted to the Powers at the conclusion of the current five-year period. The Court of Appeals itself was accordingly in-vited to "trace the broad lines" of a plan of extension which might serve as a basis for diplomatic negotiation. The court prepared a document which went to the length of proposing that *all* civil and commercial litiga-tion in Egypt, whether between natives alone, or for-eigners alone, or between natives and foreigners, should be confided to the jurisdiction of the courts. In the mat-ter of extending criminal jurisdiction, however, the

[5] For one thing the salaries paid far exceeded corresponding salaries on the continent and the cost of living in Egypt was low and living conditions attractive. For instance, the 48,000 gold francs, or $9,600, paid in 1876 to a justice of the Court of Appeals, represented in terms of purchasing power and standards of living probably twice what a similar amount would rep-resent today.

court expressed "great hesitation," finding here serious difficulties in the conflict of nationalities and legal
traditions. In this field only minor modifications of jurisdiction were suggested.

But the ambitious program presented by the court
proved to be nothing more than a pious hope. At the
very moment when the ruler of the country was exhibiting his confidence by seeking to extend its powers, he
was himself being made to feel that justice was indeed
a two-edged sword. The courts began to render judgments against the Khedivial estates. Setting aside a
royal decree prolonging the date of payment of various
drafts drawn by the estates and accepted by the Minister of Finance, judgments were given against the
debtor according to the laws. These the Khedive failed
to meet. In a petition addressed to the dean of the consular corps and to the president of the Court of Appeals
a committee of lawyers cynically observed that so far,
judgments against the Government had amounted to
nothing more or less than a new source of governmental
revenue through the payment by the plaintiffs of the
necessary costs. The petition had behind it a series of
fruitless executions. The dangerous position of the
Mixed Courts was fully appreciated. It was recognized
that their very existence was at stake:

It is morally certain that the Government, having regard to
the hundreds of similar cases pending [writes the special corre-
spondent of the London *Daily News* in the issue of February 19,
1877], can never allow the sentence to be enforced, and the only
dignified course then open to the judges will be to perform the
process known as the "happy despatch" and so close their own
careers and that of the "Réforme Judiciaire" at the same time.
Even supposing them to be willing to remain in office and continue to act the part of mere lay figures in a judicial farce, the
end would probably be none the less near or certain—for the

plaintiff is a French subject and France is one of the two Powers which refused to bind themselves to the "Réforme Judiciaire" for any definite time. She can, therefore, and doubtless will, at any period withdraw, upon finding that the interests of her citizens are not protected, and Russia, which is similarly situated with regard to her obligations, would probably follow. With the secession of these two important Powers the integrity of the "Réforme Judiciaire" would be forever destroyed—its entire collapse must inevitably follow.

It took firmness and cool judgment to steer the judicial ship through these troubled waters. The difficulties are sufficiently illustrated by the proposal, happily unrealized, of certain Egyptian judges, to withdraw from the hearing of a suit on the ground that failure to respect a Khedivial decree would amount to an act of rebellion against their own Government. Undaunted by these difficulties the courts did two things. They continued to render judgments against the Khedivial estates and to follow, even though unfruitfully, the process of execution. At the same time they called the situation to the attention of their several diplomatic representatives, requesting them to fix a time limit for the execution of judgments, and urging that, in the event that satisfaction was not forthcoming within such period, the courts should be relieved from the duty of pronouncing judgments in cases where the Egyptian Government was a party. In the issue thus sharply raised the victory went to the Mixed Courts. To quote Lord Cromer, "The institution to which Ismail Pasha was induced to assent, with probably only half a knowledge of what it meant, was the instrument which dealt him his political death blow."[6] Strangely enough the

6 *Modern Egypt* (London, 1908), p. 317. See also "Khedives and Pashas," *supra*, p. 172. "But the claim [to jurisdiction over the Government] which had frightened Ismail and out of which he had not been able to wriggle, so far as foreigners were concerned, soon brought doom to his

final event was due largely to the entry on the scene of a wholly unexpected champion. France and England, the two countries which held the greatest stake in Egypt, were unwilling to intervene jointly, or to stand by and witness the other's intervention. A year or two of discussion over financial measures and responsibilities intervened, but agreement was impossible. Matters were at a deadlock when, on May 11, 1879, the German Ambassador informed Lord Salisbury that the German Consul-General at Cairo had been instructed to declare to the Khedive that Germany regarded the Khedive's attitude "as involving the abolition of acquired and recognized rights, and as an open and direct violation of the international obligations imposed by the Judicial Reform," and that the German Government could not therefore admit the binding force of the Khedive's decree prolonging the date of payment of the drafts of the Khedivial estates, "as far as it touches either the competency of the Mixed Courts or the rights of subjects of the Empire.'"[7]

Immediately the European nations rallied to the support of Germany, and some six weeks later, on June 26, the Khedive's master of ceremonies at Abdin Palace received a telegram from Constantinople, addressed, in Turkish, to "Ismail Pasha, Ex-Khedive of Egypt."

door.'' Writing in 1877, before the deposition of Ismail, a former American Agent and Consul-General, in referring to Nubar Pasha's relations with the Khedive, used this prophetic language: "But by a strange fatality he was 'hoist with his own petard.' His unforgiven sin with his monarch is, that in tying the hands of the European diplomatic agents, and submitting all judicial decisions to what is practically an Egyptian tribunal, whose judges are paid out of the Egyptian Treasury, he at the same time threw meshes around the Khedive, and imperiled if he did not destroy his sovereign prerogative. For the Tribunal has affirmed its right to sit in judgment on the Egyptian Master of Legions, and decree against him, although declining to go through the form of insisting on enforcing judgments, for which it has not been put in possession of adequate means.'' See Edwin de Leon, *The Khedives of Egypt*, p. 113.

[7] See Dicey, *The Egypt of the Future* (London, 1907).

This telegram sounded the disappearance from the political stage of a ruler to whom Egypt owed much of her modern development and to whom the Mixed Courts owed in no small degree their very existence.

Among the incidents which marked this critical chapter in the early history of the courts is one which deserves a passing mention.

All of the foreign judges felt deeply the danger and humiliation of the situation in which the courts temporarily found themselves.[8] The Calvinistic and unbending spirit of one of them—a Dutchman—led him to a length and manner of protest which had unhappy consequences. Believing that the refusal of the Khedive to submit to the judgments of the courts rendered their continued functioning an empty form to which the dignity of justice should not yield itself, this "conscientious objector" sought to avail himself of the right of the judge to challenge his own competency, alleging that in the presence of the existing reversal of all principles of justice, equity itself forbade the functioning of courts which no longer functioned equally for all. Upon the rejection of his challenge, the protesting jurist announced his intention of postponing the hearing of all the cases called for trial before him. Resisting all persuasions to the contrary he accordingly took his seat on the Summary Court and forthwith handed down some seven opinions holding that the suspension of governmental guarantees for the execution of judgments implied necessarily a suspension of judicial proceedings. Upon the rendering of these decisions the representative of the Parquet left the courtroom, whereby the

[8] "Their precepts are obeyed and rigidly enforced everywhere in Egypt except against the Viceroy." Memorandum of Hon. Victor Barringer, American member of Court of Appeals, addressed to State Department, February 6, 1878.

court became incompetent to render further decisions of the same character.

The incident aroused great excitement both in judicial circles and throughout the city, to such an extent that a large crowd, with a band of music at its head, visited the home of the judge to hail him as a hero, which in turn led to the intervention of the consular authorities and to the expulsion from the country of some of the ringleaders of the manifesto, whose records were not above suspicion. A vigorous newspaper war was waged and the matter dragged on until the return of the Court of Appeals in October, when the judge was called before the General Assembly of that court, sitting as a court of discipline, to answer to two charges: First, of having violated his judicial duty by refusing to render justice, and second, of refusing to comply with the order which had imposed upon him other duties than those which he had theretofore performed. The judge in turn challenged all of the judges who were called to sit upon this case, but with no better result than that two of them, including the president of the court and the British member, withdrew for personal reasons. The accused jurist, maintaining that the court was disqualified to render an impartial judgment, declined to present himself before the assembly and was accordingly removed from office.

History may fairly assume that in this somewhat tragic incident all parties involved did their duty courageously, as they saw it. Let it also be added that the victim of the incident in due time found other service and, eventually, a high post in the foreign judicial service of his country.[9]

9 For a full report of this incident see the spirited and chivalrous account given by Judge Th. Heyligers, of the Alexandria District Court, *Un Episode des Premiers Temps de la Réforme Judiciaire en Egypte.* Pamphlet, privately printed (Paris, 1926).

During their early years the Mixed Courts rendered services of great value to the cause of international justice which did not fall within the strict scope of their judicial duties as defined by their Charter. By a series of separate diplomatic agreements Egypt, at the time of the organization of the system, entered into arrangements with the principal capitulatory Powers, for utilizing the services of the judges of the courts for the adjustment of pending diplomatic claims. Two alternative systems, optional with the claimants, were established. One of them provided for a commission of three members of the Court of Appeals to be selected by agreement between Egypt and each of the respective parties, and whose decision should be final. The other closely followed the existing judicial system and called for the submission of claims, first to a special chamber of the District Court, and, upon appeal, to the Court of Appeals. While following the procedure of the new courts, these special courts were required to give judgment in accordance with the laws and usages in existence at the time of the circumstances which gave rise to the respective claims. Where cases involved the claims of persons of different nationalities, it was for their consuls to agree as to which of the two systems should be followed.

The duties assumed by the several members of the Mixed Courts under these arrangements proved to be extensive. In the first year of the courts, 208 claims came before the special chamber of the District Court, and 109 claims before the commission selected from the bench of the Court of Appeals.[10] During the first five years the special chamber of the District Court consid-

[10] "It has certainly succeeded in clearing off much rubbish, in the shape of old reclamations against the Government, sitting as a Court of Claims." See Edwin de Leon, *The Khedives of Egypt* (1877), p. 114.

ered 216 claims, of which 110 came on appeal before the special chamber of the Court of Appeals. During the same period the special commission of the Court of Appeals handled 109 claims. Among the total of 318 claims instituted before the commissions and the special chambers during the first year, among others, 119 were French, 65 Greek, 62 Italian, 25 Austrian, and 22 English. Claims were presented on behalf of nationals of all the capitulatory Powers.

Six years after the opening of the Mixed Courts there occurred the British occupation of Egypt. The bombardment of Alexandria (July 11, 1882) had been preceded a month earlier by a serious political riot, immediately following which many Europeans left the country. Among this number were some of the more timid employees of the courts. On the announcement by the military authorities of their intention to bombard the city, those of the personnel of the courts who had remained at their posts, headed by their chief law officer, the Procureur-General, took refuge in the ships in the harbor which had been requisitioned by the consulates. It was impossible to return to the city until three days later, but on the following day the business of the courts was resumed, the courthouse, happily, not having suffered during the bombardment. On the day after the riots, the personnel of the courts at Mansourah arrived at Alexandria. They were not, however, encouraged to remain and returned speedily to their posts after a meeting of the Court of Appeals, presided over by its distinguished Italian president. The disturbance had led the members of the bar and the Cairo agency of the Crédit Lyonnais to petition the courts to suspend their hearings. The petition was promptly rejected by the Court of Appeals and disciplinary measures were taken against those who had left their posts. The march of justice was not allowed to be interrupted by the political disturbances. When the English troops entered the city a court-martial was set up in the courthouse of the Mixed Courts, to handle cases of pillage and incendiarism. Civil and military justice was sheltered by the same roof. The military sentences of execution were indeed carried out in the garden in front of the courthouse.

As time went on the courthouse which had witnessed these stirring events in Alexandria became inadequate for the rapidly growing business of the courts. In 1884 the Government decided to construct a courthouse for the special use of the Court of Appeals and the Alexandria District Court, and on January 1, 1886, the present handsome "Palace of Justice" was opened to the public, being visited shortly after by the Khedive. In 1899 this building was the scene of a solemn ceremony. On January 13 of that year the venerated founder of the courts died at Paris. The Government House and the City Hall both claimed the honor of guarding his body during the interval between its arrival and the interment, but the honor was properly confided to the Mixed Courts and Nubar Pasha's body lay in state under the guardianship of the institution for whose existence he was principally responsible until, in the presence of a remarkable public demonstration of respect, it was laid to rest in the Coptic cemetery near by.

The refusal of the French Government to participate in the occupation led naturally to the abandonment of the Anglo-French condominion and to a *régime* of rivalry between the two Powers. By the irony of fate France, who had grudgingly lent her support to the creation of the courts, now found in them and in the French tradition which they reflected, one of the principal centers for the maintenance of her intellectual influence in the country.[11]

On the other hand, while Great Britain occupied no position of special responsibility in respect to the Mixed Courts at the time of their foundation, she had, by virtue of the military occupation, assumed general responsibility for the administration of the country. This necessarily covered the question of the proper observance by Egypt of its treaty obligations in respect to the maintenance of the Mixed Courts themselves. Such supervision, however, was a strictly limited one. Established by international agreement, it was of course evident that British influence in relation to the Mixed Courts could not extend beyond the scope of activity properly exercisable by the Egyptian Government itself within the strict limits of its agreements with the Powers who were responsible for the founding of the courts.[12]

British influence was also limited by the very practical consideration that during the first ten years of the occupation there were no Englishmen at all in legal or judicial positions in Egypt except in the Mixed Courts.

[11] After calling attention to the fact that French is the only language of which a knowledge is exacted by the Egyptian Government on the part of foreign judges called to the Mixed Courts, and that the French language is used exclusively in the pleadings, Francis Laloë, a former president of the Court of Appeals, observes, ''The Government of our Republic doubtless did not foresee this result, so favorable to the spread of the French language, when it hesitated to give its assent to the Reform.'' See Preface to *Les Tribunaux Mixtes d'Egypte*, Herreros (1914).

[12] ''In the second place it has to be remembered that though, owing to the presence of a British garrison, British influence is predominant in Egypt, at the same time, according to the law of Europe, Great Britain, in dealing with Egyptian affairs, stands on a footing of perfect equality with sixteen other Powers. This equality is no mere diplomatic fiction. It is a reality of the utmost practical importance. For it is owing to this legal status of equality that the Capitulations cannot be modified without the consent of every European Power.'' The Earl of Cromer, Address before the Eighty Club, December 15, 1908, *The Situation in Egypt* (London: Macmillan, 1909), p. 19.

The work of representing the Government's interests
before these courts, as well as the task of preparing new
legislation, was entirely in the hands of French and
Italian lawyers.

Matters required eventual foreign guidance. In 1891
the Egyptian Government reluctantly consented to the
appointment of a British Judicial Adviser, which office
is still maintained.[13] In referring to the powers of the
first Judicial Adviser, Lord Cromer observed that it
was understood that the Minister of Justice "will take
no important step without previous consultation and
agreement." The authority of the office since that time
has naturally varied in accordance with shifting political conditions and the temperament and views of the
particular incumbent of the office.[14]

As far as relates to the Mixed Courts, the services of
the Judicial Advisers have been chiefly expressed in the
preparation and advocacy before international commissions of needed projects of reform, in making investiga-
tions necessary to advise the Egyptian Government in
the selection of new judges, in maintaining close and
friendly contact with the entire judicial family, and
in acting as an intermediary between the Mixed Courts

[13] See Cromer, *Modern Egypt*, II, 290. The first British Judicial Adviser was Sir John Scott, whose labors effected invaluable reforms in the
administration of justice in the Native Courts. At the opening of the war
the position was occupied by Sir Malcolm McIlwraith, who had held office
since Sir John Scott's retirement in 1898. In 1916 Sir Malcolm McIlwraith
was succeeded by Sir William Brunyate who was succeeded in turn in 1919,
by Mr. (later Sir) M. Sheldon Amos. On the latter's retirement in 1925
he was succeeded by Mr. (later Sir) John H. Percival, whose retirement in
the fall of 1928 was, like that of his predecessor, the subject of a flattering
testimonial of regard from the Mixed Courts. The present holder of the
office is Mr. G. A. W. Booth, formerly a member of the Cairo District
Court and later one of the Royal Counselors to the Egyptian Government.

[14] The maintenance of this office was exacted by the British Government as one of the conditions of discontinuing the occupation of the Alexandria customhouse, after the assassination of the Sirdar, Sir Lee Stack,
in 1924.

and the Government in all matters touching their common interest. In spite of the fact that the judicial advisers have on occasion sponsored projects which would have materially altered the structure of the Mixed Courts, they have rendered many and valuable services to the institution.[15]

The recent proposals (August, 1929) for an Anglo-Egyptian agreement include an important Egyptian note on this subject to the effect that during the period necessary for the completion of the existing programs of internal reform and of modification in the capitulatory system the Egyptian Government will maintain "the employment of British subjects in the posts of Financial Adviser to the Egyptian Government and Judicial Adviser to the Ministry of Justice." The note adds, "Future occupants of these posts will be selected by the Egyptian Government in agreement with His Britannic Majesty's Government in the United Kingdom, and will receive their appointments as Egyptian officials from the Egyptian Government." The British re-

[15] The dual relation of the Judicial Adviser to the British and Egyptian Governments was thus facetiously referred to by the Procureur-General of the Mixed Courts in his after dinner remarks on the occasion of the banquet given in honor of Sir John Percival June 9, 1928: "And, after all, has not this office had to suffer just a little from the evil which afflicted our allied armies at the beginning of the Great War—the lack of unity of command." To the same effect was the observation of the President of the Court of Appeals, who referred to the judicial advisers as being placed "between two Great Powers and a third and smaller one—the Mixed Courts." In expressing his warm appreciation of the many marks of friendliness exhibited toward him by the judges of the Mixed Courts, the guest of honor himself observed: "For after all, your attitude has been wholly disinterested. What have you to gain from the Judicial Advisers? Have not their activities, on the contrary, tended for the most part towards the abolition of the Mixed Courts or towards their alleged reform, an idea which, ultra conservative corps that you are, you detest almost as much as abolition." See also observations of Judicial Adviser in *Annual Report, 1911*, p. 26. "The Ministry of Justice, and its English heads, are not, I believe, generally regarded as too favorably inclined towards the Mixed Tribunals, their organization or procedure."

ply acknowledging receipt of this particular document "notes with satisfaction" the statements of the intention of the Egyptian Government. In a formal address delivered by the late Prime Minister, Mohamed Mahmoud Pasha on his return to Egypt immediately after the publication of the proposed treaty, he construes the above proposals as materially modifying the position of both the judicial and financial advisers.

Likewise the posts of Financial and Judicial Advisers are no more incumbent on Egypt. They have, however, been maintained because Egypt is really in need of experts to carry out the large scheme of financial and judicial reforms, and in need, while preparing projects for these reforms, of inspiring confidence in its work and aims; and there is no better way to attain this end than by soliciting the aid of foreign experts. Needless to say that it would be unwise to replace two reliable experts by others, especially now that they hold no political posts. The fact that they will be chosen from amongst British subjects is one more token of that confidence which we want to strengthen and confirm. Moreover, the existence of these two advisers is no more, as it used to be, an encroachment upon Egypt's independence. Their posts are intimately connected with Egypt's need of advice. Egypt is the sole judge of this need and its extent. In more than one place in the projects a reference has been made to the temporary nature of their junctions. Egypt's right has also been confirmed entitling it to make its own choice of persons in case it may be necessary to replace the present advisers. This, it will be remembered, is contrary to past usages when both the posts and their occupants were imposed upon Egypt.[16]

The rivalry between France and England was happily terminated by the Anglo-French accord of 1904 which declared that while Britain had no immediate intention of proposing to the Powers any changes in the

[16] *Egyptian Gazette*, August 26, 1929. (Translation as published.)

capitulatory or judicial *régime* of Egypt, nevertheless,
in the event that it should become necessary to introduce reforms tending to assimilate Egyptian legislation
to that of European nations, the French Government
"would not refuse to examine" such propositions, provided that Great Britain should adopt a similar attitude
toward proposed French reforms in Morocco.

Curiously enough the Entente of 1904 marked the re-
appearance of Germany as a leading factor in the diplomatic history of the Mixed Courts. Germany succeeded
to the rôle of France as the leader of opposition to
Great Britain.

We had always considered [writes a former judicial ad-
viser],[17] that it was with the French that we were primarily
called upon to deal by reason of their enormous financial interests in Egypt, but latterly it was becoming more and more clear
that it was Germany which was firmly resolved to block the way
to any increase of British influence and control in Egypt.
Whenever desirable, or even obviously necessary, innovations
were proposed in the constitution or working of the Mixed
Courts, it was not France, our former opponent in all these
matters, but Germany, docilely followed by her partners in the
Triple Alliance, who now regularly and persistently refused to
assent.

Apart from the few incidents here recorded the history of the Mixed Courts has been, relatively speaking,
uneventful. In May, 1921, riots occurred in Alexandria
and foreigners were attacked. Judges of the Mixed
Courts themselves suffered in the disorder and it became necessary to close the courts for a period of eight
days and to issue a moratorium covering this period.
But for the rest the story has been a tale of quiet
and unpretentious labor. It contains few dramatic epi-
sodes. In the diplomatic field the Mixed Courts come

17 Sir Malcolm McIlwraith. See *Egyptian Gazette*, December 9, 1918.

upon the stage most frequently on the occasions of the
several international commissions convened from time
to time in Cairo to consider the question of the renewal
of the life of the courts and the various modifications
proposed in the codes and the proposals of reform in
the system of the courts themselves. Such commissions
were assembled in 1880, 1884, 1890, 1898, 1904, and 1910,
and the ample folio reports which contain the minutes
of these assemblies and the numberless reports and protocols which resulted witness much devoted effort, some
small portion of which at least passed into the stage of
active realization. Sittings of the commissions were usually presided over by the Egyptian Prime Minister or
by the Minister of Justice.[18] The wastefulness and inadequacy of this method of legislating by diplomacy
and the later substitution of the present legislative system of the Mixed Courts, is elsewhere recorded in this
volume. So also is the war history of the Mixed Courts
and the story of the various projects of reform which
have engaged the attention of Great Britain and Egypt
during the past ten years.[19]

Perhaps the most auspicious occasion in their history
was the Semi-Centennial Celebration held at Alexandria on the 27th day of February, 1926, fifty years after
the courts had actually begun to function.[20] The scene

[18] A picture of the meeting of the Commission of 1898 is given in *The
Homely Diary of a Diplomat in the East,* by Thos. Skelton Harrison, the
American diplomatic agent, p. 265.

[19] Chaps. iv, xvii, and xviii.

[20] Shortly after the celebration, the *Journal of the Mixed Courts* published, under the patronage of the bar, a sumptuous, illustrated, memorial
folio volume of five hundred pages, known under the customary French
title of *Livre d'Or* or Golden Book. The text includes some forty articles
from as many different pens, covering various phases of the history and
organization of the courts. A full report of the proceedings at the Semi-
Centennial is presented in its appendix. The illustrations, covering also
the entire history of the courts and including photographs of a large
number of its most famous figures, are of very special interest. The book
reflects much credit on the bar and upon the editor of the *Law Journal*

was one of fitting dignity. The great rotunda of the courthouse had been transformed into an impressive amphitheater, and the audience which met on that occasion represented all that was most distinguished in the life of the country. The various orders of the judicial hierarchy, in their official costumes, were grouped upon the stage with that meticulous attention to rank which is an essential and often most perplexing element at every official gathering in Egypt. Immediately below the President of the Court of Appeals sat the personal representative of the reigning sovereign of Egypt, having at his right the Prime Minister whose presence was all the more significant in the light of the discouragement which the Government had shown toward the proposed celebration when it had been first suggested. The ceremonies were opened by the President of the Court. He was followed by the Procureur-General, a Belgian and a gifted man of letters. Addresses were also delivered by the President of the Bar, an Italian, and by the British Minister Plenipotentiary, speaking for Lord Lloyd, the British High Commissioner. The ceremonies concluded with a short speech by the Egyptian Minister of Justice. Of even greater significance, however, than this official expression of good will, was a message of congratulation, one among many such, received from Egypt's late political leader, Saad Zaghloul, who at the time occupied no public office.

The official ceremonies of the morning were followed by a banquet of 350 covers in the evening, and on the following day the Semi-Centennial Celebration was brought to a close by a reception given by the Bar to the Bench. An inspiring feature of this occasion was the

responsible for its preparation. The net cost of the publication over and above the income from subscriptions at one pound each, was met by the bar, an expense of some $5,000.

tribute of respect shown on all sides for the venerable Greek President of the Court of Appeals, himself a former President of the Bar. This tribute was happily summarized in the official report of the ceremonies, in words which, pointing as they do to the secret of success of the institution whose first half century of labor was then drawing to a close, may well conclude the present chapter:

Our former Batonnier did more than personify the intimate union that exists between Bench and Bar. He appeared as the noblest example which could be presented us who, coming after him, must carry on our common effort, of a life-time of enlightened labor and devotion. As the great judicial family extended him those greetings which came from the depths of their hearts, it seemed as if one saw in him exemplified the living Device, the Program and the Promise of the Mixed Courts, merged in one, LABOR OMNIA VINCIT IMPROBUS (*trans.*).

CHAPTER IV

THE MIXED COURTS AND MARTIAL LAW

THE Mixed Courts passed unscathed through the toils of war. Their doors were never closed, their jurisdiction was never questioned, their prestige emerged undimmed.

In August, 1914, Egypt had the political status of a nominally autonomous country occupied by one foreign power and owning suzerainty to another. Her ruler, the Khedive Abbas, was at Constantinople. For some months the British Government struggled with the question of Egypt's future status. Annexation, incorporation as a self-governing dominion within the empire, complete independence—these were all considered and rejected. A middle course was adopted—the declaration of a protectorate.[1] On November 2 a proclamation of martial law was issued by the British Commander General and a little over a month later, on December 18, Egypt was declared a British protectorate and the Turkish suzerainty terminated. On the following day

[1] "It is betraying no secret to say that the annexation of Egypt was considered, but was decisively rejected. There was no question of preparing the way for it; if it had been considered desirable it would have been effected at once. We did not annex Egypt in 1914 because we did not wish to annex it and for no other reason." Sir William Hayter, late Legal Adviser to the Egyptian Government. *Recent Constitutional Developments in Egypt* (Cambridge University Press, 1924), p. 7. See Elgood, *Egypt and the Army*, p. 88; also Chirol, *The Egyptian Problem*, p. 124, who quotes Lord Curzon as having stated that annexation "was deliberately and in his opinion wisely rejected." There are, however, those who believe that the decision was a good deal of a toss up. The Khedive's attitude has lately been the subject of lively controversy. See, for instance, *The Dethronement of the Khedive*, by A. H. Beaman (Allen and Unwin, 1929). The statement in the text is on the authority of Lord Cromer, Abbas II, Preface, p. vii.

the Khedive was deposed and his place given to Prince Hussein Kamel, his uncle, with the title of Sultan.

The question of the Capitulations at once presented itself. Here, too, drastic measures were considered and rejected. For practical reasons the proposal to abolish the Capitulations was put aside.[2] The British Government declared in a letter to the newly created Sultan, that the Capitulations were no longer in harmony with the development of the country, but that in the opinion of the British Government "the revision of these treaties may most conveniently be postponed until the end of the present war."

The logical consequence was that all of the existing judicial institutions of Egypt continued to function undisturbed, and a special decree was accordingly published declaring that these institutions should continue to exercise the same jurisdiction that they enjoyed at the termination of the Turkish sovereignty.

The maintenance of the Capitulations was, however, subject to an important qualification. *Inter arma silent leges.* For the protection of the country, and in the interests of the military forces quartered therein, the supreme military authority found it desirable to issue,

---

[2] After expressing the view that "it might indeed with perfect propriety have been maintained that the declaration of the protectorate had *ipso facto* terminated that *régime*," Sir Malcolm McIlwraith observes ("Legal War Work in Egypt," lecture before Grotius Society, published serially in *Egyptian Gazette*, December 5, 6, 9, 1918): "However, partly for political reasons, and largely because the Egyptian Government was not yet ready with the requisite machinery and technical staffs required for superseding the existing arrangements, it was decided to make no change during the war." The abolition of the Capitulations and with them, of the Consular Courts, would not, however, have affected the Mixed Courts, whose existence and jurisdiction were based on separate treaty engagements. In his report for 1904 (p. 7) Lord Cromer refers, without comment, to the opinion of a French jurist (Gabriel Jaray) that the recognition of a protectorate would justify the suppression of Capitulations, if the reorganization of the country in question was sufficiently advanced to afford proper guarantees of good administration.

under the sanction of martial law, a large number of military laws and ordinances, many of them of a nature which, in time of peace, would have required invoking the more cumbersome diplomatic legislative machinery elsewhere described.[3]

As early as August 2, 1914, in order to prevent an inordinate rise in the price of foodstuffs, the Government prohibited exportation. Shortly afterward proclamations were made regulating trading with the enemy and defining the rights and disabilities of enemy subjects.[4] By a decree issued in January, 1915, recourse to the courts of Egypt was denied enemy subjects, but this prohibition did not exempt them from suit. Its practical effect, however, was tempered by provision for the appointment of controllers and receivers of branches of enemy firms and, later, by provision for the appointment of a public custodian of enemy property in Egypt, with full authority to engage in litigation

[3] "Egyptian administration had become a highly complex business; a Protectorate existed side by side with Capitulations; British Advisers accepted part of the responsibility of the Government of the country, Egyptian Ministers the balance; and over all elements hung like a heavy cloud, the authority of martial law." Elgood, *Egypt and the Army*, p. 344. "The supreme power exercised by the military authority was unfettered by all the embarrassments which attended the rulers of Egypt in peaceful times. It has known no distinction in the rights and obligations of foreigners and natives. . . . While a decree or *arrêté* of the Government would only have bound native subjects, a proclamation by the military authority was enforceable against the whole population." *Report of Judicial Adviser* (1915), p. 24. To these observations may be added the following slightly premature prophecy taken from the same document. "From this brief survey of military ordinances, in their effect upon foreign privileges, it will be seen that it heralds the coming of an epoch in which there shall be unity and uniformity of legislative and administrative rules for all residents in the country, whether native or foreign." *Ibid.*, p. 24.

[4] In a recent decision of the Court of Appeals (March 1, 1927), Finck against Egyptian Government, *Bulletin*, XXXIX, 282, the court refers to this fact in the following terms: "Considering that access to the Mixed Courts has never been denied to citizens of Germany, even during the existence of hostilities, subject to their being represented by the Public Custodian. . . ."

on behalf of the sequestrated interests.[5] This official became a familiar figure in the litigation before the Mixed
Courts. On the other hand, the former jurisdiction of
the Austrian and German Consular Courts was taken
over by courts identical in organization with the British
Consular Courts, applying British law and procedure,
with the proviso that contracts between German and
Austrian subjects were interpreted according to German and Austrian law and that the national law of personal status was applied. The validity of documents was
also tested by the national law.

The first immediate contact between the Government
and the Mixed Courts arose in respect of the application of a commercial moratorium of August 5, which
prolonged until November the time within which protests, and other legal methods of recourse, could be
made in respect of commercial paper. This moratorium,
it may be noted, emanated from the civil and not from
the military authorities. It was not therefore clothed
with the sanction of martial law. But in practical effect
this was a distinction without a difference. It was the
military power that was speaking,[6] and the question at
once arose as to what was to be the attitude of the Mixed
Courts. The moment was midsummer. Only the few
judges required for emergency labors during the summer recess were in Egypt. Two days before the promulgation of the moratorium the vacation judge who occu-

[5] For an excellent brief summary of these measures see Elgood, *Egypt
and the Army*, chap. ix, ''Egypt in 1915.''

[6] The preamble of the governmental decree of August 6, relative to
contracts with the enemy, after reciting the fact of the existence of war
between Great Britain and Germany, continues: ''And whereas the presence in Egypt of the Army of Occupation of His Britannic Majesty ren-
ders the country liable to attack by His Majesty's enemies; And whereas,
by reason of this fact all necessary measures must be taken to defend the
country against the risk of such an attack; To this end the Egyptian
Government is advised to take the following measures . . .'' (*trans.*).
Docs. Off., 1914, p. 262.

pied *ad interim* the post of acting president of the Court of Appeals, was asked by the ministry of justice what attitude his courts proposed to take in the presence of the proposed emergency measures, and especially whether they would accept the responsibility of giving effect to such measures without the previous consent of the Powers—a consent that it would obviously be impossible to secure within the brief delay available.

The judge upon whom the responsibility for a most critical decision was thus suddenly imposed proved equal to the emergency.[7] He replied that for himself he would have no hesitation in coöperating with the Government in all measures rendered necessary by the military situation, and that he would immediately consult those of his colleagues who were present in Egypt. The following day he advised the Government that, as far as he and his associates could control the situation, the moratorium would be applied in the Mixed Courts. The decision was followed by the necessary administrative orders of the courts, which were immediately applied throughout the Mixed Courts system.

Shortly afterward a law was promulgated by the Government fixing the minimum prices of foodstuffs, the first solicitude of the Government being to protect the food supply of Egypt and the regulation of its exportation. The judges of the Mixed Courts then in Egypt convened in a *de facto,* if incomplete, assembly, in order to accord to the measure such formality of approval as was practicable, and the approval of this provisional assembly was noted in the preamble to the measure as published. On the return of the judges in the autumn the action thus taken was unanimously approved.[8]

[7] Hon. Michael Hansson of Norway, today the President of the Court of Appeals.
[8] The incident led to the promulgation in 1916, by the consent of the

For the most part subsequent legislative enactments during the War took the form of proclamations under martial law, but all alike were accorded full faith and credit in all litigation arising in the Mixed Courts.

As might have been expected, the exercise of this legislative power gave rise to various remonstrances by representatives of the Powers, on the ground that the Capitulations had not been respected. Thanks, however, to the characteristic moderation which marked the exercise of the British military power and to the conciliatory attitude of the Powers, such controversies were all settled without serious conflict.

Many of these enactments created police offenses very properly punishable by the military authorities, such, for instance, as those relating to the sale of alcoholic liquors to members of the military forces. Others, however, covered subjects which had but a doubtful relation to that "military necessity" which under the American theory, at least, is the condition of the exercise of martial law. The extension of such enactments, under the sanction of martial law (not abolished until 1922) long after the termination of the War, gave rise to much criticism.[9]

Powers, of a decree giving discretion to the Mixed Courts judges, during the summer recess, to pass on emergency administrative measures, subject to the subsequent approval of a regularly constituted assembly. It is also interesting to record the reply of the then acting British Judicial Adviser to the question, later asked him, as to what would have been the result had the Mixed Courts refused to apply the emergency measures of the period: "The Mixed Courts would have been closed." *Livre d'Or*, p. 99.

[9] See the following observations of Sir William Brunyate, Acting Financial Adviser to the Egyptian Government, in the course of a lecture delivered at the Sultanieh School of Law on February 12, 1918, and published in *L'Egypte Contemporaine* (1918), pp. 195 *et seq.*: "In France the *état de siège* has long been recognized, and even regulated: in England, so-called Martial Law has been regarded as an anomaly abhorrent to all lawyers and representing nothing but the arbitrary will of the military commander, who, but for an Act of Indemnity, would be liable before the Civil Courts, for every encroachment upon the rights of private citizens.

A much discussed example was the publication of a drastic and elaborate decree regulating house rents, designed to prevent the exploitation of the tenant class by their landlords. The measure was promulgated by the Egyptian Government in the name of the Sultan in 1920, and instead of being submitted to the Legislative Assembly of the Court of Appeals was made applicable to foreigners by contemporaneous proclamation under martial law. As the decree was valid only for a year, the same procedure was repeated a year later, and was only altered in 1922 when the law for the first time was submitted to the Legislative Assembly of the Court of Appeals and its applicability to foreigners thereby given international sanction.[10]

Another contact between the military lawmaking power and the Mixed Courts arose in relation to the problem of the settlement of claims against the Egyptian Government arising out of post-war riots and disturbances which took place in 1919 and 1921.

It was deemed inadvisable to allow liabilities thereby incurred to be made the subject of litigation in the existing courts. A governmental decree was accordingly issued in the name of the Sultan, closing the native courts to such demands and referring them to a commission of seven members, which included a British

We happen to be living under Martial Law in Egypt at the present moment, and I think that I may safely say that it is not an unpleasant *régime* to live under; but the interesting legal problem to which it gives rise is, what would be the prospects of success of an action brought before the High Court in London, against an officer acting in Egypt under the sanction of Martial Law? My clear impression is that at the present moment, such an action would necessarily fail; forty years ago I suspect that his advisers might have been seriously embarrassed in attempting to frame his defense.''

[10] Other examples of the practice are to be found in a proclamation issued in 1920 regulating the use of lighting with a view to relieving a fuel shortage, and a law forbidding the assignment of wages or salaries to trade unions.

judge of one of the native courts. Shortly afterward
(July 8, 1921) a decree was issued under martial law,
by the Commanding General of the British forces in
Egypt, reciting the fact that a million pounds had been
set aside for the payment of claims resulting from the
1919 riots, and declaring that such claims should be presented to the same commission. It further declared that
the Mixed Courts should not entertain jurisdiction over
any such suit against the Egyptian Government. The
validity of this proclamation was tacitly admitted in the
Mixed Courts. Similar action was taken in the case of
the Alexandria riots of 1921.

When the decree was published suspending martial
law in Egypt (July 5, 1923) the courts came again in
contact with the military power on the promulgation of
an indemnity act covering all demands arising out of
actions of any description taken by the military authority under cover of martial law. The act prohibited
such suits from being brought "before any jurisdiction
of the country" and was doubtless intended to include
the Mixed Courts. In this case, as in the case of the preceding proclamations, the validity of the pronounce-
ment has not been contested in the courts.

Apart from these more official contacts, the War also
touched the Mixed Courts in their family relations with
their Austrian and German members. At the outbreak
of the War the President of the Court of Appeals was
himself a German. With the rest of his colleagues he
had left Egypt for the summer vacation and, under
existing British military regulations, neither he nor his
German and Austrian associates were permitted to return to Egypt. The treatment of these officials gave rise
to considerable discussion, but the problem was grace-
fully solved by the decision of the Government to extend their leave of absence until the following February,

which was the date of the expiration of the existing period of functioning of the Mixed Courts—and consequently of the engagement of its judges. The gentlemen in question were simply not reappointed, and as already explained, the surrender of their capitulatory rights by Germany and Austria, confirmed the abandonment by these powers of their right to be represented in the Mixed Courts.

In conclusion it may be said that in a long succession of notable litigations in which enemy subjects or interests were involved during the War, the Mixed Courts maintained their tradition of aloofness from all considerations of national or political character. No enemy suitors were ever heard to complain that the scales of justice had been shaken by the clash of arms. The following fine tribute of the Judicial Adviser who was in office during this period is a fitting epilogue to the war-history of the courts.

The Alexandria Court is to be congratulated on having risen superior to all considerations of racial or political bias and on not only having maintained the high reputation of the protecting power for impartiality even as regards the enemy—but also for having worthily maintained the best traditions of a Court, which . . . has constituted hitherto, for all foreigners in Egypt, the principal bulwark against injustice and oppression of every kind and has represented abroad the chief guarantee to foreign traders of even-handed justice for all nations.[11]

11 Sir Malcolm McIlwraith, *op. cit.*

CHAPTER V

THE JUDICIARY

THE organization of the Mixed Courts corresponds broadly to that of the federal judicial system in the United States. It comprises a Court of Appeals which sits at Alexandria, and three District Courts sitting at Cairo, Alexandria, and Mansourah. The latter is an important cotton center in the Delta from which is assigned yearly a judge to hold sessions at Port Said.

The seat of the Court of Appeals was fixed at Alexandria rather than at Cairo, the national capital, three hours distant by rail, in order to remove the court as far as possible from danger of political and diplomatic influences. Recently a suggestion was made by the Egyptian Government to transfer the court to the capital. The movement had the support of the Cairo bar, but immediately aroused the violent opposition on the part not only of the remainder of the bar but of the entire community of Alexandria. A strong committee headed by Egypt's foremost private citizen, Prince Omar Toussoun, was organized to oppose the change, and for weeks the question was the subject of a lively discussion in the press. The controversy is generally believed to have shown that the change cannot be carried into effect, at least in the near future, although the program of reforms submitted in 1927 to the Powers includes a proviso authorizing the Egyptian Government to change the seat of the court in its discretion.[1]

In accordance with the Latin system a sharp distinc-

[1] See chap. xviii.

tion in nomenclature is observed in the use of French terms, referring to the upper and the lower courts. The Court of Appeals is known as *La Cour*—officially *La Cour d'Appel Mixte;* the lower or District Courts bear the title of *Tribunal.* Similarly a member of the upper bench is known as *Conseiller,* the equivalent of the American term "Justice"; the members of the District Courts bear the title of *Juge* or Judge.[2]

The number of the justices of the Court of Appeals was fixed originally at eleven (four Egyptians and seven foreigners) and the number of judges in each of the three District Courts at seven (three Egyptians and four foreigners). The number of judges in any court, however, may be increased by the Egyptian Government if the Court of Appeals certifies to such necessity, providing always that the proportion of foreign to native judges is not substantially modified. By virtue of this privilege the size of the various courts has been several times increased, bringing the original total number of thirty-two to the present total of seventy.

The method of the selection of the foreign judges gave rise to much discussion during the diplomatic negotiations. "The cornerstone of the Reform," wrote Nubar to the Italian Foreign Minister in 1873, "is the European judge—the judge from abroad, who brings

2 These distinctions had been adopted in France under the Consulate, but not until some time after the establishment of the Courts of Appeal. It is characteristic of the French jealousy of the great powers exercised by the old French parliaments (including power to refuse to approve royal decrees) that after the Revolution France for some years declined to establish an appellate order of courts, contenting herself instead with a system of "circular appeal" from one district court to another, a device which was followed in Egypt in the system which preceded the Mixed Courts. Furthermore, France at first refused to accord to the new appeal court the description of *La Cour* or even to designate its decisions by the traditional term of *arrêts,* but maintained, for a considerable time, the use of the term *jugement,* which is now universally, in the Latin system (including Egypt), confined to the opinions of the lower courts.

with him the traditions which are the rightful birth-right of a magistracy." It was the frank avowal of this principle, the recognition by Egypt of the inadequacy of her own magistrates to solve, unaided, the problem which faced the country, that paved the way to the triumphant issue of the negotiations which have already been described. This principle was effectively consecrated by a provision of the Charter declaring that the courts, both upper and lower, should be composed of a fixed number of foreign and of native judges, the former being in sufficient majority to render possible the carrying out of the further provisions of the charter which fixed the proportion of native and foreign judges required in each chamber.

But how were these judges to be chosen, and how were they to be apportioned among the several Powers? These were questions as interesting to the parties concerned as they were delicate of solution. On the one hand, the susceptibilities of the Egyptian Government as represented by two able and vigorous champions of its sovereign rights had to be respected. On the other hand, the conflicting claims of skilful diplomats, representing nations who were for the most part comparatively indifferent to the adoption of the new reform, had to be met with convincing assurances. The manner in which the problem was finally worked out is an interesting one. The French commissioners had urged that the selection of judges should be made by the several Powers involved. This suggestion was firmly rejected by Nubar Pasha, who repeatedly emphasized, always in the name of the Khedive, his unwillingness to treat this feature of the reform on any basis of separate nationality. "It should be a matter," insisted the Khedive, "simply of assuring competent judges qualified to protect the interests of all litigants. The judges are to be chosen to administer the law and not to represent the interests of their several subjects.'' While it would therefore be highly fitting to provide guarantees for the capacity of the judges, this was entirely outside the question of their individual nationalities. To place the selection of judges on a purely national basis ''would be incompatible with the dignity of His Highness the Khedive and with the independence of his Government.''

In deference to this divergence of views the solution was arrived at of including in the Charter only certain general provisions governing the selection of the judges and of allowing the question of their nationality to be settled by a more delicate diplomatic process.

Under the formula finally chosen, it was provided that the selection of the judges should be made by the Egyptian Government, but that

in order that it may be assured as to the guarantees presented by the persons whom it may select, it shall address itself unofficially to the Ministers of Justice abroad and will engage only persons who have received the approval and authorization of their own Government.

It will be noted that the communication is to be made unofficially (*officieusement* as distinguished from *officiellement*) and that it is to be addressed to the Minister of Justice and not to the Government itself. This was in line with insistence on the part of the Egyptian Government that such negotiations should not assume a diplomatic character. The subject was raised before the International Commission, convened in Cairo in 1880, and the nondiplomatic character of the communication was emphasized by the Egyptian Minister of Justice. The American representative replied that the request should properly be addressed to the several Governments directly and not to a Minister of Justice.

The French and German representatives maintained with good sense that the matter was of little importance as the Ministers of Justice would undoubtedly do nothing without first consulting their Governments. The British Minister objected that if the nomination was discussed diplomatically the judges would arrive in Egypt as official representatives of their country. And thus the discussion ended, leaving the situation precisely where it was in 1875, and where it has remained ever since.

The question as to the proper qualifications of candidates is left to the discretion of the Egyptian Government. The Charter is silent on the subject. Nubar's original intention was to name as judges those who already occupied judicial office in Europe. The magistrates will be chosen "among the magistrates of Europe," reads the official "explanations" accompanying his report of 1867. This is in keeping with the continental tradition according to which the magistracy is regarded essentially as a life career. In deference, however, to the British and American tradition, no such rule was adopted and, indeed, a suggestion to this effect made during the sessions of one of the international commissions was speedily withdrawn. The selection of judges is thus guided by the same considerations of fitness as would apply in the case of any well-administered judicial system. Obviously a good working knowledge of French is essential. A judge must be able to follow the oral arguments and read easily the briefs and other voluminous documents. He must be prepared in Summary Court, and later as presiding officer of a chamber, to direct the proceedings and conduct the necessary colloquy with counsel. More severe, however, in its test of fluency in the French language, will be his duty as "reporter," which calls for making concise but comprehensive oral

reports of cases to his colleagues in the conference room, and the weekly preparation of the written opinions which are obligatory in every case.

But if an adequate knowledge of French is essential, it is of course not the most important qualification. The really vital requirements are the possession of essentially the same fundamental professional qualities as would be expected of the judges named to an important trial or appellate court, as the case may be, in any modern country. The proper candidate is a well-trained lawyer, a man with a disciplined legal mind, with experience in the rapid handling of practical legal problems, and possessing above all what is sufficiently well indicated by the term "judicial temperament." The Mixed Courts are no place for a doctrinaire or a legal dilettante. From a professional point of view the work is singularly interesting and varied. But it is arduous and difficult and during the judicial year the machine works under high pressure. No lawyer inadequately fitted for the post could hope to be happy in the work. He would be quickly and painfully conscious of his deficiency and it would be immediately reflected in an added burden laid upon the shoulders of his colleagues.[3]

From time to time suggestions have been made looking to the exaction of previous legal experience in Egypt but the fact that several of the capitulatory Powers are not represented at the Egyptian bar, as well as the obvious interest of the Egyptian Government in drawing into its service experienced judges from the various judicial systems of Europe for whom the ca-

[3] "There is much work to be done and each judge must contribute his full share. Inability to do this will cause unkind criticism and reflect upon our country's action in the matter." Extract from letter of the late Judge Tuck, for sixteen years one of America's representatives in the Mixed Courts.

reer of the Mixed Courts has always exercised strong attraction, has defeated all such proposals.

As might be expected the practical working out of the system has varied somewhat during the history of the courts. While in some cases the Egyptian Government itself has undertaken to itself select, either abroad or from the foreign colonies in Egypt, candidates for the Mixed Court benches, the general practice is for the Egyptian Government to invite the foreign Powers concerned to suggest names from which selections may be made, being naturally guided in the exercise of its final choice by the counsel of its Judicial Adviser.[4] This does not necessarily mean, however, that the Egyptian Government has ever abandoned its right to assume the initiative in making the selections, or to exercise a veto power in respect to the names suggested.

Vacancies in the Court of Appeals are generally filled by promotion. Thus eight of the eleven foreign members of the upper court have served in the District Courts. Such nominations have the added guarantee that they must be approved by the Court of Appeals which has been known to refuse to approve a nomination presented by the Government.

As to the distribution of the foreign judges among the several nationalities represented in the courts, this

[4] An illustration of the sources of the recruitment of the judges of the Mixed Courts is contained in the following extract from the report of the Judicial Adviser of 1916. A similar summary, if made today, would read much the same. "The vacancies in the Mixed Tribunals (including the Spanish post vacated by Mr. Fournier-Cuadros in 1915 and a new post created in 1916) have been filled by the appointment of the Count d'Andino (Spain), Public Prosecutor before the International Court for the New Hebrides; Mr. Vryakos (Greece), Advocate General of the Court of Appeal of Athens; Mr. Falqui Cao (Italy), Consular Judge in Egypt; Mr. Monteiro (Portugal), President of the Chamber of Deputies and formerly Minister of Justice and Minister of Public Works; Mr. W. H. H. Thorne (Great Britain), District Magistrate at Larnaca (Cyprus), and Gamil Bey Sabet, Chef du Parquet of the Native Tribunal of Alexandria."

was a matter of special delicacy. The subject is not referred to in the Charter of the courts. It was covered by a series of special agreements recorded in diplomatic correspondence and confirmed and to some extent modified by subsequent usage. An illustration of the form and character of those agreements is furnished by the exchange of correspondence between the French Ambassador at Constantinople and his Foreign Office. The French Government pressed its Ambassador to secure an agreement in the matter. The Ambassador is compelled to reply that while Nubar had advised him that it was the Khedive's "intention" to choose the judges of the District Courts from Belgium, Switzerland, and Holland, and the justices of the Court of Appeals from the seven great Powers who had participated in the sessions of the Constantinople commission (France, England, United States, Russia, Italy, Austria, and Germany) he had refused to assume any binding obligation in the matter.[5] "As a result of which," adds the Ambassador, "a moment may arrive when the French element may be eliminated." He inquires therefore whether his Government is willing to accept as sufficient the expression of the Khedive's intention as thus recorded in an unofficial letter. Later he asks of Nubar, What is the precise diplomatic value of such an "intention"? Nubar is prepared with an interpretation. It may be considered "as having the value of an undertaking, in this sense, that if the Khedive should alter his declared intentions" the French Government should

---

[5] See observation of Nubar Pasha in his letter to Count Barbolani, the Italian representative, February 24, 1875: "In speaking of European judges, his Highness has never had the intention of indicating judges of any particular nationality and of restricting the selection of competent men to any particular countries. For him, I repeat, it has never been a question of nationality, but a question of character and the guarantees offered to litigants." See Borelli Bey, cxiv.

have the right to consider itself released from this engagement. The formula was found adequate and fairly represents the nature of the understanding reached between Egypt and the other great Powers, at least as far as the Court of Appeals was concerned. Other diplomatic understandings, however, were entered into covering the case of the judges of the District Courts, the final result, generally speaking, being to assure to each of the capitulatory Powers a minimum of two judges in the District Courts, provided that if one of the smaller Powers happened also to be represented on the Court of Appeals it would enjoy the right to only one representative in the lower courts. By a still later agreement (1889) a right was conceded to Greece, in recognition of the commanding importance of her commercial colony, to be represented in the Court of Appeals.

In filling the various seats which are not specially assigned the choice of the Egyptian Government is not limited to the capitulatory Powers. It was by virtue of this discretion that the Government has included Switzerland among the sources of judicial recruitment. In 1929 the Swiss President of the Cairo District Court was promoted to the Court of Appeals and, as it chanced, his place was taken by a Swiss compatriot who had previously held the vice-presidency of the same court. As already mentioned, a German jurist was also named to the Cairo District Court in 1926.

How far, however, may the Egyptian Government, while respecting the minimum of representation just referred to, increase the total number of judges of one nationality beyond that of the others? This question has given rise to constant diplomatic controversy due to the absence of any precise stipulations on the subject. In a declaration made in 1873 the British Government declared that its final acceptance of the proposed project for the establishment of the Mixed Courts was essentially dependent upon the principle "of avoiding giving any preponderance to one nationality over another either in constituting the Courts or in filling vacancies."[6] The Egyptian Government has latterly maintained that this represented merely a wish expressed by the British Government and not accepted by Egypt, and that the latter is bound by no limitations in the distribution of the foreign seats except those imposed by the diplomatic agreements already referred to.[7]

The question is not one for the historian to solve. He can only summarize the facts. It would seem that equality of representation between the great Powers was substantially the rule up to the outbreak of the War even though in 1889, in consideration of a temporary renunciation by France of its right under the Anglo-French Agreement of 1874 to be represented in the Parquet, a second French judge was appointed, *à titre personnel,* to fill one of the two additional posts created in the Court of Appeals—a numerical advantage in favor of the French which continued for three years. In securing this appointment the French Government assured the Egyptian Government that it recognized the principle "of the equality of representation of all the great Powers in the Mixed Courts," and as this special arrangement was approved by the other

6 Letter of Sir Henry Elliott, the British Ambassador at Constantinople, to Nubar Pasha, May 26, 1873 (*Foreign Relations, U. S. 1873,* Pt. I, Vol. II, p. 1118). This letter is published in full in *The Nineteenth Century and After* for March, 1926, in an article by Judge Crabités, "The Mixed Courts of Egypt," who refers to it as forming "to a large extent the corner stone of the Mixed Courts."

7 In support of this contention the Egyptian Government has pointed out that in the beginning there were three Dutch and three Belgian judges in the District Courts and that at that time France, the United States, and Great Britain had each only one judge in these lower courts.

great Powers it would appear that the principle of equality was then generally accepted.

In 1921, however, during the *régime* of martial law, the principle was departed from. The pendency of the unsuccessful project of reform, elsewhere discussed, led to the increase of British membership in both the upper and lower courts as a preliminary measure to the projected reorganization of the Mixed Courts under British trusteeship. Two additional British justices were named to the Court of Appeals and additional British judges were named in the District Courts.[8] Other inequalities of representation also occurred with the result that at the present time the total membership of the courts is distributed as follows: Great Britain, 7; Italy, 5; France, Belgium, United States, and Greece, each 4; Norway, and Spain, each 3; Russia, Switzerland, Netherlands, Portugal, Denmark, and Sweden, each 2; Germany, 1. Of the eleven foreign seats of the Court of Appeals, five only (Italy, France, Great Britain, the United States, and Greece) are specially assigned. The remaining "unassigned" seats, or personal appointments, are filled by justices selected from Norway, Spain, Switzerland, and Belgium, and by the two additional justices named from Great Britain.

This question of the distribution of judicial seats among the various Powers has always been a delicate one, assuming at times an emphasis out of proportion to

[8] In the International Commission of 1880, on the motion of the American representative, a proposition was adopted to amend the Charter to provide that the Court of Appeals should consist of "ten foreigners of different nationalities." This proposal, however, shared the fate of the numerous other proposals adopted by the Commission, and was never carried into effect. It was again proposed to, but not adopted by, the Commission of 1884. In 1921 the bar of the Mixed Courts urged the necessity "if the harmony which should exist between the composition of the Courts and the interests of the litigants is not to be compromised, of fixing a maximum proportional to the total number of judges, for the judges of each nationality."

its intrinsic importance. The objection to allowing any one Power to enjoy a substantial preponderance over other Powers does not lie in the possibility that the scales of justice might be disturbed by national partisanship. The Mixed Courts may fairly claim to have passed beyond such danger. It lies rather in the serious risk of disturbing the fundamental tradition and *esprit de corps* of the Mixed Courts as an institution which, so long as it exists, must enjoy the support and confidence and protection of many foreign Powers, and as such must remain beyond the sphere of influence of any of them, particularly in all that touches its administrative and legislative functions. In this fact lies the secret of the success of the institution. It is this that explains the complete absence of blocs or coalitions, that has bound the judges into a veritable "judicial brotherhood." This tie would inevitably be loosened by the according to any Power, large or small, a permanent and substantial preponderance of representation over its sister nations. But it does not follow that mathematical equality of representation between even the great Powers should be insisted on. This would not only be impracticable but might well impair the efficiency of the courts in preventing the appointment of the best candidates. One judge more or less among the thirty chambers of the District Courts represents a completely negligible element of added guarantee. Subject to a proper regard for the principle of "no substantial preponderance," especially in the composition of the Court of Appeals, and to the traditional *minimum* representation guaranteed to each capitulatory Power, the judges should be selected primarily on a basis of fitness, regardless of nationality.[9] The highest interests of diplo-

[9] Compare the following observations of Lord Cromer (*Annual Report, 1906*, p. 14): "In view of the cosmopolitan character of the foreign

macy, the common interests of all the Powers, dictate the highest measure of efficiency. National prestige is judged by the capacity and not by the number of a country's representatives. It is diminished and not augmented by every appointment which falls below the best traditions of the courts. The guiding star in diplomatic discussion should always be to strengthen the hands of the courts by bringing to their benches the ablest judges whose services are anywhere obtainable.

The distribution of judges among the District Courts is dictated by the practical needs of administration, the magistracy being regarded for administrative purposes as a single corps, under the direction of the Court of Appeals. Long precedent requires the newly appointed judges in the District Court to serve their judicial apprenticeship at Mansourah, the smallest, and commonly regarded as the least attractive of the three judicial centers, although the representatives of the great Powers have commonly been relieved from this duty and assigned directly to Cairo or to Alexandria. As a result the distribution of nationalities as between the three judicial centers varies widely.

The compensation of the judges of the Mixed Courts is fixed by statute and is paid directly by the Egyptian

population and the essentially Latin character of the law, I hold that the Magistrates should be drawn from a variety of nations, and that in particular the Latin races should be strongly represented. At the same time I am not prepared to advocate the indefinite continuance of the present system, under which all the various foreign Powers regard themselves as entitled to something like equality of treatment in the selection of judges from among the subjects of each of them. Nor do I consider that the present system of nomination, which until recently was allowed to degenerate into one under which the Egyptian Government had practically no voice in the selection of Judges, is altogether satisfactory. I can, for instance, see no reason why the Judges of the Court of Appeal should be mainly chosen from amongst the subjects of the Great Powers: Political interests should in my view, be entirely disassociated from the administration of Justice.''

Government. On the founding of the courts the salaries were fixed, by agreement with the Powers, on a basis of gold francs with an additional allowance of 20 per cent in lieu of pension.[10] This system remained practically unchanged until 1920, when, in order to render appointments to the Mixed Courts of greater attraction as a life career to the young European jurist, the principle of the sliding scale was introduced, with a minimum and maximum salary, and an increase of a hundred pounds at the end of each two years of service.[11]

In 1920 foreign judges of the Mixed Courts were admitted to the benefits of the state pension system, and were given certain supplemental advantages, in return for abandoning the 20 per cent annual bonus. The situation was materially modified in 1929, as a result of the promulgation of a new pension law applicable to all government employees, and of a supplementary law applicable only to the judges of the Mixed Courts.[12] As they stand today these laws accord a right of pension

[10] This agreement was embodied in a schedule annexed to certain Supplementary Regulations, promulgated by the Khedive on December 28, 1875, before the opening of the courts. See Borelli, p. 24.

[11] The argument has been occasionally advanced that the principle of the sliding scale is in conflict with the provision of the Charter of the Mixed Courts that ''all judges of the same category shall receive the same salaries.'' (Article 23.) The salaries were originally fixed at 40,000 gold francs, for the justices of the Court of Appeals, and at 30,000 for those in the lower courts, not including the supplementary allowance above mentioned. Under the new scale, as slightly increased in 1922, the salaries of the foreign members of the upper court now range from 1,800 to 2,200 Egyptian pounds, and those of the judges of the District Courts from 1,400 to 1,800. The salaries of the native judges in the Mixed Courts are 600 pounds lower. The Egyptian pound has a legal tender value in Egypt slightly exceeding that of the pound sterling, 97½ piasters being the equivalent of the British pound. The Egyptian pound contains 100 piasters and is thus practically the equivalent of five American dollars. The ''pound'' mentioned throughout this volume is the Egyptian pound and will be designated by the customary prefix L.E. (Livre Egyptienne).

[12] Decree Laws Nos. 37 and 41 of 1929, promulgated May 28, 1929. See Journal Officiel, March 4, 1929, No. 50, which also contains the Government's explanatory notes.

to all officials who may wish to retire after fifteen years service, if they have reached the age of fifty, or, after twenty-five years service, regardless of their age. The pension is fixed at an amount equivalent to one-fiftieth of the average annual salary received during the two last years of service, multiplied by the number of such years, and thus commencing with a minimum pension of fifteen-fiftieths. A further and special advantage is accorded by the new law to judges of the Mixed Courts in order to equalize the situation of the foreign judges with that of their native associates, who if they have previously served in other branches of the Government are entitled to take into account these years in computing the basis of their pension. The new law allows a judge who has been appointed after the age of thirty-five to add to his years of service one-third of the difference between thirty-five and the age at which he was appointed, not, however, to exceed five, and with the proviso that these added years do not affect the requirement that he shall have actually served fifteen years in order to be entitled to a pension. Nor may it be utilized to complete the requirement as to the twenty-five years of service. The maximum pension may not exceed three-fourths of the average annual salary of the last two years (or of the last annual salary itself if he is forced to retire on age limit), nor may it in any case exceed L.E. 1,080 ($5,400).

The new system is based on a compulsory salary deduction of 7½ per cent. As the former law fixed the deduction at 5 per cent the new law exacts, on the part of those who elect to accept its provisions, a repayment of the difference of 2½ per cent spread, if desired, throughout a period of ten years.

The distribution of the pension after a judge's death

(and the rule is general for all officials) is covered in careful detail. Generally speaking, three-fourths of the pension continues payable to his widow and children, if there be three or more children, and five-eighths if there is a widow and only one or two children. If there be a widow and no children the widow receives three-eighths for life or until remarriage. If a judge dies before reaching a pensionable status his dependents receive instead a cash indemnity based on years of service. If he becomes invalided before he is otherwise entitled to retire on pension the Court of Appeals is authorized in its discretion to accord him as an "exceptional benefit" the right to consider his years of service as doubled in number, provided that such added benefit shall not exceed eight years, nor in any case exceed the number of years necessary for him to reach the retirement age.

The introduction of the pension system afforded an opportunity to establish a compulsory retirement age of seventy in the Court of Appeals and of sixty-five in the District Courts. In the latter case discretion is granted to the Egyptian cabinet, on recommendation of the Court of Appeals, to authorize the continuance in service of a judge in the lower courts till the age of seventy.

Tenure is for life. "The judges shall be irremovable," reads the Charter. They may not even be removed from one district to another without their consent. They are appointed by the King of Egypt, but their discipline and impeachment rests solely in their own hands, being entrusted to the Court of Appeals. As a recent authority well observed: "The Mixed Courts enjoy a life of the most complete autonomy, and that, too, from every point of view, disciplinary, financial, and administrative, and in respect to every other authority except their own Court of Appeals.'"[13] By a three-fourths vote this body may remove a judge from office for official misconduct, defined as applying to all acts "which may compromise their honor as judges or the independence of their votes." A judge against whom disciplinary action has been instituted may present his resignation. If accepted the impeachment fails of course.

The independence of the judiciary is further guarded by a proviso that the judges shall not receive at the hands of the Egyptian Government any mark of distinction, honorary or material.[14] This not only applies to decorations but also operates to prevent the Egyptian members from receiving those honorary ranks which are traditional in the case of the Egyptian official in other branches of the public services. It does not apply, however, in the case of other officials in the Mixed Courts, a number of whom have been decorated with the rank of Bey in recognition of the length and character of service. Nor, of course, does it prevent the Government from honoring retiring magistrates. It is the custom to confer upon the retiring presidents of the Court of Appeals the highest available decoration in the bestowal of the Government. The general prohibition is enforced by a proviso that the acceptance by a judge of any remuneration other than his salary, or of any present of material value, or of any other material benefit, shall carry with it removal from office without right to compensation. Another provision of the Charter forbids alike the judges of the Mixed Courts, and all the more important officials in the personnel, from occupy-

[13] Messina, *Traité de Droit Civil Egyptien Mixte*, I, 39. As to the question of financial independence, however, see chap. xiv.

[14] The proposal of the Egyptian Government made in 1927 and not yet acted on by the Powers to abolish this prohibition has not received the general support of either bench or bar. See chap. xviii.

ing any other salaried post, and from engaging in any trade or profession.[15]

The aim of the founders of the Mixed Courts to insure the independence and the integrity of the new magistracy has been well achieved. Assuming that the judges named to these positions are endowed with common frailties, many factors have contributed to free them from the temptations and influences that might disturb the impartiality of their deliberations. The foreign judges come from countries widely separated and, on their arrival in Egypt, are altogether isolated from the busy commercial world. This isolation is confirmed by a wise tradition that discourages any active participation in the civic affairs of the community. They find themselves members of a small and closely united judicial family which lives under the aegis of the high calling which has brought them from their homelands. No occasion exists for rivalry between them and while the dignity of their office entitles them, as far as their tastes so dictate, to the best that society in their respective cities has to offer, their relations with the members of the business world who are likely to appear as litigants before them, are seldom intimate. Needless to say they play no part in political life or in diplomatic affairs. Political controversy of every kind is of course denied them. A judicial circular warns unnecessarily the members of the bench that litigants must not be permitted to fear to submit their cases for judgment because of holding adverse political opinions. ''The office which is confided to the judiciary necessarily deprives them of a large measure of that liberty which other citizens enjoy, and imposes on them the most complete reserve.''

[15] This has been applied to prevent a judge from acting as manager of a family estate, regardless of the question of remuneration, and this on the ground principally that he might thereby be exposed to the necessity of engaging in litigation in his own courts.

But this very reserve, and the essential loneliness inherent in any proper exercise of the judicial function, helps to confirm that independence which is at once their strength and, to many who come from active lives, their chief compensation. The power which appointed them cannot remove them. Their authority is defined by a charter, which is a treaty between many nations. These nations, no less than the Government of Egypt, are their protectors. But again, these several nations, while they must protect, cannot remove them. Judges are not officials of the country from which they come. Appointed for life and protected by a reasonably generous pension system, they have, if their wants are modest, nothing to fear for the future and no favors to ask of any Government. Of course the Mixed Courts might come to an end. But there is always the well-proved Egyptian maxim that "only the provisional endures,"[16] and the judges who, in the deliberation chambers, contemplate the portraits of generations of venerable and venerated jurists who have served until death or retirement, find little cause for anxiety on this score. To a singular degree they are the undisturbed masters of their fate; the conditions of their existence minister to a degree of independence as complete as may be conceived in a judicial institution, and the uncertainties of the future play no rôle in their quiet judicial life.

[16] See De Rausas, II, 496. ''Les institutions les plus provisoires sont celles qui ont les plus grandes chances de durée et—en Orient surtout, le provisoire seul risque d'être perpétuel.''

CHAPTER VI

THE PARQUET

T0 the judicial family as it has just been described must be added another figure—that of the Procureur-General.[1] The office he fills is borrowed directly from the French system, where it came into existence in the fifteenth century. It has no counterpart in Anglo-Saxon legal organization. Its functions correspond most nearly perhaps to those of the Attorney-General in the United States, but the Procureur-General is not the head of the Department of Justice and there are other important differences which make the comparison misleading.[2]

The office of the Procureur-General is officially referred to as that of the *Ministère Public* or Public Ministry—but this term must not be confused with that of the Ministry of Justice under whose official supervision it is placed. The Procureur-General and his staff constitute the Parquet which takes its name from the flooring or *parquet* before and below the court where these officers of justice originally took their place, in France. The position of these officials is considered a semijudicial

[1] The Procureur-General receives the same salary as the justices of the Court of Appeals (L.E. 1,800–2,200). The salary of his chief assistant is L.E. 1,200–1,600; two more receive L.E. 800–1,200; one L.E. 800–1,000; five L.E. 540–780, and two L.E. 240–600.

[2] The best modern exposition of the functions of this office is Francisque Goyet, *Le Ministère Public* (Sirey: Paris, 1926), p. 500. See also the admirable manual of Prof. Paul Cuche, in the series of handbooks published by Dalloz, *Paris, Précis de Droit Criminel* (Paris, 1927), p. 244. The French excel in the publication of convenient legal handbooks written by their most eminent professors and published at low prices. The price of the volume just cited, for instance (450 pages), is eighteen francs, or less than seventy-five cents.

MAIN ENTRANCE TO COURTHOUSE AT ALEXANDRIA

Translation of Arabic inscriptions: In pediment, "Justice Is
the Foundation of Government"
In panel above doorway, "Palace of the Court. A.D. 1886.
Year of the Hegira, 1303"

one in a much wider sense than applies to United States Attorneys or District or States' Attorneys; and they are looked upon as members of the magistracy—the "standing magistracy" (*magistrature debout*) so called in contrast to the judges who comprise the "seated magistracy" (*magistrature assise*) and because of the fact that they rise when they address the court. In court their place is on a level with the bench itself at a desk placed to the right of, but somewhat removed from, the seats of the judges. They wear the same costume except that the silk sash, instead of being red or green alone, is composed of both these colors.

Primarily the Procureur-General is the chief prosecuting officer of the state before the Mixed Courts. But his functions are far from being limited to the prosecution of crime. Extensive responsibility in civil matters is confided to his watchfulness. The vital characteristic of his office is that he represents the state—*l'Etat*—as sovereign, but does not represent the Government as a party litigant. The Procureur-General is the defender of the *Ordre Public*—as the phrase is—the protector of the Public Interest or the General Welfare. To plead for and defend the Government in litigation relating to its property or other civil interests is not part of his function. This duty belongs to the Government's legal department, known as the *Contentieux*.[3] The Procureur-General's duty is the broader one of defending the public and not the private interest of the state.

The Procureur-General is thus the public prosecutor in charge of the investigation and prosecution of crimes so far, of course, as they fall within the jurisdiction of

[3] For an excellent review of the history and organization of the *contentieux* in Egypt, see address by E. Piola Caselli, one of the royal councilors of the Government in charge of the *contentieux*, delivered before the Royal Society of Economics in 1924, and published in *Egypte Contemporaine* (March, 1924), No. 78, p. 193.

the Mixed Courts. But his functions go much farther than this. In many different ways the state may be interested in litigation to which it is not a party. It is the duty of the Procureur-General to see that the broader interests of the state are properly considered and protected in every litigation that comes before the courts. It is in the fulfilment of this duty that he, or his representative, sits beside the courts at every session and freely exercises, whenever in his judgment the interests of the state require, the privileges of intervention conferred upon his office by law and tradition.

As to certain classes of litigation, indeed, he is permitted no alternative. In all cases, for instance, involving minors, or persons who are represented in the litigation by a guardian, in all suits brought by married women without the authority of their husbands, or for the recovery of their dowries, in all cases involving, in his judgment, the public welfare, the state (*l'Ordre Public, l'Etat*), the public domains, the government administrations, charitable gifts and legacies, and in every case when a court has declined to assume jurisdiction as well as in a number of other specified instances, the Procureur is required to give his opinion, under penalty of the nullity of the judgment thereafter rendered, a requirement, however, which is commonly dispensed with through the fiction of a formal phrase in the judgment reciting that the *Ministère Public* had been "heard." It is also within the discretion of the court to request the opinion of the Procureur in any case in which it seems desirable.

While the Parquet is attached to the courts the office is in some respects independent of the judicial hierarchy. In the first place the Procureur and the members of the Parquet are expressly declared to be removable from office, in distinction from the judges who, as we

have seen, enjoy life tenure. Theoretically this places
the Parquet at the mercy of the Government. Practically, however, the tenure of the Procureur is as secure
as that of any judge; but this observation would not
necessarily apply to his assistants.

The members of the legal staff of the Parquet—some
twelve in number—are named directly by the Egyptian
Sovereign, there being no provision, as in the case of the
judges, for consulting the foreign government whose
national is selected. Nor does the Charter of the Mixed
Courts provide or imply that any of the members of the
Parquet should be foreigners. It was understood, however, that the Procureur-General should be a foreigner,
and to avoid objections that might arise against giving
this important post to a representative of one of the
great Powers, it had been customary to give the post to
a representative of one of the smaller nations. Thus, up
to 1929, of the nine officials who had held the office, six
had been Belgians, and one a Norwegian. Two of the
earlier nominees had been French. In 1929 in contemplation of the extension of the criminal jurisdiction of
the Mixed Courts the resignation of the Belgian jurist
who had held the office since 1920 was tendered to the
Government and his place was filled by an Englishman.[4]

When the Mixed Courts were first established it was
contemplated that large criminal jurisdiction would be
conferred upon them and that the duties of the Parquet
would not only be onerous but of vital importance to
the interests of the foreign colonies. It was therefore
agreed that the seven great Powers, including the

[4] The appointment of an Englishman as Procureur-General had been included among the provisions of a draft treaty between Great Britain and
Egypt drawn up in 1920 by Egyptian nationalists following the visit of
the Milner Mission to Egypt. The present Procureur-General, Judge
Holmes, is a graduate of Dublin University who has served on the benches
of both the Native and the Mixed Courts.

United States, should each have a representative in the
Parquet, and France indeed, by a special reservation of
which her sister Powers became entitled to the benefit,
insisted *inter alia* that in the event of an increase in the
number of courts, and a consequent increase being
called for in the Parquet, a further place in that body
should be given her. But this precaution proved unnecessary. The expected criminal jurisdiction was not conferred, and the six foreign assistants in the Parquet
who had been so far named—an Austrian, a Russian, an
Englishman, an Italian, a German, and a Frenchman
(the United States had not yet named a representative)
—soon found that they had little to occupy them. On the
other hand the rapidly increasing labors of the new
courts demanded an increased personnel, and the situation was solved by promoting the new assistants and
commissioning them as judges. Since then no foreigners
have held office in the Parquet except the Procureur-
General himself, and this fact has formed already in the
past (during the negotiations of 1884 and 1890), and as
elsewhere explained[5] forms again today, a stumblingblock in the long-projected plan of conferring on the
Mixed Courts full criminal jurisdiction over foreigners.

The relation of the Parquet to the courts on the one
hand and to the Government on the other, is in conformity with the traditions of French law. The Parquet
though forming part of the judicial family as indicated
is not subject to the system of disciplinary action governing the courts, but answers directly to its administrative superior, the Minister of Justice. This superior
authority it must obey in theory, though in practice the
control is a very light one, tempered, moreover, by the
time-honored tradition of the French penal system
which declares that while "the pen must obey, the

[5] See chap. xviii.

tongue is free" (*La plume est serve mais la parole est libre*). This means that while the superior may give orders as to instituting prosecution or as to the character of the written briefs which are to be filed on behalf of the state, the members of the Parquet are completely free to express orally to the court their personal opinions in any case.[6] The rule is based on the respect considered due the Parquet as a magistracy, and is followed to prevent the violation of moral and professional dignity that would result if a member were required to sustain an opinion contrary to his conscience. In practice such conflicts do not occur, but the independence of the office is strikingly illustrated in the case of civil litigation to which the Government is a party. If the Procureur-General is of opinion that the Government's claim as advanced by its attorneys is unfounded, and that its admission would be opposed to the public welfare, it is his right and his duty to say so even though the claim may have the support of the Egyptian cabinet. Such a situation recently arose in a litigation covering Egypt's obligations to continue paying interest on the Turkish Tribute Bonds, and involving perhaps the largest sum of money ever at stake in a litigation in the Mixed Courts. The Procureur-General vigorously opposed the Government's claim. His argument which, as it happened, declared for the point of view finally accepted by the Court of Appeals, concluded with the following spirited reply to a criticism ventured by Government's counsel, and which may well serve to complete this sketch of an office whose rôle in the history of the Mixed Courts is about to assume new proportions.

[6] This privilege applies to his deputies as well as to the Procureur-General himself. The office is what is known as "indivisible," i.e., the personality of its members is absorbed in the function of the office itself. The deputy speaks solely in a representative capacity. Thus different members of the Parquet may sit, at different times, in the same case.

Need I recall to this honorable Court the prerogative of freedom which surrounds the Procureur-General when he occupies this place:—"My pen must obey but my speech is free." To this liberty, symbol of professional liberty inherited unstained from my predecessors, two of my predecessors have sacrificed their career.[7] If this liberty were to be contested in any manner or degree, directly or indirectly, I should follow their example and should not remain an hour longer upon this bench (*trans.*).

[7] One resigned because of criticisms made by the Government on his action in regard to the arrest of a suspected criminal; another because of an order given to him as to a position to be taken while participating in the deliberations of the General Assembly of the Court of Appeals whose functions are hereafter described.

CHAPTER VII

THE JURISDICTION OF THE MIXED COURTS

THE jurisdiction of the Mixed Courts covers the territorial area of Egypt but does not include the Sudan. Originally this territory fell within the jurisdiction of the courts, but for ten years prior to its reconquest in 1898, Egyptian control over the Sudan had been abandoned and the jurisdiction of the Mixed Courts was in abeyance. Then the country was reconquered by the combined military and financial efforts of Great Britain and Egypt, and by the International Convention of 1899 the jurisdiction of the Mixed Courts was expressly excluded from the territory, a declaration that was held by the courts to be an act of sovereignty, outside of the powers of the courts to question.[1]

As previously explained the dominating position of the Mixed Courts is due to the fact that their jurisdiction, always broadly interpreted by the courts in their own favor, is of a nature to draw to them all litigation of any large importance which arises in the country.

In ordinary civil and commercial cases this jurisdiction covers all suits "between Egyptians and foreigners and between foreigners of different nationalities," except questions involving what is known in French law

[1] In his work on the legal status of the Sudan (1913) Sarkissian expresses the opinion, based on a study of conditions on the spot, that the existing judicial system of that country cannot continue to respond adequately to changing conditions and that it is desirable that the Powers should engage in negotiations looking to a restoration of the jurisdiction of the Mixed Courts. Gregoire Sarkissian, *Le Soudan Egyptien, Etude de Droit International Public* (Paris, 1913). Compare, however, the observations of Lord Cromer, *Modern Egypt*, Vol. II, chap. lx.

as the *statut personnel* and including the entire field of domestic relations (marriage and divorce, parent and child, guardianship, etc.) and all questions of legal and testamentary capacity, majority, wills, and intestacy. These questions are left to the jurisdiction of other tribunals.[2] The Mixed Courts have jurisdiction also over all cases involving land arising between foreigners, even of the same nationality.

Clear enough in outline, the principle of jurisdiction thus briefly expressed has given rise to hundreds of decisions and has been the subject of discussion at more than one international commission.

Who is a "foreigner" and who is a "native"? To appreciate fully the possibilities latent in this apparently simple inquiry, one must be familiar with the recent political geography of the Near East and the chameleon-like character of the races and nationalities which inhabit the shifting confines of its many states.[3]

One of the first questions to arise was as to whether the word "foreigner" was to be limited to subjects of those capitulatory Powers who had participated in the organization of the courts. Arguments in plenty presented themselves on both sides. Why, it was asked, should nations who had never enjoyed capitulatory privileges in Egypt, whose subjects had hitherto been amenable to the Native Courts, who had taken no part in the reform, who had not ratified it, and who were not represented on its benches, be admitted to the privileges of an institution whose object was to restrict and not to enlarge capitulatory privileges. The Mixed Courts did not take this view. They adopted the fiction that the capitulatory Powers had contracted with Egypt for the

2 See chap. xvi.
3 The subject has heretofore been complicated by the absence in Egypt of a nationality law. The comprehensive nationality law promulgated February 27, 1929, will partly relieve the situation.

benefit of all foreign Powers, and, following literally the letter of their Charter, held from the first that the courts were open to subjects and citizens of all foreign nations.[4]

The political changes incident to the War, however, brought to the front the difficult question as to the rights of subjects of those countries, as for instance Syrians and Palestinians, who had succeeded in wresting themselves free from the Ottoman dominion. The question gave rise to a number of conflicting decisions. Further importance was added to the controversy by an effort of the Egyptian Government to bring up for reconsideration the traditional attitude of the Mixed Courts toward subjects of non-capitulatory Powers. To put these questions finally at rest it became necessary to refer them to the full Court of Appeals in banc, and a decision was rendered by that body in May, 1929. The decision included several distinct categories of individuals. As to former Ottoman subjects, including not only Turks but nationals of states which formerly formed part of the Ottoman Empire and are now for the most part under mandates, such as Syria and Palestine, the court held that they were not entitled to be considered as foreigners for the purpose of invoking the jurisdiction of the Mixed Courts. The decision, however, did not affect the early decisions of the court, which had extended its jurisdiction to suits between Egyptian subjects of foreigners and the subjects of certain states

[4] "Upon first principles it may well be argued that the Egyptian Government could not be understood to have accorded the privileges of special jurisdiction to the subjects of countries which had no treaty arrangements. But just as the rights of foreigners in Egypt, which led to the foundation of the mixed judiciary, were largely drawn from custom, extending the stipulations of the ancient treaties with the Ottoman Empire, so the jurisdiction of the Mixed Courts has been extended by custom to cover all cases in which persons of different nationalities are engaged." Report of Judicial Adviser (1915), p. 26.

such as Bulgaria and Roumania which, while once part of the Turkish Empire, had become detached therefrom before the War. Their rights to invoke jurisdiction of the Mixed Courts, founded on usage, were held entitled to continued respect. The court also reconfirmed its former rulings extending jurisdiction to suits between local subjects and subjects of non-capitulatory Powers.[5]

The decision of the court was supplemented by a formal declaration made in open court on behalf of the Government to the effect that it did not propose to question the jurisdiction of the Mixed Courts over subjects of states which had enjoyed capitulatory rights at the time of the founding of the Mixed Courts but who had renounced their rights in the treaties which terminated the War (e.g., Germany and Austria); or over subjects of states formed since the War from portions of former capitulatory states (e.g., Czechoslovakia, etc.); or over former subjects of the Russian Empire.[6]

[5] See following declarations in British Note on Capitulations, which forms part of Anglo-Egyptian treaty proposals of August, 1929. ''The first [matter for agreement] is the definition of the word 'foreigner' for the purposes of the proposed extension of the jurisdiction of the Mixed Tribunals. I understand from Your Excellency that the Codes now enforced by the Native Courts in Egypt, subject to the Native Courts all persons in Egypt other than those who by Law, Usage or Treaty are withdrawn from their jurisdiction. I am content to accept this principle provided that it is understood that all foreigners who have enjoyed the benefit of the capitulatory regime in the past will fall under the jurisdiction of the Mixed Tribunals irrespective of changes of sovereignty effected after the War of 1914–18.''

[6] For several years after the severance of diplomatic relations with Russia, Egypt, as a matter of practical convenience in dealing with the large community of Russian refugees in the country, not only gave *de facto* recognition to the consular representatives of the old Russian *régime*, but made a monthly allowance to the consul at Alexandria. This recognition was withdrawn in 1923, together with the allowance which accompanied it, and at the same time it was declared that thenceforth Russians would be treated in every respect like subjects of every other non-capitulatory country. In 1926, however, a new *régime* was established (see Regulation of Egyptian Cabinet, April 12, 1926; *J.O.*, May 13, 1926;

While this decision sets at rest the more important questions of jurisdiction based on nationality, the situation of the nationals of the various non-capitulatory Powers, for example, Japan, Russia, Bulgaria, and the South American republics, may still present problems. In the first place, while they may sue and be sued in the Mixed Courts under the same conditions as all other foreigners and may be prosecuted before these courts for violations of police laws, for more serious offenses they are amenable to the jurisdiction of the Native Courts. As to litigation *between* nationals of a single non-capitulatory Power, in as much as the jurisdiction of Consular Courts is derived from the Capitulations, it would logically follow that such jurisdiction may not be exercised by the consul of a non-capitulatory Power. But it does not follow that any public authority in Egypt would question the right of the consul of such Power to deal with the affairs of his own subjects in the matter of their internal disputes. However, if, in such a litigation one of the parties, or the consul himself, should question his jurisdiction, it would seem that it would have to be declined. As the Mixed Courts have refused to entertain jurisdiction in the case of litigation between Russians (whose country has no diplomatic relations with Egypt and therefore no consulate) and would doubtless reach a similar decision in the case of other non-capitulatory Powers, even though they might possess consular establishments, their nationals would be called upon to resort to the Native Courts, whose jurisdiction, formerly limited to suits "between natives," has by a recent law been declared to extend to all foreigners who

Gazette, No. 187, May, 1926, p. 196) under which various Russian "notables" (in fact the former consuls) were recognized as chiefs of their respective Russian colonies, and were appointed to salaried posts in the government employment as heads of Russian Offices at Alexandria and Cairo.

are not specially exempted therefrom by treaties or usage.

The conclusions ventured above would not, however, apply to Germany and Austria who enjoy the benefit of a special semi-capitulatory *régime* of their own. During the War, Germans in Egypt enjoyed the privilege of resort to British Consular Courts. Maintaining that the abandonment of her capitulatory privileges by the Treaty of Versailles had been conditioned on the eventual realization of the long-projected program for the consolidation of criminal justice over all foreigners in Egypt, and on the maintenance in the meantime of her right to resort to British consular jurisdiction, Germany urged that the suppression of this latter privilege, which followed the abolition of martial law, had the effect of invalidating the condition on which the surrender was made, and entitled her to return to the capitulatory *régime*. The argument was not accepted, but liberal concessions were made in a treaty signed with Egypt in 1925. Under this agreement the German Consular Courts resumed their criminal jurisdiction, but with certain carefully defined derogations, as in the case of crimes against the public security, *lèse-majesté*, and crimes committed by Germans in the employ of the Egyptian Government. There are certain other restrictions in the matter of criminal procedure which fix limitations on the old capitulatory privileges. The concession of consular jurisdiction is to lapse "as soon as there shall be put into effect a plan of judicial reorganization having jurisdiction over all foreigners in Egypt"—a felicitous reference to the eventual realization of those plans for the closing of all consular courts which have been the goal of judicial reformers in Egypt for generations.

A similar treaty was entered into with Austria in 1929.[7]

Among foreigners entitled to the privileges of the Mixed Courts must be included the important categories of *protégés* or persons of other nationalities enjoying the protection of one or other of the various capitulatory Powers.

The development of this class of "protected persons" in the Ottoman Empire is a chapter intimately connected with the history of the Capitulations. It originated in a desire to enable foreign diplomatic offices and consulates to employ Ottoman subjects as interpreters and dragomen. The struggle of various foreign Powers to increase the influence of their colonies in Ottoman dominions led to a great extension of the privilege, whereby large numbers of Ottoman subjects were admitted to the "protection" of some of the stronger western Powers. The practice gradually resulted in one of the gravest abuses of the capitulatory *régime* in Turkey. Finally, with the consent of the Powers, it was much restricted by a Turkish law promulgated in 1863. This has been applied in Egypt with the result that protégés in that country are now limited to two classes. The first is principally represented by the dragomen and messengers employed in the consulates or in the church missions. The second includes subjects of those foreign Powers who have no diplomatic or consular representation in Egypt and who have been successful in persuading some other foreign Power to take them under its wing. The Swiss who are the principal example of this

---

[7] The German treaty was signed on June 16, 1925, and was published in the *Official Journal* of June 18. The Austrian treaty was signed on October 14, and published December 2. For texts see also *Gazette des Tribunaux Mixtes,* July, 1925 (p. 187), and *Journal des Tribunaux Mixtes,* No. 1050, December 6–7, 1929.

class are for the most part under French or Italian protection.[8]

The privileges of diplomatic and consular agents in relation to the jurisdiction of the Mixed Courts has been the subject of considerable discussion. Originally the broad character of diplomatic immunity which these officials enjoyed not only protected them from being sued or prosecuted in the Mixed Courts, but had the less welcome result of excluding them from the privilege of resorting to it as plaintiffs. They were the first to complain when the negotiations that led to the establishment of a new *régime* in 1901 were undertaken. Under the new agreement, as accepted by the Powers, a distinction is made between career officials sent from their countries (technically known as *missi*) and those chosen on the ground (including a considerable number of "honorary" consuls). The former can only be sued in respect of their commercial affairs, if they see fit to engage in them, or in matters relating to land, if such they possess, provided always that their official capacity is not involved. By this token the consul who does not pay his store bills or house rent cannot be sued in the Mixed Courts. The other class, as also the

[8] During the *régime* of martial law, Great Britain also exercised protection over German and Swiss nationals, who had previously been under the protection of the German consulates. In August, 1914, the United States undertook the representation in Egypt of German interests and on October 7, 1914, undertook the representation of Swiss citizens who had previously been registered at the German consulate. Under the laws of the United States, however, this protection which has been discontinued, did not extend to the exercise of judicial authority, being limited to matters relating to the visa of Swiss passports, notarial acts, registration of births and deaths, etc. Such Swiss subjects were therefore in no proper sense American protégés. Under a recent agreement Swiss citizens have been given the right to choose either British or Italian protection, the previous right to elect French protection also remaining unchanged. Thus, Swiss citizens originating from the Italian-Swiss cantons look to Italy for protection; those from the French-Swiss, to France. This condition of concurrent rights of protection leads to occasional conflicts of authority.

native consular dragomen, can be sued in the Mixed
Courts whenever their official capacity is not involved
and, with the same reserve, are also subject to the limited criminal jurisdiction of these courts. Both classes,
however, may now freely resort to the Mixed Courts as
plaintiffs, a resort which exposes them to liability in
counterclaim in an amount not exceeding the demand
which they themselves have made. The soldiers of the
British Army may also be sued in the Mixed Courts for
their private transactions.

By special reservations in 1875 certain religious establishments protected by France, Austria, Germany,
and Russia have enjoyed judicial immunity, and since
1902 their status has been assimilated to that of diplomatic agents under the class of *missi*.

According to the text of their Charter the jurisdiction
of the Mixed Courts is founded primarily on a difference of nationality between parties to the litigation. But
the courts have gone considerably beyond the letter of
this definition.

In spite of this perfectly unambiguous language [complains
the Judicial Adviser in 1899], the Mixed Tribunals have gradually established a principle (which is nowhere to be found in
the law itself) under which they affirm their jurisdiction in all
suits where a "mixed interest" is discoverable, although the
actual parties to the suit may both be natives. It is easy to understand that with so vague and arbitrary a criterion of jurisdiction the powers of these tribunals have been extended in an
ever widening circle.

In spite of much similar criticism and of vigorous but
unsuccessful efforts to induce the Powers to repudiate
this broad interpretation of their mission, the Mixed
Courts have held firm to this principle of the mixed interest, and its consistent application has been a large
factor in extending their influence in Egypt. They have

regarded themselves as the protector of foreign interests wherever it has become involved directly or indirectly in litigation before them, and have never hesitated to look behind the parties on the record to discover its existence. Several important categories of cases illustrate the general principle.

A fertile field for its application has been that of corporate law. Private corporations doing business in Egypt are of two classes, foreign corporations organized under the law of a foreign country and having only business offices in Egypt, and corporations of Egyptian nationality, formed under Egyptian law, holding charters authorized by the Government and issued under royal seal. Both classes of corporations have been largely employed by foreign capital in Egypt, with advantages and disadvantages in both forms. Thus on the one hand the advantages enjoyed by foreign corporations of complete freedom from all Egyptian control must be balanced against the fact that there is no corporate franchise or income tax in Egypt, and that it may be considered desirable to be recognized as belonging to the country in which it is intended to extend business interests.[9]

[9] The Egyptian Government (Department of General Statistics, Ministry of Finance, 1928) has recently published an elaborate statistical review of all corporations, foreign or Egyptian, as of December 31, 1925, having their principal sphere of activity in Egypt, and thus not including foreign corporations having merely a branch office in Egypt. Most of the Egyptian companies are composed principally of foreign capital. The table shows a total of 151 Egyptian companies, 30 English companies, 11 Belgian companies, and 3 French companies with a total capital of L.E. 104,942,234 distributed as follows: Egyptian, L.E. 87,043,529; British L.E. 12,472,536; Belgian, L.E. 4,229,984; and French, L.E. 1,196,785. By far the largest single category is composed of the land credit companies, the three Egyptian companies showing a total capital of over L.E. 40,000,000. In order of capital represented the leading categories are as follows: 7 land credit companies, L.E. 46,332,576; 2 canal companies, L.E. 16,879,579; 7 banks, L.E. 5,347,800; 13 rural land companies, L.E. 5,230,278; 10 land transportation companies, L.E. 5,008,106; 8 cotton presses and sugar refineries, L.E. 4,165,754; 16 city land companies, L.E. 3,755,398.

As far as jurisdiction of the courts is concerned, the foreign corporation raises no difficulty. Like all foreigners the foreign company necessarily enjoys the privilege of the jurisdiction of the Mixed Courts. By the application of the theory of the "mixed interest" a similar result has also been reached in the case of the "Egyptian" companies. Acting on the possibility that the stock of every company is, partly at least, in the hands of foreigners, the courts have seen here a mixed interest sufficient to enable them to assume exclusive jurisdiction even in the case of suits between such companies and purely native litigants. An exception, however, has been made in the case, recently presented, of the Bank Misr, the ownership of whose stock is restricted to Egyptians.

The importance of thus asserting jurisdiction is self-evident. It brings within the jurisdiction of the Mixed Courts all the largest enterprises of the country, including the Suez Canal Company, the various municipal water, traction, and other public service companies, and practically the entire banking system of the country. Its significance is further emphasized by the various changes that have been made recently in regulations governing the formation of Egyptian companies. Certain of these requirements are opposed by the foreign commercial interests.[10] The fact, however, that such corporations will be under the protection of the Mixed Courts should be a factor of large importance in determining the extent to which foreign capital will avail itself of Egyptian corporate form and nationality.

This principle has been applied to purely governmental administrations, in which foreign interests are

[10] By the decree of May 31, 1927, it is required that two places on the directorate be reserved for Egyptians; that a quarter of the company's stock be offered for sale in Egypt; that its reports be published in Egypt; and that one-quarter of its employees be Egyptians.

officially or otherwise represented. Examples of these have been the Commission on the Public Debt or the *Caisse de la Dette,* the Royal Estates, the Sanitary and Quarantine Commission, the Railway Administration, and the Alexandria Municipality. This last organization, however, a strangely amorphous body, was specially removed from the jurisdiction of the Mixed Courts in its relations with natives by consent of the Powers in 1900. On the other hand the courts themselves declined to see in the Customs Administration, even though its revenues were in part pledged to the payment of the debt, sufficient foreign interest to justify the application of the principle.

In bankruptcy, likewise, the application of the principle of mixed interest has found wide scope. The existence of a single creditor of a nationality different from that of the alleged bankrupt has been held sufficient to support the jurisdiction. The result is that the entire bankruptcy system of Egypt is in the hands of the Mixed Courts. The importance of the rôle which this principle has played in the development of commercial credit in Egypt is discussed hereafter.

The principle is also invoked in the extremely important matter of attachments of property in the hands of third parties. The Mixed Courts early held that whenever any of the three parties of the triangle is a foreigner they alone have jurisdiction over the entire controversy. This decision led to abuses. Where natives were in dispute before the Native Courts the pursuing creditor in order to bring the case into the Mixed Courts would frequently avail himself of any pretext to attach goods in the hands of a foreigner who, as he would allege, owed money to his debtor; or a foreigner, by a collusive arrangement with the debtor, would attach an imaginary sum alleged to be owing him by the plaintiff. The matter was brought before the International Commission convened in 1900 and an agreement was reached under which, in such cases, the decision of the principal question as to the existence and amount of the debt as between the two native litigants should be left to the Native Courts, reserving to the Mixed Courts, if their jurisdiction was otherwise established, all questions turning on the validity of the attachment.

Another illustration of the broad interpretation given by the Mixed Courts to their own powers is seen in their attitude toward the familiar device of a "straw-man." This consists in the use of the name of a person of foreign nationality—often a sort of *attaché* of a particular law office—but without any real interest in the case, who is introduced into the litigation (under color of an assignment or sale or endorsement) solely to confer jurisdiction on the Mixed Courts. In theory the device should not be permitted. The real parties in interest should be relegated to the courts of their own nationality—in practice always the Native Courts. But from the first the Mixed Courts showed themselves reluctant to close their doors upon native suitors. For reasons of equity and practical convenience alike, and to avoid interminable controversy, they accepted jurisdiction, unless the existence of the "straw-man" was either admitted or incontrovertible, or unless it could be proven—and such is rarely the case—that a resort to the Mixed Courts would materially injure the rights of the other party—as, for instance, by depriving him of some particular tangible advantage which he would enjoy under the law or procedure of the Native Courts. However, the Mixed Courts are slow to entertain jurisdiction where there is a closely connected litigation pending before other courts. Then too a special limitation exists in the case of purely civil, as distinguished from commercial litigation. Here, by virtue of a change made in the law by consent of the Powers in 1900 directed against the abusive assignments of contracts made between natives, such assignments are declared to be invalid without the debtor's consent. The steady improvement in the character of the Native Courts and the practical convenience, in the case of natives, of bringing suit before a court composed wholly of Egyptians, has somewhat discouraged the use of this device. But it is still widely employed.

The jurisdiction of the Mixed Courts over foreigners extends in many cases to nonresident foreigners who cannot be served within the country. Under the very extreme provisions of the Code Napoleon, a foreigner, regardless of his residence or domicile, may be sued in the French courts not only on contracts made by him in France with Frenchmen, but in respect of any obligation "contracted by him in a foreign country towards French people." The jurisdiction of the Mixed Courts recalls this proviso, but does not go as far. Foreigners may be sued in the Mixed Courts in matters relating to property situated in Egypt, or arising out of contracts made in or to be executed in Egypt, or out of acts performed in that country.[11]

Service on nonresidents in the case of suits in the Mixed Courts is made through the Parquet, which forwards the copy of the writ to the Egyptian Ministry of

[11] The text of the Charter is limited to foreigners "who have left the country," but after some conflict of decision it was decided by the full court in 1926 that the jurisdiction included as well those who had never been in Egypt. Compare the provisions of the English law authorizing service out of the jurisdiction upon special allowance of the court, when the action is founded on a breach in England of a contract which wherever made "ought to be performed within the jurisdiction." Order XI, Rule 1, Sub-section c, British Supreme Court.

Foreign Affairs to be transmitted for service through diplomatic channels.

This principle of jurisdiction over nonresidents applies, of course, to foreign corporations.[12] They are liable like individuals. If they have established branch offices in Egypt they are liable to suit in regard to all business done there. To what extent, however, are they liable, if the office is something more than a branch office—and if it is the real center of the company's activities? Can they in such case be sued in Egypt on their general obligations contracted abroad? This is one of the most closely contested questions that has troubled the pleaders and the judges of the Mixed Courts in recent years and one that has profoundly stirred the Egyptian commercial world, because of the particular type of litigation in which it chanced to be presented. This litigation concerned itself with the legal interpretation of the word "franc" as used in the stock and bond issues of various foreign companies whose principal interests are centered in Egypt. In what cases must this word be taken to refer to the existing French paper franc, with its depreciated value; in what cases must it be taken to refer to the so-called Egyptian gold franc, the franc of the Egyptian Government monetary decrees, dating back to 1885, under which a legal tender value of 77.15 piasters (or $3.85) is given to "the gold pieces of the various countries of the Latin Union which are the equivalent of the French twenty franc gold piece?" What must be taken to have been the "legal intention" of the contracting parties when the word was used?

[12] Foreign nationality does not always result from the compliance with the registration laws of the foreign country. In a celebrated case the Mixed Courts dissolved a company formed in Egypt by persons living in Egypt but who had availed themselves of the British company laws in an attempt to give the company British nationality.

When the various securities were marketed the question was of no importance. The French franc was practically at par. But when the disparity began to make itself felt, and coupons were paid in French francs, the large possibilities inherent in the question at once revealed themselves to many persons besides the existing bondholders.

The question first came up in the case of companies where the jurisdiction of the Mixed Courts was not questioned. The Suez Canal Company, an Egyptian corporation, was held to be entitled to collect its dues, and, subsequently, to be obliged to pay its bonds in gold francs. Again, the Egyptian Sugar Refining Company, also an Egyptian company, one of the leading industrial establishments of the country, was ordered to pay its stockholders in the same currency. But the litigation immediately extended to foreign corporations. Several of the largest public service corporations of the country were brought before the courts. And here it was that the jurisdiction of the courts to entertain jurisdiction over suits based on securities issued abroad stood at the threshold of the litigation. Could these companies, by virtue of the conditions of their franchises, be said to have accepted the jurisdiction of Egyptian courts in such matters? Had they assumed a legal domicile in Egypt? Could they be said to be ''found'' within the country, within the wording of the Charter, for if so, like all other foreigners, they would be liable in Egypt on all their contracts? On these and other questions the legal battle has been fought, and in spite of some hesitation, the more recent decisions of the Court of Appeals have gone far to maintain the jurisdiction contested. Thus while the commercial chamber of the court in 1927 declined jurisdiction in the case of the Alexandria

Tramway Company (a Belgian company with head offices in Brussels), in the following year the same chamber, otherwise composed, assumed jurisdiction in the closely similar case of the Cairo Tramway Company. Shortly afterward the entire court in plenary session rendered a decision upon the question submitted by another chamber of the court in the case of the principal land mortgage company of Egypt. In reply to its inquiry the chamber was advised by the full court that a foreign company with its head office abroad, but with an "administrative office" established in accordance with its statutes in Egypt, and having there the exclusive or principal center of its activities, might be sued before the Mixed Courts on both the principal and interest of securities issued by it abroad, even if no particular place of payment had been stated. In its opinion the court emphasized the nature of an "administrative office," by referring to it as one which participated in the direction of the company's corporate interests, exercising some or all of the powers usually exercised by a home office, such as the payment of the company's general debts, the maintenance of an office for the payment of interest on its stocks and bonds, the keeping of the company's books, and in a word the direction of its active corporate life.

The limitations of this principle, however, are well illustrated by another contemporaneous decision in which the Court of Appeals refused to assume jurisdiction in the case of a similar demand against the French Gas and Electric Lighting Company, which in addition to its other activities throughout Europe exercised the public franchise of lighting in the cities of Cairo, Alexandria, and Port Said. It was held that in this case the company could be sued in Egypt only in matters concerning its activities there conducted. Nor does the jurisdiction, broad as it is, mean that the Mixed Courts of Egypt will assume jurisdiction in suits by stockholders or directors relating to the financial management of a foreign corporation, or the interpretation of its statutes, or the handling of its internal affairs where these are directed from its home office abroad. Unlike the determination of the money in which it must pay interest on its bonds to suitors in Egypt, these are matters which belong to the jurisdiction of its corporate home. The Mixed Courts refuse to consider them.

The broad outlines of jurisdiction having thus been indicated, the questions may well be asked—How, in fact, are these outlines filled in? What are the kinds of litigation that go to make up the daily labors of the Mixed Courts? Who are its most frequent, or its more important, suitors? Where—among many fields of litigation—does the emphasis lie?

A preliminary remark suggests itself. Egypt is a litigious country. The law courts and their processes are a common subject of conversation. The law as embodied in the lucid phraseology of the French codes, as adapted to the needs of Egypt, is far more accessible to the commercial world than it is in Anglo-Saxon countries.[13] All important cases are followed with close interest and are given much attention in the press. Law and the courts bulk large in the Egyptian world.

---

[13] Compare the following observations of an English author as to the familiarity of the French people with their codes, an observation which may be applied, though in somewhat lesser degree, to the merchant class in Egypt: "In France, the law is exceptionally easy of access. A knowledge of the principles of the law is not there, as in England, the monopoly of the specialist. It is the common property in France of every citizen, who can carry the law about in his pocket in the form of a handy volume edition of the codes. . . . It is rare for any citizen to lack, at any rate, some small acquaintance with the Civil Code." O. E. Bodington, *Outline of the French Law of Evidence* (London: Stevens & Sons, Ltd., 1904), p. 125.

The litigation which comes before these courts faithfully reflects the varied occupations of the people who inhabit the land.

The great body of the Egyptian population cultivate the fields. Cotton, which forms over 90 per cent of the country's export trade, is king. In working the commercial machinery incident to the handling and marketing of the crops the native comes into close contact with the foreigner. The advancing of funds to the farmer for the growing of his crop, the storage, ginning, and sale of the cotton under pledge, the handling of the commercial paper and the preparation of the contracts necessary to its marketing—these varied operations furnish to the Mixed Courts a steady stream of litigation which vitally touches the life of the entire people.

Commerce, too, is an inexhaustible subject of litigation. Egypt is an enormous warehouse and one of the great commercial crossroads of the world. The merchant ships which pass ceaselessly through the Suez Canal often carry with them lawsuits in their cargoes. Every conceivable form of merchandise would appear to attract the interest of the Egyptian broker and it would seem at times as if no transaction were too large for the humblest merchant to undertake. Sales of cargoes are divided and subdivided; the commercial usages and documents of several countries may be involved in a single transaction; the market drops and the tangled thread of relationships is suddenly pulled into a tight knot and thrown into the law courts to be cut or loosened.

Land litigation takes a large place in the life of the courts. For the great mass of the people land is the only form of investment and the purchase of an acre or two is the dream of every laborer in the fields. Every owner is constantly seeking to enlarge his holdings; always

mortgaging what he has to buy more. The practice of
loans on mortgage is everywhere prevalent.[14] The existence of large foreign land banks which control this business is made possible only by the security which the
Mixed Courts offer to their investments. Litigation of
this character involves all the intricacies of an extremely complicated and archaic land system. The uncertainties of title to land is one of the most common
sources of lawsuits. Such litigation is much complicated by the institution of the *Wakf* or religious or
family trust to which reference is elsewhere made. Its
existence contributes to make land cases one of the most
difficult types of problems which are presented to the
Mixed Courts.[15]

Insurance naturally plays a large rôle in the commercial life. The variety of nationalities and of contracts

[14] Mortgages were unknown to the Mohammedan system which could
not conceive of a real estate security without the delivery of possession.
The institution was imported into Egypt from the French (and Roman)
law—under the name of *hypothèque*. (It differs in many details from the
common law mortgage.) In the Mohammedan law, land security was of
two sorts: one known as *garouka* and the other the simple pledge (*gage immobilier*). The former, which developed under the French system into
what was known as the *vente à rémeré*, took the form of a sale with power
of repurchase. The ostensible purchaser took the land and enjoyed the
fruits, and failing redemption within the time fixed, automatically became
its possessor without necessity of foreclosure. It was an iniquitous institution usually employed to conceal a loan, and lent itself to great abuse.
In 1923 by a law approved by the Mixed Courts such transactions were
declared illegal wherever in fact they constituted a mere pledge, thus
limiting their validity to cases where they represent the *bona fide* right of
a seller to reconsider his bargain within a time fixed. In the system of real
estate pledge (*gage immobilier*) the possession passes, but in order to secure title elaborate foreclosure proceedings are necessary, and the debtors
are well protected.

[15] The result is to render the property permanently inalienable. The
institution is slowly but surely spreading over the land. Upward of a
thousand such trusts are recorded every year. If continued indefinitely it
presents the prospect of an entire country held in mortmain. Its existence
has given rise to a body of law second in intricacy to no other subject in
the Mohammedan system. Many of these cases are thrown into the Mixed
Courts. A vigorous movement is now on foot looking to the suppression,
or if not, to the substantial reform, of this deplorable institution.

often involved in a single loss opens delicate questions of private international law. So too does the field of maritime law which has long claimed for the maritime jurisprudence of Egypt a place beside that of the leading maritime nations of Europe.[16]

Litigation in the field of corporate law takes precedence over others so far as concerns the amounts involved. Owing to the lack of industrial development in Egypt, large corporations are relatively few in number, but the hundred or more important banks, public service corporations, shipping companies, and large commercial concerns constantly present problems of great public interest. Some of these have been already referred to. Finally there may be mentioned the field of litigation involving the settlement and distribution of large family estates in which the problems raised by the varied nationalities of the parties and by the widely diversified nature of the family estate are often very complicated. Indeed, what would probably most strike the Anglo-Saxon lawyer, in looking over a weekly stock of *dossiers* in the Court of Appeals, would be the very large number of parties who often appear in a single litigation, and the strange juxtaposition of names, which reflects that almost incredible mingling of races which characterizes the Levant.

Such are a few of the principal topics that go to make up the weekly roll of the courts. Many others might be added—partnerships, patents and trade-marks, unfair competition, accidents, torts of every description as well as the extraordinarily fertile field of governmental suits varying from those early processes which con-

[16] Apart from their official publication in Egypt (see Appendix) the admiralty decisions of the Mixed Courts are regularly reported and annotated in the standard French maritime law review, *Revue du Droit Maritime*. Other decisions of the Mixed Courts are constantly appearing in the French and other continental law reviews.

tributed to the downfall of the country's ruler to the recent case of the Turkish Tribute Bonds already referred to. In a word, the entire life of Egypt is the grist that comes to the judicial mill for grinding. There are few legal problems that do not find their place. They form, indeed, a jurisdiction of special and singular interest and of a character to inspire the best efforts of the judges who have been drawn from many lands to solve them.

CHAPTER VIII

ORGANIZATION AND JUDICIAL METHODS

THE right of every suitor to enjoy two trials of his case—*le double degré* as it is known—is one of the oldest principles of judicial organization on the continent, inherited from the Roman law. It is carefully observed throughout the organization of the Mixed Courts. Except in those cases before the Summary Courts not involving over ten pounds every case may be appealed—Summary Court cases to a bench of the District Court and District Court cases to the Court of Appeals.

Following the continental system the work of the Court of Appeals and of the three District Courts is distributed among chambers of equal and independent authority. Originally the Court of Appeals sat in a chamber of eight, five foreigners and three Egyptians—the total membership of the court being eleven judges; in the District Courts the chambers were composed of five judges—three foreigners and two Egyptians. Nubar Pasha's original proposal had called for chambers of five in the Court of Appeals and of three in the District Courts, but the international commission had rejected the proposal on the ground that in the case of a disagreement between two Europeans in the District Court the vote of the native judge would decide the question. But here again experience finally justified Nubar's foresight. It soon became evident that the large chambers in the Court of Appeals were unwieldy in discussion, wasteful in operation, and not adapted to that promptness of decision which was essential to earn the favor of a large commercial community. In the Court of Appeals the number of judges was gradually raised to sixteen, thus permitting the formation of two chambers—which only served to accentuate the evil. Proposals to reduce the size of the chambers made to the Powers in 1880, 1884, 1890, and 1893 were unsuccessful. In 1911 again the plan was successfully opposed by Germany, Austria, and Italy. Finally in 1915, through the changes brought about by the War, the number of judges composing the chambers was reduced to three and five respectively as originally proposed by Nubar. For a time thereafter the size of the Court of Appeals was maintained at fifteen (thus permitting the formation of three chambers) but the rapidly growing administrative duties of the President made it essential to relieve him from the responsibility of presiding over one of the three regular chambers—a relief that was brought about by the restoration of the sixteenth seat in 1922. In 1929 the continued increase in the work of the court led to the appointment of a seventeenth justice.

In the District Courts the number of chambers depends upon the character of business, and upon the number of judges who happen to be available, the delays in securing the nomination of new foreign judges as well as illness often rendering it impossible to maintain a uniform number of chambers. In the Court of Appeals the three chambers are known respectively as the first, second, and third, and to each is assigned certain general categories of cases, corresponding roughly to the classifications of commercial, civil, and real estate. Various special categories, for example, referee actions, accident suits, and suits on promissory

notes, are distributed among the chambers as administrative efficiency requires.

On the first rung of the judicial ladder stands the
Summary Court. It corresponds to that of the French
juge de paix, though it exercises no criminal jurisdiction. But on the other hand the Summary Court has the
advantage of being composed of a judge of the District
Court of which it forms part, and thus enjoys an authority quite exceptional for courts of this character.
In cases not concerning real estate it exercises final
jurisdiction up to ten pounds and, subject to appeal,
may entertain cases involving amounts not exceeding a
hundred pounds. It may also hear suits for rental, where
the annual rent does not exceed a hundred pounds, but
in this case subject always to appeal. Again, subject to
appeal, it exercises jurisdiction in all possessory actions brought by persons who have been in possession
for over a year. In the Summary Court there is no distinction between civil and commercial cases, although
the character of the case must be noted in the opinion.

The Summary Judge is heavily worked, his weekly
roll frequently running as high as a hundred cases
listed for trial. Each case must be made the subject of
a written opinion, and these not infrequently number
thirty or forty a week.[1] This court is the school of the
prospective lawyer. It is here that the *stagiaire* or
lawyer apprentice first tries his mettle and often the
temper of the judge. Parties frequently appear in person, unaided by attorneys. It is quite common for the
long-robed fellah from the country to plead his own
case. Sessions are crowded and busy and provide the
most intimate contact which the Mixed Courts have
with the people.

[1] During one year a single judge sitting in the Summary Court at
Alexandria disposed of over 2,500 cases of which 1,200 involved written
opinions.

On appeal every case is heard anew. New documents may be introduced; new arguments may be presented; new measures of "instruction" may be ordered as, for instance, orders for the taking of new testimony, the summoning of the parties before the court or one of its members, or the reference of the case to an expert for a special report. The decision of the appellate court is a complete retrial on the law and on the facts.

In criminal cases, moreover, there is a further measure of review—the word "appeal" must here be strictly avoided—in a resort to the Court of Cassation. In France and other continental countries the Court of Cassation exercises the supreme judicial function in questions of law. The purpose of its creation is to maintain uniformity of jurisprudence and to set aside—to break (*casser*)—judgments of the courts which have been rendered in conflict with the law. It is in this sense that the Court of Cassation is said to "judge the judgment"—and not the case itself. It is for this reason that the measure is not described as an appeal (*appel*) but as *pourvoi*—a resort. The decision of the Court of Cassation is not substituted for the judgment which it "breaks." The judgment is simply annulled and, in order to avoid asking judges to decide against opinions they have already expressed, the case is sent back to be retried before a different court. The new trial court, moreover, is free to disregard the opinion of the Court of Cassation and to persist in the interpretation given by the judges who first tried the case. In France such an occurrence leads to the convening of all the chambers of the Court of Cassation and to a second decision in *cassation,* which it becomes obligatory for the third trial court to follow. In the criminal cases coming before the Mixed Courts the difficulty which in France had led to the necessity of occasionally twice submitting a case to a Court of Cassation, has naturally not existed.

In the Mixed Courts system the principle of *cassation* has been adopted for criminal cases alone, in which, as we shall see in the review of the criminal jurisdiction of the courts, it plays an important rôle. The reason it was not adopted for civil litigation was doubtless that originally the Court of Appeals sat in a single chamber and conflicts of opinion on questions of law were thus excluded. Since that time, however, the situation has become materially changed through the increase of the chambers of the Court of Appeals from one to three, as well as through the frequency of conflict in the decisions rendered by both the District Courts, and by the Summary Courts, in cases in which there is no further appeal. Pending realization of the somewhat utopian plan for the creation of a Court of Cassation for all the jurisdictions of Egypt, there was worked out in 1906 a system for the holding of plenary sessions of the Court of Appeals. Under this system whenever one of the chambers of the court finds itself in presence of a conflict of decisions, or where it is of opinion that a previous decision should be departed from, it is entitled to refer the question to the Court of Appeals in banc. In such hearing (in which peremptory challenge is not admitted) the presence of the full court of seventeen is obligatory, although in the absence or disqualification of one of the justices, his seat may be taken by a judge of the District Courts specially designated for the purpose. Designation of the District Judges to sit in the ordinary sessions of the several chambers of the Court of Appeals is also permitted when the needs of service require.

The plenary sessions of the court are of special solemnity and attract the close attention of the bar. Twenty or more important and vigorously controverted problems have thus been settled. But there are certain objections to this measure. It is a cumbersome matter to convene the whole court. Deliberation on delicate questions by such a large body is inconvenient. The loss of time is considerable. Then too the device does not meet the situation where District Courts, in matters within their final decision, insist, as they have the right to do, on maintaining positions on questions of law which are at variance with those of one of the chambers of the Court of Appeals. To remedy this situation the creation of a Court of Cassation within the Mixed Courts system itself has often been urged. The establishment of a new court with separate judges would perhaps be impractical and overcostly. But the creation of a special chamber of cassation within the existing body, composed for example of five members, including the presidents or representatives of each chamber, would probably be a wise and practical measure, provided the Government would at the same time make whatever increase might appear necessary in the membership of the court. The change, however, would require the consent of the Powers.

Throughout the system runs the fundamental distinction of French judicial organization between civil and commercial courts. In both the upper and the lower courts there are separate commercial and civil chambers, observing different rules of procedure and evidence. Furthermore, in the case of the District Courts, the commercial chambers differ materially from the civil chambers in manner of composition.

In France this distinction is expressed in the existence of an entirely separate body of Commercial Courts which go back to the sixteenth century, the Commercial Courts of Paris having been founded in 1563. They originated at an epoch when commercial affairs were simple and were summarily disposed of by merchants. "Commercial transactions require little formality," observed Montesquieu. "They follow along the same line day by day and should be decided each day." Although the simplicity which obtained in Montesquieu's day has long since disappeared, and with it the possibility of having disputes "decided each day," the principle of submitting such affairs to the judgment of merchants has been maintained with singular persistence on the continent.[2] Its value was recognized by the founders of the Mixed Courts, who had the happy inspiration of adopting a compromise. It was decided that in commercial cases merchants chosen from a selected group of men of high reputation in the community should participate in the trial. Two such associates, known as assessors, sit with three judges on the trial of every commercial litigation. They serve without pay and enjoy equal right of vote with their judicial associates.

The Charter of the courts merely directs that these foreign assessors shall be elected. In each of the three judicial districts a list of twenty-four assessors is annually selected from the "notables" or leading members of the merchant class of the various communities of the capitulatory countries whose names are listed as such by their several consuls.[3] In Alexandria it is the practice of the foreign chambers of commerce and of certain similar institutions to agree upon a complete list of candidates in advance, all of whom are invariably

[2] One of the most experienced procureur-generals of France recently observed to the writer that he would be glad to see merchants sitting among the members of the Courts of Appeal. Similar views are quite common. The suggestion has been made by responsible writers in Egypt that the commercial assessors might even with propriety be given a majority vote. See El-Sayed Bey, p. 107.

[3] By custom Roumania has been added to the countries furnishing such lists at Cairo, and Persia in the case of Alexandria.

elected as little interest is shown in the elections. In Alexandria voting takes place in the main court room of the Court of Appeals, under the presidency of the *doyen* of the consular corps, assisted by four representatives of the capitulatory Powers, who in practice are Greece, France, England, and Italy. The chief clerk of the Court of Appeals acts as secretary.

The native assessors are selected through the local governors, and the several lists, both native and foreign, for the various districts are separately approved and published by royal decree.

The calling of the assessors for service in the courts is a matter of administrative *régime* under the direction of the President of the Commercial Court, who convenes them and distributes their periods of service in the manner best calculated to reconcile their convenience with the interests of justice. Their term of service is yearly and they usually serve in turn for two or occasionally for four consecutive weekly sessions.

It is generally conceded that the institution of assessors has been a success. These gentlemen bring practical experience in the dealings of merchants and a knowledge of commercial usage which is often of great value. As might be expected they defer to the other members of the court on questions of law, and the fact that they are in the minority obviates all possibility of serious conflict. Moreover, the educational value in bringing the leading members of the commercial world in close and friendly contact with the courts themselves is an important element in favor of the system. All things considered it would probably be impossible to devise a plan better adapted for the solution of commercial litigation in a country presenting such cosmopolitan business interests and such complexity of commercial usage as exists in Egypt.

As the distinction between civil and commercial cases determines before what court a case must be brought, it follows that a case brought in the wrong court may be thrown out. The difficulty of defining this distinction has given rise to much litigation. The Commercial Courts have jurisdiction over all transactions between those whose habitual occupation is that of merchant or banker, as well as over transactions entered into by anyone relating to the purchase of merchandise with a view to its resale. All operations of transport by land or sea are considered as commercial, as also are suits based on commercial paper, with the exception of bills drawn by Egyptian cultivators or by women not engaged in commerce. Bankruptcy falls also within the jurisdiction of the Commercial Courts, since only merchants may be declared bankrupt.

Besides determining to which court the case belongs the traditional French distinction between commercial and civil affairs is expressed by the many stringent regulations prescribed by the codes of the Mixed Courts for the conduct of commercial business, particularly in the matter of keeping commercial books. For example, merchants are legally obliged to keep a daybook and an inventory book, every page of which has been numbered and stamped by a designated clerical official of one of the Mixed Commercial Courts. Failure to observe such and other similar requirements often determines the decision of a case.[4]

The procedure in commercial cases is more expedi-

[4] The Importers' Association of Alexandria has recently (February 21, 1929) petitioned the Court of Appeals to bring about the opening of a Commercial Register for the compulsory registration of all merchants. A prior proposal by the same body has led to the publication under the auspices of the court of an elaborate monthly bulletin containing a list of all protests of commercial paper made during the month. This publication, which is furnished to subscribers, has been warmly welcomed by the commercial communities of Egypt.

tious than in civil cases. Legal interest is calculated at 7 per cent instead of 5 per cent, and there is less restriction than in civil cases on the assignments of legal rights with the view of giving jurisdiction to the Mixed Courts. The statutes of limitations are also more strict; rules of evidence different; methods of proof more elastic. As there is no law similar to that in France, under which practically all corporations are considered as commercial, the distinction between civil and commercial cases is of special importance in Egypt in corporate matters. The Mixed Courts are called upon frequently to analyze carefully corporate operations in order to determine whether the litigation is commercial or civil. For example, in a recent important litigation over the payment of interest on Suez Canal bonds suits were brought by different bondholders in both the civil and the commercial chambers of the District Courts. On appeal it was finally decided that notwithstanding various secondary operations conducted by the company the question of its character must be determined by reference to the principal object of the enterprise which was the exploitation of a canal, an object which fell within no category of commercial activities defined by the law.

One of the most active and useful jurisdictions exercised by the Mixed Courts is that of the Court of Referees (*Tribunal de Référés*) composed of a single foreign judge assigned yearly to this duty. This institution is adopted from the French system, but the scope of jurisdiction in Egypt has extended considerably beyond its prototype. The judge of this court exercises jurisdiction in matters where immediate action is required to protect a party's rights provided it can be had without prejudice to the merits of the case. Jurisdiction is invoked in an astonishingly wide variety of cases, characteristic among which are petitions for the appointment of temporary receivers; orders for the sale of perishable property or its examination by experts; expulsion of a tenant where a clear case is presented by the landlord, or expulsion of any other person who is unable to show a colorable right to occupation; and orders for immediate repairs necessary to prevent serious damages to property. Jurisdiction of the Referee Court is also invoked in all difficulties involved in making executions, a power which it shares with the court by whom the judgment has been issued. In the carrying out of his duties the referee judge may order the inspection of property by experts, the taking of testimony, or the placing of property under seal. To him are also committed special duties touching various and often difficult questions of procedure. The practical importance of this jurisdiction will appear from the fact that an average of 2,500 decisions are rendered by the three referee judges of the District Courts within the course of a year.

Two other ''single judge'' courts must be added: a court charged with the duty of holding judicial auctions of real estate, and a court exercising the important functions involved in bankruptcy proceedings under a judge yearly assigned to such functions elsewhere described.

Rapid increase in judicial work, incommensurate with the increase in the number of judges, has led in recent years to various plans of relief. In 1926 the Court of Appeals proposed the creation of a new chamber of five judges, a plan which could be realized by the simple act of the Egyptian Government without consulting the Powers. The Government, however, rejected the project. Its decision was said to have been largely influenced by anticipated diplomatic difficulties incident to the distribution of seats among the larger powers in the light of the tradition of substantial equality among them. The Government did, however, propose a series of counter propositions calculated to reduce the pressure of work in the upper court. These included, first, a proposal to increase the general jurisdiction of Summary Courts from a hundred to two hundred and fifty pounds, and their final jurisdiction from ten to twenty pounds; and second, the creation of a fourth chamber in the Court of Appeals to be composed of three judges for the hearing of appeals from decisions by a single judge. Both these propositions were vigorously opposed by the Mixed Court bar, which declared itself in favor of the original plan of the Court of Appeals. As to the first proposal it was urged that the jurisdiction of the Summary Judge already exceeded that of such judges in France, Italy, and Belgium, and that it would be certain to increase diversity of judicial decision in the matter of the cases not subject to appeal. As to the second it was insisted by the bar that the cases to be referred to the three judges would frequently be of the greatest practical importance and that it would be highly inconsistent to have such cases heard by three judges, while small commercial suits involving only a few hundred pounds were being submitted to a bench of five. Furthermore it was pointed out that the project would require the consent of the Powers—a condition of doubtful realization. On the first proposal the Court of Appeals consulted the members of the District Courts, a majority of whom were found to be opposed. Under these circumstances the court replied to the Government rejecting the proposal of increasing the jurisdiction of the Summary Judges, but approved, as a *pis aller,* the proposal to create a new chamber of three. Such a proposal was therefore included by the Government among the six proposals of reform, officially submitted to the Powers in December, 1927, to which reference is elsewhere made.[5] In the meantime the Government in recognition of urgent need consented to the appointment of the additional justice to the Court of Appeals, of which mention has been made, and to the naming of three new judges, two foreigners and one native, to the District Courts.

An added measure of protection to litigants exists in a liberal right of judicial challenge. A distinction is made between the Court of Appeals and the District Courts. In the former the litigant's risk of irreparable damage led the founders of the Courts to establish a right of peremptory challenge, without assignment of reasons (except in the case of a plenary session). This right must be limited to the challenge of a single justice. It may be exercised only once in a single case. In addition, however, the right to challenge any judge for cause is clearly accorded to suitors. Causes are enumerated on which it may be based as, for instance, relation to a party, family interest in the litigation, having at any time been a witness or given advice in regard to the controversy, or the existence of any serious fact calculated to prevent an impartial judgment. The question is decided by the unchallenged members of the court.

When the challenge for cause goes to the whole court, if it be against a District Court, the question is at once brought before the Court of Appeals. If it be against an entire chamber of the Court of Appeals the organization of a special court is provided for, composed of at least eleven justices not involved in the challenge, including, in case of need, the president and vice-presidents of the District Courts. Such a court was consti-

5 See chap. xviii.

tuted in 1918, but, in general, challenge for cause is extremely rare.

The annual term of the courts runs from October 15 to July 1. Weekly sessions are held by all of the chambers without interruption, except in so far as occasionally a legal holiday requires the sessions to be held on an earlier or subsequent day. Rarely a weekly sitting is lost. During the vacation, sittings of the Court of Appeals are suspended, the administrative affairs of the court being in the hands of a specially designated judge, commonly a member of the Alexandria District Court.

In the District Courts the sessions of the Police Court continue throughout the summer, as well as such sessions of the Summary and Referee Courts as are required. For carrying on this work judges are delegated to the summer service in each district, this duty being shared in turn, and the judge so serving being entitled, if and when the interests of the service permit, to a vacation of six weeks.

The language of the Mixed Courts, the spoken language of the bench and bar and personnel, the written language of all opinions, briefs, and writs, is French. No other language is used by lawyers in addressing the courts. It is not, however, the only official language. By the Charter of the courts the official languages were declared to be "the languages of the country, Italian and French." English was introduced by agreement with the Powers in 1905, "the languages of the country" being thereafter designated simply as "Arabic." This means that legally any one of the four languages mentioned can be freely used in the courts. But the controlling predominance of the French language in legal circles in Egypt, as well as reasons of practical necessity, have led to a tacit agreement adopting its exclusive use. While the first opinion of the Court of Appeals was in Italian and the early volumes of reports contain as many opinions in that language as in French, the use of Italian has been gradually abandoned. Even if today an Italian judge occasionally files an opinion in his native language this is the only exception and it is a rare one.[6] Opinions are never filed in English or in Arabic. Other considerations apart, to write an opinion on French law in the English or Arabic languages would in itself present serious difficulties of nomenclature and phraseology. Moreover it is realized that if the workers in the Mixed Courts should seek to avail themselves of their legal rights in the use of their several languages judicial babel would again return to Egypt and at best the judicial machine which is urgently required to proceed under full speed and pressure would be seriously clogged.

The costume worn by judges as adopted on the organization of the courts consists of a high-collared frock coat, known as a stamboulin, the recognized costume of all employees of the Turkish Government in old times. The lawyers alone wear robes with the traditional legal cap or beretta, and the white *rabat* of the French bar. Across the breast of the coat is worn a broad silk sash, green in the case of the Court of Appeals and red in the case of the District Courts. To the center of the sash is attached the traditional badge of judicial office, a gold medallion bearing the coat of arms of Egypt. The judges also wear the national *tarbouche* (fez),[7] which is usually laid aside by the foreign judges as they take their seats upon the bench.

[6] The early importance of Italian appears from a letter from the American diplomatic representative to the Secretary of State, March 5, 1875, in which the former states that he has been desired to say ''that the magistrates must possess a perfect knowledge of the French and Italian languages, otherwise they will not be accepted.''

[7] At royal receptions the judges of the Mixed Courts (who are always free to attend or not) wear, unless otherwise requested, the official costume

The Charter provided that each of the several courts should name from among its foreign members a Vice-President, who should act as President Judge. The nominal post of President was left to the selection of the Egyptian Government and was always filled by an Egyptian. This office, however, was purely honorary and in the course of time it was discontinued and the foreign "Vice-President" became recognized as the President, and his "substitute" as Vice-President. However, by a recent innovation the Government has adopted the practice of officially addressing the acting President as Vice-President.

Originally the selection of the presidents of the District Courts was left entirely to these bodies. But this tended to impair the independence of the office. As far back as 1884 the proposal was made that the choice be left to the Court of Appeals. The suggestion dragged for twenty years. Then the Government proposed that the Khedive name the Presidents of the courts. This was refused by the Powers and in 1911, after extended negotiations, the present plan was agreed upon by which the Presidents and Vice-Presidents of the District Courts are elected annually by the Court of Appeals

prescribed for such ceremonies. Those interested in sartorial details may care to peruse the following official specification:

"*Habit:* Forme redingote droite en drap ou cachemire noir, non boutonnée; grands revers forme 'croisé'; deux rangs de trois boutons chaque, le premier bouton posé à dix (10) centimètres du bord, les autres suivant graduellement en descendant de façon à ce que le dernier bouton soit à six (6) centimètres du bord; revers garnis de soie faille verte jusqu'au bord, col en velours soie noire; manches se terminant par un parement de dix (10) centimètres avec trois boutons et boutonnières; la basque du dos ornée le long des plis d'une soubise partant de la taille et s'arrêtant à 2½ centimètres du bas; la soubise garnie de deux boutons à la taille et de deux boutons dans le bas. *Gilet:* A châle piqué blanc bien ouvert à quatre petits boutons. *Pantalon:* Même étoffe que l'habit et bordé de tresse en soie noire de deux (2) centimètres." The detail bestowed on such matters is further illustrated by a recent circular issued by the Grand Chamberlain, and changing the form of buttons to include "le monogramme de sa Majesté Fouad, surmonté de la Couronne Royale."

from an alphabetical list of candidates presented by the District Courts—five each in the case of Alexandria and Cairo, and three in the case of Mansourah. This plan has worked admirably. The President and Vice-President of the Court of Appeals are also elected annually by that body itself. Until 1929 elections were held on the reconvening of the courts in October, but the proper organization of the annual work being thus delayed, the elections were changed by law to May.

The proposals of reform presented to the Powers in 1927 call for the opening of these posts to Egyptians and foreigners alike, with the proviso that one or other should always be held by an Egyptian; also that upon election by their colleagues the officials should be named to office every three years by governmental decree. So far this proposal has met with general disfavor.[8] The offices of President and Vice-President carry with them no additional emoluments, a contingency foreclosed by the provision of the Charter providing that all judges of the same category should receive the same salaries.

The duties of the President of the Court of Appeals are in large part administrative—to such extent that he occupies no seat in the regular weekly chambers of the court, except when called on to replace a colleague. He presides, however, over the Court of Cassation for criminal cases, which sits two or three times a month, and also presides over the occasional extraordinary sessions of the full court in banc.

The administrative responsibilities of the President are elsewhere referred to. He is the pivot upon which

[8] As a possible alternative it has been suggested that the purely honorary Egyptian presidencies be revived, in order thus to emphasize the national character of the institution, without, on the other hand, disturbing the present rule as to the filling of the two effective offices by foreigners. Soubhi Ghali Bey, ''Les Tribunaux de la Reforme et l'Egypte,'' *Revue de Droit International* (Paris, April–September, 1926); *Journal des Tribunaux Mixtes* (No. 603, January 29, 1927).

the entire machine turns. One of the most important factors in the success of the Mixed Courts has been the complete absence of any personal or political partisanship in making selections for this highest judicial office in Egypt.[9] Wholly apart from all other considerations, the spirit of self-preservation would instinctively recoil from naming to a post of such critical importance any but the judge most capable of filling it.

The distribution of the judges among the several chambers is a matter of internal regulations as fixed by the several courts at the beginning of each judicial year, and in the case of District Courts subject to the approval of the Court of Appeals. In making these assignments the capacity and desires of individual judges are taken into account. There is no fixed principle of rotation. A judge who becomes expert at a particular branch as, for instance, bankruptcy or commercial law, may remain for many years as the president of a particular chamber. In the Court of Appeals changes are even less frequent than in the District Court, the chambers often remaining practically unchanged for long periods.

The courts are composed entirely without reference to the nationality of the litigants. The Egyptian-French protocol of 1874 (the benefits of which were later conceded to the other capitulatory Powers) records that the

[9] A fine tribute was contained in the address of the British High Commissioner, Lord Lloyd, on the occasion of the fiftieth anniversary of the courts. "The choice has always fallen on the most eminent and the most able of the Judges, regardless of his nationality and with no preference to those belonging to the greater powers. During the last twenty years, we have seen successively, as President of the Court of Appeal, M. de Korizmics, an Austrian, M. Moriondo, an Italian, M. Gescher, a German, Mr. Sandars, an Englishman, Mr. Larcher, a Portuguese, M. Laloë, a Frenchman, M. Eeman, a Belgian, and finally yourself, Monsieur le President, a Greek. This fact which I have mentioned is merely typical of the independent and unprejudiced attitude which the Mixed Tribunals have always shown towards all those who have had to deal with them."

GENERAL ASSEMBLY COURT OF APPEALS
1927

Center: Nicolas Cambas (Greece), President.

Reading down: (to right of President) Michael Hansson (Norway), Fouad Gress Bey (Egypt), del Aziz Kahil Pacha (Egypt), Richard A. Vaux (Great Britain), Mahmoud El Toayer Bey gypt), Bernard Favenc (France), Constant van Ackere (Belgium), Mohamed Bahi El Dine akat Bey (Egypt).

n rear: Georges Coroni, Chief Clerk.

Reading down: (to left of President) Firmin van den Bosch (Belgium), Procureur-Gen- , Soubhi Ghali Bey (Egypt), Ralph P. B. Cator (Great Britain), Moustapha Beyram Bey gypt), Alex. C. McBarnet (Great Britain), Jasper Y. Brinton (United States), Giovanni iera (Italy), Don Enrique Garcia de Herreros (Spain).

French Government having requested that one of the European judges should always be, as far as possible, of the same nationality as the European party litigant, the Egyptian Government undertook to call the matter to the attention of the new magistracy as being alone responsible for matters of internal organization. Presumably the Egyptian Government complied with its undertaking, but whatever attention, if any, may have been given the request by the judges at that time, no trace of its influence exists in the functioning of the courts today. Apart from the utter impracticability of applying any such principle to a system as large and as overtaxed as the Mixed Courts, any such practice would violate the whole spirit of the institution which is essentially that of a single judicial unit. The nationalities of the parties litigant is an utterly negligible element in the work of the courts—one which indeed for the most part passes quite unnoticed.

In the study and decision of cases and in the preparation and rendering of opinions (what might perhaps be called the technique of judging) the system followed differs considerably from Anglo-Saxon procedure. It is the reporter or *rapporteur* system of the continent. Immediately at the conclusion of each weekly session the cases which have been argued, or which have been submitted for decision without argument, are assigned by the President to one or other of his associates, excepting those cases which he retains for himself. On the afternoon of the hearing the complete original record or *dossier* is delivered to the judge to whom it has been thus assigned.

In appearance the *dossier* is a heavy manila folder, varying in color according to the court in which the case has arisen, and in size some twenty inches by twelve. At the top is printed in large letters the number of the

case, the name of the court, and the judicial year, counting from the inauguration of the courts. Thus, cases
docketed between October 31, 1929, and October 31,
1930, belong to the fifty-fifth judicial year—*Année Judiciaire 55.*[10] Below this appear in a large hand the names
of the parties, and underneath, an indication of the nature of the case. On the rest of the outside cover is a
series of columns containing a chronological index of
every paper filed in the case, with a note of the payment of all the clerk's costs or service fees. Thus on a
single cover is presented at a glance a concise but complete summary of the record within.[11]

All the documents in the case (unfolded, for folded
papers are unknown to the Mixed Courts) are contained
in the *dossier.* These begin with the original writ with
its return of service, followed by all supplemental or
cross writs. Then comes the *procès-verbal* or minutes
of the various sessions of the court where the case has
been called upon the roll, with the names of counsel and
their respective prayers to the court, and the decisions

[10] Apropos of the judicial calendar, no fewer than five different calen-
dars are encountered in the *dossiers* of the Mixed Courts. The Mohammedan calendar year, which gives the official date to legislation, begins
June 19, the present year being 1438; the Jewish year begins September
15, the present year being 5690; the Coptic year begins October 12,
the current year being 1646; the Julian or old Orthodox calendar, which
was in use in the Greek community until October 31, 1928, began the
year on January 14. Promissory notes and bills are frequently dated according to the Mohammedan calendar. The Coptic calendar, curiously
enough, is currently used in certain classes of land transactions throughout the country.
[11] This system eliminates keeping of elaborate court dockets. Each
dossier carries its own docket, and is made available by a careful system of
index ledgers, one covering the names of *all parties* to litigation in the
Mixed Courts, and the other a double list—chronological and alphabetical
—of *all decisions* rendered in all of the several courts. Generally speaking,
the clerical work in the Mixed Courts is admirably done. The defects are
that there is too much formalism—too much signing and countersigning of
documents—and too much detailed supervision imposed upon the judge,
defects that are the inheritance of an older legal generation.

of the court as to the date set for hearing, provisionally
or definitely, as the case may be—the record of each hearing being signed by the chief clerk and the president of
the chamber. This is followed by the briefs. Owing to
the large number of parties frequently drawn into a
single litigation in Egypt, and to the common practice
of filing briefs in rebuttal, these are often both numerous and voluminous, frequently running into the hundreds of pages. Except in rare cases they are typewrit-
ten and not printed. They are prepared, however, with
great attention to appearance and the copy on heavy
paper in the *dossier* is as readable as the best printed
page. A touch of color is given by the ribbon with which,
by common practice, briefs are bound together, and
which often designates the office from which they come.
At the end of each brief are the countersignatures of
opposing counsel, with whom copies are required to
have been exchanged in advance of argument, according
to carefully specified requirements. Together with the
rest of the papers in the case, except the exhibits, the
briefs are sewn to the back of the *dossier,* so that each
dossier makes, in effect, a volume of its own. The exhibits in a case are filed in separate folders or *bor-
dereaux,* which in turn contain other folders for the
separate subdivisions of documents chronologically in-
dexed. Frequently for convenience of reference a case
will contain a large number of these folders, classified
according to the points which they cover, to permit easy
identification by the judge. As a guarantee of authenticity and as a safeguard against loss, every *bordereau*
is pierced by a linen thread of which the ends are sealed
by the office producing it.

Accompanying the *dossier,* if the case is in the Court
of Appeals, is submitted the *dossier* of the court below,
together with any other *dossiers* involving a connected

litigation for whose production the parties may have asked. The *dossier* thus furnishes a judge a presentation of the case as complete and compact as may be possibly conceived. It contains, or should contain, practically every element in the litigation except those exhibits which are by their nature not susceptible of being so included as, for instance, books of commerce and such additional *dossiers* or exhibits as are too bulky to be contained within the original folder. Even its inside covers are utilized for the computation of court costs and the necessary clerical notations.

Such is the form in which the cases are finally presented to the judges for study at their homes. Following the receipt of every *dossier* it becomes the duty of a judge to make a minute and thorough examination of the entire record, to probe every problem of fact and law involved, and to prepare for submission to his colleagues, at the ensuing weekly deliberation, a comprehensive presentation of the whole litigation with a proposal for its solution.

The system responds well to the conditions which have to be met. First, it is in harmony with the rule of prompt decision, the firmest tradition of the Mixed Courts and of the French system from which it was inherited. This is indeed more than a tradition, for by the Code of Procedure itself, the founders provided that decisions should be rendered from the bench forthwith —*sur le champ*. This was to be the normal event. A subsequent article permitted judges to retire for deliberations. A third dispensation permitted the decision to be postponed to a subsequent fixed date "not later than eight days"; if a further delay became necessary the court was required to pronounce an order of postponement in open court, and to enter upon the judges' "deliberation roster," and in the presence of the Procureur-

General, the reasons making such a postponement necessary. Usage has rendered these rules superfluous. The practice of handing down opinions at the next weekly sessions after argument is too well ingrained in the system to require rules to enforce it. Nine out of ten cases are thus disposed of. On the other hand, where the interests of justice require, every judge in both the lower and the upper courts feels free to retain a case for study as long as may be necessary—but this is a freedom sparingly made use of.

Obviously under these conditions it would be physically impossible for a judge to examine personally the records in every case coming before his court even were they printed. And to print the records would be out of the question. Original documents may be filed in any one of the four judicial languages, and are often filed also in Greek, a language much used in commercial affairs. While it is the practice to have the material portions of all Arabic documents accompanied by French translations, initialed by one of the official court interpreters, and while translations of documents in Greek are generally also filed with the original, an examination of the original document is often necessary to obtain a correct impression of its tenor and importance. Then too many documents are in a form which it would be impossible to reproduce in a printed copy. In view, moreover, of the common practice of submitting complete correspondence files in evidence, the cost of printing would assume formidable proportions. As it is, of course, essential for all the documents in any case to be minutely examined it is better that this responsibility be concentrated upon one than shared by several. Any other method would probably defeat the primary object of the system, which is to give the court in the deliberations of its council chamber the benefit of a full and

well-informed discussion of a case, the general outlines of which are still familiar to the other members of
the court through their recollection of the argument at
bar. This report is the keystone of the system. The reporter is submitted to a cross-examination as searching
as it is friendly. The result is to focus upon every case,
at the moment of its decision, the best collective efforts
of the judges who decide it. Helpful criticism could
hardly find wider scope or more useful play. The discussion is subject to no limitation of time. Each problem is pursued to its conclusion. Where a case presents
exceptionally difficult problems, or where some new approach has been suggested by the discussion, it will be
held over for further examination and report, or will
be passed to colleagues for review. The existence of a
normal weekly schedule undoubtedly develops the capacity of concentration and prompt decision. The closeness of coöperation resulting from the small chambers,
from the frequency and regularity of the deliberations,
and from the personal intimacy which exists among the
judges, goes far to eliminate unnecessary friction and
waste of time. It makes possible in a high degree that
consensus of informed and reasoned opinion on a given
set of facts which is perhaps the principal aim of every
judicial system.

Decisions are given by majority vote and dissents are
not recorded. The opinions rendered are the opinions
of the chamber. Unless the court has ordered the taking
of testimony by one of its members, or some other special intervention has become necessary, the clue to authorship lies, ordinarily, only in a particular style which
in course of time becomes more or less recognizable to
the bar. In the Court of Appeals, however, the authorship of opinions is more or less an open secret. If the
reporter of a case finds himself overruled by a majority

of his colleagues upon any point it is always within his
discretion to ask to be relieved from the preparation of
an opinion in which he does not fully concur.

Opinions commonly follow the French model under
which each paragraph opens with the phrase "Considering that" (*Attendu que*). This form encourages close
and concise reasoning and discourages tautology, that
very grave offense in the eye of any true French jurist.[12]
The form of an opinion, however, is not mandatory and
the phraseology referred to is occasionally discarded.
The only requirement is that the grounds of every opinion must be stated. An opinion which fails to contain the
reasoning upon which it is based is void. For the rest
the form and style as also the length of an opinion are
left to the discretion of the author subject to the final
revision of the President Judge. Every opinion, however, must conclude with a formal decree, known as the
dispositif—which follows immediately the phrase "For
these reasons" (*Par ces motifs*). The preparation of
this portion of the opinion is specially trying, as the
dispositif is required to contain a minute and complete application of the opinion to the facts including a
formal ruling upon each specific claim made, as well as
the exact calculation of the amounts of all claims and
counterclaims, the fixing of dates and amounts of interest, and the award of costs. In complicated litigations with many parties involved, the framing of a *dispositif* is often a task of special difficulty and, as a *dispositif* once pronounced can be amended only under
very special conditions, it is one which requires the clos-
est application.[13]

[12] See for an interesting presentation of the French conceptions as to
judicial opinions *Le Style des Jugements*. Pierre Mimin, President of la
Cour d'Appel de Paris (1927). See also the well-known works of Fabre-
guettes, *La Logique Judiciare et l'art de juger*, and of Ransson, *L'art de
juger*.

[13] See chap. x.

The President of each chamber is responsible for the form of all opinions rendered by his chamber. In the published report his name alone appears. Each opinion, as prepared by his colleagues, is submitted to him for his signature and approval. The responsibility of the President of a chamber, under these circumstances, is exceptionally heavy and is emphasized by the fact that except in the rare case when the President happens to be a Frenchman, the judge upon whom this duty falls is not working in his mother tongue, and is reviewing opinions written by associates who for the large part are working in a foreign language.

Obviously such a system diminishes the importance of oral argument and increases the importance of the written brief. It is a far cry from the familiar picture of an English judge thrashing out a case point by point with counsel in searching colloquy and often able at the conclusion of an argument to deliver an opinion from the bench. But it is a system well adapted to the conditions which exist in Egypt. The more important the rôle of documentary evidence becomes, the more difficult it becomes to discuss adequately a case in oral argument within a short allotment of time; the more useful, too, becomes the detailed discussion of the documents as presented in the briefs. The oral argument is sufficient to review the case in outline, to bring home to all the members of the court the opposing contentions and something of the atmosphere which surrounds them. It satisfies also the demands of counsel and of client to have their day in court. For the rest it is better that the case once briefly outlined be immediately taken in hand for close study and prompt decision. The system is not without its defects. But it has its checks and balances. On the whole it works well and no serious proposal to change its essential outlines is likely to be made.

CHAPTER IX
THE LAW OF THE MIXED COURTS

THE Mixed Courts of Egypt administer their own law. Founded upon codes, supplemented by statutes, interpreted by over fifty years of judicial decisions, and illuminated by an extensive legal literature, this body of law can fairly invite comparison with that of the leading law systems of the world.

The new Courts, in the exercise of their jurisdiction in civil and commercial causes, and within the limits of the jurisdiction conferred upon them in criminal matters, shall apply the codes presented by Egypt to the Powers, and in case of silence, insufficiency and obscurity of the law, the judge shall follow the principles of natural law and equity.[1]

Such was the answer given by the founders, to the question as to what law should be administered in the new courts. It called for the preparation of a system of codes. These codes were to be prepared by Egypt. According to tradition they should doubtless have been the result of the extended and painstaking labors of a learned judicial commission. In point of fact they were prepared by a single hand, the secretary of the international commission convened to examine the various projects of reform. The author was a competent French lawyer thoroughly familiar with the peculiar conditions which the Mixed Courts would have to meet.[2] His work, while it has been sometimes criticized, was a highly creditable achievement. It has stood well the severe test of a half century of daily use and has furnished an ad-

[1] Charter, Title I, Article 34, see Appendix; also Civil Code, Article II.
[2] Mr. Manoury, afterward member of the French Chamber of Deputies.

mirable basis for the progressive development of the law.[3]

It had been generally accepted that the codes should be based upon the French models. French was the language which dominated the intellectual life of Egypt and the leading figures in Egyptian public life, then as now, had for the most part received a French education. In his report of 1867 Nubar Pasha had already observed that the French Commercial Code would naturally be adopted in the new courts, as it was already applied in the existing mixed courts imported from Turkey. As to the civil law, Nubar referred to the intention of the Khedive to convoke a commission of foreign jurists who should coöperate with the Egyptian jurists in reconciling the provisions of the Code Napoleon with the existing law of Egypt. While a shorter and simpler method was found to complete the work, the principle remained the same. The French codes were taken as a basis, but many changes were made, some of them in a deliberate design to improve or modernize the original, others in an effort to adopt the old provisions to the peculiar conditions and institutions of Egypt.[4]

[3] One of the most authoritative and at the same time appreciative critics of Manoury's work, M. E. Piola Caselli, former Royal Councilor to the Egyptian Government, in a review of Professor Walton's study of the Egyptian Law of Contracts (elsewhere referred to) points out that Professor Walton, while rarely referring to an imperfection in Manoury's work, as compared to its French prototype, calls attention, on the contrary, to some fifty instances where the Egyptian Code shows marked improvement upon the French. "La Réforme des Codes Civils Egyptiens." *L'Egypte Contemporaine*, XII, 189.

[4] "It is in reality a system of almost pure and unadulterated French law." Sir Malcolm McIlwraith, former Judicial Adviser. Lecture at Cambridge University as reported in *Egyptian Gazette*, September 13, 1924. Compare observations of Sir Maurice Amos in "The Code Napoleon and the Modern World," *Journal of Comparative Legislation and International Law* (3d series), X, Part I, 235. "Egypt offers an example of the reception of French law by a people totally alien to Europe in language, religion, and social and political traditions. When, fifty years ago, Nubar Pasha secured the consent of the Powers to the institution of the Interna-

The French system, moreover, had deeper roots in Egypt than those already indicated. The traditions of the Roman law had been gradually assimilated into Egyptian jurisprudence long before the Arab conquest. The influence of Roman jurists who had lived and worked in Egypt had not been ephemeral. The Mohammedan and the Roman systems were replete with legal parallels. During the Middle Ages, moreover, the close relations between Mohammedan peoples and French merchants gave rise in Egypt to the coexistence, under a capitulatory *régime,* of legal institutions based on the Roman law. Insensibly the Roman tradition found its way into the jurisprudence of the country, an influence whose culminating expression was found in the Turkish codes, which preceded the institution of the Mixed Courts.[5] It cannot be said, therefore, that the adoption

national Courts, it was agreed without debate that the only possible law with which to equip them was that of the French Codes. Eight years later, the year after the British Occupation, the French Codes were extended to the newly reorganized native jurisdictions, and this became the law governing all civil causes in Egypt excepting those relating to the family and personal status. The inevitable consequences followed; and after forty years of the British Occupation, British officials were administering French law in Arabic, teaching French law in English, and arguing French law in French; and to-day a young Egyptian who has learned English at school, finds that he has to learn French when he grows up, in order to engage in business and to mix in society. And the English administrator has often had occasion to observe that proposals for innovation were at least as likely to be criticized on the ground that they offended against the gospel according to Napoleon as for any reason based on the traditions of Islam.'' Cf. observations by same author in article ''Code Napoléon,'' *Encyclopaedia Britannica* (14th ed.), V, 954. See also same author's article published *Egyptian Gazette,* November 13, 1929. ''After forty years of British occupation Egypt is still in a legal and cultural sense a French colony.''

[5] See for a development of this parallelism the introductory chapter to Volume I of Judge Messina's admirable treatise on the Egyptian Civil Law, which contains also a complete bibliography on the subject. See also observations of Goudy, ''Administration of Justice in Egypt,'' *23 Law Quarterly Review,* pp. 416, 417. ''For the student of Roman law Egypt offers numerous points of interest. The Mixed Courts will recall the court of the peregrin praetor at Rome. The peregrin praetor had to deal, just as the Mixed Court judges have to deal, solely with actions in which

of the Mixed Codes involved any violent contradiction of the principle that any system of law must represent the slow outgrowth of the collective legal conscience of the people. The new system of law was in large measure a body of legal principles which already prevailed in the adjustment of legal controversies involving foreigners and which had been found peculiarly responsive to their requirements.

In the field of substantive law the differences between the system administered in the Mixed Courts and that familiar to the Anglo-Saxon lawyer are, of course, many and various. They are in the main the differences familiar to all English students of the Latin system—the traditional differences between the systems of the Roman and the common law. To attempt to trace even the barest outline of these differences would carry us beyond the scope of the present volume.[6] It may be observed, however, in passing that as a practical matter the closer one draws to the points of difference the less important they tend to become. Often on closer acquaintance, what appears at first sight to be a substantial distinction turns out to be no more than a difference in nomenclature or procedure. Differences in fundamental legal conceptions are comparatively rare.[7]

either or both parties or one of them was a non-resident (peregrinus) and the law administered by the ancient and modern tribunals alike is *jus gentium*. Only in Egypt we have a code instead of the praetors' edicts'' (Sherman, *Roman Law in the Modern World* [2d ed.], I, 186).

[6] In one important field, that of contracts, the work of comparing the two systems has been admirably done. Professor Walton's scholarly volumes on *The Egyptian Law of Obligations* (see Bibliography, Appendix) leave nothing to be wished for on that score. See also the same author's article in English on Employers' Liability, *L'Egypte Contemporaine* (1921), p. 30, and in the same volume (p. 189) an able article by M. E. Piola Caselli, late Royal Councilor to the Egyptian Government, inspired by Professor Walton's two volumes, on the subject of the reform of the Egyptian Civil Codes. See also the more recent article of Sir Maurice Amos already cited.

[7] ''In the course of some twenty years experience, I have found that,

The most radical distinctions between the two systems are those which spring from historic differences in the field of domestic relations, a field which so far has been withheld from the Mixed Courts.[8]

The Mixed Codes were far from servile imitations of their prototypes. The Civil Code contains less than eight hundred articles as compared to the two thousand of the Code Napoleon. While this disparity is largely due to the omission of all articles dealing with questions of domestic relations, many useless provisions have been omitted and various special provisions drawn from the Mohammedan law have been inserted.[9]

Like the Code Napoleon the Egyptian Civil Code is divided into the principal topics of property and contracts (*obligations*) with two further general topics, the first composing various specified forms of contracts such as sales, hire, partnerships, bailments, agency, and pledge, and the second covering the rights of creditors, including the various forms of liens and mortgages.

Second in order but of no less importance in its influence on the affairs of the community is the Commercial

historical accidents apart, the differences between large portions of French and English law are little greater than is necessarily incident to the expression of the legal concepts of one country in the language of another.'' Report of Judicial Adviser, Mr. (later Sir) William Brunyate (1916), p. 32. A similar view was frequently expressed to the author by his former and valued American colleague, Hon. Wm. Grant Van Horne, of the Alexandria District Court, a lawyer well schooled in the principles of the common law.

[8] The official transfer of jurisdiction in such cases to the Mixed Courts is suggested in the Anglo-Egyptian treaty proposals of August, 1929. The realization of such a plan will, of course, involve problems of peculiar delicacy. See chap. xviii.

[9] As for example the Mohammedan institution of preëmption under which, generally speaking, a contiguous landowner may intervene, on the sale of property, and acquire it in place of the intended purchaser. See *De la Préemption en Droit Egyptien*. Baron Adrien Forgeur, late Judge of the Alexandria District Court. Doctoral Thesis (Paris, 1897). There are many other similar borrowings.

Code, with its 427 articles contrasted with the 648 articles of the French Commercial Code. Here the disparity is due largely to the fact that the provisions of the French Code covering maritime law have been made the subject of a separate code. The Commercial Code fixes with precision the distinction, all-important in the French system, between commercial and civil affairs and covers such topics as commercial contracts, partnerships, corporations, brokers, carriers, commercial paper, prescription, and finally the important topic of bankruptcy, to which is devoted more than half of the entire body of the code. Under the third code, the Code of Maritime Commerce, are grouped the provisions of the French Code covering this subject, with some interesting changes. Then follows the Code of Civil and Commercial Procedure—the most elaborate of the Mixed Codes, containing some eight hundred articles, and covering every feature of procedure, pleading, and proof before the Mixed Courts. Finally we have the Penal Code and the Code of Criminal Investigation. These were adopted in anticipation of the conceding to the Mixed Courts of complete criminal jurisdiction over foreigners, a jurisdiction that has even yet not been conferred. They are thus in large part inoperative.

To the codes of the Mixed Courts must be added the very considerable and steadily growing body of statute law, promulgated by the Egyptian Government and made applicable to foreigners with the consent of the Powers as manifested through one or other of the legislative methods elsewhere discussed.

To these again must be added a further body of internal legislation, which even if it has not received the specific consent of the Powers, is none the less applicable to foreigners and is recognized by the Mixed Courts. For while it is true that without the consent of the Pow-

ers as expressed either directly or through the medium
of the Mixed Courts the Egyptian Government cannot
enact laws which may be enforced by appropriate penalties directly against foreigners (all such penalties must
be enforced through the Mixed Courts), it is incorrect
to say, as has been frequently stated by commentators
on the Egyptian system, that the laws of Egypt must
be considered as nonexistent in the case of foreigners,
except so far as those laws have been accepted by the
Powers. The Capitulations lay down no such rule of exclusion. They accord the foreigner large immunities in
the matter both of jurisdiction and of legislation, but
this does not mean that the foreigner stands outside the
law. The Mixed Courts have thus not hesitated to recognize the right of the Government to promulgate laws
relating to the internal administration of the country,
which are obligatory upon both foreigners and natives,
provided, of course, that no specific capitulatory privilege is infringed. There are many illustrations of such
laws as, for instance, in the *régime* affecting irrigation,
the jurisdiction of the sanitary boards, the authority of
the veterinary police, decrees touching the seizure of
fruits, and the important *régime* covering the public
highways. By the same token the Mixed Courts have
recognized the right of the Government even to modify
the territorial jurisdiction of the Mixed Courts by making changes in the administrative boundaries of various cities. The tendency of the courts is in favor of recognizing broadly the application of the general laws of
Egypt to all persons in matters relating to the civil administration of the state.

Apart, however, from the written law, as expressed
in the codes and in the subsequent legislation, there is a
second source of law in Egypt, which stands upon an
equal footing with the edicts of the legislator. This is

usage—*la coutume,* as it is known—an element which plays an extraordinarily large rôle in regulating the relation of peoples in Mohammedan countries, and which has acquired a peculiar significance in Egypt in that it is the basis of the whole capitulatory system which led to the founding of the Mixed Courts.

In a peculiarly real sense it can be said that in Egypt usage is law. It is usage that the courts are called upon to look to determine the very existence of rights that have behind them the sanction of international obligations. Usage is present, moreover, as a living force in every detail of the system. The codes themselves contain many specific references to it. The decisions of the courts, too, are replete with references to usage, both general and local, in almost every field, particularly in those which relate to commercial operations. Again the Mixed Courts themselves have developed a large body of usage pertaining to the administration of justice, and the foreigner would indeed be poorly guided who would seek to gain from a study of the codes themselves a picture of the system as it is actually in operation. Usage has constantly supplemented and often, in fact, in matters of procedure has actually modified the law itself.

But even as thus supplemented, it is obvious that the written law cannot supply a rule for the decision of every case. If so, where then may the rule be found?

This question opens a classic dilemma of continental law. It is a historic axiom of the French system that the judge must render justice according to the precepts of the statute; as Montesquieu observed, the judge is but "the mouthpiece of the written law."[10] But under penalty of punishment he may not decline his task on the

10 "La bouche qui prononce les paroles de la loi," *Esprit des Louis XI,* p. 6.

pretense that the law is silent or obscure.[11] What then if, in spite of his most patient search and study, it seems to be so to him?

The answer to this dilemma has long troubled the jurists of the Roman system. Variously has it been declared that if the study of the text is profound enough, the answer will be forthcoming; "that its principles are eloquent for those who will but take the pains to meditate"; that beside, and inherent in, the text there is the "general spirit of the law"—"the general principles of law"—and the principle of "analogy" to which the judge may have resort. More latterly still has arisen the school of "positivist" or evolutionary interpretation. Appeal has been made to the law as a living institution. The school of historic interpretation has given way to the school of those who have for guide the "social object" sought to be attained by the legislation as the same is to be interpreted in its relation to actual and changing conditions. At the expense of the letter, and sometimes by the ever ready aid of legal maxims, and of those fictions not unknown to the common law, the French law has thus been enabled to meet the expanding and the changing needs of society.[12]

In Egypt, however, this dilemma has not disturbed the judges of the Mixed Courts. It was foreseen and

[11] "Any judge . . . who on any pretext whatever, even that of the silence or obscurity of the law, shall refuse to render justice according to the law" . . . reads the French Penal Code (Article 185), "shall, if he persevere in his refusal, after due warning from his superiors, be subjected to a fine of from 200 to 500 francs, and suspension from office of from 5 to 20 years." In the Mixed Courts a similar refusal would be punishable as a denial of justice.

[12] See article by Justice Van Ackere of the Court of Appeals. "De l'Action Novatrice de la Jurisprudence," *L'Egypte Contemporaine*, XII, 277. Compare observation of the Court of Appeals in an opinion rendered in 1928: "La jurisprudence n'est, ni doit être rigide et inflexible, et dans tous les pays du monde elle évolue avec les nécessités du temps et avec la plus saine et approfondie interprétation des textes légaux anciens."

solved by the framers of the Charter in that provision
of the article cited at the head of this chapter, which
declares that when the written law is silent or obscure,
the judge shall have resort to natural law and equity.
As we shall see this principle has played an important
rôle in the development of the law of the Mixed Courts.
But it was intended to supplement, and not to divert attention from, the written law. The law of the codes does,
in fact, furnish to a degree which it would be difficult for
the Anglo-Saxon lawyer fully to appreciate, the key to
a satisfactory solution of the great mass of litigation
that is daily brought before the courts.[13]

This is due principally to two facts: one, the admirable form and content of the codes and the other, the
manner in which these codes are applied to legal problems—the judicial approach, as it were, to the law.

The codes themselves present within the limits of
some 2,500 articles as clear a summary of legal principles as it would be reasonably possible for human language to express within such limits. These principles
are presented in a language which by reason of its
flexibility and precision singularly lends itself to the
expression of legal concepts.[14] They are embodied in a
form which is itself a model of style and clearness in the

---

[13] Compare observations of Judge Henry of the Alexandria District
Court in article on ''Jurisprudence Constante and Stare Decisis,'' *American Bar Association Journal*, January, 1929. ''The codes are supposed to
contain the whole of the law, and such theory is by no means so far from
truth as a Common Law legist might suppose. In actual practice certainly
ninety-nine per cent of the cases coming before the courts are disposed of
by the broad general principles to be found in the codes.''

[14] Compare the observation of the Hon. George W. Wickersham at the
Convention of the French Bar, Rouen, 1923, in an address on the Unification of Law in the United States, quoted by James Brown Scott, *Le
Français, Langue Diplomatique Moderne* (Paris, 1924), p. 312: ''Malgré
sa richesse, la langue anglaise n'a cependant la précision du français, et
les incertitudes de la loi peuvent, au moins dans une certaine mesure, être
attribuées à l'inexactitude de la langue anglaise.''

use of that language.[15] The result is to focus the attention of the Egyptian jurist from the earliest days of his legal training upon a carefully coördinated, scientifically arranged, and comprehensive system of principles which has for generations formed the basis of decision and commentary both in his country and on the continent. It would, of course, be absurd to suggest that these codes furnish a clear guide to the decision of every case. They do, however, almost invariably supply a principle conveniently set forth in a logical relation to the entire body of law, which even if it does not expressly cover the issue in hand, at least serves as a point of departure for the reasoning and the legal inquiry in which the solution is to be found. They make quickly accessible in relation to that principle the whole body of precedent and commentary, and place within easy reach of the Mixed Courts not only their own, but the rich field of modern French jurisprudence and legal scholarship.[16]

[15] ''The specific mission of a code is to emphasize principles: and there can be no doubt that the wealth of the French Code in statements of principle, expressed in lapidary language, has been one of the potent causes of its world-wide influence. Style is a powerful force; and it is related that Stendhal made a practice of reading a chapter of the *Code Napoleon* before sitting down to write, in order that he might attune his mind to the cadences of its short and limpid sentences'' (Sir Maurice Amos in ''The Code Napoleon and the Modern World,'' *Journal of Comparative Legislation and International Law* [3d series], X, Part I, 222, 224).

[16] Compare the following observations of a member of the Court of Appeals of the Mixed Courts, Justice Van Ackere (Belgium), for many years President of the Alexandria District Court: ''The law no longer remains an enigma for the public. It is open to all. It is discussed and criticized. It is not enough that the judge shall simply decide. He must explain the sense and the meaning which he gives to the written law. And from this dual control, of a Court of Appeals and a Public Opinion, results uniform and well understood rules. If the judge has paid with a part of his prestige for the greater stability which is thus assured to commercial affairs, the price is not too dear'' (*trans.*) (Van Ackere, *op. cit.*, p. 283). Also compare the following observation of a previous Judicial Adviser. ''French law is by reason of the precision and lucidity of the language clearer in form and more congenial in substance to the mass of the inhabitants of Egypt, both native and foreign, than would ever be, in my opin-

It is this statement of general principles that under the French system is substituted for the great body of judicial decision which forms the basis of the English common law. It is here that the French jurist claims for his system of law the merit of greater simplicity and accessibility. The attention of the judge is focused not so much upon what other judges have said in the presence of more or less similar legal situations, but upon the proper application of a general principle to the particular state of facts presented to him. It is his duty to think through his own problem, without leaning too much upon others who were presumably no better equipped than himself.

To the Anglo-Saxon lawyer fresh from the digest system which places literally hundreds of thousands of cases at his command the French system seems at first incomplete in detail. He feels the lack of familiar props. He searches in vain through the texts and commentaries for a *pronunciamento* on the exact (the almost exact— the more or less inexact) point before him. The reported decisions, while they are sufficiently abundant and well reported, seem somewhat arid with their logical conciseness and their absence of extended discussion. He counts himself fortunate when he chances upon one of those familiar and admirable "notes" which accompany leading decisions from the pen of some distinguished law writer or teacher wherein the principal decisions (or *jurisprudence*) are reviewed in the light of the opinion of the great legal authorities in the universities or at the bar (*doctrine*). But the closer he comes to the actual working of the system, the more he is forced to realize that in spite of deficiencies it has great merits.

ion, our own uncodified, largely unwritten, more or less inaccessible and partly archaic system'' (Sir Malcolm McIlwraith, *Lectures at Oxford* [1924]. Reprinted *Egyptian Gazette* [Alexandria, September 5, 6, 8, 13, 1924]).

The independent struggle of the judge to apply settled principles to difficult problems of facts, is an intellectual exercise which has many compensations. Litigants may be disappointed but the public mind is not confused. The public has a better chance of "knowing the law," and if conflicting applications of the same law occur, there exists always a supreme tribunal to pronounce the final word—in France the Court of Cassation, in Egypt the Court of Appeals in banc.

But it would be incorrect to allow the reader to gain the impression that "precedents" or "case-law" play a negligible part in the jurisprudence of the Mixed Courts. It is true that in general, every judge is free to decide each case presented to him without being bound by the decisions rendered by others. In France this tradition, indeed, is embodied in a formal article of the Code Napoleon (which, however, is not reproduced in the Mixed Codes), which forbids judges, when giving judgment, from laying down general rules of law which shall be binding in future cases. It proceeds from a determination to prevent the judiciary from assuming the functions of the legislator and of thus violating the principle of the separation of the powers which since 1790 has dominated the French constitutional system.[17]

[17] This point of view is reflected in the fate of a proposal made by the Egyptian Government to the international commission which elaborated the existing provision of the codes for hearings before a full Court of Appeals. The proposal was made that the decision rendered should thereafter be obligatory on all chambers of the court. This was rejected after strong opposition on the part of several of the District Judges, who were members of the commission, and who objected that it was inconsistent with the accepted continental principle forbidding the judicial power to trespass on the legislative field by giving the force of law to a judicial decision. An illustration of the same attitude appears in the observations of a former French president of the Court of Appeals, relative to the same procedure: "The decision thus rendered recalls the decisions of the ancient French Parliaments; it constitutes a *veritable legislative act*, since it fixes *a point of law*—at least for the time being—even if, owing to the progressive evolution of legal ideas, it be not permanent" (*trans.*) (Francis

In Egypt this independence is occasionally illustrated
by the refusal of District Courts to follow decisions of
the Court of Appeals. But these are very exceptional
cases. Organized to administer justice in an essentially
commercial community, the Mixed Courts have been
fully alive to the importance of maintaining settled
rules of law for the guidance of the commercial world.
The decisions of the courts are well reported and published in convenient form.[18] The principle of *jurisprudence constante* is firmly embedded in the traditions of
the courts. Previous interpretations of the written law
are followed not because they *make* the law but because
of the assumption that they have been made *according
to* the law and of the vital interest of the public in seeing
such interpretation maintained. The commercial world,
and the bar which represents it, are quick to criticize
any vacillation in judicial decision.[19] It is immediately
noted in the law journals and, where of sufficient importance, leads to a submission of the question to the
full bench of the Court of Appeals. For the rest it may
be said that in so far as a greater latitude does exist
than under the common law system, it is probably a

Laloë, former President of the Court of Appeals, *Livre d'Or*, p. 132).
Similarly when the Court of Cassation of Belgium, sitting in full bench,
sets aside a jurisprudence which has been adopted by the Courts of Appeal, the decision is legally characterized as an ''interpretative *law*''
(*loi interprétative*).

[18] See reference to law reports, Bibliography, *infra*. Appendix.

[19] Compare the observations of Sir Maurice Amos, *op. cit.*, p. 225:
''Let me observe at this point that the impression which prevails in England to the effect that in interpreting the Code the French Courts do not
recognize the doctrine of *stare decisis*, and are not influenced by the authority of precedent, is greatly exaggerated, if indeed it is not truer to
say that it is simply mistaken. In point of fact great respect is paid in
France to the authority of decided cases; indeed it is sometimes said that
things have come to such a pass nowadays that counsel no longer need to
display any knowledge of legal principle, since all that the judges will lis-
ten to is an exposition of the *jurisprudence*, as it is called.'' Compare also
Judge Henry's suggestive article on ''Jurisprudence Constante and Stare
Decisis'' cited above.

wholesome one. Where the work is done under such
high pressure as exists at present in the Mixed Courts,
and where an individual judge assumes a particularly
large measure of responsibility in the preparation of
the opinion, it would probably be undesirable if every
decision even of the Court of Appeals were always to
be considered as a binding precedent.[20]

Let us now return to the provision to which reference
has already been made, to the effect that when the written law is silent the judge shall have resort to natural
law and equity.[21]

We have here a source of law which lies entirely outside the traditional realm of French code law. Histo-
rians may claim to have traced the origin of this principle to Aristotle himself,[22] but the founders of the
Mixed Courts had no modern precedents to guide them.[23]

[20] See similar observations on this point by Michael Hansson, today
the President of the Court of Appeals, in an highly suggestive article on
usury in Egypt. ''L'Usure dans le Droit Civil Mixte et la Conception
Moderne de l'Exploitation Usuraire,'' *L'Egypte Contemporaine* (1921),
p. 1.

[21] See the scholarly article of Judge Messina of the Alexandria District
Court, ''Lacunes de la Loi en Droit Égyptien,'' *L'Egypte Contemporaine*
(1921), XII, 353, incorporated also in the author's treatise on the Civil
Law of the Mixed Courts. See Bibliography, *infra*.

[22] ''One would do well, there where the legislator is at fault and has
erred through using expressions which are too absolute, to supplement and
correct his silence, and to pronounce the law in his place, as he would
have pronounced it had he been there himself; that is to say, by making
the law such as he would have made it had he been acquainted with the
particular case in hand.'' *Eth. Nicom.*, Book I, chap. x, trans. from
French translation as given by Barthélemy Saint-Hilaire, *Morale d'Aris-
tote* (1856), II, 184. Cited Messina, *op. cit.*, p. 374.

[23] The only similar legislative approach to the subject was to be found
in the proviso of the Italian Code of 1865, to the effect that when the code
is silent, and analogy fails, the court ''should apply the general principles
of law.'' It finds an interesting extension in the Swiss Civil Code of 1907,
which enlarges the judicial to a semi-legislative function by providing that
in the absence of any specific text or established custom the judge should
decide the case ''according to the rules which he would enact were he
called upon to act as legislator,'' adding that he shall be guided by the
prevailing solutions of the problem to be found in the works of law
writers and in the decisions of the courts. See Messina, *op. cit.*, p. 373.

The formula chosen was an inspiration of their own, and that, too, at a moment in the history of European jurisprudence little propitious for the introduction of any principle of natural law. It was a solution prompted by the practical necessities of the situation. The courts, if they were to succeed, would have to meet situations for which the written codes, even under the most elastic of interpretations, could scarcely be expected to furnish the solution. This clause equipped them for the unforeseen. The wisdom of its inclusion has been abundantly justified. It has enabled the judges of the Mixed Courts to meet many practical problems created through the lack of any body of statute law governing various fields of contract and property rights which were unknown at the time of the adoption of the codes. Where the work of the legislator has yet to be accomplished the courts have been able to supply the gap. The principle has been invoked in the solution of many questions touching partnerships, sales, life insurance, accidents, collisions, literary property, governmental responsibility, and other branches of a rapidly developing commercial life.[24]

One of the most interesting examples of its use is in the field of trade-marks and patents, a field where obviously the ingenuity of the jurist is put to a severe test to supply the inaction of the legislator. Feeling their

[24] For an interesting discussion of the problem of copyright in Egypt, particularly in the light of the proposal made to Egypt to join the International Copyright Union, see article by M. Lilant de Bellefonds of the Egyptian Ministry of Justice in *L'Egypte Contemporaine*, February, 1927; also note on same (in English), by Mr. F. M. Goadby, in *Jour. Comp. Leg. and Int. Law* (3d series), IX, 260. A project of law for the protection of literary property, prepared under the direction of the Ministry of Justice, was among the many topics discussed at the Thirty-seventh Congress of the Association Literaire and Artistique, held at Cairo, December 23–28, 1929. Pending legislative action, it can be said that the protection afforded by the Mixed Courts, while in some respects not yet fully defined, is on the whole wide and effective.

way step by step, the Mixed Courts have gradually developed a system of the protection which, even if it lacks the completeness and precision of the written law, has responded admirably to the needs of commercial justice.[25] Broadly speaking the guiding principle applied in the courts has been the right of every man to be protected against unfair competition in the enjoyment of the products of his ingenuity. While recognizing the strictly territorial limitation of the protection afforded by foreign patent law, the courts have been working out the problem on a basis of prior usage and fair commercial dealing, of which the existence of a foreign patent plays, none the less, an important rôle. There have long been established offices for the registration both of patents and of trade-marks.[26] Registration, while not essential, is an important factor as to proving the date and publicity of usage, and of preventing the invention from becoming public property by abandonment. Even the perplexing question as to how long the protection of a patent should last has not been found insoluble. The courts look to the duration of existing rights of protection in the country of the origin of the patent as furnishing a reasonable basis of protection. So far, litigation has concerned itself with the use of inventions which have been patented elsewhere. The question of the extent of protection to be given to inventions originating

[25] Speaking of an effort made in the early nineties to secure the adoption of a trade-mark law, a former British member of the native bench observes that ''Lord Cromer, who was a very practical man, thought that the object had been attained by decided cases and that it was best to leave it at that'' (J. E. Marshall, *The Egyptian Enigma* [London: Murray, 1928], p. 15).

[26] The growing importance of this work led, in 1929, to the consolidation of the various district registry offices at Alexandria, under the direct supervision of the Court of Appeals. The Swiss classification system of 1908 is followed, with its 550 subclassifications for patents, and 70 for trade-marks. Registry of a patent costs $4.25 and of a trade-mark $1.15.

in Egypt, and not patented abroad, has not yet been fully developed.

The same general principles have received frequent application in the matter of the violation of trade-marks, a practice unfortunately frequent in Egypt. It has also been applied to protect the right to use a trade name. Here again the courts look wherever possible to the country of the origin of the trade-mark as furnishing a guidance as to the extent and nature of the protection to be accorded in Egypt. Where no such element of guidance is present, they accord protection according to the demands of equity.

As the courts have in these instances been merely supplying the inaction of the legislator, it remains for the legislator himself to supplement and to complete and define the work of the judiciary. Laws on several of the topics noted are needed. They will be passed in the course of time. Undoubtedly they will follow along the lines which have been already traced by the courts themselves.

CHAPTER X

PROCEDURE

WHILE many incidents of the procedure before the Mixed Courts seem at first confusing to the Anglo-Saxon legal mind, the system in its main outlines, in spite of the 816 articles of the Code of Civil Procedure, is distinguished by its simplicity. It represents a deliberate and successful effort to simplify the French system on which it was modeled.

It may be recalled that in Europe, in the Middle Ages, parties were required to appear in person. Later in the sixteenth century they were permitted to be represented by a *procureur,* but the gradual transformation of this office into one of public character led to the creation in 1791 of the office of *avoué,* an office which after a short and unsuccessful effort to suppress it, has existed ever since. The *avoué* is a ministerial office with established rights and privileges. It is transmissible from holder to holder and is often an asset of great value. It corresponds in many respects to that of the English solicitor. It is the *avoué* alone who technically represents his client. His services, unlike those of the *avocat,* are obligatory. It is he who appears on the record. It is he who prepares all documents and secures service of process; it is he who elaborates the technical position of his client before the court in the form of formal written demands. The essence of the rôle of *avoué* is proficiency in procedure. Here he is a specialist just as the lawyer or *avocat* is the expert in law and argument. The independence and efficiency of the bar is supposed to be advanced by not overburdening the lawyer with the detail labor of procedure or the preliminary taking of testimony. The requirements of the two professions are considered to be quite different, involving the exercise of distinct and often incompatible qualities. This fact has been considered sufficient to outweigh the resulting duplication of expense, the diffusion of responsibility, and the dangers incident to inadequate coöperation between the *avoué* and the lawyer. Needless to say the profession of *avoué* has not exhibited any zeal in the simplification of professional mysteries over which it enjoys a monopoly. Its existence is largely responsible for the delays and complications of French legal procedure.

The absence in Egypt of any body from which the *avoué* could be recruited was in itself sufficient reason to eliminate this office entirely. The result was to avoid a large part of the elaborate system of French written pleadings. The normal procedure in bringing a suit is simplicity itself. The action, whether it be an original suit or an appeal, takes the form of a combined summons and statement of claim bearing the signature of the bailiff, but in practice prepared by the plaintiff's attorney, in form somewhat as follows:

In the year 1929, and on the first day of November, at Alexandria, at the request of John Papadopoulos, merchant, a Greek subject, with domicile in Cairo, rue Mousky 25, who has elected domicile at Alexandria, in the office of Messrs. Valentino and Sporakis, Counselors before the Court of Appeals, I, Henri Robini, Bailiff attached to the District Court of Alexandria, have duly served upon the Royal Steamship Company, a British Company, with headquarters at London, and a local office at Alexandria, 27 rue Alexander the Great, in the person of their agents Dobbs & Co., notice to appear before the Court aforesaid at a session to be held on February 1, 1930, in respect of the following matter :—

Then will follow a recital of the facts forming the plaintiff's claim, and the statement will conclude with a prayer that "for these reasons, and others to be developed on the argument, the defendant be condemned to pay to the parties aforesaid the amount of the claim, with interest from the date of the demand, together with the costs."

After serving a copy of the summons the bailiff adds to the original document an explicit statement as to the manner of service, and returns the document to counsel, who thereupon files it in the office of the clerk of court, and the case is docketed and placed upon the trial list. No further action by the parties is called for until the date which has been fixed in the writ for the hearing. On that date the case is called on the calendar and if the court happens to be well up in its list, and if the parties are prepared, the case can be and in cases before the Summary Courts frequently is heard immediately; otherwise it is automatically placed upon some later list.

Pleadings as known to the Anglo-Saxon system do not exist. It is through the required exchange of briefs before the argument and the submission for the opponent's inspection of the documentary evidence relied on, that the parties are put in possession of the contentions of their adversaries. On the trial each party is at liberty to present to the court any argument which he believes to be of a nature to support his demand or to defeat the demand of his opponent. It is for the court, on the examination of the record, after hearing the arguments, and in the light of the written briefs and the evidence, to sift out the wheat from the chaff, and to resolve the real questions in issue.

The lawyer schooled to the severe discipline of the Anglo-Saxon law is, of course, at first confused by the apparent looseness of any such procedure. But the situation must be appreciated in the light of two factors of controlling importance. One is the predominant importance in the Latin judicial system of written as compared with oral evidence. The other is the absence of a jury.

The fact that the controversy is thus presented *en bloc* to the court has led to the development among the more competent element of the bar of very special skill in brief making. To a certain extent briefs supply the place of pleadings, in the sense that they frequently contain allegations of fact which, if not denied, are taken to be true. To the preparation of these briefs the lawyers devote their ablest efforts, commonly exhibiting a professional devotion, and often a skill in arrangement, and even a literary art that would do credit to any bar.

At the opening of his argument each pleader is required by the French tradition to define his demands or, as the phrase is, "take his conclusions," which appear repeated at the end of his written brief. Preliminary exceptions are often presented to the court, covering questions of jurisdiction, allegations as to the pendency in another court of the same issue, or of an issue so closely connected that the two cases should be joined, questions as to the absence of necessary parties, demand to bring in a guarantor, and exceptions based on the failure of parties to communicate properly their briefs and exhibits.

Pleas to the jurisdiction of the court assume a rôle of peculiar importance in Egypt. These fall into the two broad categories of pleas based on the subject matter of the dispute and pleas which involve the jurisdiction of the court over the individual. The first of these has regard to the selection of the particular court within the judicial hierarchy before which the subject matter

of the litigation should be presented as, for instance,
the choice of the Summary Judge, the Civil Court, the
Commercial Court, or the Referee Court. The second
has regard to the jurisdiction of the court as tested by
the domicile of the parties or the place of the formation
of the contract. The former of these is considered to involve public policy and attacks on the jurisdiction based
on these grounds are encouraged. They are permitted
to be raised in any case by the Procureur-General, or by
the court itself of its own motion without application of
the parties, and can be brought up at any stage in the
proceedings. The scope allowed to the second class of
exceptions is somewhat more limited.

In the case of the Mixed Courts, however, there is a
third category of exceptions of an even more rigid character based on the jurisdiction of the courts from the
viewpoint of an international institution, and looking
to the distribution of judicial powers in Egypt between
the several categories of courts which make up its
highly cosmopolitan legal system. The principle that no
one should be deprived of his right to be judged by his
"natural judges," as the phrase goes, is deeply embedded in the Egyptian judicial systems and it goes
without saying that in the course of fifty years an elaborate and important jurisprudence has developed defining the domains of these several jurisdictions.

Reference has already been made to the rôle of the
Procureur-General and the "watching brief" which he
holds for the state. In cases where "communication"
of the case is required to be made to him, the entire record, including all the documents, is transmitted to the
Parquet twenty-four hours before the hearing. On the
argument of the case the Procureur-General is heard
after the parties. The law denies them the opportunity
of making a reply, but they are permitted to file with the

court memoranda calculated to correct any alleged mis-statements of fact. In special cases the court may authorize the production of new documents. In cases where the Procureur-General has given an opinion the law requires, under penalty of nullity of the decision, that this fact shall be recorded in the minutes, but at the same time forbids any record to be made of the nature of the opinion given. This proviso is evidently inspired by a desire to avoid putting on record the existence of any difference of opinion between the court and the representative of the state. It reflects the same spirit which forbids the rendering of minority opinions.[1]

An important feature of the procedure in Egypt is the wide use of certain processes of attachment and garnishment of personal property, which have proved to be eminently suited to the needs and mentality of the country. Both of these processes, the former known as the *saisie conservatoire* and the latter as the *saisie arrêt,* may be resorted to before the filing of a suit, and as such are considered as an exercise of the *jurisdiction gracieuse* or extrajudicial jurisdiction of the court. In other words the litigation is not yet begun. There is, therefore, as yet no judicial controversy before the court.

The first of these measures lies against property in the hands of a debtor. It is open to owners against their tenants; to creditors where their debtors have no domicile in Egypt; to holders of drafts or notes which are overdue and have been protested, and this regardless

[1] As an example of simplified procedure reference may be made to the very practical utility of the device of cross appeals, or *appels incident* as they are known. An appeal by one party opens the door to a cross appeal upon any of the questions passed on in the lower court. Such appeal may be made in the brief of the opposing party, without the expense or delay of any special procedure. The possibility of having to meet such a cross appeal is not without its effect in discouraging the taking of appeals in cases of doubtful merit.

of the fact that the debtor is domiciled in Egypt. Authority to make the attachment must first be obtained from the President of the court. This is commonly granted as a matter of course, the judge inquiring merely whether the claim appears on its face to be *bona fide*. The likelihood of the removal of his property by the debtor is not an element to be considered. The result of the procedure is to prevent the debtor from disposing of any of the particular property seized, provided the creditor brings his suit within eight days. If suit is not brought within that period the attachment falls. If, however, the suit is finally successful the attachment is converted into an "attachment execution" which, as its name implies, may be enforced by levy.

The second of the processes—the *saisie arrêt*—which corresponds broadly to the common law garnishment, covers the attachment of property in the hands of third parties. This proceeding is even simpler than the former—not requiring an order of the court if the debt is based on a written document and is for a liquidated sum. In such cases the attorney for the creditor merely files his attachment with the bailiff, without recourse to the court. Where the claim is not based on a written document or the sum is unliquidated, application must be first made to the judge for the provisional fixing of the amount for which security can be asked, but in neither case is the seizure limited to property in the amount claimed. The danger of abuse here is at least in part counterbalanced by the liability of the creditor to damages where his action is afterward proven to have been abusive.

The Mixed Courts execute their own judgments "free from all administrative interference, consular or otherwise." For this purpose their own bailiffs are invested with the necessary authority and in case of need are authorized to invoke the aid of the civil authorities. The consul representing the person against whom the execution is issued is notified of the execution and may be present personally or by his representative, if he so desires, but his absence does not interrupt the proceedings.

Judgments are of two classes, those which are subject to immediate execution, regardless of appeal, and those whose effect is suspended by an appeal. Judgments in commercial cases fall within the former class, although in such case the party ordering the execution must give bond or make deposit of the proceeds of the property sold by the sheriff. The execution of other judgments is held in suspense by an appeal. The principle of specific performance is freely applied, and relief is often enforced indirectly by the use of the French system of *astreints* or penalties, ordinarily an amount fixed at so much per day, for failure to obey an order of the court.

In this connection mention should be made of an important procedure which is commonly resorted to shortly prior to an execution. This is known as the *affectation hypothécaire,* unknown in French law, a process by which the judgment holder is enabled to secure an immediate lien on any designated property of his debtor in advance of execution. Recorded in the office of the recorder of deeds it takes precedence over other subsequent deeds or mortgages, and, indeed, over those of the same date. In practice it is a most effective measure of protection. Its value is that it is good against all the world—whereas an ordinary attachment does not protect the holder in certain cases when the debtor has mortgaged his property after judgment.

The procedure of the Mixed Courts includes an extraordinarily liberal right to move to open judgments given by default for nonappearance. Such a right is a matter of course. The merits of the judgment may be attacked without assigning any reason to explain the default. The privilege has been liberally viewed as a prudent measure of safety against possible errors in the service of documents or the results of temporary absence from the place of residence at the time of service. At one time indeed the privilege developed into a serious abuse. The law went to the extent of allowing a party to make *opposition* even against judgments rendered after he had once entered his appearance, provided he had not committed himself to any formal attitude in respect of the litigation and had later failed to appear. This particular abuse indeed grew so serious that the practice had to be abolished by legislation, approved by the Powers in 1913.[2] The right, however, still lends itself to abuse.

An extension of the same principle is found in the right accorded to an interested outside party to the litigation to intervene and to make what is known as a "third party opposition" (*tierce opposition*) even after the rendering of the judgment, on the condition always of rendering himself liable to costs in the event of failure to make good his contentions.

Another interesting procedure is the "civil request" (*requête civile*)—a form of special appeal against final judgments intended to serve as a medium for the cor-

---

[2] This privilege of making *opposition* is subject to the limitation established by an amendment introduced into the procedure in 1913, by virtue of which, when a plaintiff has secured a judgment against two or more defendants, one or more of whom has failed to appear, he may make a special service of the judgment thus rendered, which will have the effect of preventing the judgment from being attacked by *opposition*. The object is to prevent the possibility of two contradictory judgments being rendered in the same case. The procedure is known as *profit joint*, that is, through a joining of the two judgments—one *contradictoire*, or with the defendant present, the other *by default*—it operates to secure to the plaintiff the full benefit (*profit*) of both judgments without risk of either of them being reopened by the process of *opposition*.

rection of certain classes of judicial error or for permitting a defeated party to take advantage of after-discovered fraud. The procedure is of ancient origin. It dates back to the establishment of an absolute monarchy in France and the growing predominance of the Royal Courts, which accompanied it. This had led to a severe restriction of the former liberal time limit allowed for the taking of appeals from the ordinary courts and to a procedure for the granting of special dispensations upon formal request to the royal judicial authorities. Originally known as "the proposal of error" (*la proposition d'erreur*) the procedure took its present name in the French Ordinance of 1673—the word *civil* having here its significance of courteous or respectful, the suggestion being that he who sought to avail himself of this special measure should couch his request in deferential form and conduct himself with due civility. Such a request was addressed to the royal chancellery and, it is almost superfluous to add, was granted only upon the payment of very substantial fees.[3] While the procedure has been happily shorn of its burdensome formalities—and expense—it has firmly endured as an essential part of French procedure, and as such was incorporated with some modifications into the Mixed Courts system. Out of justice to the Mohammedan lawgivers, however, it is perhaps only proper to add that the procedure introduced no new principle into Egypt. Under Mussulman law the judge was accorded a large latitude as to the retracting of a sentence when convinced that he had committed an error in the interpretation of the religious doctrine.

The *requête civile* is available whenever it can be shown that the adverse party has been guilty of fraud, or that documents assumed to be true have since been

[3] See Glasson et Tissier, II, No. 1055; El-Sayed Bey, par. 469.

recognized as false, or that material papers have since been recovered from the possession of the opposite party. It may also be resorted to whenever the court has failed to pass upon one or more of the claims presented to it, or has rendered a judgment that is contradictory in some of its terms, or has undertaken to pass upon some question which was not submitted for its decision. In this aspect the procedure meets the danger inherent in the peculiarly sacramental character of the decree or *dispositif* and the elaborate dispositions which it is often required to contain—a danger necessarily accentuated by the traditional rapidity of decision.[4] The procedure is one of undoubted usefulness.

Still another procedure peculiar to the French law, and which perhaps merits mention even though it is more a matter of historical interest than of practical importance, is that which provides for the bringing of an action against a judge for misconduct in the course of a suit. It is a proceeding (known to the French law as *prise à partie*) quite apart from the ordinary disciplinary measures which may be invoked against judges, as against lawyers, although it may also lead to the institution of such measures. In substance it amounts merely to an action in civil damages against a judge for malfeasance in office, although in France, otherwise than in Egypt, the effect of such a procedure, if successful, is also to invalidate the judgment. It is available whenever a judge has been guilty of deceit, fraud, or corruption, or when he has been guilty of a "denial of justice" (*déni de justice*) as, for instance, when he has refused to act upon a proper legal request or to hand down a decision in a case which has been regularly submitted for decision.

Finally may be noted the right of any party to ask

4 See chap. viii.

that the judgment shall pronounce against his opponent damages for a "vexatious defense." This is a development of the French doctrine that it is not permitted to exercise one's rights (if so they may be strictly termed) in a malicious or offensive manner. Such demands are frequently made, but not often successfully, the tendency of the courts being to allow very large latitude of expression to the defense.[5]

In a commercial community the efficient administration of the bankruptcy laws is the backbone of the country's commercial life. Business cannot be carried on if merchants can escape the judgments of the law courts by abusing the processes of bankruptcy. This is particularly true in the case of such a cosmopolitan commercial community as Egypt, whose traders are largely drawn from all the races of the Levant. In Egypt the bankrupt trader has been a tough antagonist for the law. He has put the Mixed Courts on their mettle. The fact that the existence of a single foreign creditor gives the Mixed Courts jurisdiction has made the problem of bankruptcy theirs exclusively. The result has been the development of a system of bankruptcy law whose administration has proved an incalculable boon to Egypt. The fact that four hundred bankruptcies were wound up in the year 1928–29 is sufficient indication of the practical importance of this feature of the work of the Mixed Courts.

[5] With this may be compared another legislative expression of the same principle in that which allows the recovery of at least a limited measure of compensation for abusive dismissal from employment. "When the duration of the employment has not been fixed, each party may terminate the contract at any time, providing that this be not done in an abusive manner" (d'une manière intempestive). Civil Code, Mixed Courts, Article 492. In such cases damages normally only cover a reasonable period in which to permit the employee to secure other employment, but in the case of employees of long standing fairly substantial damages are sometimes awarded. The word intempestive includes practically all dismissals where the employer has not given some good reason for the discharge.

The more characteristic features of the bankruptcy system are closely modeled on those of the French law. Principal among these has been the development of a system of judicial liquidation designed expressly *to avoid* bankruptcy—so indicated by its name, *concordat préventif,* although in France the procedure is known as judicial liquidation (*liquidation judiciaire*). Under its provisions the merchant who, as the phrase goes, is merely "unfortunate but not dishonest" (*malheureux et de bonne foi*) is permitted to put the wheels of justice in motion to the end of working out a settlement with his creditors under the supervision of the court. The encouragement which this procedure offers to a merchant to invoke the protection not merely of his creditors but of the courts, before his affairs get hopelessly entangled, has responded admirably to the practical business experience, which has taught how quickly the assets of a bankrupt estate become absorbed in the costs of administration even under the most favorable conditions. The procedure was introduced in the Mixed Courts in 1900 and was inspired by the French law of 1889.

To avail himself of this procedure the debtor must act promptly. A statement of assets and liabilities must be filed and his books deposited within fifteen days from the date of his first failure to meet his obligations. The requirement is peremptory. It is rigorously enforced. If the court admits the application, one or more representatives of the creditors are named by the court to investigate the debtor's situation and to report upon his proposition for settlement. Originally this investigation was confided entirely to the creditors. To prevent abuses, however, the practice was developed of naming an official expert to assist the creditors' committee in their inquiry. This expert is chosen from the

official list of trustees or syndics, to whom we shall refer later. The particular services now in question, however, are rendered purely as an expert and not as
trustee.

In due course the bankrupt's proposition is submitted
to a meeting of his creditors presided over by the judge
of the District Court who has been specially delegated
to handle bankruptcy matters for the year in question.
The availability by the parties, throughout the proceedings, of the services of such a judge, who naturally enjoys special experience in bankruptcy matters and who
is readily accessible at all times for the hearing of special motions, has proved itself to be a most effective aid
to good administration.

If three-fourths of the creditors in amount and a majority in numbers agree to the settlement the proposal
is provisionally accepted, subject to the approval of the
District Court, sitting in banc. Approval of these settle-
ments is given approximately in half of the cases presented. If the *concordat* is not accepted the case moves
on to a declaration of bankruptcy. Such a declaration
may also be brought about on a direct action of the creditors, or by the simple filing by the bankrupt of his statement of assets and liabilities, indicating a state of in-
solvency, and without any request on his part for a
concordat.

The declaration of bankruptcy is made by a judgment of the commercial chamber of the District Court.
Immediately upon the declaration of bankruptcy the
court is authorized to order the arrest of the bankrupt
or to place him under police surveillance, the latter being the general custom. In practice the bankrupt is
thereafter called upon to report daily to the native police headquarters, his visits being recorded in a pass-
book which he carries with him. This feature of the sys-

tem is suggestive of the facility which would otherwise be afforded in a country like Egypt for dishonest bankrupts to make away with their assets and return to the country of their origin.

The declaration of bankruptcy introduces into the procedure a personage of great importance in the bankruptcy system who has already been mentioned, known as the Syndic, and whose functions correspond broadly to the office of Trustee under the American law. In Egypt, however, the Syndics form a permanent roll selected by the Court of Appeals. Composed for the most part of men of long experience and high capacity, some of them are former merchants, others are expert accountants. Legally they are free to engage in other business, but practically their official duties occupy their entire time. While not ''officials'' of the court they are none the less regarded as officers of justice and their fees are specially taxed by the court in each case, and are paid by the bankrupt estate. Due largely to the prestige which attaches to the office and the fact that it ordinarily commands a revenue of from two to three thousand pounds it has been possible to secure men of high type for these posts. To the efficiency of their services has been largely due the success of the system.

The Syndic takes possession of the entire estate with the assistance and supported by the authority of the court clerks. Under the law he is allowed to intercept correspondence, both private and business. He calls the bankrupt before him for explanations and if the latter does not appear he presents a petition to the court for his arrest. The same is true if the bankrupt presents obstacles in the road of the Syndic's investigation. Originally arrest was ordered by the bankruptcy judge, but under a recent change of procedure the latter makes his report to the District Court of which he is a member and the question of arrest is passed on by the court thus insuring ample protection against arbitrary or hasty action.

In due course the Syndic prepares a list of all the creditors whose names he has been able to secure, and the court clerk summons them to appear before the bankruptcy judge to vote on the question as to whether they are satisfied with the nomination of the Syndic made by the court. If after hearing the report of this official the creditors are dissatisfied, the court will exercise its discretion as to replacing the Syndic by another or as to naming one or more additional Syndics to coöperate with him. Nominations are not confined to the official roll, but outside selections are uncommon. In general the nomination of the court is immediately confirmed. The creditors, however, are at liberty to name one or three of their members to exercise a surveillance over the management of the estate.

The Syndic when definitely confirmed in his office calls upon the creditors to present proofs of their claims. When the documents are received the hearing is fixed before the bankruptcy judge for individual proof of debts. At this hearing each claim is taken up and the decision rendered by the judge, subject to a right of appeal by any creditor to the District Court, with a further right of appeal to the Court of Appeals if the amount involved exceeds a hundred pounds. When the creditors and the amounts of their claims are thus fixed the district judge invites the bankrupt to propose a judicial settlement (or *concordat judiciaire*), which requires for its approval the same measure of acceptances as in the case of the nonjudicial settlement already referred to. If the *concordat* fails of adoption the judge orders what is known in the French system as a *union* of creditors. This means the compulsory winding up of the estate and the payment of dividends by the syndic under the direction of the court. If the case ends in a *concordat* the bankrupt is again placed at the head of his affairs and further claims of the creditors, who are bound by the settlement, are outlawed. If, however, the *concordat* is not carried through and the case goes to a compulsory liquidation the bankrupt is not relieved of his debts.

During these proceedings the bankrupt must live. If the *concordat préventif* has been accepted the bankrupt remains at the head of his affairs and draws such allowance as the creditors permit. If a decree of bankruptcy has been entered, and as long as there is a possibility of a settlement, the practice is for the syndic to propose to the bankruptcy judge the fixing of an allowance from which there is no appeal.

The procedure of bankruptcy in Egypt is strictly limited to the commercial world. Only merchants are subject to its operation. The aversion to inflicting the stigma of bankruptcy upon those who have not undertaken to engage in trade as a livelihood, and the very special responsibilities which, under French law, have always been imposed upon merchants, has so far withstood all efforts to break down a barrier which to the western mind may appear indefensible. It is not considered that in the case of private citizens not engaged in commerce there is any sufficient need for invoking rigorous measures of publicity and control of private affairs involved in the administration of bankruptcy laws. Creditors of persons other than those engaged in commerce are left to work out their remedies by the ordinary processes of execution.

The distinction here referred to gives rise to a very common and often bitter controversy in the courts. Does or does not a particular debtor fall within the category

of a merchant? The dividing line between the two
classes is often a fine one. Apart from questions as to
the character of a particular occupation, in order that
a man shall be a merchant it is necessary that it shall
be his habitual means of livelihood. Occasional business
transactions are not sufficient.

Another question which gives rise to much greater
difficulty in the court is that which is presented by the
necessity under the law of fixing a date on which the
bankrupt shall be considered as having first failed to
meet his obligations. This date is of great importance
in the French system owing to severe provisions as to
the annullability of transactions carried out during the
period since that date—the *période suspecte* as it is
known.

Corporations may be declared bankrupt, but in practice never are. The administrators buy the stock of failing companies and vote to liquidate. The practical
utility of a resort to the bankruptcy laws never makes
itself felt. Partnerships—both general and limited—are
frequently declared bankrupt.

Obviously the efficiency of the administration of the
bankruptcy laws depends largely on the punishment
which the laws inflict in the case of dishonest merchants
or those who refuse to comply with the many detailed
requirements exacted of merchants against whom the
processes of bankruptcy have been invoked. This brings
up an important distinction under the French law which
is followed in the Egyptian system. The French term
for bankruptcy is *faillite*—the man who has failed. It
implies no moral turpitude or improper conduct. The
term *banqueroute* is reserved for an entirely different
class of persons, those who have been guilty of offenses
exposing them to criminal punishment. Of these there
are two categories. Fraudulent bankruptcy (*banque-*

route frauduleuse) carries with it a penalty of from two to five years. Simple bankruptcy (*banqueroute simple*) is punishable by imprisonment from one month to two years. In the first class fall such offenses as falsification of books, the wilful destruction of records and accounts, fraudulent concealings of bankrupt's property, and the creation of fictitious obligations in favor of imaginary creditors to secure a majority vote. The essence of the second offense is gross negligence. It includes the failure to keep books required by law or to comply with some of the other specific requirements exacted of all traders, unjustifiable extravagance, reckless management of the bankrupt's affairs, the borrowing of money at extortionate interest, or extravagant efforts to keep the business afloat.

Criminal jurisdiction in these matters was originally left to the Consular Courts. Experience showed that before an order for his arrest could be obtained from the consul the bankrupt had generally left the country with the contents of his cashbox. In 1900 the consent of the Powers was secured to the transferring to the Mixed Courts of criminal jurisdiction over bankruptcy crimes, as also the power to commit the bankrupt to prison on application of the Parquet. The result has been on the whole excellent although in Egypt, unfortunately, bankruptcy does not carry with it the social or commercial stigma that it commonly does in western countries. The public is indulgent and abuses of the privileges offered by the bankruptcy laws are too frequent. But the laws as to punishment are no dead letter. It is the duty of the Procureur-General to see that they are vigorously enforced and the duty is not neglected. Example has gone far. The infliction in 1907 of a five-year term of imprisonment on one of the most influential bankers of Egypt was a lesson that even today has not been forgotten. From first to last the administration of the bankruptcy system lies in the hands of the Mixed Courts and the measure in which this responsibility has been fulfilled forms one of their chief titles to gratitude at the hands of the country.

CHAPTER XI

PROVING THE CASE

TO any Anglo-Saxon lawyer the most striking point of contrast between the Egyptian system and his own would undoubtedly be the predominant importance accorded in the Mixed Courts to documentary evidence as compared with the relatively negligible rôle played by oral testimony. To this would be added his astonishment (and possibly also his sense of relief) at the practically complete absence of any law of evidence—a relief which in its turn might be somewhat disturbed by the strictness of a rule (happily, however, of small practical consequence and, it is hoped, soon to disappear) which allowed a challenge to the testimony of the interested parties.

In a word he will find here all the more characteristic features of the classic French system of proofs.

In early French law oral testimony took precedence over written evidence. *Témoins passent lettres*—read the ancient maxim. The change came about with the spread of printing and a growing unwillingness to trust important issues to the corruptibility of human character and the fallibility of human memory. It was principally exemplified in the celebrated Ordinance of Moulins of 1566, which forbade proof by oral evidence in cases involving over one hundred francs (except in commercial cases where oral testimony is always freely admitted). Ever since that time oral testimony has been regarded with distrust in countries where the Latin system has prevailed. It has been looked upon as a sort of unavoidable evil, somewhat akin to a game of chance. In modified form the rule has been incorporated into the French Civil Code, forming as it stands today the

French Statute of Frauds. It appears also in the Civil Code of the Mixed Courts, forbidding parties who have not been prevented by unavoidable circumstances from obtaining written proof of the existence or the execution of an obligation from supplying this lack by "either proof or presumptions" (where the sum involved exceeds ten pounds or is unliquidated), unless the written evidence shall have been lost or what is known as the "beginning of a written proof" (*commencement de preuve par écrit*) has been established.

The rule itself is not today of great practical importance, but it is significant of the attitude toward oral and written proof. Oral testimony is only one of the several methods and an altogether subordinate method of proving the case. It is probably not resorted to in 10 per cent of the cases which actually come before the courts for trial.

The right to produce oral testimony is, moreover, not a matter of course. It requires, in every instance, a special order of the court authorizing what is known as an *enquête*, or examination of witnesses, either before the court or, as is usually the case, before a judge delegated for the purpose. The matters to be proved must be carefully stated and the order will be entered only in case the facts are denied by the adversary and the courts find that they are "pertinent and admissible." The object is to avoid encumbering the record with obviously irrelevant matter and to give protection against the use of this procedure merely to delay proceedings.

The granting of the *enquête* implies the right of the opposing party to hold a counter inquiry to prove the falseness of the facts alleged by his adversary, and this without any special demand. However, if the party against whom the inquiry is being granted wishes to establish his case by proving facts other than those go-

PHOTOGRAPH OF MODEL OF
COURTHOUSE OF CAIRO DISTRICT COURT
NOW UNDER CONSTRUCTION

LAND REGISTRY OFFICES
MIXED COURTS, CAIRO

ing directly to denial of the facts alleged by the first
party he is required for this purpose to specify the
facts he proposes to establish. The order of the court
must fix with precision the facts which are to be proved
and name the time within which the hearing is to be had.
Parties enjoy the right of compelling the attendance
of witnesses and are required to notify the names to
their adversaries a day in advance.

The rules of privilege and of challenge are strictly
defined by law. Witnesses subject to challenge include
the husband or wife of either party, or their relatives
or connections by marriage, in direct or collateral line,
to the fourth degree inclusive. Following the French
method the degree of relationship is determined by
counting the number of generations between two persons where the line is direct, or by counting back to the
ancestry and thence down to the other party where the
relation is collateral.

A witness may also be challenged if he has an action
pending with one of the parties; if he is his heir pre-
sumptive or his clerk or his domestic servant, or if he
has a direct or personal interest in the case. The exclusion of the parties themselves is, as under the French
system, a matter of course. A "party," indeed, would
not be considered as entitled to the qualification of "witness." But this disqualification is in practice greatly
tempered by the rule hereafter referred to, permitting
the parties to be examined by the court.

Apart from these rights of challenge, the right to
claim the privilege not to testify is accorded not only to
those various relatives of the parties which have been
named, but also to those who by reason of their employment, or their profession, have come into possession of
facts whose revelation would be considered a violation
of their professional duty.

The extreme narrowness of this rule has often been attacked and in 1913 the Government proposed to the Court of Appeals to abolish completely all rights of challenge, thus following the example of the Native Courts. The Legislative Assembly of the Court of Appeals,[1] however, refused to accept the Government's proposal and most of the disqualifications were retained. The only change consisted in permitting a witness, who was subject to legal disqualification to be heard, as a mere informant (*à titre de simple renseignement*) and not under oath—and while such a witness may not be compelled to answer, the permission granted is frequently a very useful one, the omission of the oath not being a matter of real importance. Lord Kitchener's remark in his *Annual Report* (1913, p. 56), that the reform is "probably useless" has not been justified.

Witnesses do not give their testimony in presence of each other. They are required to give their evidence verbally without being permitted to refer to written notes. Questions are put to witnesses by counsel or by the judge, the latter having sovereign discretion to exclude questions which are considered irrelevant or improper. Here again, as in the case of the order for the holding of the *enquête,* we find a situation which conceivably might have led to the development of a law of evidence. Such, however, is not the case. Judicial control over the examination of witnesses is directed along the most general lines. It is correct to say that no more in Egypt than in France does there exist any "theory" or any "law" of evidence as it is known to the Anglo-Saxon legal mind.[2]

[1] See chap. xvii.

[2] "There is no such thing in France as a theory of evidence. There is no hard and fast system of rules liable to become intricate and confusing to litigants regarding what is relevant or admissible evidence and what is not" (Bodington, *The French Law of Evidence*. See Bibliography, *infra*).

According to the letter of the law the examination is supposed to be recorded verbally complete. But the use of stenography has not yet been adopted for these purposes and the examination is transcribed in handwriting or on the typewriter by one of the clerks of the court, many of whom have developed a high degree of speed and efficiency in such work. When concluded the record is signed by the judge, the lawyers, and the witnesses and becomes part of the record as submitted to the court.

Effective cross-examination is rarely possible, not only because of the slowness incident to the proceedings, but because of the fact that frequently the witnesses give their testimony in other than the French language, which alone is used for transcribing the record. The native witnesses do not generally speak French. Greek and Italian witnesses frequently give testimony in their own tongue. Proceedings consequently are tedious and lack the spontaneity of the Anglo-Saxon system. Moreover, the oath is less sacred among Levantines than among western peoples. Prosecutions for perjury are impracticable. These are among the reasons which have tended to discourage the taking of oral testimony, a practice which if largely resorted to under present conditions as to pressure of work would seriously retard the movement of the judicial machine.

While the parties themselves are not permitted to testify, there are certain conditions under which they are allowed to contribute their statements to the elucidation of a case. One of these is to be found in a procedure, little used, allowing interrogatories to be put to an opponent on application to the court. The party thus questioned can avoid the interrogatory by admitting the fact. Otherwise he must appear before the court and the presiding judge will then propose to him the questions which have been submitted by his adversary.

A much more useful and practical method of securing the statement of a party is found in a proceeding already referred to whose merit lies in the fact that it is authorized by a single broad and elastic direction of the code, to the effect that the court may order that the parties "shall attend in person on a day which it shall appoint." This is the traditional French procedure of the personal appearance or *comparution personnelle*. The parties appear before the court in banc, or more often before one of the judges designated for that duty, to answer such questions as the court shall propound. It is not an *enquête*. The witnesses are not under oath. It is simply the appearance of the parties themselves before their judges in the interests of justice. It is a procedure which may be resorted to both in the upper and the lower courts. It opens wide avenues of usefulness and its only practical obstacle is the time which it consumes in the operation of an overburdened system.

Another instance in which the oral testimony of the parties may assume decisive importance in a litigation merits special mention not only because of the frequency of its use but because of its historic counterpart in early English law. It is the system of the peremptory oath or the *serment litis décisoire*. It is a form of proof *in extremis*, which permits a party who has no other means of proving his case, to stake the issue of the litigation on the reply of his adversary to a question or questions so framed that the answers, assuming them to be true, would necessarily determine the questions involved. To avail himself of this procedure a party must renounce all other means of proof and be prepared to stand or fall by the result. It places his case, so far as it turns upon the subject covered by the oath, on the honor of his opponent who in turn is compelled to present himself at the bar of the court for the taking of the oath prescribed. The solemnity of the occasion goes far to emphasize the moral responsibility imposed on a party who is thus compelled to accept a gage of legal battle, or by refusing it, to lose his case.

The form of the oath as well as its materiality is always subject to the approval of the court and, curiously, it is by law required to be so framed that the fact sought to be proven results from a negative answer to the question. If the party replies in the affirmative to the question the judgment on the point must be in his favor.

Before passing from a consideration of oral to that of written testimony, it may be of interest to refer to an institution which plays a very considerable rôle in the French system of proofs, and which has been adopted in the Mixed Courts. This consists in the existence of permanent lists of experts whose services are invoked whenever questions are presented which in the opinion of the court require expert inquiry and opinion.

These lists are prepared by each of the District Courts, subject to approval by the Court of Appeals and include some fifty experts, chosen for their special capacities in the various trades and professions in which their occupations lie (and including also experts in handwriting). The lists are revised every year and every effort is made to see that it includes the names only of those who are both skilled and trustworthy. While the selection of experts in a particular case is not limited to the official list, it is normally made from among the names thus registered, although the parties are also permitted to agree upon some other expert whether he be included in the official list or otherwise.

In France the institution of the experts at one time

had an official character. Experts were sworn when first named, and were considered as holders of public office. The system, however, has long since disappeared and both in France and Egypt experts are considered merely as citizens who have been charged with a public service, although in Egypt the tendency has been to bring the expert in even closer contact with the court and to emphasize the public character of his functions.

The order of the court naming the expert in a particular case carefully specifies the question to be submitted to his inquiry, but leaves him wide latitude in the following out of his mission. The expert may hear witnesses if so authorized, but not under oath, and can make whatever inquiries he considers appropriate into the subject matter of his mission. The mission frequently calls for an expression of opinion on a trade usage. For information as to this he naturally supplements his own information by consulting those who are engaged in business in the particular occupation involved. In general the expert is given a free rein. He has essentially a roving commission. He convenes the parties, keeps a careful record of his proceedings and in due course files before the court his report, frequently an elaborate and highly scientific document, together with the exhibits on which his conclusions are based.

This report is advisory only and its value naturally depends on various considerations—its intrinsic merits, the experience and qualification of the expert himself, and the force of the criticisms directed against it, reinforced as they frequently are by the reports of other experts privately engaged by the opposing party. The expert is paid by fees which are taxed by the court.

The system at least meets the common objection that expert opinion can be secured in support of any opinion. The temptation of the expert to render a biased judgment is reduced, relatively speaking, to a reasonable minimum. His work is subjected to the most searching scrutiny, not only by the parties and their clients but by the court itself. Being named by the court and conducting his operations under its protection, it is more to his interest to merit the good opinion of the court than of the parties to the litigation. If his work reveals partiality, incompetence, or negligence, the standing of the expert in the eyes of the court is bound to be immediately affected and to be felt in the future, if not by the dropping of his name from the list, at least by a reduction in the number and importance of the missions confided to him.

Passing finally to the realm of documentary evidence, which dominates the whole French system of proofs, we find here an even greater latitude than in the matter of oral testimony. Counsel is at liberty to file with the court whatever documents he may consider of value to his case. "In a general way I found myself permitted to say anything I wished to say and to rely on any document upon which I wished to rely," observed, with substantial truth, a former Judicial Adviser.[3] Practically the only restrictions touching the admissibility of written documents, besides a few which limit the value of documents which have not been properly legalized, are found in the existence of two carefully defined measures which are open to a party who desires to question their genuineness. One of these is known as a simple "verification" and the other an allegation of forgery. One may only be used to attack purely "private" as distinguished from "authentic" documents, or those which have been recorded with, or whose date or authenticity has been certified to by, a notarial officer. The other may be used to attack both categories. Each of

3 Sir William Brunyate, *Annual Report* (1916), p. 19.

these proceedings is regulated by an elaborate procedure reflecting the historic solicitude of the Latin system for written documents and the discrimination which has always been maintained between the two characters of documents referred to. In each case the party who fails to make good his attack is subject to a fixed penalty, aimed at discouraging the making of ill-founded attacks. In the former case, the penalty is four pounds, in the latter twenty.

As there is no printed record the number of documents produced does not affect the cost of the proceedings. Conceivably this might result in an overloaded and confused record. Practically the danger is not a substantial one and the advantages of the broad liberty given in the matter of written proofs are often of service to the ends of justice. Deprived of the opportunity enjoyed by the lawyers of the Anglo-Saxon system of calling upon their clients to build up the story and to present the atmosphere of the case, the lawyer in the Mixed Courts is confined to documentary evidence to accomplish the same purpose. It is frequently, in the examination of documents which under the common law system might not respond to the test of admissibility, that a court is enabled to gather up here and there elements of importance in filling in gaps in the general outlines of the litigation and which illuminate in a helpful way the personality of the parties and that other important element known in the French law as the "morality" of the case.

In this connection mention should be made of the singularly important rôle played by the use of presumptions in the judicial search for facts.

The Code Napoleon defines presumptions as the "consequences which the law or the judge draws from a known fact to an unknown fact." The manifest inadequacy of this definition, which contains nothing to distinguish a presumption from any other kind of evidence, is in sharp contrast to the precision which generally distinguishes the French Code. Together with most of the remaining dispositions of the Code Napoleon on the subject, it was wisely omitted from the Mixed Codes. These contain few references to the topic, but such as they do contain are adequate. Proof by presumptions is admitted in all civil cases, whenever oral testimony is allowed to be produced; it may also be invoked in all commercial cases. The question as to what it is to consist of (outside of a few carefully defined legal presumptions) is left to the discretion of the judge. He is not even enlightened by the doubtful counsel of the French Code, that presumptions "are left to the perspicacity and prudence of the magistrate," who may admit them only when they are "serious, pertinent and harmonious." This simply means that the judge is free to draw his own deductions from the evidence—in other words, to apply in his own best judgment the rules of common sense and everyday experience as, for example, in the case of unexplained failure to reply to letters. In a system where proof is largely written presumptions offer on every side a wide field of application.[4]

In measuring the efficiency of the system of proofs thus outlined, it must be remembered that it is administered by judges who, for the most part, have grown up

[4] The same latitude as to the use of presumptions is permitted in criminal cases. There is no formula requiring proof of guilt beyond a "reasonable doubt." The sufficiency of the proofs is purely a matter for the court (or jury). So far the need has not asserted itself for the creation of any of those purely legal presumptions which have raised so many interesting questions of constitutional law in the United States. It is interesting to recall that in old French criminal procedure there was a graded and mathematical system of proofs (and "half-proofs") classified according to the relative values attributed to them by law—a certain number of one kind being the equivalent of one of another kind and so on.

in it, or who, at least, have had long experience in its practical administration. Then, too, a large proportion of the cases are tried before a bench of five—three judges and two judge-assessors in all commercial cases before the lower courts, five justices in the Court of Appeals—and that even purely "civil" cases in the lower courts are tried before a bench of three. Even if we do not accept the traditional French theory that the weighing of evidence is a matter for the trained specialist on the bench rather than for the "man in the street," it is beyond all question that the system followed in the Mixed Courts is far preferable to that of any jury system which it would be reasonably practicable to establish for civil causes in Egypt. In a system where the proofs must be in large part documentary, the confusion and delay incident to submitting them to the judgment of a necessarily cosmopolitan jury would be fatal to the efficient administration of justice. The jury system in civil and commercial cases would be quite unworkable. The system, which has been in vogue for fifty-four years, responds well to the conditions which it has to meet.

CHAPTER XII

CRIMINAL JURISDICTION

T HE efforts of Nubar Pasha and of the Khedive Ismail to confer on the Mixed Courts full criminal jurisdiction over foreigners were not successful. But a considerable measure of criminal jurisdiction was conferred and this measure has since been substantially enlarged. The framework, at least, of the system is complete. Within the jurisdiction of the courts are included examples of each of the three general categories of criminal offenses—felonies, misdemeanors, and police offenses—and a separate system of criminal procedure has been established for each category.

It may be recalled that, anticipating that plenary criminal jurisdiction would be given to the Mixed Courts, Nubar Pasha secured the adoption by the Powers of an elaborate Penal Code and an equally complete Code of Criminal Procedure. Every category of crime known to the criminologist of 1873 was defined and an appropriate punishment affixed; for the trial of these offenses a system of procedure responding to the most modern development then in evidence in European countries was adopted. These systems of penal law and procedure appear as part and parcel of the codes of the Mixed Courts as they exist today. But they are in large part a dead letter. The essential clause conferring general jurisdiction was not accepted by the Powers. Criminal jurisdiction was limited to two classes of cases— police offenses, and offenses touching directly the administration of justice in the Mixed Courts themselves. As an experimental measure the courts were empowered to judge cases involving only minor penalties; and they were also armed for their own defense. The list of offenses included in this second category was set forth in detail in the Charter of the courts. It includes offenses of widely varying gravity—police offenses, misdemeanors, and even a few felonies—with punishments extending to the penalty of death as, for instance, the case of murder of a judge while exercising judicial functions. To this broad category was added, in 1900, the important jurisdiction of offenses against the bankruptcy laws, including several crimes of grave character.

It happens, however, that if the systems established for the trial of police offenses and of misdemeanors have seen active service and have been made the subject of some measure of revision, the procedure for the trial of felonies before a High Court, or *Cour d'Assises,* and a jury has been practically unused and is out of date. It is therefore but natural that the Egyptian Government of today, striving to carry out the work of the founders of the Mixed Courts and to bring about the transfer to them of the criminal jurisdiction of the Consular Courts, should see in a careful revision of the whole body of criminal procedure one of the first steps necessary to realization of its plans. In the winter of 1928–29, it accordingly appointed a commission to undertake the important work of preparing a draft project for the revision of criminal procedure in all its several categories.[1] The labors of this commission will doubtless in due course be made the basis of diplomatic negotiations looking to the transfer of criminal juris-

[1] This commission is composed of the Judicial Adviser (Mr. G. A. W. Booth) and his legal secretary (Mr. E. F. W. Besly), a Royal Counselor (Mr. Linant de Bellefonds), the Procureur-General of the Mixed Courts (Mr. Hugh Holmes), the Undersecretary of Foreign Affairs (Waguih Pasha), and a member of the Court of Appeals (Justice Vryakos), who is the official reporter of the commission.

diction from the Consular to the Mixed Courts.[2] With this reservation as to the probability of important changes of procedure in the near future let us glance at the system as it is in operation today.

Police offenses comprise the principal burden of the criminal work of the courts. Over 8,500 such cases were tried in 1928–29. General jurisdiction over them was conferred on the courts by their Charter, but the offenses were left to be specified in the Penal Code. By this code police offenses are defined as those which involve a punishment not exceeding a week's imprisonment or the fine of a pound. It contains a list of such offenses as accepted by the powers in 1875. This list soon became inadequate. But no addition to it could be made without the consent of all the capitulatory Powers. The system of legislation by diplomacy proved unworkable and, as previously mentioned, in 1889 authority was given to the Court of Appeals to act for the Powers in approving new police laws. As a result the list of such laws is today large and is rapidly increasing. The phrase "police regulation" contains possibilities which have been liberally explored and the offenses punishable under this heading include many which in other countries would be treated as misdemeanors and punished by far severer penalties. Highway ordinances and automobile regulations; municipal regulations requiring the maintenance of houses and other buildings in sanitary condition; regulations covering hotels and inns; ordinances regarding the guarding and care of domestic and other animals; the pure food and milk laws; public nuisances; the use of false weights and measures; the anti-drug laws—these are a few among the hundred or more classes of offenses which form the subject of the prosecutions weekly presented to these

2 For *résumé* of report of this commission see *infra*, p. 217.

courts. While the penalty is often inadequate, considerable added effect is given to these regulations through the fact that they frequently include provisions for the closing of offending establishments, the confiscation and forfeiture of property used in violation of laws, and the suspension of the right to continue to exercise a trade or profession.[3]

Prosecutions are ordinarily begun by the Parquet on receipt of a report from the local police officials in the form of the traditional *procès-verbal* which plays such an important part in every branch of French procedure —civil as well as criminal. Almost every incident which may be brought before the courts becomes the subject of such record. The summons is served by a bailiff of the Mixed Courts without the intervention of the consul, and arrest is not permitted. The accused must appear in person, but if he does not appear sentence may be given by default. Danger of abuse upon this score is met by the large tolerance allowed in the matter of the reopening of all decisions thus rendered.

Police cases are tried before a single foreign judge sitting in the *Tribunal des Contraventions*. Sessions of the court are held weekly. At the trial the official report of the police officer is read, and the official who prepared it is examined; the witnesses for the prosecution and for the accused are then heard, the accused having a right to question last the witnesses produced against him.

Sentence is pronounced immediately but with this distinction from the Anglo-Saxon system—that each judicial decision in this, as in every other class of cases, must be embodied in a written opinion. This must contain a summary of the facts and reference to the various provisions of law governing the offense. Alleged failure

[3] See chap. xvii, p. 314.

to comply with this requirement often provokes resort to the Court of Cassation. For the rest, however, the opinion is generally summary in form, and is commonly dictated to the clerk at the time of rendering of the sentence.

Except where the sentence involves other than fine and costs it is final as to the accused. Otherwise he may appeal to the Court of Misdemeanors. By a recent change (1926) the Procureur-General has further been given the right of appeal whenever he has asked for a sentence other than that of a fine and the accused has been acquitted or has suffered a sentence other than that asked for by the Government. An appeal is also allowed where the conviction has involved a judgment in civil damages exceeding the amount of the final jurisdiction of the Summary Court in civil matters—generally speaking, ten pounds. On appeal to the Misdemeanor Court the case is retried in the same manner as if prosecution had been for a misdemeanor. This appeal exists concurrently with the right of appeal on points of law to the Court of Appeals sitting as a Court of Cassation, whose functions have been explained.

On the whole the proceeding is simple and effective. It accords to police offenses the dignity of being tried before a trained jurist. The diversity of nationalities involved, and the delicacy of the questions often raised, fully warrant this expenditure of judicial effort. The system has amply justified itself and only in minor details have reforms been proposed.

As to the graver offenses which are triable in the Mixed Courts, such as contempt of court, obstruction of justice, and violations of the bankruptcy laws, these fall into two categories, according to their gravity, and for each a different method of trial is provided.

Misdemeanors (*délits*) are defined as those offenses

other than simple police offenses which do not rise to the grade of felonies and which the law punishes by imprisonment exceeding a week, or by temporary exile not exceeding a week, or by removal from public office. Felonies (known to the French law as *crimes*) are defined as those acts which the law punishes by death, imprisonment at hard labor, or banishment.

Before proceeding to sketch the systems which have been created for the trial of these two categories, a preliminary observation is necessary. At the threshold of the system of criminal procedure in Egypt, outside the field of police offenses, we are brought face to face, as in France, with an official of great importance, who has no counterpart in the Anglo-Saxon system. This is the examining magistrate or *Juge d'Instruction*. In France this office traces its origin back to the end of the fifteenth century when French criminal procedure began to follow the lead of the ecclesiastical courts by abandoning the so-called "accusatorial" system under which prosecution was regarded, and treated, as an open public contest between private individuals, in favor of the "inquisitorial" system, where the public prosecutor stepped in to protect the interests of the state, and the initial examination before an officer of the law took on the character of a secret written inquiry where the accused did not appear and was not represented by counsel. The abuses of this system and the long, slow processes of reform by which these abuses were gradually removed is a chapter closely interwoven with the whole progress of civil liberties in France. It is enough to remark that today the battle for those liberties in the field of criminal law has been so far gained that the reproach of undue laxness in the administration of criminal justice is more often heard than that of excessive severity. But the landmarks of the old order have remained, and among them none is more conspicuous than the *Juge d'Instruction*.

To understand properly the part played by this official it is necessary to grasp another conception of the French criminal system. This is the sharp separation which has been maintained, since the Napoleonic reforms, between the processes of accusation, or *poursuite*, and those of *instruction* or the preparation of the case. The joining of these functions in the hands of a prosecuting or district attorney is a conception not admitted in French law. As long ago as 1808 the strict separation of these two functions was decreed by statute. The French theory is that if the prosecuting officer, our District Attorney, were called upon not only to institute proceedings but also to assemble the evidence to support his charges, he might be influenced by professional pride to be overzealous at the expense of the accused. The preliminary examination of witnesses and assembling of proofs was thus separated from the duty of formulating the charge, and placed in the hands of a professional judge, an official whose importance is illustrated by the story told of the law student who, being asked by his examiner which was the most powerful official in France, ventured the name of his sovereign, only to be informed by his facetious examiner that he was in error, and that his reply should have been the *Juge d'Instruction*.

This central feature of the French system was adopted, quite naturally, by the Mixed Courts. In each of the several District Courts, a foreign judge is designated each year to act as *Juge d'Instruction* in prosecutions against foreigners; and an Egyptian judge is similarly designated in the case of prosecutions of natives.

The proceedings before the *Juge d'Instruction* are opened upon request of the Parquet, following complaint made to that office. But the injured party may lay his case directly before the *Juge d'Instruction,* independently of the Parquet, provided he is willing to assume the responsibilities inherent in his rôle of *partie civile* or civil plaintiff, a rôle that will be explained later.

The character and extent of the inquiry which follows a complaint are determined by the energies and capacities of the official to whose charge it is committed. It is as thorough as circumstances permit. The judge has at his disposal the coöperation of various designated administrative and police officials.[4] When necessary he is allowed to visit personally the scene of a crime and, generally speaking, does whatever he deems necessary to bring together into the *dossier* or record all the proofs that it is possible to accumulate concerning the offense. The proceedings are not public and the Parquet is not represented, but the accused, while not present during the examination of the witnesses, is called before the *Juge d'Instruction* before the conclusion of the proceedings and is allowed to make a statement, being entitled to the assistance of counsel. A proposal to permit the accused to be present with his counsel throughout the examination, and to cross-examine witnesses, is included among the reforms now projected. When the examination is closed the accused is notified by the clerk that the record is subject to his inspection, and he is permitted to note his objections or to request the hearing of additional witnesses or to ask leave to make an additional statement.

Unlike the procedure in France, the *Juge d'Instruction,* in Egypt, is not obliged to pass on the *prima facie* guilt of the accused and has no authority to dismiss a

---

[4] These form what is technically known as the *Police Judiciare* (Judicial Police) to whom are formally confided by law, in Egypt as in France, the responsibility, in addition to their other duties, of investigating crimes, making searches and seizures, taking the statements of witnesses, etc.

complaint. Nor does the Parquet enjoy this right once an examination has been begun. However, in all cases which have been officially submitted for its action the Parquet may decline to prosecute at any time before the case has been sent to the *Juge d'Instruction*. The law further requires the Parquet to transmit each week to the Court of Appeals a list of all charges which it proposes to abandon, and it is within the discretion of the court to order that any such case shall proceed. In practice, however, this procedure is never invoked and the discretion of the Parquet is never questioned.

When the *Juge d'Instruction* has completed his examination, the written record is sent to the Parquet, which then frames the indictment. This must be submitted to the *Chambre de Conseil*, or Council Chamber, a body which resembles to some extent the grand jury of the common law, but with such important differences that here again the French designation must be adhered to. It is composed of three judges, also yearly assigned, to whom is added the *Juge d'Instruction*, who makes a report to his colleagues reviewing the evidence, but has no vote. No witnesses appear before them, and their duty is limited to an examination of the evidence taken before the *Juge d'Instruction*. The accused and his counsel, however, as also a member of the Parquet, appear and are heard. Hearings are not public unless the accused so requests and provided always that the court does not consider that an open hearing would not be in the interest of public morals. The decision on the question as to whether the accused should be held for trial is rendered immediately. If the decision is in the affirmative the case is sent for trial before the Court of Misdemeanors unless the offense is a felony, in which case it follows the special procedure described below for the trial of such cases. An intermediary appeal to the Court of Appeals on questions of jurisdiction alone is also allowed, but such appeals in fact are unknown. Should they occur the law provides for a decision "upon the record" and without argument, although a supplemental inquiry or "instruction" may be ordered, if it is thought necessary.

The usefulness of the institution of the *Chambre de Conseil* has been sometimes questioned on the ground that it is superfluous. It existed formerly in France, but was suppressed as useless in 1856.[5] It was adopted in Egypt primarily to afford the consul of the accused, to whom notice of the proceeding must be communicated three days before the meeting of the chamber, an opportunity to claim jurisdiction over the case if he considers that it does not fall within the jurisdiction of the Mixed Courts.[6] While the institution does not play a very important rôle today in Egypt it presents at least some measure of added guarantee for foreigners, and there appears to be no general demand for its abolition. It does not exist in the procedure of the Native Courts.

If the *Chambre de Conseil* approves the prosecution the record is returned to the Parquet by whom the case is again prepared for presentation to the Court of Misdemeanors, before whom it is called for trial in due course.

The Court of Misdemeanors, known as the *Tribunal Correctionnel,* is composed of three judges of the District Court, aided by four lay associates or assessors

[5] The institution, however, still survives in France for the case of felonies, under the name of the *Chambre des Mises en Accusation* (Court of Indictments) which forms part of the several Courts of Appeal. The court also entertains appeals from decisions of the *Juge d'Instruction* sending misdemeanors to the Trial Court for trial. Its suppression in Egypt has been urged by some writers. See Hazan, p. 121; Heyligers, p. 83.

[6] See *Report of Constantinople Commission of 1878*, Borelli Bey, p. xxxvii.

drawn from a list prepared by the consular corps. They receive no pay, and are subject to a fine of from $10 to $200 for nonattendance. In the case of a foreign defendant two of the assessors must be foreigners and, if he so demands, must be of his own nationality. If assessors of such nationality are not available they are selected from some other nationality designated by the accused. When natives are being tried together with foreigners, two of the assessors must be natives.

These assessors occupy seats upon the bench and enjoy the right of vote, decisions being rendered by a majority. Their presence reflects in part the idea of the common law jury and in part the institution of the commercial "assessors" which has proved so successful in commercial cases both in Egypt and in France.[7] In the criminal field, however, it has proved less successful. If countrymen of the accused, it is inevitable that they should regard themselves as in some measure his protectors. A proposal for their suppression was included among several projects of reform submitted by the Egyptian Government to the Powers in 1927 and still awaiting action. On the question being submitted by the Court of Appeals to the three District Courts all of those bodies reported in favor of the proposal.[8]

On trial before the Court of Misdemeanors the defendant is first questioned as to his identity, and the indictment is read by the chief clerk. The list of witnesses is then read and they are ordered to leave the

[7] They recall also the *tribunal des échevins* of the Middle Ages in France, and more latterly the courts of the same name which have long functioned in Germany for the trial of minor offenses, composed of one judge and two assessors. Compare also the Swedish system, which prevails in country districts, of a judge sitting with twelve assessors with the curious proviso that if a judge has one assessor in agreement with him, his opinion prevails.

[8] See chap. xviii, p. 343.

court room. The representative of the Parquet rises and outlines his case and the president calls the witnesses in their order, the Parquet and the accused having, of course, the right of cross-examination. The defendant himself may not be questioned unless he desires to make a statement, nor may any declarations made by him before the *Juge d'Instruction* be read, nor may the testimony of witnesses before that official be communicated to the court, unless it is impossible to secure their attendance at trial. After the hearing of witnesses the representative of the Parquet makes his verbal charges or, as the phrase is, pronounces his *réquisitoire,* followed by the defendant or his attorney, to whom is always reserved the privilege of making the final address. The court retires forthwith for deliberation and ordinarily pronounces judgment immediately.

The verdict thus rendered is final, subject always, as in the case of all criminal verdicts, to the appeal on points of law, which has already been mentioned[9]—to the Court of Cassation of the Court of Appeals composed of one of the three regular chambers of the Court of Appeals with the president of the court acting as its presiding officer.

Cases may be carried to this court upon motion either of the Procureur-General or of the accused, whenever it is alleged that the act proven is not punishable by law, or that the law has been misapplied to the facts, or that there is some cause of nullity in the decision, or an irregularity in the procedure. No principle of double jeopardy prevents a second trial by a different court in the light of the decision which has, for reasons given, "broken" the first conviction.

The law contains still one or two other interesting

9 See chap. viii.

provisions drawn from the French law looking to the correction of verdicts, although in practice no occasion has so far arisen for their application. Thus, if after the conviction of A, another individual, B, is later convicted of the same offense, under circumstances which make the two convictions inconsistent with each other, both convictions may be annulled by the Court of Appeals and the case sent to a new court for retrial. If one of the accused shall have died in the meantime, the court names an attorney to represent him. A similar provision obtains in homicide cases where, after there has been a conviction, the supposed victim is "found again," or if one or more witnesses are convicted of a perjury which in the opinion of the Court of Appeals might have influenced the verdict.

Passing from the field of misdemeanors to that of felonies, we are here confronted with the spectacle of an elaborate judicial machine which has scarcely turned a wheel; of a High Court which exists on paper; of a jury system which has only twice been resorted to in fifty years. It is generally conceded that the system of jury trial designed in 1873 for the trial of felonies in Egypt would be quite unworkable today and, as will be seen,[10] measures for its replacement are well under way. But it occupies a place of historic interest in the story of the Mixed Courts, and for the Anglo-Saxon has the added claim to attention of being fairly typical of the organization of Courts of Assize for the trial of felonies in countries which follow the Latin system. As such it merits a brief review.

The High Court is composed of three foreign and two native justices of the Court of Appeals, the justices being assigned to this duty in rotation. The system calls for the impaneling of a jury of twelve, all of whom, if

10 See chap. xviii.

the accused are foreigners, must also be foreigners. If the accused is a native, or if natives are being jointly tried with foreigners, half of the jurors must be natives. Furthermore, on request of the accused, half of the jurors are required to be of his own nationality. If jurors of his nationality are not available, they must be of the nationality indicated by him. When there is more than one foreign defendant the proportion of jurymen of a particular nationality is correspondingly reduced. The jurors are drawn from a panel selected annually by the consular corps from lists presented by each consul and totaling 250, each nationality being entitled to between eighteen and thirty jurors. Fifteen peremptory challenges are allowed to both the accused and the prosecution, provided the number of available jurors permits. The procedure at the trial is practically the same as in the case of the Misdemeanor Court. Following the French practice precautions are taken against the witnesses being "coached" during the trial. All the witnesses are summoned to the bar at the opening of the case and are escorted to a waiting room where they must remain until called to the stand and after giving their testimony they are required to remain in the court room.

There is no charge to the jury.[11] At the conclusion of the arguments the presiding judge presents to the jury the questions to be determined, in the formula, "Is the accused guilty of . . ." such and such an offense? Each question of fact that might be considered as an aggravating circumstance is separately presented to the jury, as also the question of the existence of extenuating circumstances. To these are added the questions as to the

11 In France the Code of 1808 authorized a jury charge, but the practice was forbidden by law in 1881.

application of the statutes of limitation and as to the minority of the accused if they are raised in the trial.

The verdict of the jury is rendered by majority vote, an equally divided vote resulting in acquittal, the jury being always admonished, according to a direction in the statutes of the courts, to decide all questions submitted to them, in accordance with their conviction and their conscience, "without insisting upon any single specific form of proof, and without concerning themselves with the consequences of their verdict."

The verdict of the jury is final as to the facts. As in the case of misdemeanors, however, the case may still be brought on points of law before the chamber of *cassation* of the Court of Appeals, to be composed of justices other than those who sat upon the trial of the case.

In the early part of this chapter reference was made to the large rôle of the private prosecutor under the early French accusatory system. But the injured party often occupies another rôle in criminal causes in Egypt, which deserves a brief notice. This is the rôle of "civil suitor" or *la partie civile*. In this capacity the person who has suffered civil damages by a criminal act, may, if he has not already begun a civil suit on the same facts, formally join as a party to the prosecution and ask for damages for the injury he has suffered, depositing at the same time the estimated costs and making himself responsible for both costs and damages if his suit fails. The institution is borrowed from French procedure and exists generally on the continent.[12]

The presence of this third party in the case is at once an added guarantee of the effective administration of

---

[12] See "The *Partie Civile* in the Criminal Law of France." Article by Dr. P. O. Lapie, translated by A. W. Blair, LL.B., *Jour. Comp. Leg. and Int. Law* (3d series), X, Part I, 33.

justice and a most convenient method of economizing the time of the courts. The civil suitor is permitted to initiate proceedings before the *Juge d'Instruction,* and when he appears in a case almost invariably takes an active part in the direction of the proceedings. He enjoys also the right to appeal. The absence of any practical difference as to the laws of evidence in civil and criminal cases obviates the difficulties which might confront such a proceeding in Anglo-Saxon courts, and in practice its existence gives rise to no inconvenience.

Prior to the institution of the Mixed Courts foreigners were allowed to intervene freely as "civil suitors" in prosecutions pending before either the Consular or the Native Courts. The privilege was a valuable one. Ever since the institution of the Mixed Courts, however, the Consular Courts have been divided in their attitude as to the propriety of continuing their former practice. On the one hand it has been forcibly argued that such a procedure necessarily involves a civil suit of a character reserved exclusively to the jurisdiction of the Mixed Courts. To this the reply has been made that to refuse to permit a party to appear in this capacity in any criminal proceeding would be to deprive him of a fundamental right incident to *every* criminal process, a right of which he should not be deprived in the absence of some express prohibition.

The French Consular Courts have generally advocated the principle of reciprocity. They have allowed such intervention to be made by the nationals of those countries in which it would be permitted to a Frenchman to intervene in similar circumstances. Similarly, the same Consular Courts have denied the privilege to natives, the Native Courts having consistently refused, since the establishment of the Mixed Courts, to allow foreigners to become civil parties before them. In an im-

portant recent criminal trial, however, Egyptian subjects were admitted as civil parties before the Greek
Consular Courts, and the Italian Courts favor a similar
solution. As each Consular Court is at liberty to decide
the question according to its own interpretation of its
own law, it is not likely that a uniform solution will soon
be reached.

Originally sentences imposed upon foreigners were
carried out in special jails maintained by the Mixed
Courts. The system proved wasteful and inconvenient
and since 1912, by agreement between Egypt and the
powers, sentences are executed in government prisons
under the close supervision of the courts, the duty of
inspection being confided to the parquet.

Such in outline is the system by which foreigners, in
a limited number of criminal cases, are today tried before the Mixed Courts. For the rest their offenses still
belong to the jurisdiction of the Consular Courts. Many
unsuccessful efforts to bring about a substantial transfer of this remaining criminal jurisdiction to the Mixed
Courts have been made. Such a plan was proposed to
the International Commission convened in 1880, but
time was lacking in which to discuss it. It was presented
again with careful elaboration in 1884[13] and in 1890. In
each case it failed principally because of difficulties
arising out of the appointment of foreigners to the
Parquet. In 1900, with the consent of the Powers, a limited increase of jurisdiction in the case of bankruptcy
crimes was secured, but the step was a small one. Since
the closing of the War the project has been presented in
several different forms. The Egyptian proposals of
1927 for a limited transfer of consular jurisdiction have
been followed by the Anglo-Egyptian Treaty proposals

[13] See reference to this proposal in Third Annual Message of President
Garfield, December 4, 1883. *Messages and Papers of the Presidents*, X,
4759. ''This government is not indisposed to accept the change . . .''

of August, 1929, under which Great Britain engages to use all her influence with the capitulatory Powers to secure the transfer to the Mixed Courts of "the jurisdiction of the existing Consular Courts," that is to say, both civil and criminal jurisdiction. The project has thus come to assume new importance and today occupies the center of the stage in diplomatic discussions of capitulatory reform.

The wisdom of the proposal is in principle universally conceded. The existing criminal jurisdiction of the Consular Courts is indefensible. While it has served a useful purpose in the past, it is now a historic anomaly, a relic of past centuries, an obstacle to the administration of criminal justice and an injury to the foreigner himself whose interests it is supposed to benefit. It removes from the operation of the laws of the land large bodies of foreign malefactors belonging to the lower and less desirable elements of the population, and leaves the Egyptian Government powerless to enforce laws which are vital to the health and order of the country. The criminal law administered in the Consular Courts is not the law of Egypt and with rare exceptions was not made for Egypt. It is often the highly strained adaptation to a foreign country of criminal legislation framed with far different conditions of society in view, and administered on the application of a local police force by an often incompletely equipped judicial or semijudicial personnel attached to a foreign consulate and of the same nationality as the accused.[14] Worst among the evils for which this state of affairs is responsible is the feeling of injustice which it engenders on the part of the native Egyptian, when considering the contrasted lot of Egyptian and foreign offenders against the same laws. Already, in order to prevent foreigners from enjoying

14 For other objections, see chap. xvi.

complete immunity from the laws of the country, there
has been conferred upon the Mixed Courts, under the
rather dubious designation of police offenses, the administration of criminal laws, which not only should
call for the infliction of heavy penalties, but which, as
actually applied in the native courts in the case of
Egyptian offenders, do result in the imposition of such
punishments. The inequality thus resulting is a proper
cause of discontent to the Egyptian people. The temptation of the consular authorities often to be overgener-
ous in the protection of their nationals, accused of crime
by the Egyptian police, is inevitable and, in spite of the
most loyal efforts of many upright and vigorous consuls
and consular judges, has in the long run not always
been resisted. The importance of finding a way to end
this system is a matter of common consent.

But as has been well remarked the consular jurisdiction "dies hard." It has been maintained in Egypt, not
because of anything that can be said in its favor, but
because of the practical difficulty of persuading a large
number of Powers to agree as to the system which shall
take its place, and of determining just what measure of
additional guarantees should be exacted in exchange
for the surrender of the existing jurisdiction. This involves in the first place an appreciation of the guarantees which are in fact presented by the Mixed Courts
under the present system. These may be summarized as
follows:

Initiation of the proceedings (in a great majority of
cases) by the Parquet, under the supervision of a foreign Procureur-General; the preparation of the case by
a foreign examining judge (*Juge d'Instruction*); the
proceedings before a judicial "Grand Jury" of four
judges (*Chambre du Conseil*), three of whom are foreigners (not including the foreign *Juge d'Instruction*

who reports upon the case to his colleagues but has no vote) ; trial before a court composed in majority of foreign judges and foreign assessors; review upon questions of law by a Court of Cassation, also composed, in majority, of foreigners.

The value of these guarantees, so far as they go, speaks for itself. There are, however, two features of the existing system as to which (if we are to judge by experience) additional guarantees will be exacted by the Powers.

The principal of these touches the organization of the Parquet. Today there is but a single foreign member of the Parquet—its chief, the Procureur-General. He has many duties to perform besides those concerning the administration of criminal justice. These must be largely delegated to a corps of young native attorneys without any large experience in criminal law. Much depends upon their efficiency and integrity. They are to be called upon to assure to Anglo-Saxons and to Europeans alike a smooth and even-handed administration of criminal law under conditions that present many very special difficulties. To exact the appointment in the Parquet of a number of capable foreign lawyers would appear to be a measure of common protection for both Egypt and the Powers. To do this would not involve any new concessions by Egypt. It would merely mean the application of the principle of foreign representation in the Parquet, which was accepted, on the invitation of the Egyptian Government itself, at the time of the formation of the courts. This representation was only given up because the anticipated jurisdiction was not forthcoming.[15] To the extent to which the jurisdiction is now at last conferred this foreign representation should be restored. To attempt to dispense with adequate for-

15 See chap. vi.

eign coöperation in the Parquet in the early stages of a
new experiment which involves the surrender of long-
established, traditional privileges, would be a short-
sighted policy from even the Egyptian point of view.
The personal supervision over prosecutions which
might be expected of the Procureur-General with only
the present restricted criminal jurisdiction confided to
his charge (a supervision which even today is necessarily very limited in its character) would become practically impossible if that jurisdiction were materially
enlarged. As already stated, in 1906 the Powers conferred on the Mixed Courts full jurisdiction over all
offenses against the bankruptcy laws, but with the condition that prosecution against foreigners should be
authorized by a member of the Parquet of foreign nationality, or by a judge delegated by the court for such
a duty. The equivalent of the measure of security that
was considered acceptable by Egypt in 1906 could
hardly be reasonably refused today.

The second problem presents itself in connection with
the police. While the Mixed Courts personnel includes a
considerable number of bailiffs and guards, it has no
separate police force, and for police services relies on
the coöperation of the local police force throughout the
country. At the present time the misdemeanors which
come before the Mixed Courts for trial are connected
with the administration of justice by the courts themselves. It follows that from the earliest stages these
proceedings come under the close supervision of the
officials of the Mixed Courts system. In so far as the intervention of the local Egyptian police force is involved
there is relatively small chance of abuse. As soon, however, as the jurisdiction of the courts is extended to a
considerable variety of misdemeanors and crimes lying
entirely outside the domain of the law courts, the situa-

tion becomes more delicate. Under the present system when foreigners are arrested they are promptly turned over to their consul. They are thereafter under consular orders and protection. Under the new system these persons when arrested must be brought before a representative of the Parquet at the Mixed Courts, whose duty it will become, after examining the *procès-verbal* of the police, to determine whether the case should be proceeded with. With many cases pending, and a large number of arrests being made, frequently in company with Egyptian subjects, there will be greater risk of abuse, and some plan must be worked out for reducing these abuses to a minimum. The assignment of a definite portion of the police force to the handling of the cases of foreigners, under the direction of the Parquet, is perhaps the proper solution of this problem.[16]

The granting of full criminal jurisdiction to the Mixed Courts would involve of course a careful definition of the crimes over which jurisdiction is conferred. The Penal Code of 1873 would be out of date today. The work of revision is of great importance, but fortunately the greater part of the labor has already been performed. In December, 1914, in anticipation of the eventual abolition of the Capitulations at the conclusion of the War, a commission was appointed to draft a Penal Code suitable to be applied to foreigners as well

16 In a note (February 5, 1928) addressed by Sir Austen Chamberlain to Lord Lloyd, the British High Commissioner, during the pendency of the abortive negotiations of 1927–28, it was suggested that the Egyptian Government "would be well-advised to satisfy the Powers that the Procureur-General would be able to count on an adequate number of Europeans in the city police forces and on some suitable liaison with the Public Security Department." The British note on the Capitulations, which formed part of the treaty proposals of August, 1929, likewise refers to the importance of a future agreement between Great Britain and Egypt as to "the new functions of the Procureur General of the Mixed Tribunals and the staff which will be necessary to enable him to discharge those functions satisfactorily."

CRIMINAL JURISDICTION   217

as to natives. Such a code was prepared by competent hands with painstaking labor and was published, together with an elaborate commentary, in English, in 1919.[17] It was based largely on the Native Penal Code, and while retaining "the form and much of the substantial law of the French Code, from which the Egyptian Code was originally taken," it reflected throughout the view of the commission that it "should be harmonized as much as possible with the principles and spirit of the English criminal law which is accepted throughout the British Empire." It is thus a ready-made complement to the work of the Commission on the Reform of Criminal Procedure.

The work of the latter commission will amount to a complete revision of the present Code of Criminal Procedure, bringing it into line with the latest foreign legislation and embodying ideas taken from the English and the German systems. It is expected that the principal proposals touching the composition of the courts will be the following:

In the Court of Misdemeanors the institution of the four assessors is to be abandoned, the court to consist of three judges, two foreigners and one native; the High Court, or Court of Assizes for the trial of felonies, to be composed of five judges, three foreigners and one na-

[17] This commission included Mr. (later Sir) John H. Percival, Judges Hill and McBarnet, of the Native Court of Appeals (the latter now a member of the Court of Appeals of the Mixed Courts) and Professors Goadby and Bentwich of the Egyptian Law School, the latter being later replaced by Mr. Ross Taylor, then Acting Legal Adviser to the Ministry of Public Works. Their work was further revised in 1920 by a special commission which included the Minister of Justice, the Judicial Adviser and his legal secretary, the Procureur-General of the Native Courts and two justices of the Native Court of Appeals, a Khedivial Counselor, and two judges of the Mixed Courts, including the "reporter" of the commission now engaged in revising the Code of Criminal Procedure. See "The Native Penal Code," article by A. C. McBarnet, *L'Egypte Contemporaine*, March, 1919; and two articles (in French) by J. H. Percival, "Le Projet de Code Pénal Egyptien," *op. cit.*, February and March, 1919.

tive, of whom two at least shall be justices of the Court of Appeals.

The proposal to eliminate the lay element in the trial of crimes and misdemeanors carries with it the weight of practical experience in Egypt. It finds support in the very special conditions that have to be met. As already observed, even in the very limited field in which the experiment of a lay element has been tried out, namely that of the few classes of misdemeanors which, up to the present, have been triable before the Mixed Courts, with the adjunction of four foreign assessors, it has not been a success. The practical difficulties which have been so far encountered would assume much more serious proportions were the principle (whether expressed in the form of assessors or of a jury) to be extended into a larger field. The fact is that the fundamental conditions necessary for the efficient working of the jury principle for foreigners in Egypt, do not exist. Inevitably it would be required that the jurors (and the same would be true, though in a lesser degree, in the case of assessors) should, at least in a fair proportion, be of the nationality of the accused. Apart from the special complications presented in the case of joint trials of offenders of different nationalities, there would be insurmountable difficulties in the matter of recruitment. Jurors would have to be selected from among relatively small and closely knit national groups. The Anglo-Saxon idea of selecting them by lot from among a large number of disinterested citizens scattered throughout a relatively wide district would be quite unattainable. Jurors would be often familiar with the facts of a case, before they were summoned to hear it; the accused would often be known to the jurors. Differences in language would greatly limit the effective use of cross-examination. The small number of available talesmen would render any adequate exercise of the right of challenge impossible. It would be impossible to exclude from the jury room elements which should have no place in a judicial proceeding, and which in a small community, would be as likely to operate to the prejudice of the accused as in his favor.

The reasons which led the founders of the Mixed Courts to provide for the introduction of a lay element into criminal trial in the Mixed Courts no longer exist today. These reasons were a very understandable mistrust of the new and wholly tried judicial system of the Mixed Courts; and, on the part of some at least of the nations involved, a reluctance to abandon the use of an institution which had taken root in their particular national legislations. But early distrust of the untried judicial system has given way to complete confidence; and the fact that the subjects of some of the foreign Powers (notably Great Britain and Greece) are still entitled to the right of trial by jury in their consular tribunals in Egypt, and that others (as, for example, France and Italy) are remanded for trial by jury before national courts sitting elsewhere, seems hardly likely to furnish sufficient argument for maintaining the same institution in the Mixed Courts. Again, it is to be remembered that the jury system on the continent has been looked upon primarily as a measure of protection for the citizen against his own government; and as a guarantee against the responsiveness of the judiciary to administrative influences. But in the case of the Mixed Courts, the majority of their judges are foreigners, drawn from abroad, and quite removed from the sphere of governmental influence. So, too, as to the objection occasionally urged to support the jury system in Europe, that the judges, who are almost invariably men of life career, are apt to possess a narrowness of mental outlook due to the fact that they have passed all their lives in governmental service. For the most part the judges of the Mixed Courts are recruited from men in mid-career of active professional life.

Such are the reasons which would seem to dictate the inexpediency of seeking to perpetuate the institution of the criminal jury in Egypt. Whether the proposals of the Commission, if made in the sense indicated, will be accepted by the Powers, remains, however, to be seen. On the whole the matter is probably not of as great importance as might at first appear. Whatever system is adopted, the essential guarantee of justice will rest in the integrity and capacity of the judges by whom it is administered.

The suggestions as to the composition of the courts and the elimination of lay element, compose only a small part of the revisions to be proposed by the Commission. These will touch at many points the various steps of criminal procedure—preliminary charges, the private prosecutor, investigation, arrest, searches, proof, and so on—with the object, at each step, of increasing efficiency and strengthening guarantees. It is a comprehensive and exacting undertaking, but with the practical results of long experience to draw upon, it seems safe to assume that the competent and representative commission now engaged upon this important task, will be able to present for the consideration of the Powers, a carefully revised system of modern criminal procedure that will enlist international confidence and acceptance.

CHAPTER XIII

THE GOVERNMENT BEFORE THE COURTS

THE Egyptian Government, both as plaintiff and defendant, is one of the principal litigants before the Mixed Courts. The members of its legal department appear more frequently at the bar of the courts than any other counsel. The doctrine that a government may not be sued without its consent is wholly incomprehensible to the Egyptian legal mind. The Government may be sued for the violation of its contract obligations or for the negligence of its agents, in precisely the same manner as any individual. It may be doubted if in any country in the world the state can be so freely called upon to answer in damages before the ordinary courts of law.[1]

The question may well be asked as to how it came about that in a system avowedly based upon the French model, a separate system of administrative courts was not established as in France for the hearing of suits against the Government.

The answer lies in the practical situation which existed at the time of the founding of the Mixed Courts. Prior to 1876 and as a result of the Capitulations all disputes with the Government were settled by diplo-

[1] Large amounts are often involved. For instance, in a litigation finally determined by one of the chambers of the Court of Appeals in May, 1929, relating to a contract for dredging in the Suez Canal, the claims of the Dutch contractors amounted to some seven hundred thousand pounds and the Government's counterclaims to some half that amount. The Turkish Tribute case is said to have involved the ultimate payment of close to twenty million pounds. The recent action by the Alexandria Tram Company asks damages in the amount of over a million pounds.

matic negotiations.[2] The Consular Courts, following the principle of confining jurisdiction to the forum of the defendant, naturally could not entertain jurisdiction over such suits and the Native Courts failed to inspire the confidence of the foreigner, who invariably addressed himself to diplomacy, a *modus operandi* which was far more unsatisfactory to Egypt than to the Powers. Claims to the value of many millions of pounds had accumulated and one of the first thoughts in the mind of Nubar Pasha in presenting his program of reform in 1867 was to provide an impartial forum for their settlement, one where the judicial functions should be severely separated from the executive power and which should be free from diplomatic and political interference. Obviously no system of purely administrative courts could have been made wholly independent of governmental control unless it reproduced practically all the guarantees of the Mixed Courts themselves. An imitation of the French system would have thus completely failed to meet the needs of the situation. The interests of Egypt itself did not either demand or permit it, and the foreign Powers would not have accepted it. It was indeed the French representatives who were the first to declare that the Egyptian Government should submit itself to the new courts. On their side, the Egyptian representatives went so far as to propose to submit to the new courts even controversies between the Egyptian Government and its own citizens.

As far as can be seen, the Anglo-Saxon theory had no direct influence in bringing about the adoption of the principle of a single jurisdiction for government and individual alike. It was rather to Italy, Belgium, Greece, and Denmark, all of whom in their constitutions or stat-

2 See chap. i.

MICHAEL HANSSON
(NORWAY)
PRESIDENT OF THE COURT OF APPEALS

utes had broken away from the Napoleonic idea of administrative courts, that the founders of the Mixed Courts looked for the expression of the theory of complete governmental responsibility before the courts of the land—an idea that was in sharp conflict with the Anglo-Saxon theory of the immunity of the state from suit.

The general principle of liability was proclaimed, in the Charter of the courts, in the broadest terms:

"The Government, the Administrations, and the Estates of His Highness the Khedive and the members of His family, shall be subject to the jurisdiction of these Courts in litigation with foreigners" (*trans.*).

Such was the general principle—on its face all-comprehensive. The Government might be sued like any other defendant. It was therefore subject to all the rules of law—to all the principles of liability—embodied in the codes. But obviously, in the case of the Government, there must be some limitations imposed on the exercise of judicial authority. Recognition must be had of those general principles which, even in the most advanced continental systems, forbade the courts from interfering with the actual operations of government. The situation was covered, or sought to be covered, by an article[3] which provided that without being permitted to interpret or interfere with the execution of an administrative measure, the Mixed Courts might entertain jurisdiction over all suits based on the alleged violation of an established private right by an administrative act. In

[3] "Ces tribunaux, sans pouvoir statuer sur la propriété du domaine public, ni interpréter ni arrêter l'exécution d'une mesure administrative, pourront juger, dans les cas prevus par le Code civil, les atteintes portées à un droit acquis d'un étranger par un acte d'administration." Charter, Article 11. For translation of this article as revised in 1900, see Appendix.

other words, judicial remedy in such cases was to be
limited to the award of damages.

As might well have been expected, the exercise of this
jurisdiction immediately became the battleground of
the Courts of the Reform. It was a hard battle and as
has already been related was principally responsible
for the political ruin of the ruler under whose auspices
the reform had been accomplished.[4] The jurisdiction of
the Mixed Courts over the Government was fully vindi-
cated; the execution of judgments against the Government is no longer a matter of controversy.

While bowing to the judgments of the courts, however, it was none the less inevitable that the Government should chafe under the rigorous exercise of this
jurisdiction, particularly in matters touching the exercise of governmental functions. This irritation at length
assumed the form of a definite program of amendment.

In 1896 the Mixed Courts decided a case of great importance. With the consent of the German, Austrian,
English, and Italian members of the International Commission on the Public Debt, and in order to meet the expenses of the military expedition in the Sudan, the Government encroached to the extent of some half a million
pounds on the reserve funds held by the Commission.
Suit was immediately brought by the foreign bondholders, as well as by the French and Russian commissioners who had not concurred in the decision. Both the
District Court and the Court of Appeals decided that
the action of the commissioners and of the Government
was illegal, and constituted a violation of the international agreement by which certain revenues were
pledged to the debt. The Government was accordingly
ordered to return the sum which had been taken. This
decision gave much dissatisfaction to the Government

[4] See chap. iii.

and led to a protest to the Powers, demanding a limitation of the jurisdiction of the courts in these matters.[5]

Contrary to the spirit of the articles of their Charter and to the principle of the separation of the Powers [complained the Government], the Mixed Courts have assumed the right to pass upon all governmental acts without distinguishing between acts of sovereignty whose object is the regular functioning of the State and the accomplishing of its normal ends,—acts which by this very token are removed from the jurisdiction of the Courts,—and those other acts of Government, private and individual in their character, which alone may give rise to a violation of private rights (*trans.*).

In due time the question was referred to an international commission. But the Government's protests were in vain. The Powers agreed to a change in form, but all pleas for change in substance were denied. The Government was compelled to find what satisfaction it could in the formal declaration of a principle which the courts had never contested, that "acts of sovereignty" did not fall within the proper scope of judicial power. "The Courts may not entertain jurisdiction over (*connaître*) acts of sovereignty," reads the new article, "nor over measures taken by the Government in execution of and in conformity with the laws and regulations of public administration." The old proviso, however, still remained in force, giving the courts jurisdiction to pass on pecuniary claims based on infringements of the rights of foreigners resulting from an "administrative act."[6]

[5] "The Egyptian Mixed Tribunals are practically asserting the same sort of political authority as belongs under the American Constitution to the Supreme Court of the United States. And a Supreme Court of this description has to be deliberately created; no nation would allow it to come into existence by accident" (H. D. Traill, *Lord Cromer, a Biography*, p. 279. See Bibliography).

[6] The negotiations which led to the adoption of this amendment are reviewed in great detail in a doctoral thesis of some 750 pages submitted to the University of Lyon in 1914 by an Egyptian lawyer, Abd El-Salam

The language finally agreed upon by the representatives of Egypt and the Powers was far from precise. It represented a compromise, or perhaps rather an effort on the part of the Powers to make concessions in form without making them in substance. It does not yield easily to logical analysis. Covering as it does one of the most subtly controversial problems of modern government, it is little wonder that it has lent itself to varying interpretations. It is impossible here to enter on a discussion of these interpretations. A few practical illustrations drawn from the decisions of the courts, indicating the application of the general principles of governmental liability and immunity, embodied in the two clauses of the Charter, will suffice.

First, then, what are those acts of sovereignty over which the Mixed Courts must decline jurisdiction even to the extent of refusing to entertain claims for damages arising as a result of them? The phrase has no exact definition. It is not even the phrase (*actes de gouvernement*) commonly used in French jurisprudence to express the same idea. As interpreted by the Mixed Courts, acts of sovereignty are those which relate to the status of the state as sovereign, as illustrated, for instance, in treaties and matters touching diplomatic relations; in acts directly relating to the administrative and judicial organization of the state itself; in the organization of the various administrations and in the exercise of legislative functions; in acts relating to the external or internal security of the state; in measures relating to the conduct of war.

The principle can be perhaps best illustrated from

Zohny, Lyon, 1914. ''L'Article II du Réglément Général d'Organisation Judiciaire.'' The work is carefully and elaborately documented. See also the same author's *La Responsabilité de l'Etat Egyptien à Raison de l'Exercice de la Puissance Publique*, 2 vols. (Paris-Lyon, 1914). See also Messina (Bibliography, *infra*).

THE GOVERNMENT 227

cases which have arisen out of the administration of the
police service. Thus, the establishment of a police system is an act of sovereignty. The Government is not
held responsible for inaction in setting up such establishment. Once, however, it undertakes to exercise this
function, the exercise becomes an act of administration.
If conducted in a negligent manner the individual injured has a right of damages. If he is an innocent by-
stander and is injured by a shot negligently fired by a
policeman in the quelling of a riot, the Government is
liable in damages, precisely as would be an individual
employer. This idea of responsibility for the negligence
of governmental agents is applied in every field of its
activity. If the Government sells for salvage purposes
old cannon which contain unexploded shells, or if it
negligently and erroneously includes the names of innocent persons in a published list of those who have been
convicted of the illegal practice of pharmacy, it must
make amends to the injured person.

The same distinction is frequently applied in the conduct of the all-important irrigation service. The individual is not entitled to claim damages for inaction on
the part of the Government. It alone must exercise
sovereign appreciation as to the installation of public
facilities. For all acts of negligence, however, in the
maintenance of its canal system, once a system has been
installed, it must respond in damages. Similarly, if it
undertakes to close a bar which has been open in virtue
of a permit, it must do so in strict conformity with law
or be answerable for the consequences. If its agents act
with inexcusable carelessness in expelling from the
premises the occupants of a house, supposedly but not
in fact menacing ruin, or if they arrest illegally or by
error a foreigner, believing him to be a native, or if it
refuses to grant a permit to which the applicant is

legally entitled, these are injuries resulting from defective administration of the laws. The Government must pay. On the other hand the Government has been held not responsible for injuries suffered by an individual through the cession of territory to another sovereign, nor for the payment of sums due to foreigners by the Sudanese Government after the establishment of the condominion over the Sudan in 1899, nor for claims based upon a decree of confiscation directed against chiefs of insurgent tribes. So, too, in the absence of proof of arbitrary action or bad faith, the Mixed Courts have consistently refused to accord damages arising out of claims by foreigners based on their expulsion from Egyptian territory. A similar result was reached in a suit brought against the Government by an individual who had made a shipment of guns to the insurgent forces of the Hedjaz, to be delivered at the port of Jeddah on the Red Sea, opposite Egyptian territory. The shipment was transhipped in the Suez Canal but was detained by order of the Government. The Court of Appeals held that the political character of this act—its quality of an "act of sovereignty"—was indisputable, particularly in view of the considerations of public safety involved in permitting arms to be forwarded to a neighboring country where a state of rebellion existed, and which might readily expose Egypt to measures of reprisal.

The most important recent decision touching the principle of "acts of sovereignty" arose in what is known as the Turkish Tribute Case, involving the obligation of the Egyptian Government for the continued payment of interest on various Turkish loans, under khedivial decrees, stipulating the payment of a fixed sum annually to the bankers Rothschild for a period of sixty years from date, the same to be deducted "from the

Egyptian tribute which we and our successors owe and shall owe to the Imperial Ottoman Government.'' The consideration for the agreement was various concessions made by Turkey to Egypt, and the obligations assumed were carried out until 1924, at which time the Egyptian parliament declared that since, as a result of the War, Egypt had been freed from its obligation to pay tribute, she was necessarily released from further payment of the interest on the bonds, as from the date when Turkey, by the signing of the Treaty of Lausanne, recognized that her suzerainty over Egypt had ceased. The Egyptian Government, however, agreed that a sum representing the amounts alleged to be thereafter due should be deposited in the National Bank of Egypt, pending final decision in the courts. The question came before the Mixed Courts on a suit against the Government by the bankers, who claimed fulfilment of the contract embodied in the decree. The Government raised, among others, the defense of ''act of sovereignty.'' The Court of Appeals held that in order that an act of sovereignty could be held to exist within the meaning of the law, it was necessary that the act be one taken by the Egyptian Government within the limits of its sovereignty, as restricted by the Capitulations and with due respect to the various rights of foreigners guaranteed thereunder, and that if the alleged act had for consequence the impairment of any right already acquired by a foreigner—as, for instance, in the case in question, by express contract with the Government—action would lie against the Government in accordance with the general principles of liability. The resulting judgment was immediately acquiesced in.

Some of the most interesting recent cases touching governmental liability are those involving the prohibition which forbids the courts from interfering with any administrative measure performed in execution of and in conformity with the laws and regulations of the public service. This prohibition has nothing to do with the obligation to respond in damages. It looks only to physical interference with governmental functions. Two recent examples of its application, both of public interest, will indicate its general scope.

In 1915 the Egyptian Government granted to the late Lord Carnarvon a concession to make excavations in the Valley of the Kings at Luxor. In 1922 Lord Carnarvon's representative, Mr. Howard Carter, discovered the tomb of Tutankhamen. Lord Carnarvon's death followed shortly and his widow was authorized to continue the clearing of the tomb under the control of the Antiquities Service. Difficulties arose between the Egyptian Government and Mr. Carter, who had continued in charge of the work, relating to the admission of visitors. An agreement was entered into covering the subject and, *inter alia,* a visitors' day was reserved exclusively for the press. Mr. Carter, having wished to secure entrance to the tomb on the day mentioned for the families of his associate workers, and the Ministry having refused such authorization, announced to the public that the tomb would be closed and that no further work would be done. The Ministry thereupon offered Mr. Carter the opportunity of continuing with the work, and upon his refusal issued a decree annulling the permit to Lady Carnarvon, and instructed the director of the Antiquities Service to take possession of and proceed with the opening of the tomb. Mr. Carter and his associates thereupon brought suit against the Government and among the measures of relief asked that Mr. Carter himself be named by the Court of Referees as receiver of the tomb, pending a decision on the merits of the controversy. The judge of the District Court, over the

Government's objection, held that the Mixed Courts
had jurisdiction to entertain such a petition, but this
decision was immediately appealed to the Court of Appeals, the decision of the District Court being rendered
on March 11, 1924, and that of the Court of Appeals,
April 2. The appellate court reversed the court below
and held that the order of the Government clearly constituted an administrative act with whose execution the
Mixed Courts were not permitted to interfere.

By this phrase (administrative act) [observed the court],
must be understood every expression of the public will by which
an administration acting in a public capacity and within the
exercise of the jurisdiction which the law has accorded to it,
takes a decision in the public interest, within the limits of the
forms legally established, as distinguished from a simple act
of management (*act de gestion*) where the administration no
longer acts in a public capacity but as an ordinary party-con-
tractor (*trans.*).

The guardianship and preservation of antiquities falling notably within the scope of its public authority,
the court held that the granting of the petition would
be an unwarranted interference by the court with the
action of the executive power. This decision put an end
to the litigation and the controversy was subsequently
adjusted under conditions which happily permitted Mr.
Carter to continue the work he had so brilliantly begun.

Of far greater importance was the case of the litigation between the local suburban tramway company, the
Alexandria and Ramleh Railway Company, and the city
of Alexandria. The company had been operating at a
handsome profit under a concession dating back to
1860, which contained a provision permitting the Government to cancel the concession on payment of compensation for the work done in accordance with estimates

made by experts named by both parties. For some years
the Municipality and Tram Company had been endeavoring to come to an agreement as to the turning over of
a portion of the gross annual revenue to the municipality, and failing such an agreement the Government
withdrew the concession. The company immediately
brought suit asking, *inter alia,* for the restoration of its
property. The courts held, however, that the giving of
such relief did not fall within their jurisdiction; that
the enterprise while private in its inception had, by
virtue of constant resort to the Government's aid in the
application of the procedure of eminent domain, assumed the character of a public utility and that action of
the Government was thus an administrative measure,
taken in accordance with the law. The decision, however,
was entirely without prejudice as to the measure of indemnity ultimately to be awarded.

The prohibition against interference by the courts
with governmental activities, however, has its limits. As
intimated by the court in the Turkish Tribute case,
where the Government interposes the defense that its
action is an act of sovereignty, it must establish that it
is really an act of sovereignty, having in mind the limitations necessarily placed on the sovereignty of Egypt
by the existence of the Capitulations. Again, if the litigation concerns not an act of sovereignty but an administrative measure, it must be established that the
measure has been taken in accordance with the laws. If
it is in direct violation of the laws as, for instance, an
arbitrary seizure of property, the court would not hesi-
tate to order the same measure of redress that would be
applicable in the case of an individual. If in the last
analysis a conflict should arise between administrative
officials and the officers of justice, this would be settled

by diplomatic negotiations, but happily no such controversy is within the realm of reasonable possibility.

A further tempering of the principle as to the removal of acts of sovereignty from the jurisdiction of the courts is found in a well-established tendency to recognize a right of equitable compensation wherever the act can be assimilated to the taking of private property for public use. An illustration of this is seen in the case where an individual who had received a permit from the Government to do business in the Sudan had been obliged to abandon his enterprise by the withdrawal of his permit as the result of the reoccupation of the Sudan in 1898. The courts held that while the judicial power was powerless to pronounce on the legality of the particular measures, and while individuals could not claim damages for the direct consequences of war measures, this principle should not be applied to measures of purely preventive character, which took the form of an expropriation of an individual in the public interest. Compensation was thus awarded not in the form of damages for an abuse of power, but as an equitable indemnity.

The general question of governmental immunity suggests naturally the question as to the binding authority of legislative acts themselves, when questioned in the courts—in other words, as to the existence in Egypt of what may be termed the American theory of constitutional law.

The Egyptian Constitution itself dates only from 1923, and questions of "constitutional law," based on its provisions, have not had time to present themselves in the courts. The Capitulations, however, present what may be regarded as a constitutional Bill of Rights for foreigners. As to their inviolability no question has ever existed. No law or decree which conflicts with a capitulatory right can be enforced in the Mixed Courts. Any action which has been taken in pursuance of such a law or decree would open a right to direct relief through judicial measures as well as expose the Government to liability for reparation for the wrong so done.[7] In practice, however, such laws are not attacked in the courts for the reason that in order to be applicable to foreigners, they must, in general, have already received the approval of one of the two legislative bodies of the Mixed Courts, or of the Powers themselves.[8] But the approval by the Court of Appeals, acting in legislative capacity, would not prevent the question from being raised in judicial proceedings before one of the chambers of either of the upper or lower courts, as far as the Constitution is concerned.[9]

It remains to be seen as to how far the future will justify the prediction of the late Professor Duguit, that the day is not far distant when ''the doctrine of constitutional review will be accepted in every court in

[7] Such a power, which constitutes one of the titles of gratitude which Egypt no less than the Powers owes to the Mixed Courts has none the less been made the subject of unfriendly criticism. See, for example, the observation of Mr. Sidney Low, *Egypt in Transition* (Macmillan, 1904): ''If they choose to hold that any Khedivial decree is ultra vires or contrary to the Capitulations, or otherwise unsatisfactory, they can and do ignore it.''

[8] See chap. xvii.

[9] In a recent criminal case brought before the chamber of *cassation* it was urged by the accused that the law under which he had been convicted was invalid in that the Legislative Assembly of the court had acted beyond its authority in approving a certain legislative measure on which the proceedings had been based and which, so it was alleged, was of a nature to require the assent of the capitulatory Powers direct, and not through the medium of the Legislative Assembly. The court, by declining to reject the argument as ''inadmissible,'' recognized that the validity of the act could be questioned on that ground. It held, however, that even if the legislative body had exceeded the scope of its authority, this defect had, in the particular case presented, been covered by the tacit acquiescence of the capitulatory Powers in failing subsequently to raise any objections to the law. See also, in same sense as text, minutes of Legislative Assembly, November 8, 1929.

Egypt.'"[10] In the case of a recent governmental decree, submitted for the approval of the General Assembly of the Mixed Courts, the assembly returned the law to the Government for reconsideration, with the suggestion, *inter alia,* that its provisions were such that, according to the provisions of the constitution, it should have been submitted for action to the Egyptian Parliament, and could not be properly promulgated as an administrative decree. This action, taken before the *coup d'état* of July 19, 1928, suspending parliament for a period of three years, does not mean that the Mixed Courts will allow their jurisdiction to be invoked in matters of a purely political character.[11] By the *coup d'état,* regardless of its conflict with constitutional provisions, a situation *de facto* was created which the Mixed Courts in their legislative capacity recognized to the extent of approving laws which recite in their preamble the decree dissolving parliament and suspending certain provisions of the constitution. No question of the capitulatory right of any foreigner being involved, the Court of Appeals took the view that it would lie outside its province to take cognizance of a situation concerning the political

[10] See Leon Duguit, *Leçons de Droit public général, faites à la Faculté de Droit de l'Université égyptienne,* ed. Boccard (Paris, 1926), p. 295. This doctrine is strongly espoused by Judge Messina of the Mixed Courts, Volume I, *Droit Civil Egyptien,* p. 175. A strong current in the direction of the American theory is found among law writers in France today. In the work of Professor Duguit, above cited, is found (p. 289) a concise exposition of the two theories, with a masterly statement of the writer's reasons for preferring the American system. However, this theory has not yet been accepted by the French courts.

[11] The constitution (Article 155) declares that no provision thereof may be suspended except temporarily in time of war or state of siege, and that in no case may the assembling of parliament be interfered with. Compare public statement in England of Egyptian Prime Minister, Mohamed Mahmoud Pasha, published in *Egyptian Gazette,* June 23, 1929: ''Egypt is at the moment under a dictatorship. I temporarily suspended Parliament because it did not serve the public interest.'' The decree of suspension was revoked by the decree of October 31, 1929, restoring the parliamentary *régime.*

relations between the Sovereign and his people. The question of the constitutionality of such laws has not been presented to the courts for decision in judicial proceedings.

So far, we have discussed only the relation of the Egyptian Government itself to the Mixed Courts. A word should be added as to the position of foreign states.

The administrative jurisdiction of the Mixed Courts is not confined to the Egyptian Government. Refusing, in this respect, to follow the older traditional doctrine alike of French and of Anglo-Saxon law, the Mixed Courts have entertained jurisdiction over suits against foreign governments in cases where it has appeared that such governments have engaged in a commercial enterprise or have entered into obligations of an ordinary civil nature not involving the exercise of purely governmental powers. They have not allowed themselves to be disturbed, as have the courts of France, by the impossibility of enforcing respect for such judgments[12] and it is a tribute to their authority that so far such eventualities have never been realized.

A good illustration of this doctrine appears in a case where the Sudanese Government leased a villa at Cairo to be placed at the disposal of a guest of the Government, the chief of an important religious sect. At the end of the term a dispute over the damages alleged to have been done to the property led to a preliminary demand for the appointment by the Mixed Courts of an expert to appraise the damages. In vain the Sudanese Government, whose sovereign independence as a state

[12] "It is the duty of the court to give judgment regardless of eventualities." Court of Cassation of Naples, March 27, 1886. See also "Jurisdiction of National Courts over Foreign Governments," *L'Egypte Contemporaine*, March, 1927, No. 99, p. 215, and article on same topic by Raymond Schemeil, *Gazette des Tribunaux Mixtes*, August, 1927, p. 229.

in its relation with Egypt was not disputed, pleaded its immunity from suit.[13] A similar plea had been raised by the British Government in the case of a suit arising out of a collision between a Spanish merchantman and a vessel belonging to the British Government, which had confided its operation to Lord Inchcape, the vessel being engaged in a commercial voyage on the Government's account. The Court of Appeals held that even if the profits of the voyage were to be enjoyed by the British Government, this was only in its capacity as a private person (*personne privée*) and that as such it must respond in the courts of law like any other trader.[14]

More striking still as illustrations of this principle is a case in which the Cairo District Court, overruling a decision of its Summary Court, retained jurisdiction over the French National Savings Fund (*Caisse Nationale d'Epargne Française*), an institution conducted directly by the Government in connection with the French Post Office; and one (decided in January, 1930) in which the Court of Appeals similarly retained jurisdiction over the Tobacco Monopoly (*Monopole*) operated by the Turkish Government.

In conclusion then it may be said that while the Mixed Courts have resolutely refused to interfere with the administrative activities of the Government—and in this respect are in practical effect perhaps more restricted in their jurisdiction than the courts of countries where the principles of the common law prevail, they stand, on the other hand, for the most liberal expression of the

[13] Zaki Bey Gabra vs. Moore, Agent of the Sudanese Government, Cairo District Court, February 14, 1927. *Gazette*, XVII, 104–151.

[14] In a recent suit brought in Italy against the Egyptian Government, by the owners of an Italian sailboat which had the misfortune to come into collision, in the harbor of Genoa, with the magnificent Egyptian royal yacht, the *Mahroussa*, the property of the state, the Egyptian Government raised no question as to the jurisdiction of the court, and the outcome was a judgment against it.

doctrine of governmental responsibility—an expression which is in sharp contrast to the conception of that responsibility which still maintains in both America and England. This tendency has been fostered by the presence on their benches of judges drawn from various nations where liberal views on this subject have long been followed. It has been made possible by that complete independence of action, elsewhere referred to, which has permitted the courts to exercise and develop the powers intrusted to them without regard to possible reactions upon the institution itself—and, in the truly international sense, without fear or favor. If on the one hand, it has enabled the courts to afford complete protection to foreign interests, it has none the less enabled them to protect the Egyptian Government itself against a rapacious army of foreign claimants. The balance between Government and Citizen has been fairly held; today no voice is longer raised against the usurpation of the courts.

CHAPTER XIV

THE ADMINISTRATIVE MACHINE

BY the Charter of the Mixed Courts Egypt assumed
the obligation of establishing and maintaining
the new system. Egypt was to undertake the active rôle; the Powers a passive one. It was for Egypt
to build and equip, to set up and keep in motion the new
machine. The Powers assumed no obligations, financial
or otherwise, except that of agreeing to permit these
new Egyptian courts to exercise a certain measure of
the jurisdiction formerly exercised by the Consular
Courts, and of lending to Egypt the modest measure of
coöperation implied in the duty of approving or dis-
approving the proposed nominations of foreign judges.
The courts are thus administratively an integral part
of the Egyptian judicial system. The essential points
of contact between them and the Government, apart
from the question of the nomination of the judges, are
those of the budget and the personnel.

The expense of the maintenance of the courts is an
obligation resting solely on the Egyptian Government.
This obligation was implied in the nature of the new
régime—Egyptian Courts substituted for Consular
Courts—and for this reason no reference to the subject
occurs in the charter as it was accepted by the Powers.
The budget of the Mixed Courts is a part of the Egyptian National Budget. It is proposed annually by the
Court of Appeals, but like the rest of the national
budget must be approved by parliament.[1] Failure to
make the appropriations necessary to enable the Egyp-

[1] For extract, see Appendix.

tian Government to meet her treaty obligations as to
the maintenance of the courts or the more special obligations as to the payment of salaries, which involve contract as well as treaty rights, would not only give rise to
diplomatic representations, but would doubtless lead to
suits before the courts themselves.[2]

Among other matters necessarily left, at least in the
first instance, to the discretion of the Government, is the
question of providing adequate courthouses and other
necessary accommodations in the various judicial districts. The urgency of the need for enlarged accommodations or the desirability of constructing new buildings
is a matter for the decision of the Government, largely
guided, as it always is, by the views of the Court of Appeals. The recent completion of a handsome building at
Cairo for the housing of land registration offices of the
Mixed Courts, and the progress already made on an imposing new courthouse for the District Court in the
same city, are evidences of the Government's recognition of its responsibilities in this field. It is hoped that
the Government will soon replace the present inadequate courthouse at Alexandria, a measure utterly necessary if consular jurisdiction is transferred to the
Mixed Courts.

In this connection it may be recalled that while the
expenses of the courts are met out of state funds, in fact
no funds pass to the courts from the treasury. The
practice is to draw directly upon judicial receipts up to

2 As an illustration of the protection given by the courts in such cases
may be cited the case of a former French judge of the Mixed Courts to
whom, not being by law entitled to a pension, the Government gratuitously
accorded a pension of three hundred pounds a year. Parliament having
later declined to pass the credit necessary for the maintenance of the pension, the Court of Appeals held that under the terms of the law granting
the Government the right to accord special pensions, a pension which has
once been formally entered on the pension rolls was irrevocable, and gave
judgment against the Government. (June 9, 1927.)

RALPH P. B. CATOR
(GREAT BRITAIN)
VICE-PRESIDENT OF THE COURT OF APPEALS

the limit of the items passed in the budget. The Mixed
Courts almost from the beginning of their history have
been a source of revenue to the Government, at times
approaching a million pounds, the greatest part of
which, however, is due to fees from the registration of
deeds and mortgages. For the year 1929–30 the net
revenue is estimated at $4,500,000 as against gross re-
ceipts of some $7,700,000, an increase of a million dol-
lars over the preceding year.[3] On the side of purely
judicial services, and laying aside the items of pensions,
new construction, property registration, and notarial
fees, receipts and expenditures are about even.

When we turn from the budget to the question of personnel a somewhat different situation is presented. For
the organization of the courts the employees necessary
to start the judicial machine were selected by the Government. Shortly afterward, however, pursuant to a provision of the charter, the Government, on the proposal
of the Court of Appeals, promulgated a general statute[4]
covering the internal organization of the courts, by
which the selection, advancement, and discipline of the
personnel were placed entirely in the hands of the courts
themselves. For practical purposes this control is complete.

At the present time there are some fourteen hundred
employees in the service of the Mixed Courts, scattered
throughout Egypt, representing all nationalities and
grades of employment, a few of them in the higher
grades receiving fairly adequate salaries, but the great
majority receiving extremely modest ones. To maintain
throughout this body a standard of efficiency necessary

[3] See Budget, Appendix J.
[4] Known as the *Règlement Général Judiciaire*. This statute can be
amended by the Government with the approval of the Court of Appeals.
A complete project of revision has been awaiting final action for several
years.

for the good functioning and reputation of a judicial
institution calls for the most constant supervision. Immediate responsibility for this supervision falls in the
first instance upon bureau chiefs, but more particularly
upon the three chief clerks of the District Courts, and
upon the chief clerk or *Greffier en Chef* of the Court of
Appeals, who is the trusted adviser and collaborator
of the administrative head of the entire system, the
President of the Court of Appeals himself. The peculiarly onerous and responsible character of the duties of
this latter official have already been referred to. It is on
his vigilance and uprightness, on his firmness and tact
and sympathy in dealing with the cosmopolitan little
army under his charge, that depend, in large measure,
the *esprit de corps* and the real efficiency of the whole
system. Behind him stands the Court of Appeals, the
supreme arbiter of the destinies of the institution.[5] Control is exercised through its General Assembly composed of all the members of the court which sits on an
average of two or three times a month. Questions of
nomination and promotion, questions of minor and
graver discipline, questions of the interpretation of
laws and regulations, questions touching administrative relations with the Government, problems submitted
by the various District Courts or by individual members of the courts, incidents of every imaginable kind
and description, serve to give these sessions the relief
of variety and a human touch; the decisions taken in the
course of the deliberations of this little international
assembly go far to determine the standing of the institution in the Egyptian world.

Almost the entire personnel of the Mixed Courts be-

[5] "It alone possesses the real control—and is the guardian of their
prestige and reputation." Report of Sir Eldon Gorst, British High Commissioner, 1907, p. 31.

long to a highly organized civil service known as the
Cadre, a body infinite in its mysteries of hierarchical
rank and privilege and compensation. The employee entering the service of the Mixed Courts at the bottom of
the ladder does not at once become a member of the
Cadre. He begins as a copyist, earning on the piecework
system from $25 to $75 a month. If he is enterprising,
he will commence the study of the law in his spare hours.
In a few years he is admitted to the civil service and
thereafter his progress through its many stages and
classes will be largely determined by his own energy
and talent, subject always to the play of chance that
controls the existence of vacancies. As a result of the
protection afforded by this system the young employee
entering the service of the Mixed Courts can look forward to a career of steady, if slow, advancement and to
an assured income with a modest pension on retirement.

The system has had good results. It has furnished in-
centive to ambition and reward to capability. It has induced young men to undergo the long and laborious
training necessary to the more responsible posts in the
service. It has brought to these higher posts a body of
men who, it is safe to assert, can be matched in capacity,
training, and general competence with any body of judicial employees in the world. But it must be added that
it is seriously doubtful whether this high standard can
be maintained in the future, owing, among other things,
to the very low salaries at which new employees are
forced to begin their service.

The highest post to which an employee may aspire is
that of chief clerk of the Court of Appeals or chief inspector. The salary of these two positions, following the
accepted practice of the sliding scale, begins at $4,500
and rises in six years to $5,700. Next in order come the
chief clerks of the three District Courts with salaries

from $300 to $400 a month; following them we find a group of head clerks and deputy head clerks in the Court of Appeals, three of whom are assigned to the three chambers of the court. These responsible officials occupy desks on the extreme left of the bench, opposite the Procureur-General. They wear an official costume and announce the decisions of the courts at the opening of every sitting. But, as suggested, progress is slow. To have reached a salary of, say, $3,000, a competent employee, if he be fortunate, will serve perhaps some twenty years.[6]

The elaborate provisions for the infliction of disciplinary measures are characteristic of the attention, often wasteful in its expenditure of the time of higher officials, given to every detail affecting the "vested rights" of the great army of public officials in Egypt. Minor penalties, warnings, and fines up to half a pound may be inflicted by the President of each District Court or by its chief clerk. The heavier penalties, temporary suspension from office, the placing of the employee in a lower grade, and discharge from the service, are pronounced by a special Disciplinary Commission of the court to which the employee is attached, composed in the same manner as a judicial chamber. In the case of employees in the service of the District Courts appeal may be made to the Disciplinary Commission of the Court of Appeals either by the employee or by the Procureur-General. This commission in turn is composed in the same manner as a chamber of the court—three foreigners and two Egyptians. Its sessions are held in the regular court room, and are conducted with the same dignity as any judicial session. The hearing, however, is

6 See list of officials with their salaries in the extracts from the Budget, Appendix. It is to be remembered that the cost of living in Egypt today probably equals, if it does not exceed, that of any European country.

not open to the public. The employee is entitled to the free aid of counsel. The proceedings represent an almost excessively painstaking guarantee against abuse of office by a superior against his inferior.

The nationality of the personnel of the Mixed Courts is widely varied. There is no legal requirement, as in the case of the judges, of a fixed proportion between foreigners and Egyptians. The recruitment depends on the available material. The nationality of those who seek service in the Mixed Courts is naturally affected by changing economic and political conditions. In the early history of the courts the entire personnel with the exception of interpreters and certain officials delegated for special duty in the Mixed Courts by the native religious courts were Europeans. Little by little this situation has changed, and the European has been largely replaced by members of the Syrian and the other Levantine races, who are for the most part Egyptian subjects, and who have greater facility than the European in the use of the Arabic language. Today Egyptian "subjects" are in the majority in the personnel of the courts.

An interesting reflection of this change in the nationality of the personnel is seen in the efforts which have been made by its foreign members to secure for themselves the benefit of the Indemnity Law of 1923, covering the retirement of foreign officials and whose passage was one of the conditions exacted by Great Britain for the abolition of martial law. The principle of this law as it had been declared by the report of the Milner Mission, which visited Egypt in 1919–20, was a recognition of the right of the Egyptian Government to dismiss foreign officials as well as the reciprocal right of these officials to voluntarily retire, and to receive, on retirement, a special cash bonus, independent of and in addition to whatever pension they would have been entitled to under the general pension law in the case of their services being dispensed with by the Government. The right of voluntary retirement, with bonus, was based on the assumption of an essential alteration in the conditions of service. The bonus was defined in a schedule of cash indemnities, prepared by London actuaries and based on the various factors of age, years of service, salary, and date of compulsory retirement, but in no case to exceed L.E. 8,500 ($42,500). It was payable without discrimination of nationality to all of the several thousand foreign employees who should thus retire or be retired from the service.

This law was of general application but contained two or three exceptions, excluding from its operations certain institutions of an international or semi-international character. These institutions were the Commission of Public Debt, the Quarantine Board, the Municipality of Alexandria, and the Mixed Courts.

Basing their argument on the steady elimination of the foreign element in the personnel, which they represent as an essential change in conditions of service, and on an increased measure of governmental control as expressed in the supervision of the budget and in the administration of the general pension system of the state of which they are now the beneficiaries, the employees of the Mixed Courts, following the example of those of the Alexandria municipality (an amorphous body composed of foreigners and natives), have vigorously urged, but so far without success, and without the support of the Court of Appeals, a claim to be admitted to the privileges of the new act.

So far this review of the system of the Mixed Courts has been directed primarily to their purely judicial labors. As will be seen in the pages which follow, their work includes responsibilities of quite a different nature. Two of these will now be explained.

Under the French system, with its love of logical distinction, the functions of a judicial institution are divided into two categories. One is that of the normal judicial work—the deciding of contested cases (or *jurisdiction contentieuse*); the other comprises the non-judicial labors of the courts which are grouped under the title of jurisdictions of grace (*jurisdiction gracieuse*).

In the case of the Mixed Courts this second category comprises two highly important services, which under the Anglo-Saxon system have no relation to the judicial system.

The first of these is the institution of the Notary Public. At the time of the foundation of the Mixed Courts there were no notaries in Egypt. The office was necessary. It had to be created. There was no other body to whom its organization could so well be confided as the Mixed Courts themselves. This was accomplished by creating in each of the District Courts the office of Judicial Notary, filled by clerks who have reached a high rank in the classified civil service. This official is charged with the performance of many of those far from perfunctory responsibilities which in France are confided either to the private notary—in that country often an important and wealthy member of the community—or to the solicitor or *avoué*, a person who without being a member of the bar performs much of the work which elsewhere falls on the shoulders of the lawyer (in England upon the solicitor).[7]

As in France, the deeds or agreements which it is desired to execute before a notary are for the most part considered to have been prepared by the notary himself.

[7] See chap. x.

In form they record the declarations solemnly made by the parties in the presence of the notary, who signs the document and authenticates the signatures. This duty is, however, anything but formal. The notary, who is frequently a man of legal training and always an official of long experience, is expected to examine every document in order to assure himself that it is in conformity with the law and must exercise his discretion as to accepting or rejecting it. He must be quick to detect a usurious transaction or an agreement which conceals an enterprise contrary to public policy. Other documents, however, may require simply a notarial authentication as, for instance, corporation by-laws, proxies, powers of attorney, and documents for which it is desired to secure the peculiar authenticity and probative value embodied in the certifying of a date—the traditional *date certaine* of the French law.

The notary's office is a barometer of the country's prosperity. The volume of transactions requiring notarial acknowledgment is in proportion to the availability of funds for commercial and other speculative transactions. It is a busy and important office, as witness the eighty thousand notarial acknowledgments and certificates given during the year 1928–29.

The second category of the extrajudicial service is one of far larger extent and importance. It covers practically the entire system of the recording of deeds and mortgages in Egypt. The placing of this responsibility on the Mixed Courts was due to the lack of any adequate registration system for the protection of the interests of foreign landowners and the imperative need of establishing one. The Mixed Courts were thus compelled to open public land registries, which while technically concerned only with transactions involving foreign interests, and while not exclusive of such native agencies as were already in existence, soon came practically to monopolize the entire field. This predominance is sufficiently indicated by the fact that out of every thousand deeds offered for registry in Egypt, upward of 97 per cent are registered with the Mixed Courts, the small remainder being divided between the native and religious courts.

The vast importance of land transactions soon caused this particular activity of the Mixed Courts to assume large proportions and to make necessary the maintenance and close supervision of a large and well-trained staff. The attention of many able European jurists was directed to the evils of the existing Egyptian land *régime* and led to the establishment of close coöperation between the Mixed Courts and the Government in working out a plan of relief.

The problem presents very special difficulties. They involve racial, religious, political, linguistic, geographical, physical, and other factors of a unique and peculiarly baffling character, most of them of ancient origin. The whole subject is extremely technical and the struggle for reform has been carried on for many years. The ultimate object is the introduction of a system of registered title guaranteed by the state, in other words, the Torrens System, in its fullest and most modern development. The plan necessarily involves a change from the present Egyptian system of recording land under the names of the individual owners, to that of recording by property unit. In 1922 the patient efforts of years witnessed the first measure of practical fruition. A law passed in that year seeks to remove the first obstacles in the path of this reform. It aims at bringing all existing titles within reach of the law. Heretofore the principal difficulty has been the absence of any legal requirement that deeds be registered. The only inducement to registration has been a proviso that, unless registered, certain deeds and documents, enumerated altogether inadequately, should not be valid as against third parties. The mildness of this sanction combined with the high registration tax—originally 5 per cent—led to the unfortunate result that by far the greater number of private deeds were never registered, the purchasers preferring to trust to the good faith of their seller to protect them in the enjoyment of their rights.

The new law exacts registration as a condition for the effective transfer of property, not only as regards third parties but as between individuals themselves, and enumerates with careful detail the various forms of documents to which the requirement is to apply and the serious consequences of noncompliance.

The new plan also sought to remedy the utterly defective system of conveyancing which has prevailed throughout Egypt, most deeds being prepared either by the parties themselves or through the aid of some inexperienced "scribe." As a result, the description of property and the identification of the parties are often sadly inadequate, a defect which is much increased by the relative lack of Egyptian surnames. A remedy for this evil is sought in defining carefully the various requirements of deeds and providing for the preparation of printed forms.

To carry out the provisions of the law the Mixed Courts have established throughout the country some ten branch registry offices or *délégations*. The selection of competent officials for these posts and the supervision necessary to put the new system into operation have involved much labor, but the system is today running smoothly and showing excellent results. Modern methods are used, including the wide use of photography, the regulations providing for the making of photographic copies of the original deed in all cases except where three originals are presented for registry.

The new system, however, has had serious difficulties to overcome. For one thing the basic principle of the law declaring unregistered deeds invalid even as between the parties, runs counter to popular feeling. The principle that it is for the people themselves to make their own agreements in their own way is particularly deep-rooted in Egypt. Moreover the formalities are perplexing to a large portion of the uneducated class, while still others have a natural inclination to withhold registration in the unworthy desire of leaving a door open to back out of a bargain. Finally there is the ever present discouragement of the high rate of registry tax, fixed at $3\frac{1}{2}$ per cent, an obstacle that was temporarily overcome by the reduction of the fee to 2 per cent for a period sufficiently long to encourage the holders of unregistered deeds to present them for registration. The offer was liberally taken advantage of but the former rate is now in force. To it is due the handsome net revenue paid over annually by the Mixed Courts to the Egyptian Government.

The growth of the Mixed Courts has been in proportion to the expansion of the commercial life and prosperity of the country. The thirty-two judges have increased to seventy, but the increase in output of judicial work has far exceeded this proportion. Thus the Court of Appeals with its eleven members, sitting in a chamber of seven, handed down in its first year 187 decisions, in its second, 213, and in its fifth year, 405. It is well past its fiftieth birthday; the number of its judges has been increased to seventeen; it hands down today an average of 1,200 opinions yearly.

During the judicial year 1928–29 over 38,000 civil and commercial cases and some 13,000 criminal cases appeared on the dockets of the three District Courts. Of the 38,000 civil and commercial cases, upward of 22,000 were definitely disposed of during the year by the filing of written opinions. Of the remainder nearly 8,000 were struck from the rolls or merged into other litigation. To this record must be added the important labors of the Referee and Bankruptcy Judges and the Courts for Judicial Sales and for the Distribution of Proceeds represented, in the first case, by over 3,000 opinions, in the second by the winding up of some 400 bankruptcies, and in the third by over 1,000 opinions touching judicial sales and in the fourth by some 650 opinions filed. Adding to these the 11,294 cases of police offenses and the 577 cases of misdemeanors disposed of during the year in the District Courts and the 1,161 cases disposed of during the year by the Court of Appeals, the total of judicial output of the Mixed Courts for the year reaches approximately 40,000 written decisions. To complete the picture mention must also be made of the various notarial and recording functions exercised by the officials of the courts, which included the recording or registration of some 134,000 deeds, some 14,450 mortgages, the authentication by notaries of some 38,700 legal documents, and 14,200 notarial deeds, and 36,200 certificates of titles, and, finally, the humbler labors of the bailiffs who during the year served over 270,000 writs.

CHAPTER XV

THE BAR AND LEGAL EDUCATION

THE formation of a bar presented a very practical
problem to the founders of the Mixed Courts.
High standards of legal education were reflected
in the personnel of the new magistracy from Europe;
but it was not possible to import lawyers to plead before
them nor to leave suitors lawyerless. The litigation
transferred to the Mixed Courts from the Consular
Courts and the old commercial courts had been largely
in the hands of simple agents or *mandataires* who often
were without legal education. These gentlemen formed
a large proportion of those who sought admission to the
bar of the Mixed Courts. It was decided that they should
be admitted to plead in the District Courts and that the
requirement of a legal education should be limited to
practice before the Court of Appeals. Ten years later
these "agents" were restricted to appearing before the
Summary Courts, and with the steady improvement of
legal education they were in time eliminated altogether.

At the outset the only requirement for admission to
the bar was the possession of a legal diploma. This
sufficed to admit the possessor, if his character and his
record were considered satisfactory, to practice before
the Court of Appeals. It was not until 1887 that it was
found possible to introduce the French system of office
apprenticeship or the *stage* as it is known. When first
introduced the apprenticeship was fixed at the excessively long period of five years, at the end of which the
law apprentice or *stagiaire* was permitted to plead before the District Courts, and, three years later, before

the Court of Appeals. This requirement went considerably beyond the practice in European countries and five years later it was reduced to three years, an additional *stage* of two years being required for admission to the Court of Appeals. Such is the rule today. To be registered as *stagiaire,* the candidate is required to present the diploma of a recognized law school, whether it be in Egypt or abroad, supplemented by a certificate attesting the regularity of his attendance, to assure that his diploma is not an empty form. In addition there is required a certificate of good character. The law office which he is about to enter also adds its certificate, and if the candidate is over twenty-one he is required to state the various occupations in which he has been engaged since his majority.

During the period of his apprenticeship the law student is required to continue without interruption in the service of the office he has entered. He is thus prevented from having his own office, the purpose, of course, being that he shall profit by the experience of his elder brethren. He is also required, throughout the same period, to attend two-thirds of the yearly sessions in the Court of Appeals or in one of the District Courts, remaining in attendance for at least an hour and a half. During this apprenticeship, if he is twenty-one years of age, he is permitted to plead before the District Courts when accompanied by one of his older associates, but is not permitted to file briefs except when countersigned by a member of the bar. Ordinarily he is not paid.

During the past three years there has been an encouraging renewal of interest by the bar in the case of the *stagiaires,* marked by the organization both in Alexandria and in Cairo of a series of moot courts and addresses by well-known jurists. These have proved highly successful and have helped to confirm the value of the *stage* as an element of first importance in legal education in Egypt.

Admission to the bar is in the hands of a Commission of five, composed of the President and an associate justice of the Court of Appeals, of the *bâtonnier* and an associate member of the bar, and of the Procureur-General. From the decisions of this Commission there exists a right of appeal, which in practice is scarcely ever invoked, to the Court of Appeals.

To appreciate the large rôle played by the bar in the formation of this Commission, one must recall the traditions of the French bar, on which the Egyptian system is founded. Generally speaking, at the beginning of the last century admission to the French bar was controlled as effectively by the bar itself as was admission to any well-organized club. The bar was a sovereign "Order." The decisions of its members as to who was to be added to their list was final. This point of view while contested by some of the French Courts, was formally admitted, in 1810, by a decree of the Government which expressly authorized the bar to refuse the admission of candidates. As late as 1850 the highest court in France declared that such a decision was not subject to appeal. This was the application of the ancient maxim, *"L'ordre est maître de son tableau."* Under the second empire, however, and well before the inauguration of the Mixed Courts, a change set in, and in 1864 we find the French Court of Cassation establishing the right of appeal from decisions of the bar.[1]

At the end of the *stage* comes the much-dreaded final

[1] The principle thus established has since been steadily maintained in France and in the formation of the Mixed Courts bar there were obviously very special reasons for maintaining judicial control. The system gives general satisfaction although from time to time the bar has asked that it be given "full mastery over its roll."

examinations before the Commission. These are in two parts. A written examination, conducted in the assembly room of the Court of Appeals and occupying three days, includes problems of procedure, the drafting of legal documents, and a "consultation" on an imaginary legal problem. The object of this examination being essentially practical, candidates are permitted to consult the codes and the digests, and the problems are prepared with this in view. Candidates who pass this examination are admitted to the oral examinations which are held with fitting dignity in one of the court rooms, the examiners in their judicial costumes or professional robes occupying seats upon the bench, and the candidates, also wearing their robes, occupying in turn a seat in the center of the semicircle in front of the bench. Each examiner in turn covers by his questions the subjects allotted to him and credits are noted by all the examiners present for the compilation of averages. If this examination is successfully passed the candidates in due course are admitted to practice before the District Courts. Two years later, upon application to the commission, they are admitted to the bar of the Court of Appeals, if their conduct during the intervening years has been free from criticism.

Foreign lawyers who have been members of the bar of their own countries for a period of five years (which may include the period of an apprenticeship) are admitted without further examination to the bar of the Mixed Courts. Visiting lawyers who are not members of the Egyptian bar are also allowed to appear before the courts in special cases. At one time a distinction was sought to be made between the solicitors and barristers of the English system, but these two categories are now assimilated. The minimum age for admission to the bar of the District Courts is twenty-one and to the bar of the Court of Appeals, twenty-six. By a recent decision the limit of twenty has been fixed for admission to the *stage*. At the present time the bar numbers some 800 members. Of these 545 have been admitted to practice at the bar of the Court of Appeals; 277 of these reside at Cairo, 209 at Alexandria, 39 at Mansourah, and 10 at Port Said. Seventy-nine lawyers have been admitted to practice only before the District Courts, while the law apprentices number 194. This number has long exceeded the needs of the community, and many of them are altogether nonactive.[2]

The nationality of the members of the bar is widely diversified. Approximately half the bar are Egyptian subjects, but of these only a small proportion are of the Egyptian race. The majority is composed of Syrians and Jews whose families often have been long resident in Egypt. The following table, presented by the Judicial Adviser in his Report for 1916, represents approximately the situation today, with the exception that the proportion of Egyptian members is steadily increasing.

	Lawyers	Law Apprentices	Total
Egyptian or Ottoman	191	160	351
Greek	111	30	141
Italian	75	20	95
French	62	8	70
British	24	5	29
Other Nationalities	43	16	59
Total	506	239	745

Women are not excluded, the first woman *stagiaire* having been enrolled in 1906. At the present time there is one woman admitted to practice before the Court of

[2] "I am not unaware that a very similar, and even more acute problem exists as regards the Mixed Bar, the members of which have recently increased out of all proportion to the work available." Report of Judicial Adviser (1916). This remark is equally true today.

Appeals, one before the District Courts alone, and four *stagiaires*.

Following the French system the bar of the Mixed Courts is closely organized. The "Order of the Bar," to which all lawyers must belong, carries with it much of the traditional spirit of a guild or closed corporation.[3] It occupies a more active place in the life of the lawyer and of the profession than is the case of the organized bars in America or England. In its sense of pride and self-respect, in its feeling of responsibility for the conduct of its members, in its vigilant defense of its own prerogatives it is a strong influence for good in the judicial system of the Mixed Courts.

As indicated the president of the bar bears the French title of *Bâtonnier* and occupies a position of influence and honor. The original rules of court made no reference to this office and employed phrases, drawn from the Italian and Austrian systems, unfamiliar to the dominating French element in the growing profession; but it was not long before French influence asserted itself in the creation of this office, as in all other branches of the judicial organization.

The bar of the Mixed Courts occupies handsome quarters in the several courthouses, where it maintains permanent secretariats and well-kept libraries. The vitality of the bar is also expressed in its substantial revenues and current assets of some ten to fifteen thousand pounds. Its revenues are derived from admission fees and annual dues, these latter fixed from time to time by the Bar Council. At present they are three

---

[3] The closeness of spirit is reflected in a phrase frequently recalled of an elder President of the Bar (A. Manusardi): "I have always striven to keep you united. United we are a power, disunited we are helpless. Let us stand firm together. This is the last will and testament of your Bâtonnier who now bids you farewell." Farewell address of Bâtonnier Manusardi, December 3, 1885.

pounds for lawyers admitted to practice before the
Court of Appeals, two pounds for those practicing only
before the District Courts, and one pound for the
stagiaire. The last, however, pays also forty pounds on
becoming enrolled. Under the new pension fund system
the *stagiaire* pays eight pounds into the fund on being
admitted to the bar and twelve pounds on passing from
the bar of the District Court to that of the Court of Appeals, the total fees paid in the course of his legal progress being thus $230 apart from such annual dues as he
may have happened to pay.

The "Order of the Bar" takes an active interest in
all that touches the profession or its members, or the
broader interests of the Mixed Courts. Its spirit of
fraternity is illustrated by the practice of devoting some
five hundred pounds annually to the lending of a "helping hand," frequently in the form of "loans of honor,"
without interest, to its less fortunate and needy brethren, of whom the number is unhappily very considerable.

This spirit has more recently expressed itself in the
creation by the bar of a mutual benefit fund, designed
along lines which have already been successfully followed out in various continental countries—notably
France, Belgium, and Greece.[4] The fund draws its capital from several sources in addition to the payments to
which reference has just been made: voluntary subscriptions (some of which have been in handsome figures);
a contribution of $25,000 from the treasury of the bar
itself (comprising thus nearly half of the existing capital of the bar); special gifts and legacies; current annual
economies in the bar budget. As a prospective source
of income there is in view a small special tax on all
litigation pleaded in the courts, if and when the same
should be authorized by the Government. Such a tax was

[4] Plan of bar approved by the Court of Appeals, May 22, 1928.

authorized by law in France in 1921 and in Belgium in 1924. In Greece, under the law of 1926, its place is taken by stamp taxes on documents, and by other special impositions including a tax of five hundred drachmas on the marriage of a lawyer and one hundred drachmas on the birth of each child.[5]

As the system imposed a considerable added financial burden on the *stagiaire* who is already required to pay forty pounds on being enrolled, it was natural that it should have aroused some opposition; but neither the bar at large, nor the Court of Appeals, found the burden incommensurate with the benefits offered. It was perhaps also felt that the imposition of these new financial obligations might even have a salutary effect in discouraging the too rapid recruitment of the bar from certain less desirable elements of the law clerk class.

The usage to be made of the fund is left to the discretion of the Bar Council, which is authorized to make loans of honor or to pay annual pensions in deserving cases. To obtain a loan, however, the lawyer must have been at the bar for ten years and must never have been suspended. To secure the grant of a pension he must have practiced for fifteen years, be fifty years of age, and must not have been suspended for over two years. Loans may not exceed fifty pounds. They are repayable "without interest" if the borrower finds his way back to "happier fortunes," as the phrase goes. Similar loans and pensions may be made to the widows and children of deceased lawyers.

Among other activities of the bar are also the enterprises calculated to advance the interests of the pro-

5 See for French law the standard works on the bar of Appleton, paragraph 89; and of Payen, paragraph 29, etc. Law of December 31, 1921; Decree of Paris Bar, June 13, 1922, the fund being opened January 1, 1923. See also Belgian Royal Decree, March 30, 1927; Moniteur Belge, April 2, 1927. See also Greek Law of May 5 (old style), 1926.

fession as, for instance, the publication of the *Golden Book,* on the occasion of the fiftieth anniversary.[6]

The discipline of the bar is a subject which has received close attention. Generally speaking, supervision of the conduct of the members of the bar is a responsibility imposed both upon all the various courts and upon the Bar Council. This body is even authorized to inflict "warnings" on its members. All further disciplinary measures, however, must be taken by the Court of Appeals.

True to its traditional attitude, the bar has long sought a larger measure of self-discipline. In 1921 a new set of by-laws for the bar was approved by the court, and still awaits governmental action. According to this proposal the infliction of disciplinary penalties is to be in the hands of a commission composed of three justices of the Court of Appeals and of two lawyers, with a right of appeal by the accused, or by the Procureur-General, to the Court of Appeals. "This," remarks a former *bâtonnier,* "will be a progress, while we await the day when the Order alone shall exercise disciplinary jurisdiction in all cases, subject to appeal to the highest Court.'"[7] Whether in final analysis the acceptance of any such broad pretensions would really be welcomed by the bar may well be doubted.

Disciplinary action before the court can be set in motion either by the Bar Council, by the District Courts, by the Procureur-General, or by any injured party. The case is presented to the General Assembly of the Court

[6] A tangible illustration of the attention which the bar pays to even small matters touching its organization, is seen in the annual publication of its bar lists. One of these is a substantial pamphlet, containing the names, addresses, and telephone numbers of all the members of the bar, with date of their admission or enrolment, arranged both alphabetically and according to seniority. Another presents a complete list of the bar in poster form, suitable for framing for display in the courts and law offices.

[7] *Livre d'Or,* p. 225.

of Appeals, and, unless summarily dismissed or disposed of by the infliction of a warning, is referred for investigation to one of the members of the court, who summons before him the lawyer and such witnesses as he may think necessary. The result of his inquiry is reported in person to the Assembly. This report usually consists of a written summary of the case, distributed before the meeting of the Assembly, supplemented by oral explanations to the Assembly. The accused lawyer is not present on this occasion. If the Assembly concludes that the case should be further proceeded with, it orders the case for final hearing, which takes place in secret session in the court room of the Court of Appeals before a bench of eight members. The accused is represented by counsel, and of course has the privilege of cross-examining the witnesses against him and of calling witnesses in his defense. While the system imposes a very considerable burden on the court, its salutary effect leaves little room for doubt.

An interesting expression of the French system is found in the adoption in its entirety in Egypt of the principle of the disqualification of lawyers from engaging in other pursuits, or, as they are known, *les incompatibilités.*

One of the most cherished traditions of the Latin bar is that which has ordained from time immemorial that the lawyer must renounce all gainful occupations and serve only his chosen profession. It is a principle finely expressed in the French maxim, *"La profession veut son homme tout entier,"* or as the old English maxim has it, "My lady common law must lie alone." He must be a lawyer and nothing but a lawyer. He must be free to dedicate his whole life to his profession. He must be in a position to approach every case confided to his charge and every question submitted to his counsel, free from control by outside interests. He must himself be completely disinterested. Such, broadly, were the motives that lay behind a tradition which became second nature to the bar itself, and which every French lawyer recognizes instinctively as at least the ideal of his professional life. It is thus significant that the declaration of incompatibility, as it appears in the rules of the Mixed Courts, and which follows substantially the rules which obtain in France today, is conceived in terms which are in themselves an appeal to tradition.

It shall be incompatible with the exercise of the profession of the law [reads the article] to accept any public salaried office other than that of Professor of Law or to engage in any occupation which might reflect on the dignity of the Order of the Bar.

What these occupations were, the rule makers found it unnecessary to specify. Tradition had long established them. The requirements of the dignity of the bar were sufficiently well understood for the general outlines and spirit of the prohibition not to be a subject of serious discussion regardless of any changes of detail which might be brought about in the course of time.

That the prohibition excludes engaging in all ordinary commercial occupations, is too clear to admit of question. It would also exclude the lawyer from becoming a wage earner, in the ordinary sense of the word, and in general every occupation calling for continued devotion of a lawyer's time and energy in a direction other than his profession. Not only would a wage earner be considered as lacking that independence of position which is essential to his professional status, but the position would be felt by everybody as one conflicting with the dignity of his profession. As to purely commercial occupations, moreover, not only would the lawyer be deprived of the opportunities to devote his full energies to his profession, but he would be necessarily exposing himself to pecuniary responsibilities in a manner which might readily lead him to the undesirable exchange of his rôle of lawyer for that of client. Nor even within his profession is his liberty unchecked. He may not become the salaried legal official of a corporation as, for instance, the salaried head of the legal department of a bank. To permit this would deny to him the field of free professional activity.

Economic and social changes have brought about interesting problems in the development and application of this general principle. One of the most interesting questions has been a long-standing conflict over the right of a lawyer to act as a director of a corporation. In 1865 the Paris bar pronounced squarely against this right and until recently a similar ruling prevailed in European bars dominated by the Latin system. Little by little, however, the increasing importance of corporate activity has forced a change in this point of view. This development made itself strongly felt in Egypt. In 1918 and again in 1923 the Mixed Courts bar adhered to the traditional doctrine; but in 1925 the Court of Appeals, after carefully reviewing the problem, pronounced itself in favor of the lawyer's right to act as a director, and thus placed itself in line with the later continental practice. The decision of the court, however, left it to the Bar Council to take action in special cases where the presence of a lawyer as director of a corporation was felt to constitute an abuse of the privilege.

About the same time a decision of the Court of Appeals settled another controversy over the right of lawyers to be engaged in journalistic enterprises. The decision was reached that the lawyer should not be permitted to engage in the business management of a paper or journal, whether as owner or otherwise, but that there was no objection to his becoming the owner of a newspaper if its business management was left in other hands, provided that if his journalistic activities were considered for any reason to involve an abuse of this privilege, the question might be brought before the council of the bar. This decision is substantially the same as the prevailing rule in the French bar. The business management is considered a commercial function objectionable for reasons already indicated. But these objections, however, do not apply to mere ownership or even to the editorship of the paper, provided it does not prevent a lawyer from giving proper attention to his profession.

The prohibition against engaging in other public employment is sufficiently clear not to give rise to any serious controversy. It is interesting to recall that at the beginning of the history of the court the legal agent of the Suez Canal, who was at the same time vice-consul of Denmark, sought in vain to be admitted to the bar. His duties were considered to be incompatible with the legal profession. A contrary decision would probably be rendered today in the case of an ordinary consular official drawing a salary from his government. Such, at least, was the opinion in France, in 1913, of the leader of the French bar, now a member of the French Academy, Henri Robert.

So far, Egypt has not had occasion to resort to the system of special exceptions, which in France has been frequently invoked to permit presidents of the republic and higher officials of the Government to continue in their profession.[8]

[8] Among others, such an exception was invoked in the case of President Millerand, who is numbered among the many distinguished members of the European bar who have pleaded at the bar of the Mixed Courts. A similar exception was made in the case of President Poincaré in 1920, at that time President of the Reparations Commission.

From what has been said it is clear that an incompatibility would exist between two professions, for instance, as between medicine and law; but it is interesting to note that in 1855 the French bar held that no such incompatibility existed, although accompanying its decision was the curious condition that no mention of his other profession was to be carried on the lawyer's visiting card. A contrary decision, more compatible with the spirit of the exception, was, however, recently reached in France. In 1918 a similar result was reached denying the right of ministers of religious professions to become members of the bar, but no such question has been presented in Egypt. The argument of separation of church and state was unsuccessfully urged. The French bar considered that the character of the bond of independence uniting the minister to his church was such as to create an insurmountable obstacle to his admission to the bar. Such an objection would not be considered valid in the case of those who had effectively retired from the exercise of their profession.

The problem of free legal aid has been solved in a manner that reflects credit on the bar, and closely reflects the best continental practice. Free legal aid is a tradition in Roman law. Writing in the fourth century the historian Lambridus relates that the Emperor Alexander Severus declared that it was the lawyer's duty to defend freely the penniless suitor. A compensation, however, was paid him out of the public treasury. The lawyers of the Middle Ages pleaded freely the causes of the poor "for the love of Our Lord," and when in 1278 the Order of St. Louis undertook to provide lawyers for the defense of the poor and the widows and orphans, it was merely giving expression to a custom already centuries old and one which has long been established in the continental legal system. In 1851 the whole subject was covered and the rights of the poor to legal aid considerably strengthened by a French law which is in force today. And in 1898, the French Workmen's Compensation Law having guaranteed to workmen the benefit of free legal aid, a by-law of the French bar effectively provided for carrying out this guarantee. So extensive indeed has been the application of the practice in France that in Paris alone free legal aid was accorded in a single year (1923–24) in ten thousand criminal cases and in seven thousand civil suits. In the organization of the Mixed Courts this important branch of professional activity was given deserved attention. In the earliest by-laws of the Mixed Courts it was declared that "Free legal assistance to the poor is the moral duty and the legal obligation of the Bar." Thanks to the good will of the bar, which has long enjoyed an envious reputation for generosity, and to a carefully devised plan of coöperation between the bench, the bar, and the Parquet, the obligation, thus declared, has been successfully met throughout the entire history of the Mixed Courts.

The system is a simple one. Attached to each of the three District Courts as well as to the Court of Appeals there is a Commission on Legal Aid, representing the three branches of the system, composed of a judge who acts as president, the *bâtonnier* or his representative, and a member of the Parquet. A place upon this commission is one of dignity and its labors are active and continuous throughout the judicial year. Each commission has a permanent office in the courthouse and is aided by an experienced secretary selected from the most responsible members of the clerical staff. This office is open to the public at all times to receive applications for legal aid. It knows no holidays. Applications are heard by the commission on fixed occasions and in case of favorable action the case is assigned to an attorney, assignments being distributed as far as possible throughout the membership of the bar, regard being had to the various circumstances which good judgment should naturally dictate in assuring the maximum of protection to the indigent client and a fair and practical distribution of burden among the lawyers.

Two conditions only are exacted of an applicant, poverty and the probability, not too strictly interpreted, of a favorable issue in his case. Poverty is not necessarily destitution. Proof of inability to support the costs of the proceedings is sufficient. In the case of foreigners it is a fixed rule that poverty must be established by the production of a consular certificate to that effect. In the case of Egyptian subjects the certificate is issued by the local authorities and is perhaps more readily obtained on that account. This circumstance doubtless helps to account for the fact that an overwhelming proportion of requests for aid comes from Egyptians.

The care with which the framers of the system sought to protect the rights of the needy suitor is evidenced by the existence of a right of appeal from the decision of a commission of one of the District Courts to the commission of the Court of Appeals on the question of the probability of a favorable outcome of the case. If the commission of the upper court reverses the decision below and grants relief it proceeds directly to the naming of the lawyer. In practice such reversals are not infrequent.

Naturally the great bulk of applications are made in the District Courts. An average of some thirty cases is taken up each month by the commission in the upper court, orders for free aid being entered in perhaps a quarter of this number.

The system above described applies only to civil and commercial cases. In criminal cases a still simpler method is pursued, counsel being assigned directly by the trial court on satisfactory evidence of the single condition of poverty.

The measure of relief which follows the favorable action by a commission is comprehensive and adequate. It not only includes the assignment of the case to an attorney whose conduct of it is subject to the supervision of the commission, but it exempts the suitor from all judicial and notarial fees and provides for the payment out of the treasury of the court of the cost of travel of court officials and witnesses, the payment of experts' fees and the cost of judicial advertising, and other incidental expenses. Charitable organizations are entitled to the privilege of free legal aid.

The question of legal fees has given rise to some interesting regulations. Here again the French tradition is guided by the hand of reform. It may be recalled that, consistent with the lofty Latin conception of the bar, the lawyer's fee was regarded as an honorarium—a spontaneous tribute of gratitude by client to counsel. As late as 1885 the *bâtonnier* of the Paris bar observed: "The lawyer does not discuss questions of money with his client. He exacts nothing, neither before nor after the pleading."[9] The obligation of the client properly to compensate his lawyer is thus of comparatively recent origin and has left its mark in the established tradition of the French bar—a tradition and not a legal prohibition—which forbids lawyers from suing for their fees. The founders of the Mixed Courts remedied this harsh situation by a comparatively simple device. There is an ironclad prohibition against contingent fees, in the sense of agreements to receive a share or percentage of the amount or thing recovered (*pacte de quota litis*).[10]

9 Cresson, quoted Payen, p. 382.
10 This is the general rule on the continent. See, for instance, France:

But lawyers are permitted to enter into agreements with their clients fixing in advance the amount of their fees and which may take into consideration, in a reasonable measure, the various contingencies of success or failure. In case of dispute the question is settled by the court. An excellent usage has established the practice of first submitting such questions to the Bar Council, whose decision is then submitted to the president of the chamber in which the case was tried, with the right of appeal to the chamber in banc.[11]

As might be expected in a country where the profession of the law occupies a position of such relatively large importance the problem of legal education has not been neglected.

There are two excellent law schools, the Native School or Royal Faculty of Law, and the French School, both at Cairo, and two large institutions at Alexandria, the French Lycée and the College of St. Mark, also offer law courses which should in time develop into completely organized law faculties.

The Native School occupies handsome quarters on the opposite side of the Nile from Cairo. It was founded in 1868 during the reign of the Khedive Ismail, and was incorporated into the present Egyptian University in 1926. At the present time there are about five hundred

"Such contingent agreements, which by some Court decisions indeed are prohibited in all kinds of transactions, are specially forbidden in the case of lawyers. They were forbidden under the Roman laws. They were forbidden in the Middle Ages. They are as severely forbidden today as ever" (*trans.*). Payen, p. 397. Compare also the Turkish law of 1924: "All agreements which contain a clause fixing legal fees on the basis of a percentage of the amount of the claim in suit as well as any agreements which imply an association (between lawyer and client) in the outcome of the litigation or the acquisition (by the lawyer) of a part or the whole of the amount sued for, are null and void." Act of April 3, 1924.

11 The activity of the bar in this field is indicated by the fact that in the report presented to the bar assembly for the year 1928–29 it was stated that 996 such requests had been passed on by the council during the year, an increase of more than 400 over the preceding year.

HUGH HOLMES
(GREAT BRITAIN)
PROCUREUR-GENERAL OF THE MIXED COURTS
1930

students in regular attendance, and a night school of some two hundred students. These figures have occasionally been considerably exceeded in times past as, for instance, in 1925 when there were over nine hundred students in regular attendance and an equal number in the night school.

Admission to the school requires an Egyptian baccalaureate degree, corresponding to the diploma of an American high school. There is also an additional requirement of one year's work at the Egyptian Faculty of Letters, the object being to give the students a fixed and uniform added preparation of general culture. The regular course of three years leads to the diploma or *licence en droit* which enables the holder to be registered as a law student. Attendance at lectures is obligatory. The teaching throughout the regular course of three years is in Arabic and given by Egyptian professors. There is, however, an elaborately organized series of supplementary courses attended by some fifty students leading to the doctorate. These are given by foreign professors, including four French professors, three Italian professors (two of whom teach in English and one in French), and two English professors, who give their courses in English. The school as a whole shows a strong French intellectual influence, although its administration is entirely in Egyptian hands. The French professors come from French faculties and are career men —*agrégés,* as they are known, being in fact lent by the French Government to the services of Egypt. The salaries, however, exceed those which they receive in France, for the most part running close to $6,000, the salaries of Egyptian professors being some $2,000 less, with the exception of the Egyptian president who receives a salary slightly in excess of that of the professors.

The system of instruction is essentially the lecture system, the *cours magistral* as it is known, a somewhat authoritative exposition of the principles of the law by professors in formal lectures, supplemented by informal conferences or quizzes. No trace of the American case system has made its way into Egyptian legal education. In Egypt as in France, teachers of French law— and they occupy a position of exceptional authority[12]— hold to the view that it is the teacher's duty to expound principles based, as all principles in the French law are based, upon the codes. It would be wholly incorrect, however, to assume that the study of cases forms no part in Egyptian legal education. The evolution of the written law as interpreted by the cases is constantly in the foreground and lecture notes of the professors are replete with the decisions of the courts of France and other continental countries. The cases are looked upon as an interpretation and not the source of the law.[13]

The Native School is the normal source of recruitment for the bar of the Native Courts as also for the higher walks of the governmental services. Graduates of the school are also permitted to present themselves for the Mixed Courts bar, but must be prepared to comply with the requirements of the *stage* and to pass an examination in the law of the Mixed Courts at the end of their three years' apprenticeship.

In the case of graduates of the French Law School desiring to join the native bar the situation is more difficult. They are required to pass an examination at the Native School roughly equivalent to the Egyptian baccalaureate, and are further required to have knowl-

[12] Generally speaking the salaries of French professors are well above those of judges, a professor of the first class in France receiving a salary equivalent to that of the president of the Court of Appeals. Their social position is also more highly esteemed.

[13] See chap. ix.

edge of Arabic and to pass an examination, both written and oral, on laws administered in the native courts.

The great majority of students in the Native School are Mohammedans, who do not speak with any fluency either French or English, which accounts for the fact that the greater number do not apply for admittance to the bar of the Mixed Courts.

The Egyptian Law School has passed through many stages. At the outset it reflected the French tradition in Egypt, being in turn under the direction of three French professors, and all the courses being given in French. Shortly before the War the tide turned in the direction of English and three English directors followed in turn, one of them being later a judge of the Mixed Courts, a second becoming Judicial Adviser to the Egyptian Government, and the third being Professor Walton, the distinguished Canadian jurist. Again the tide turned with the declaration of Egyptian independence, and while the system is French the school is now altogether Egyptian in its atmosphere.

The French School of Law founded in 1890 has an attendance of about three hundred. The school shows a large progressive elimination of students during its three-year term, the opening class of two hundred being frequently reduced to some fifty students who present themselves for final examination. Of these perhaps only thirty are successful. Out of this number a considerable portion find their way into government service or engage in other activities than the practice of the law.

The relation of the school to the French Government is interesting. The school is conducted under the form of an association, whose managers are its director and professors. The administration of the school belongs to the association. The school is not the property of the French Government nor under government direction. However, the French Government names the professors, and the teaching staff is thus directly responsible to the Minister of Foreign Affairs who, should occasion present, would exercise disciplinary control. Thus a teacher endeavoring to instruct contrary to the government curriculum would be disciplined from Paris and not from Egypt.

The baccalaureate is given, moreover, each year by the French Government, who sends each year a commission, generally of two members, to conduct the examinations, to which are added other examiners chosen on the spot. In this sense the school forms an integral part of the French educational system. Law professors receive a fixed salary of fifty thousand francs ($2,000), together with a proportion of the tuition fees, distributed according to seniority, and free lodging at the school or an equivalent allowance. These two items suffice to perhaps double the salary. The places are highly prized, and there is no little competition for vacancies. The teaching staff includes six principal professorships and one Egyptian Sheikh of the University of El Azhar, who gives an optional course in Mohammedan Law in the third year.[14]

As in the case of the Native School, candidates for admission are required to present the French baccalaureate diploma given by the French Government. Several French schools in Egypt, as well as other foreign schools, provide courses which prepare students to present themselves at the examinations for the French baccalaureate. In the absence of such a diploma students are allowed to pass an "examination of equivalents"

[14] The present dean and virtual founder of the school, Pelissié dé Rausas, is an outstanding figure in the legal life of Egypt and one of the principal authorities on the capitulatory system. His personality and abilities have been largely responsible for giving to the school the very high standing which it enjoys.

given by the French Minister in Egypt or by his representative.

The larger proportion of the students of the French School are Levantines of Egyptian nationality but not of Egyptian race. Perhaps some 30 per cent are Mohammedans, with about an equal percentage of Greeks, Italians, and other foreign subjects. The school year is six months, running from the middle of November to the middle of June, lectures being given six days in the week, two hours a day, for the first two years, with an additional hour during three days in the week, in the last year. The courses, as laid down by the French Government, follow the same lines as those given by the French professors in the Native School. Most of the students are engaged in some outside occupation, so that the institution, which holds all its sessions after five o'clock, is practically a night school. Attendance is not in fact obligatory.

CHAPTER XVI

THE MIXED COURTS AND OTHER
JUDICIAL INSTITUTIONS

AS Lord Cromer frequently observed, Egypt is and must remain a cosmopolitan country. This cosmopolitanism is specially marked in the field of law. In the place of a single unified judicial system nearly twoscore independent courts group themselves into four broad systems, and divide, and occasionally dispute, the jurisdiction of the land.

To appreciate properly the position of the Mixed Courts in this unique judicial hegemony it is necessary to glance briefly at these other systems and to indicate the principal points of contact between them all.

These remaining systems are the native Egyptian Courts, the Religious Courts of Personal Status (both Mohammedan and Christian) and the Consular Courts. To these might indeed be added, to increase the judicial census, a further category of administrative tribunals of widely diversified character but which, not being fully invested with the character of judicial institutions, need not divert our attention in this brief review.[1]

---

[1] Among these might be mentioned a special court, international in membership, instituted in 1895 for the trial (under certain conditions) of crimes and misdemeanors committed by Egyptians against officers of the British Army of Occupation or against members of the crews of British warships; a special court established in 1906 for the suppression of the slave trade, consisting of five judges of the native Court of Appeals of whom two must be Europeans; an important customs commission established in 1884 for the trial of breaches of custom regulations subject to appeal to the civil courts, Mixed or Native Courts, as the case may be; a court of four Egyptian officials for the trial of offenses against the law for the prevention of the locust plague; a commission of five members for the establishment of canal regulations; special commissions for the trial of

The place in the Egyptian world of the *Egyptian Native Courts* has been partly suggested in the preceding chapters. These are the national courts of the people and exercise civil and criminal jurisdiction in matters concerning Egyptian subjects alone, except in cases of domestic relations or personal status.

While the Mixed Courts were established prior to the British occupation of Egypt in 1882, and enjoy a treaty status under the protection of the Powers, the Native Courts were not instituted until 1883, their existence being due to a most laudable effort on the part of England to put an end to the abuses of the existing system of purely Mohammedan courts. The new Native Courts were modeled largely on the Mixed Courts themselves and comprise a complete and independent judicial system in no way organically related to the Mixed Courts, with whom their jurisdiction is mutually exclusive.

In their early stages the benches of the Native Courts were strengthened by a considerable number of foreign judges, for the most part Belgian and English.[2] Little by little, however, this foreign representation has been withdrawn and at the present time there remains in the institution but a single foreign judge, a Belgian, in the

offenses against the regulations for the guarding of the Nile and Canal banks in time of flood; a commission for the examination and placing under police supervision of notoriously dangerous persons; and finally certain special courts in the frontier desert districts and the more important oases (such as the famous town of Siwa) and the Sinai Peninsula.

[2] See Memorandum of Sir J. Scott, appended to *Annual Report of Lord Cromer* (1896), p. 27: ''Between twenty and thirty European judges arrived in the country, but it was not long before a new but serious difficulty was encountered—the difficulty of assimilating Europeans to the life, ways, and climate of the East. The new-comers were all chosen from Holland or Belgium, mostly from the latter country. In a very few years almost all of them had returned home. But the need of the European element was still felt so essential that a fresh contingent was introduced, this time only four in number, all of English nationality. They fortunately were acquainted with Arabic, and were young enough to accommodate themselves to the ways and conditions of an Eastern country. They all still remain.''

Court of Appeals at Cairo. The only other element of foreign influence is that which is represented by the presence in the Egyptian Ministry of Justice of the British Judicial Adviser.

Broadly speaking, the Native Courts comprise a comprehensive system of Summary, District, and Assize or Criminal Courts covering the entire territory of Egypt, and with Courts of Appeal sitting in Cairo and in Assiout, for the hearing of civil appeals from the central courts in matters involving over two hundred and fifty pounds. Their judicial personnel includes upward of 330 judges, some thirty of whom sit in the various chambers of the Courts of Appeal, each chamber being composed of three judges. A chamber of *cassation* of five members for criminal cases also sits in Cairo, exercising the traditional supreme appellate jurisdiction attributed to such courts in the Latin system, to review criminal cases on questions of law. A plan for the creation of an entirely separate Court of Cassation for both criminal and civil cases is now actively being advanced.

The complete separation of jurisdiction between the two systems thus far mentioned, added to the fact that the language of the Mixed Courts is French and that of the Native Courts Arabic, has resulted in practically no contact between them.[3] The Native Courts have their separate bar and their separate codes of law, and the two systems are completely independent of each other.

[3] The creation of the Native Courts, and the consequent establishment of a new and entirely independent system of justice in the country, is characterized as ''a backward step'' by Judge Herreros, in his introduction to an article on a ''High Court of Justice for Egypt'' (''Une Haute Cour de Justice en Egypte'') published in the *Livre d'Or*, privately republished in 1928. The author deplores the diplomatic opposition which prevented granting to the Mixed Courts jurisdiction over suits between natives, and thus removed one step farther the unification of justice in Egypt. What, however, would have been the course of development and transformations of the Mixed Courts if they had been called upon to handle the entire litigation between natives it is difficult to say.

The Egyptian Government has made a determined attempt to uphold the prestige of the Native Courts by maintaining the salary of its judges at a figure slightly above that of the native judges of the Mixed Courts, and by even giving, for the moment, to the highest magistrate of the Native Courts a salary which exceeds that paid to the European President of the Mixed Courts.[4] This tends to draw Egyptian judges from the Mixed Courts to the Native Courts, which is perhaps less detrimental than the increasingly common tendency of recruiting from both systems the higher officials of the Government in cabinet and other administrative posts. The record of almost every public man of affairs in Egypt includes a term of service in one or other of the two judicial systems.

In the Religious Courts is encountered that broad domain of jurisdiction over questions of personal status which has always played such a large rôle in the complicated legal machinery of the former Ottoman Empire. From the earliest days the impracticability of giving Mohammedan courts jurisdiction over legal problems essentially religious in their early conception, was recognized and acted upon. The distinction involved no idea of inferiority or humiliation, but was the inevitable result of the great diversity of social and religious organization existing throughout the country. Such questions had to be left to the only authorities capable of solving them. It has thus been primarily a question of

[4] The foreign justices of the native Courts of Appeal receive salaries ranging from L.E. 1,300 to L.E. 1,600, as compared with the salary scale of L.E. 1,200 to L.E. 1,600 in the case of Egyptian justices on the Court of Appeals of the Mixed Courts. The normal salary of the president of the native Court of Appeals at Cairo is L.E. 2,200 (by virtue of a special arrangement temporarily L.E. 2,300), that of the president of the Cairo Court of Appeals L.E. 1,900 (actually L.E. 2,200). The president of the Court of Appeals at Assiout receives L.E. 2,000, the vice-president L.E. 1,800.

religion and not of nationality, as evidenced by the fact that the principle applies equally to foreign and Egyptian subjects. These latter, if non-Mussulman, have the same right to resort to their own religious courts as has the native Mussulman himself. In the case of foreigners, logically perhaps, they, too, should be under the jurisdiction of their own religious courts in matters involving the "religious law." Theoretically it should make no difference whether an Orthodox Greek was an Egyptian or a Greek subject. Here, however, the broad capitulatory jurisdiction of the Consular Courts comes into play. To these courts is reserved full jurisdiction over foreigners except so far as that jurisdiction has been conceded to others. It has not been so conceded in matters of personal status, either to the Mixed Courts or to the religious courts. Consequently it is retained in consular hands, subject in each case to the right of each consulate to invite the coöperation of the religious tribunal of the particular religious denomination to which the foreign subject belongs. Thus it comes about that in matters, for instance, of marriage and divorce, a member of the Orthodox Greek church, if he happens to be an Egyptian subject, will find himself before the Greek patriarchate, whereas if he be of Greek nationality his case will go before his consul.

The principle thus outlined is embodied in a section of the Civil Code of the Mixed Courts, which declares that "questions relating to the legal status and capacity of persons, and to the law of marriage, to the rights of natural and testamentary succession and to guardianships," shall remain within the jurisdiction of the judge of the appropriate court of personal status (*juge du statut personnel*).[5] For example, in a suit on commercial

[5] Compare the enumeration given the unratified Treaty of Lausanne, between the United States and Turkey, of August 6, 1923, Article 8 of the

paper, a question of the legal majority or the mental capacity of one of the signers of a given instrument may be raised; or in a suit involving the distribution of an estate, involving mixed interests, a question may come up as to the rights of the heirs under some particular religious law. Such cases are covered by a proviso of the Civil Code to the effect that when such cases do arise, the court, if it recognizes the necessity of a decision upon such question before proceeding further, must suspend the trial of the substantial issues, and fix a time within which the party against whom the point has been raised, shall be bound to have the point heard and decided by the judge having jurisdiction over such questions.[6]

The Religious Courts administer the law *par excellence* of the Mussulman. This is, or at least is presumed to be, the law of the Koran, the supreme law of the Mohammedan, a law to be interpreted and administered only by the priest. The broad texts of this sacred book

matters reserved to the jurisdiction of American courts sitting outside of Turkey. "En matière de statut personnel et de droit de famille (y compris toutes questions concernant le mariage, les régimes matrimoniaux, le divorce, la séparation de corps, la dot, la paternité." The phrase "statut personnel" is commonly translated by the term "personal status" (see, for instance, Article 42, Treaty of Lausanne). Properly speaking the word "statut" refers to a law rather than a status. The "law of the personal status" is thus a more correct rendering, but the shorter term will be hereafter used in the text.

[6] To avoid the impression that the principle here given expression, of consulting the judgment of totally separate courts in all that relates to a large variety of legal questions of first importance, is wholly anomalous, it may be well to recall that even today this principle finds expression in the French Civil Code (Article 3), providing that "laws relating to the status and capacity of persons apply to French people, even residing in a foreign country." As a leading commentary (Aubry-Rau) observes, "this proviso justifies the interpretation that foreigners in France, remain under the dominion of their national laws for all that concerns their civil status and legal capacity." While this practical application of the principle is only very relative it is none the less frequently invoked. See Sewell, *French Law Affecting British Subjects* (Stevens & Sons: London, 1897), pp. 119 *et seq.*

have been applied to the most detailed and intricate special situations of life throughout generations. In the Near East, however, as occasionally elsewhere, it has been the habit of the conqueror, in assimilating the laws and institutions of the conquered, to attribute their sources to his own religious texts. This has happened in Egypt as it has happened in Syria. The student of comparative jurisprudence will find many traces in the Mohammedan law of borrowings from other systems, notably from the Roman law, which in the early centuries of the Christian era was so largely spread over the territory which later became subject to Mohammedan rule.

Where the rigid system of koranic law has proved inadequate to meet the demands of a complex civilization, the problem has been met by two devices—one by transferring from the religious courts to civil courts various important fields of litigation, and the other by forcing a change in the substantive laws under the cover of the alteration of a law of *procedure,* any change in substance being contrary to the established teachings of koranic law, and beyond the powers of the lawmakers of the country.[7]

  [7] A good illustration occurs in the case of litigation arising over wakfs or religious trusts. Under Mussulman law proof is primarily oral. It soon became obvious, however, that to allow the establishment of a system of land trusts to be at the mercy of such an uncertain method of proof of title would be little short of judicial anarchy. But law of proof could not be modified by statute. The difficulty had to be cured by the device of inserting in an act regulating procedure before the Religious Courts a proviso which effectually excluded actions based on wakfs whose existence was not established by documentary evidence, and which had not been executed before a notary. The act also affected proof of wills and some other dispositions of property. It is interesting to recall further that at the time of the inauguration of the Mixed Courts the Egyptian Government, pursuant to a contemporary undertaking to publish a native code of domestic relations, did in fact ''publish'' such a code, the private labor of a well-known Mohammedan jurist, but the code was never formally promulgated. While accepted as authority in the Mixed Courts, and published in

A no less difficult problem in relation to the Religious Courts has been the recruitment of the judges. Originally the courts were composed solely of the Egyptian *ulema* or priests learned in koranic law. Their benches were closed to all Egyptians who did not hold the diploma of the great Egyptian University of El Azhar or some similar certificate. It is largely due to the efforts of Lord Cromer, aided by the late Egyptian leader, Zaghloul Pasha, while Minister of Education, that there was brought about the establishment of separate Mohammedan schools, *Ecoles de Cadi*, for the scientific training of the judges as well as for the training of teachers.[8]

The former of the two reforming processes to which reference has just been made, that of secularizing religious law, has recently been given a notable expression. In 1896 a special category of religious courts was created for the handling of the estates of minors, lunatics, absentees, and others incapable of managing their affairs. These Courts of Wards were known as the *Meglis El Hasby* and were really boards composed of government officials and leading members of the community. They corresponded somewhat to the French "family council" (*conseil de famille*) composed of relatives and presided over by a judge, except that they were composed of strangers and were presided over by an official. Their responsibilities were large and their

the same volume as the other codes, it enjoys no higher authority in the religious courts than any private treatise.

[8] This innovation was stoutly resisted by the university, which had theretofore enjoyed practically a monopoly of filling these important posts. The difficulty of maintaining progress in these matters is illustrated by the act of a recent ministry in again attaching the newly founded schools to the university. This action, however, was promptly disapproved by the first succeeding parliament, which recommended the detaching of this famous institution from its former direct royal control and placing it under the direction of the prime minister, subject to parliamentary supervision.

administration of estates gave rise to much abuse. The
result was an extensive reorganization of the system in
1925, and the adoption of two highly important principles. In the first place, the jurisdiction of these bodies
was extended to all Egyptian subjects, Christian as well
as Mussulman. To this end the jurisdiction of the non-
Mohammedan religious courts was given a secular
basis by the introduction of the lay or professional
judge. It was provided that they should be composed of
three members—a judge of the Native Courts, who acts
as president, a Cadi or Mohammedan religious judge,
and a "notable" nominated by the Minister of the Interior. The secular character of their Court of Appeals
is even more strongly emphasized. It is composed of
three members of the native Court of Appeals, one member of the religious Appeal Court, and one high official
of the Government. The necessity for the application of
their own law, in cases involving non-Mohammedans, is
recognized by the proviso that in such cases the place of
the Mohammedan judge shall be taken by a member of
the religious faith of the person whose interests are involved. This reform is significant. It is a step toward
the eventual unification and secularization of family law
in Egypt. Another reform of much interest to the Moslem world was the promulgation in March, 1929, of a
new law on marriage and divorce which removed many
of the inequalities and abuses inherent in the preëxist-
ing system.[9]

There remain to be considered the *Religious Courts
of the Non-Moslem Egyptian Communities*—the most
complicated and multifarious system of courts in
Egypt. It includes a network of purely religious tribu-

9 Law No. 25, March 25, 1929. For text of this law see *Journal des
Tribunaux Mixtes*, No. 942, March 30, 1929; for Government's explanatory
note see same journal, No. 943, April 1, 1929.

nals, under the independent direction of as many different patriarchs or religious heads, who occupy positions of great authority in their several communities.[10] The jurisdiction of these courts covers all questions affecting personal status (marriage and divorce, etc.) except such as may have been transferred to the Court of Wards. Their jurisdiction is only obligatory in case all the parties are members of the same community.

At the head of these, numerically considered, stand the Orthodox Copts, a Christian sect of great antiquity, and one of the most solid and important elements in Egyptian life. The population of this community numbers perhaps three-quarters of a million as compared with the thirty thousand of their religious brethren who owe allegiance to the Catholic Church. The native Protestants number some forty thousand; Syrians of various beliefs probably well over twenty thousand, and the Jews, including the Rabbinites (who recognize the inspiration of the Talmud) and the Caraites (who deny this inspiration) some fifteen thousand. There are also approximately five thousand Orthodox Armenians, as well as considerable bodies of Greek, Armenian, Syrian, and Maronite Catholics.

After the severance of the political ties between Egypt and Turkey the continued existence of these various religious communities was open to some doubt, especially as to those which had theretofore received no formal recognition by the Egyptian Government in the shape of the official promulgation of their statute. This doubt, however, was put at rest by a law promulgated by

---

[10] These various religious bodies are as follows: Egyptian Moslems, Egyptian Orthodox Copts, Egyptian Catholic Copts, Egyptian Orthodox Greeks, Egyptian Catholic Greeks, Egyptian Maronites, Egyptian Orthodox Armenians, Egyptian Catholic Armenians, Egyptian Catholic Chaldeans, Egyptian Orthodox Syrians, Egyptian Catholic Syrians, Egyptian Sephardim Jews, Egyptian Caraite Jews, Egyptian Achkenazi Jews, and Egyptian Protestants.

the Government during the War (1915) prolonging, provisionally, the functioning of such jurisdictions in Egypt.[11]

The case of the Protestants is worthy of note. Most of the members of the "Native Protestant Community," (*Communauté des Protestants Indigènes*) as the body is officially known by the Egyptian Government, are members of the "United Presbyterian Church of Egypt," although, under the law, the "Community" also includes "all Christian churches not otherwise specially represented." Among these are a few other small sects known as the Church of God, the Holiness People, and one or two others. Many of the early members of the United Presbyterian Church belonged originally to the Coptic church. Ecclesiastically the organization is part of the United Presbyterian Church of America. There is a sharp distinction, however, between the religious order proper—which forms the Synod of the Nile, with five Presbyteries, and which comprises *all* members of the church in Egypt, and the "Community" which in the eyes of the Egyptian Government includes only Egyptian subjects and which comprises also the few additional sects, other than Presbyterians, just mentioned. The Council of the Egyptian Protestant "Community" stands before the Egyptian Government as the common governing body of the several sects mentioned, exercising judicial powers limited, of course, to Egyptian subjects in all questions of the personal status and enjoying other privileges of self-government and the management of its property in accordance with the

11 "Whereas changes which will be required in the judicial and other institutions of the country, in view of the existing régime, demand an extended study which must necessarily be retarded by the present state of war, It is Hereby Decreed, that until otherwise decided, . . . the special jurisdictions, heretofore recognized in Egypt, will continue to exercise all the privileges which they enjoyed at the moment of the termination of Turkish suzerainty." Proclamation, February 9, 1915.

terms of an elaborate governmental decree. Thus the
American or other *foreign* members of the "United
Presbyterian Church of Egypt" do not participate in
the elections held for the twelve members which represent the Community on its Council. The one remaining
seat in the Council is reserved to the members of the
small "Dutch Mission" at Calioub. The governing body
is thus composed almost entirely of one sect but questions affecting the other sects are determined according
to the religious laws and practices of such other body.
How far the purely ecclesiastical authorities of the
United Presbyterian Church in the United States, or
their representatives in Egypt, could exercise control
over the actions of the "Community,"—the "United
Presbyterian Church of Egypt,"—a body established
by decree of the Egyptian Government, is a question
which fortunately has never been raised. Obviously the
system presents some strange anomalies, but as frequently happens in Egypt, these are more evident in
theory than in practice. Moreover, as explained, some
reform has already been effected in transferring important powers to the recognized Egyptian Courts of
Meglis El Hasby, but a unification of jurisdiction along
purely judicial lines is needed and would probably be
welcomed by the members of the various sects involved.

The majority of these communities hold charters issued under Turkish law, although a few, such as the
Orthodox Copts, the Protestants, and the Armenian
Catholics, hold charters from the Egyptian Government. These provide, in general, for an administrative
organization based on a central council endowed with
judicial powers in all matters of personal status, and for
the appointment of a Wekil, or official trustee, for the
community's religious estates. The legal jurisdiction of
the communities is exercised independently of all su-

pervision by the Egyptian Government. They are subject only to the heads of their respective churches, and,
in this respect, their freedom from control is perhaps
even greater than in the case of the Consular Courts,
whose jurisdiction, while independent of the Egyptian
Government, is none the less subject to careful scrutiny
by their several home governments. Their sentences are
executed, where necessary, by the Egyptian Government, upon approval by the Minister of Justice.

Space forbids any closer examination of the functioning of these anomalous tribunals. The conclusion,
however, may be safely ventured that whatever the
capacity of many of the religious dignitaries by whom
these courts are conducted, they respond inadequately
to the standards of administration to be expected in a
modern civilized state. But the problem of their suppression is one of the greatest delicacy. The unification
of these various courts exercising jurisdiction over
Egyptian subjects, and the unification and secularization as far as reasonably possible of the law of domestic
relations (the secularization of marriage law has so far
never been seriously urged in Egypt)[12] has more than
once been advocated. But the difficulties in the way of
devising any plan that would not shock the religious
sensibilities of large and important elements in the
population have so far discouraged any effective attack
on the problem.

The system which remains for our brief examination
is that of the *Consular Courts,* which, in spite of the very
great retrenchment of their powers brought about by
the establishment of the Mixed Courts, exercise a wide
and important jurisdiction.

The jurisdiction of the Consular Courts covers

---

[12] See leading article in *Gazette des Tribunaux Mixtes*, August, 1928.
"A propos de l'unification des jurisdictions de statut personnel."

broadly: (1) All civil (including also, in the European sense, commercial) litigation between foreigners of the same nationality; (2) the prosecution of crimes and misdemeanors committed by foreign subjects other than the offenses confided to the Mixed Courts; (3) questions of personal status—e.g., divorce, domestic relations, wills, the administration of estates, etc.

As will be seen, the first, and to a large extent the last, of these categories is limited to matters which interest primarily a single foreign colony. They are, so to speak, family matters within a particular community and, as such, are not of special interest to the public authorities of the country. The existence of such jurisdiction is in sharp derogation of the general principle of territorial sovereignty, but the logical objection to its existence has not so far led to any active movement on the part of the Government for its suppression. It is only in the case of the criminal jurisdiction, elsewhere discussed,[13] that the Government has felt the need to move actively for its suppression.

As might be expected the Consular Courts represent a group hardly less varied in composition, procedure, and law than the Religious Courts to which we have just referred. Drawing the source of their power from without the country in which they sit, they administer justice in the name of a foreign government, and by the same token their organization depends solely and entirely on its will and direction. Each of the foreign capitulatory Powers, guided by the size and importance of its native colony in Egypt and by practical considerations of distance and expense, decides for itself just how highly organized and how efficiently manned its system of consular jurisdiction shall be and to what ex-

13 See chap. xii.

tent a final resort of appeal may be had to the courts of the fatherland.

The British Consular Courts, representing as they do the occupying power in Egypt, and administering justice to the politically, even though not numerically, predominant commercial colony, have always presented an example of efficient British justice. There are local and provincial courts and over them a Supreme Court—His Britannic Majesty's Supreme Court for Egypt, presided over by a trained jurist permanently assigned to this important post.[14]

The provincial courts are presided over by the several British consuls and have jurisdiction in matters not exceeding five hundred pounds. From their decisions appeals lie to the Supreme Court, whose judgments in turn may be appealed in certain cases to the Privy Council in London. This latter right of appeal, however, is closely limited and the prestige of the court is such that its decisions command the respect of the community and are not often attacked.

Under the British Orders in Council the law administered in the British Consular Courts is the English law, "in so far as circumstances admit." The courts, however, are required to enforce the customs existing in Egypt even though they conflict with the provisions of the Egyptian law, this being particularly the case where the religious law of the particular litigant, in a matter of personal status, differs from the law of England.

Owing to activity of the British commercial community and its extensive maritime interests, a considerable

---

[14] The present incumbent is His Hon. Sir Wasey Sterry, from 1917–26 legal secretary to the Sudan Government, and prior to that Chief Justice of the Sudan. One of his recent predecessors, Mr. R. P. B. Cator, who formerly held the post of judge of H.M. Supreme Courts for the Ottoman Dominions, which then included Egypt, was appointed to the bench of the Court of Appeals of the Mixed Courts in 1916.

number of cases of importance are presented each year to the British Supreme Court, although, numerically speaking, their importance is slight as compared with the many thousands of such cases presented at the bar of the Mixed Courts. Unlike any other courts which sit in Egypt, the British Supreme Court impanels a jury (of six) for the trial of civil cases.

The Consular Courts of the remaining capitulatory Powers are conducted for the most part on a somewhat more modest scale. Greece and Italy, however, whose colonies are numbered among the most important in the country, maintain in Egypt professional consular judges, from whose decisions appeals are taken directly to the home Courts of Appeal sitting respectively at Athens and at Rhodes. Certain cases, indeed, are removed immediately to the home courts. In the case of France the problem of securing a professional magistrate, in cases of importance, is usually met by enlisting the aid of one of the French professors of the Law School. Appeals from the French Consular Courts are carried to Aix. Those nations, however, whose local colonies are of minor importance must forego the luxury of a professional judge and be content with justice as it is administered, according to the best of his training, capacity, and common sense, by the consular officer of a particular district, sitting as consular judge.

In the case of the United States, consular jurisdiction is exercised in the first instance by the consul, with an appeal to the United States minister, whose decision is final. Whenever the consul is of the opinion that a case involves ''legal perplexities'' or when the damages exceed $500, he is required to summon not less than two or more than three associates to his assistance. These associates are required to note their opinion on the record, together with their reasons for dissent, if their views differ from that of the consul, "But the consul shall give judgment in the case." If his associates concur with him the judgment is final. If there is a difference of opinion the case may be appealed to the minister.

In the case of criminal trials before the consul the provisions for the convening of associates are slightly different. If the offense is punishable by a fine not exceeding $100 or by imprisonment not exceeding sixty days, the judgment of the consul, sitting alone, is final. If it may involve severer punishment, he is required to summon one or more assistants, not exceeding four, and in capital cases not less than four, taken from a list previously approved by the minister. If the consul and his assistants concur, the decision, except in capital cases, is final. Otherwise, as before, it is referred to the minister for final decision, subject always to the exercise of the pardoning power of the President which, in important cases, has come to take the place of a measure of appeal. The consul is furthermore permitted to invoke the aid of associates in any case in which he feels that it is desirable.

The law administered in the Consular Courts of the United States is unfortunately of a somewhat indefinite quantity. The statute provides that jurisdiction shall be exercised, in the first instance, in conformity with the laws of the United States. Where they are found not to be adapted to the case or to be otherwise deficient, resort is to be had to the "common law" and the "law of equity and admiralty," and finally, if neither of these sources furnishes appropriate enlightenment to the consul, then he is to decide in accordance with decrees and regulations promulgated by the ministers (if any there shall be, appropriate to the question) which are declared to have the force of law.

It goes without saying that the wealth of selection

thus presented to a consul called upon without previous legal training to assume judicial functions, is hardly likely to encourage the administration of justice upon scientific principles. The Statutes of the District of Columbia and of Alaska have done yeoman service, but their limitations are obvious, and the difficulties are even greater when the consul seeks to find in "the laws of the United States," the principles which shall guide him in difficult commercial litigations. And his perplexities are scarcely lightened by the knowledge that in 1860, the United States Congress declared by law that diplomatic and consular officers should be responsible to the United States "and to the laws thereof, not only as diplomatic and consular officers but as judicial officers, when they perform judicial duties, and shall be held liable for all negligences and misconduct as public officers."

Then, too, on the more personal "family" side, there are serious objections to the exercise of the consular jurisdiction. In a small community, litigation between two or more of its members is only too apt to involve delicate relationships, and to make its reactions felt throughout the entire national group. The consul is the natural friend and protector of the entire community; he is a sort of national *paterfamilias* to his local colony and is normally in close personal relations with many of its members. It is far from desirable that he should be forced to assume the position of judge in what may turn out to be bitter and protracted controversies. Nor does it help matters that he may feel called upon to associate with him on the consular bench some of the leading members of the community to share his responsibilities. The exercise of the judicial function is always a serious and delicate business. It should not be undertaken sporadically by a non-professional judge, however able and upright he may be. It is indeed a tribute to the good sense and efficiency of consular officers that such a patchwork judicial machinery has been able to meet the practical situations as they have arisen.[15] But as commercial interests grow more important the inadequacy of the system is steadily making itself more and more felt.

These observations prompt a suggestion in connection with the pending proposals to transfer part or all of the remaining consular criminal jurisdiction to the Mixed Courts. In case it should be impracticable to seize the present occasion to transfer to the Mixed Courts the civil jurisdiction of the Consular Courts, might it not be desirable to at least include some plan for permitting the transfer of special cases to the Mixed Courts, possibly upon a certificate from the diplomatic representative of the country involved. Such a plan might be of less interest to those Powers who are maintaining professional consular judges in Egypt, than to those whose consuls are from time to time suddenly called upon to exercise the judicial function. But to these latter it might well prove a source of great relief in the matter of specially complicated litigation, and if adopted might very naturally pave the way to the eventual abolition of extraterritorial jurisdiction in Egypt.

The presence of the diversified groups of jurisdictions which have just been reviewed has presented to generations of troubled law reformers in Egypt the problem of conflicts of jurisdictions. The situation is indeed prolific in possibility of conflicts. They have often occurred. Efforts have constantly been made to provide a sovereign remedy for the difficulty. Unfortunately the

15 The widely varied judicial labors of the late American consul at Alexandria (Mr. R. H. Geist) during the past six years form a noteworthy illustration of such efficiency.

common "Sovereign" has been lacking. But, on the other hand, the situation has been tempered by an admirable display of tolerance and common sense. A practical way has been found out of all difficulties. The danger always inherent has proved far less in reality than it appeared in theory. Vital interests have seldom suffered. The problem, however, is an interesting one and merits a brief mention.

The founders of the Mixed Courts, anticipating such conflicts, sought to devise, to a limited extent at least, a method for their solution. But the particular method provided has proved of no practical usefulness. It covers only the case of conflicts between the Mixed Courts and the Consular Courts over criminal cases, and was devised in contemplation of the unrealized project of conferring upon the Mixed Courts full criminal jurisdiction over foreigners. Occasion for its application has thus far never arisen. The same may be said of similar machinery for the solution of conflicts between the native Courts of Personal Status and the native Civil Courts, as also those between the Native Courts and the administrative authorities. Simple and more direct methods of resolving such conflicts have been found preferable.

The most frequent source of conflict lies in the application of the law of personal status, depending as it does on the peculiarly elusive quality of a litigant's membership in a religious body. Changes in membership are easily made and are not always dictated by religious connections, particularly when important questions of the distribution of family estates are at stake. Such conflicts are constantly arising between the several religious communities themselves. For instance, a man belonging to the Greek Catholic Church, who marries according to the rites of that church, may subsequently join the Orthodox Greek community in order to obtain a divorce, which would not be obtainable under the law of the former church, and this in defiance of the rule that patriarchs have only jurisdiction between persons professing the same religion. Or a Christian husband may become a Moslem and then seek to force his wife to accept the introduction of other wives into the home, with serious consequences in regard to the custody of children. Or, again, the conflict may arise between the native Religious Courts and the Native Tribunals over the administration of a religious trust (wakf), or in regard to a question of the payment of alimony where both courts have reasonably tenable claims to the exercise of jurisdiction. The instances cited do not necessarily involve the Mixed Courts, although they may do so as soon as a right, asserted under a judgment obtained in one of the other categories of jurisdiction, is sought to be asserted in the Mixed Courts, in an action where mixed interests have become involved. In such a case the Mixed Courts assume in effect the rôle of arbiter.

The widest ground for conflict exists in the case of contested nationality—all the more acute because of the absence, until recently, of any comprehensive law on the subject. These conflicts are particularly apt to arise where the nationality is based on a question of marriage as, for instance, in the case of a marriage between a foreign woman and an Egyptian, a situation that has given rise to some of the most hotly disputed problems of private international law that have come before the courts of Egypt.

The practical result, however, has been that in the case of a conflict arising between the Mixed Courts and the Native Courts, precedence is always conceded to the former, as a body whose jurisdiction is based on treaty,

a source of authority which, under native law, takes
precedence over the statute law.[16] The same may be said
as to conflicts between the Mixed Courts and the several
consulates. While these have at times assumed a lively
character, particularly in cases affecting British companies doing business in Egypt, a practical solution of
the problem has always been forthcoming.

Obviously it would be better were there a tribunal
of conflicts to which all such disputes might be referred,
but the wide diversity of political and spiritual allegiance enjoyed by these numerous independent systems
render the working out of any such device a problem
that has so far defied all efforts to accomplish it. Projects looking to this end were discussed at several meet-
ings of the international commissions held in Cairo, but
the difficulties have proved greater than the practical
evils sought to be cured, and as in many other walks of
life, time and the necessity for a common understanding
have brought about a solution the result of which might
have defied the regular machinery of justice.

Such then is the rough outline of the judicial map of
Egypt—four separate categories of jurisdiction and
some thirty systems of law. Such is the plan into which
fits, with singular nicety, the institution which is the
subject of this volume. Of the three remaining systems
one only, that of the Native Courts, responds to the normal western conception of judicial administration in a
modern state, a system of purely civil and criminal jus-

---

[16] This solution is thus frankly conceded by the most recent Egyptian
authority on the subject (1926): ''Thus, one must concede that in case
of a conflict between the law and decisions of the Mixed Courts and those
of the Native Tribunals, it is the former which must be given precedence.''
Farag, p. 252. ''The Mixed Courts have, indeed, developed from the class
of exceptional to that of general jurisdiction, and their claim to decide all
mixed cases has come to be recognized by the Native Courts, so that
conflicts between the two systems are rare.'' *Report of Judicial Adviser*
(1915), p. 26.

tice functioning as an integral part of the national governmental machine. One of the systems—the Consular Courts—lies wholly outside the governmental machine and represents a historic survival unjustifiable under any scientific conception of judicial administration and which awaits only the hand of the statesman-diplomat to bring about its disappearance without disturbance of the interests it was created to protect. The third system, the Religious Courts, presents hardly less of an anomaly in a modern state, and little by little its jurisdiction is being absorbed, as it should be, into that of the civil tribunals of the land.

CHAPTER XVII

LAWMAKING FOR FOREIGNERS AND THE LEGISLATIVE FUNCTIONS OF THE MIXED COURTS

THE founders of the Mixed Courts established, in the Mixed Codes, a *régime* of laws for foreigners, but unfortunately paid little attention to the question of their amending. The Charter of the courts, in which adequate provision should have been made, contains no reference to the subject. By Article 12 of the Civil Code, however, it was provided that additions and modifications to the codes might be decreed by the Government, upon the approval of the "judicial corps" (*le Corps de la magistrature*)—a somewhat ambiguous phrase, which was later taken by the Government to refer only to the Court of Appeals. This proviso would seem, on its face, to have opened the door to a simple system for keeping the law of the Mixed Courts up to date. But the event proved otherwise. The machinery thus set up was never put into motion. The reason is not altogether clear. It may have been partly due to a reluctance on the part of the Government to risk the opposition of the Powers to the utilization of a system of legislation that had not been discussed in the principal negotiations for the reform, and which had only been included, as it were incidentally, in a subsequently adopted Civil Code. Partly also it was probably owing to a tendency on the part of the newly appointed judges to discourage the use of this novel legislative procedure, for in 1877, when the Court of Appeals was asked to approve a new bankruptcy law, it replied by suggesting that the Government should, as a preliminary measure, seek the opinion of the various consuls. It further explained its position in language which strikes the keynote of its future attitude toward its judicial and legislative responsibilities:

> As to all that concerns its purely judicial mission, the Court, as it is both its right and duty to do, is determined to pronounce upon the extent of its own jurisdiction, without concerning itself with the views of other authorities; but in matters of legislation, while it conceives itself to enjoy a similar right, it considers that, in the interest of its own dignity and of that of the Egyptian Government, it is its duty to exercise the greatest reserve in order to avoid conflicts of power, which are always regrettable, and which, under existing circumstances, might have most unfortunate consequences (*trans.*).[1]

This situation of legislative impotency was obviously inadmissible. Efforts were early begun to remedy the situation. In 1880 the Egyptian Government prepared a plan for the consideration of the International Commission convened in that year, and which called for the appointment of a mixed commission, advisory to the Government in matters of legislation, and to include three judges. The suggestion was part of a much larger plan of judicial reorganization and fell with its abandonment. In 1884 the Government succeeded in securing the approval of the International Commission to a plan which would have permitted the promulgation of new legislation for the Mixed Courts on the approval of the "judicial corps," provided it did not conflict with what were defined as "essential principles." What these were is not altogether clear, but wherever they should become involved, the consent of the Powers was to be secured by direct negotiation. Like its predecessor the plan also

---

[1] Minutes of General Assembly held January 4, 1877. See Vercamer (Bibliography, *infra*), p. 97.

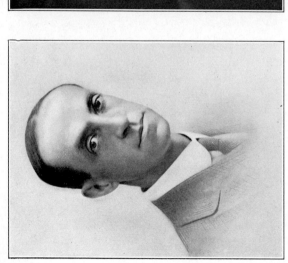

ROBERT L. HENRY

JUDGE OF THE DISTRICT COURT, ALEXANDRIA

PIERRE CRABITES

JUDGE OF THE DISTRICT COURT, CAIRO

JULIAN M. WRIGHT

JUDGE OF THE DISTRICT COURT, CAIRO

AMERICAN REPRESENTATIVES ON THE MIXED COURTS

(AS OF JANUARY 1, 1930)

failed, this time because of the refusal of the Powers to approve the suggestion of the commission.

Meanwhile the Government was constantly urged by the pressure of necessity. Reforms of great importance were needed. The only resort was a direct appeal to the Powers. Such an appeal was accordingly made, from time to time, through the medium of the international commissions to which reference has been made. In these commissions the several Powers were represented by their diplomatic representatives in Cairo, as ''First Delegates,'' and by their representatives on the Court of Appeals, or, failing a representative on the appellate court, by one of its judges from the lower courts, as second or technical delegate.[2]

The latter [writes Lord Cromer],[3] form a Sub-Commission. The Powers are under no obligation to accept the views expressed, either by the Sub-Commission or by the full Commission. Moreover, before legislation can be undertaken, unanimity among the Powers must be secured. Each exercises the right of *liberum veto*.

This cumbersome system bore its first fruits in 1886, with the promulgation of a series of new laws relating to mortgages, real estate execution, commercial pledge, and bills and notes, and which had been approved by the Commission of 1884. These were promulgated ''upon the agreement of our Government and the Powers which gave adherence to the Judicial Reform.'' A precedent for a system of legislation by diplomacy was thus established, which, despite its many and obvious shortcomings, still served to carry through a number of useful reforms in both law and procedure, of some of which mention has been made.

[2] In the case of Great Britain its legal interests were represented by the British Judicial Adviser.

[3] Cromer, *Annual Report* (1903), p. 45.

The inadequacy of such a legislative system was specially felt in the matter of police regulations. The jurisdiction of the Mixed Courts was limited to the offenses specified in the Penal Code. Certain provisions of the Civil and Penal Code encouraged the Egyptian Government to believe that it had powers to add to these offenses, but in 1887 this contention was denied by the Court of Appeals. To resort to an international commission each time a police regulation required amending or a new one was called for, was obviously impossible. Extended diplomatic negotiations ensued, and in 1889, to quote Lord Cromer, "after vast travail the diplomatic mountain did at last bring forth a small but not altogether ridiculous mouse." This "mouse" which later proved to be a creature of far more substantial proportions, took the form of a decree, promulgated by the Khedive with the approval of the Powers, and which in effect delegated to the General Assembly of the Court of Appeals, authority to approve "police regulations," touching, as the Government explained, those matters "which make up, so to speak, the daily life of the population."[4]

By the decree the scope of the approval to be given was carefully defined. In its examinations of new projects the assembly is directed to limit its examination to assuring itself that the measures proposed are applicable, without distinction, to all the inhabitants of Egypt; that they contain no provisions contrary to the Capitulations or existing treaties; and finally that they contain no penalty in excess of those applicable to police offenses.

At the outset the new system encountered serious ob-

[4] See for text Appendix F. As an additional and quite independent legislative function of this Assembly, should be mentioned the power conferred upon it by an article of the Commercial Code to approve all regulations adopted by public exchanges in Egypt.

stacles. France at once protested against the approval
of various regulations, among others those covering
compulsory vaccination, the registration of births and
deaths and the regulation of the practice of medicine,
on the ground that they embodied provisions which violated the Capitulations and that the approval of the
courts involving, as they did, a legislative and not a judicial function, was invalid as having exceeded the powers
conferred in such cases. A long controversy followed
and, as usual, was settled by a series of compromises
touching the individual measures. In the meantime the
usefulness of the reform increasingly asserted itself.
Many needed and effective police measures were approved and little by little opposition was withdrawn.
But, of course, the scope of the new legislative system
was very limited. It did not touch the broader questions
of legislation for foreigners. It was wasteful and cumbersome to the last degree. "Legislation by diplomacy
is probably the worst and most cumbersome form of
legislation in the world," observes Lord Cromer in
Modern Egypt, and elsewhere he thus summarizes some
of the difficulties:

It is natural enough that both in the Sub-Commission and in
the Plenary Commission some differences of opinion should
arise. Every one of these differences, even although they may
only refer to minute points of detail, has to be referred to the
fifteen Powers concerned. If some concession is made to satisfy one or more of the Powers it is by no means certain that
it will be accepted by others. Renewed reference to every capital in Europe then becomes necessary. Thus, the delays are interminable, so much so, that, as I have already said, a reform
which may be greatly in the interests of both the European and
indigenous population of Egypt, has to be abandoned not because it encounters any really strong opposition from any
quarter, but simply because no workable machinery exists

which will enable the matter to be decided. . . . The system is radically defective, and no amount of good-will on the part of those who have to take part in its workings can remedy its defects.[5]

The late Nubar Pasha once described in epigrammatic phrase the judicial institutions of Egypt before the establishment of the Mixed Tribunals. He said they constituted "a judicial Babel." It may be said, with equal truth, that "a legislative Babel" still exists.[6]

In point of fact, this system reduces Egypt to a state of legislative impotence. It is difficult to say whether the Europeans or the Egyptians are the greatest sufferers. Both suffer alike.[7]

It is not surprising that the evils of such a system should have early attracted Lord Cromer's reforming zeal. At first, however, he despaired of finding a solution to so complex a problem. In 1903 we find him concluding a review of the evils of the existing system with the discouraging observation that, "under the special circumstances of the situation, I do not think that, for the present and probably for some time to come, any better system could be devised."[8] But the problem continues to attract his interest and in the following year we find him observing that the question which "lies at the root of the whole matter" of capitulatory abuse in Egypt is the fact that the country "possesses no machinery for general legislation such as is possessed by the various states which in judicial and administrative matters it is taking as its model." He then adds a suggestion that the powers should transfer to Great Britain the legislative functions possessed by them collectively, and proposes as one of the necessary consequences of any such transfer, "the creation of some local machinery which would take a part in the enact-

5 *Annual Report* (1905), p. 2.   6 *Ibid.* (1904), pp. 7–8.
7 *Ibid.* (1906), p. 11.   8 *Ibid.* (1903), p. 46.

ment of laws applicable to Europeans.'"[9] The details of any such proposal, however, are left to future development. These he gives in the last two annual reports from his masterly hand, those of 1905 and 1906. His plan as finally developed,[10] proposed a legislative council of thirty-six members, including four Egyptian Government officials (the advisers in the Departments of Finance, Justice, Interior, and Public Works), an Egyptian judge from the native Court of Appeals, six judges of the Mixed Courts (either *ex-officio* members or nominated by the whole body of judges), five unofficial members nominated by the Egyptian Government, and twenty elected members. Tentatively, Lord Cromer suggested that for the election of these latter

"the same plan should be adopted as is now employed for nominating the assessors attached to the Mixed Courts,[11] that is to say, to call on the representatives of the various Powers to propose lists of Notables, or leading members of their respective communities," to serve as an amalgamated electoral body, each voter to have the right to vote for twenty members, no single nation, however, to be represented by more than four members, exclusive of the case of the four government advisers.

Lord Cromer's plan was bold in outline. It is difficult to say what would have been its fate had he remained in Egypt to give it the support of his enthusiasm and great personal influence. But with his retirement was lost all reasonable hope of the adoption of so ambitious a measure. Sir Eldon Gorst,[12] who succeeded, refers in his first annual report to Lord Cromer's observation that his "final opinion" must necessarily depend upon the reception accorded to his plan by the

[9] *Report* (1904), p. 8.
[10] *Ibid.* (1905), pp. 3 *et seq.; ibid.* (1906), p. 11 and pp. 20 *et seq.*
[11] See chap. viii.
[12] *Report* (1907), p. 2. See also observations of Sir Malcolm McIlwraith, *The Grotius Society*, III (1918), 87, quoted Beer, pp. 382–383.

leading Egyptian and European residents, and adds the significant remark, "So far, however, there has been no sign of unanimity on this subject on the part of local public opinion, either European or native." In Sir Eldon Gorst's report for 1908 the plan is not even discussed. It had disappeared from the realm of practical possibilities.[13]

The failure of Lord Cromer's reform did not, however, mean the continuance of the *régime* of "legislative impotence." Relief came, but from a direction little expected and, as often happens, as a result of negotiations involving quite other questions.

In 1903 an International Commission was convoked in Cairo to consider various proposed reforms in the law codes, but no proposal touching legislative reform was included in the program. However, agreement was reached to consider a proposal which had in view remedying the instability of the jurisprudence of the courts resulting from the possibility of conflicting decisions upon the same principle of law by different chambers of the Court of Appeals. The discussions thus aroused led to fruitful results in two directions. One was the adoption in 1906 of the procedure, elsewhere described,[14] for submitting conflicting opinions to the united bench of the entire Court of Appeals. The other, which required five years more of discussion for its realization, was the creation in 1911 in the Mixed Courts themselves, of a veritable Legislative Assembly, which

[13] However, it is interesting to record that in his article "The Capitulations in Egypt" published in the *Nineteenth Century* for July, 1913, Lord Cromer, then in retirement, again reverts to his proposals, and expresses the hope "that the question will now be taken up seriously." He discusses at some length the proposed international assembly, and, among other points, insists that, for the present, the proposed chamber should not be composed of both Europeans and Egyptians, but that there should be two separate chambers.

[14] See chap. viii.

has come to solve, in large measure, the very legislative problem which formed the object of Lord Cromer's campaign. As will be seen, while negotiations were begun during his period of service they were not concluded until several years after he had left, and it is not remarkable that the significance or possibilities of the new project should have escaped his attention. The new proposal took the form, in 1904, of a suggestion that in case of "silence or obscurity" in the codes, the Egyptian Government should be empowered to promulgate supplementary or interpretive laws on the approval of the Court of Appeals—a plan referred to by Lord Cromer as "a step in the right direction" but which could not furnish any solution of the main difficulties, seeing that all comprehensive measures of reform would still have to be submitted to the several Powers. In 1905 the project was temporarily withdrawn[15] and in his report for 1905 Lord Cromer adds the observation "Personally I may say that I never attached any great importance to it."[16] The project, however, belied his expectations. The subject was revived and in 1909 a plan, proposed by the sub-commission, was approved by the plenary commission and submitted to the Powers. In the course of the extensive diplomatic negotiations which followed, numerous modifications were added and the plan, as finally agreed upon, was promulgated, in the form of an amendment to the Civil Code in 1911.[17]

By the new system the Court of Appeals of the Mixed Courts, with certain additions to its membership, was constituted a Legislative Assembly with authority to approve, on behalf of the Powers, all modifications and additions to the "mixed law" (*législation mixte*), a phrase which while directed primarily to the Mixed

[15] See *Report of Judicial Adviser* (1905), p. 59.
[16] *Ibid.*, p. 76.   [17] See for text, Appendix G.

Codes themselves, is sufficiently broad to include all
general legislation intended to be applied to foreigners
except, so it has generally been assumed, measures involving the imposition of new taxation of a nature to
conflict with existing capitulatory privileges.[18] It is expressly stipulated, however, that the Assembly may not
approve any amendment to the charter. The fundamental structure of the courts thus still remains under
the direct protection of the Powers. By implication,
also, and in spite of the fact that the Assembly was itself established by an amendment to an article of the
Civil Code, rather than to the Charter, the Assembly
may not use the new power thus conferred to modify its
own powers. It cannot lift itself by its own boot
straps.[19] It may, however, submit new legislative proposals to the Government.

Having in mind the essentially diplomatic character
of this Assembly, its composition was designed to represent all the capitulatory Powers. It is thus a body distinct from the General Assembly of the Court of Appeals whose functions include the approval of police
laws. As some, at least, of the capitulatory Powers are
always unrepresented on the Court of Appeals, the new
plan provides that the Legislative Assembly shall be
composed of the Court of Appeals (including all its
Egyptian members) augmented by the senior District
Court judge from each country whose government had

[18] "A few years ago, the magistracy of the Mixed Courts was empowered, as a deliberative assembly, to adopt proposed changes in mixed
legislation, so as to make them binding upon foreigners; but their power
did not extend to the approval of any fresh taxation." *Report of British
Judicial Adviser* (1915), p. 23. See French reservation (letter, October 25,
1875) excluding jurisdiction of Mixed Courts as to approval of fiscal
measures, Borelli Bey, *op. cit.*, p. cxii.

[19] "It is, moreover, clear that the Assembly could not alter its own
organic constitution, though such constitution is contained in an article of
the Civil Code, and not in the Statute of Judicial Organization." *Report
of Judicial Adviser* (1911), p. 25, note.

joined the Reform of 1875 and which at the moment is not represented on the Court of Appeals. It results that the senior Russian District Judge is allowed to retain his seat on the Legislative Assembly, notwithstanding the suspension of Russian capitulatory rights in Egypt. The representative character of the Assembly and the principle of equality between the Powers are further illustrated by the fact that in the case of the three British justices, who at the moment occupy seats in the Court of Appeals, the senior member alone has heretofore sat in the Legislative Assembly. This exclusion of the two remaining British justices was made a condition of their nomination—a condition, however, which is not in accord with the text of the law creating the new Assembly. The latter observation applies also to the case of the present Swiss justice, who, so far, has not occupied a seat in the Legislative Assembly. But in this case it is to be recalled that Switzerland is not a capitulatory Power, and cannot, therefore, claim a right to be represented in the Mixed Courts. As the Procureur-General, or his representative, also sit in the Assembly, this makes a total membership of twenty.

Fifteen members are required to form a quorum and decisions are taken by two-thirds vote. Laws which have been approved by the Assembly may not be promulgated until three months after such approval. During this period any one of the foreign governments may ask for a reconsideration of a project. In such case the law may be readopted by a simple majority vote and may be immediately promulgated. This proviso which, with the exception of the suggestion or approval of candidates and the approval of organic changes in the judicial structure, is the only point at which the Powers come into official contact with the Mixed Courts system, was intended as a safeguard, but has come to constitute rather a clog in the legislative machine. It is a privilege which has never been invoked by any Power and the nature of the inquiry which precedes the action of the Assembly and the general unanimity with which its decisions are taken render it little likely that it could prove of any practical value. On the contrary the institution of a parliamentary *régime* in Egypt has served to render this requirement an obstacle to legislative efficiency inasmuch as every amendment made by Parliament or by the Legislative Assembly to any measure which has been passed by the other body must be submitted to it for approval. As this approval, in turn, might be coupled with some further modification again requiring the approval of the first assembly, and as the constitution provides that laws shall become effective thirty days after their promulgation, the possibility of complication and delays incident to the existence of the additional period of three months accorded to the Powers in which to ask for a reconsideration of the measure by the Legislative Assembly are self-evident. The Government accordingly included among the various projects of reform submitted to the powers in December, 1927, a proposal for the abolition of this proviso. For the same reason it also proposed to increase from three months to one year the period during which a law, after having received the final approval of the Legislative Assembly, must be promulgated by the Government under penalty of being considered to have been abandoned. These suggestions are still pending.

The new legislative system of 1911 did not supplant the old one of 1889. Both are in active operation today—although the line of separation between a "police measure," which is submitted to the General Assembly of the Court of Appeals, and a "law," which goes before the Legislative Assembly, is not defined with any precision.

As convening the Legislative Assembly always involves bringing to Alexandria several judges of the District Courts, representing the smaller Powers, and as sessions of the General Assembly are held for administrative purposes two or three times a month, the natural tendency has been to resolve a doubt in favor of resort to the simpler method. One of the characteristics of a police measure is always the inclusion of a police penalty. But this is not alone sufficient to characterize the measure as a police law. General laws which could not by any stretch of reasoning be qualified as a police measure, may have a police penalty included in their text. Generally speaking the test followed is whether or not the purposed act touches the liberty of commerce or the exercise of property rights. If so it must be submitted to the Legislative Assembly. The distinction can be well illustrated by reference to a series of measures touching the country's capital industry. A law aimed at preserving the purity of cotton seed and requiring cotton growers to secure the authority of government agents before preparing the grain, and containing elaborate provisions for confiscation of a portion of the grain and the closing of the offender's establishment, was considered to be a general law and not a police measure. So too was the law directed against the deterioration of cotton through the improper mixing of various grades. But on the other hand the law of 1927, continuing a restriction twice before imposed in 1920 and 1921 and limiting the acreage which landowners were to be permitted to plant in cotton for the years 1927, 1928, and 1929, was treated as a police measure, as falling within the general category of ordinances touching the "régime of lands, docks and canals," which is specifically included in the Decree of 1889. In the same way a law passed in 1912, imposing measures to prevent the spread of infectious diseases and providing for the necessary fumigation of houses, the isolation of invalids, etc., was treated as a police measure but an elaborate law passed in 1926 aimed at the suppression of malaria, principally through the destruction of mosquitoes, was considered, in view of the wide powers which it contained as to the filling of drains and the making of structural changes in cisterns and pools as well as to the construction of new systems of drainage, as intimately affecting the exercise of property rights and as therefore requiring the approval of the Legislative Assembly.

Comparing the two systems, it may be observed that in the General Assembly, consisting of eighteen members, the foreign element is represented by the eleven foreign justices, and the foreign Procureur-General, if, as is usually the case, he is present in person. In the Legislative Assembly foreign interests are represented by one member from each of the thirteen capitulatory Powers still represented in the courts. In each case the six Egyptian members of the Court of Appeals are members of the body. Foreign interests are thus represented in a slightly larger proportion in the Legislative Assembly, where, also, a two-thirds vote is required. Literally construed the scope of the action of the General Assembly is, as already noted, limited to an examination of the questions of uniformity of application, compliance with capitulatory and treaty rights, and restriction to police penalties, a limitation which suggests that the function of this assembly is rather more judicial than legislative. Practically, however, this limitation has so far not been of much importance. The Government has been glad to welcome the coöperation of the General Assembly in proposing amendments to police measures in matters both of substance and of form, and regardless of whether the suggestions strictly involved the points of inquiry referred to in the law of 1889. Moreover, in practice, the application of the tests prescribed is apt to involve a consideration of the substantial merits of any measure.

It may be of interest to examine a little more closely the nature of the tests which must be applied by these two assemblies to the laws which the Egyptian Government presents for their approval.

In the first place, as to police measures, these must be "common to all the inhabitants of the country without distinction." This direction gave rise to some discussion in connection with the approval of the Egyptian Antidrug Act of 1925, in which, in order to give criminal jurisdiction to the Mixed Courts, it was provided that "provisionally and until other dispositions are possible" the offenses in the case of foreigners should be considered as police offenses, and, as such, punishable in the Mixed Courts. As a result of this arrangement, as has been elsewhere pointed out, Egyptians are liable to receive far heavier punishments than can be inflicted upon a foreigner for violations of precisely the same law. The assembly, however, was of opinion that this feature of the law did not violate the spirit and purpose of the Decree of 1889, which essentially sought to prevent discriminations being made against foreigners, and this point of view, thus accepted in 1923, was again followed in approving in June, 1928, the more severe antidrug law which replaced the earlier law of 1925.

The question as to what "accessory" penalties may be properly included in a police measure has also given rise to some difficulty. In practice these accessory penalties put teeth into the law. As we have already observed the assembly has in turn approved measures which included the forfeiture of property used in viola-

314 THE MIXED COURTS OF EGYPT

tion of law, the closing of establishments where the law
has been violated, and even the suspension of licenses
to exercise a business or profession.[20]

The most delicate question, however, which presents
itself alike to both assemblies is that of the possible
violation of capitulatory privileges. In the case of police
measures, while the language of the Decree of 1889 only
requires that the laws shall not violate ''the text of
Treaties and Conventions,'' it is generally accepted that
this covers all capitulatory privileges, whether based
on a specific text or on usage. In the case of laws submitted for the approval of the Legislative Assembly,
the various capitulatory privileges must likewise be respected.

Principal among these privileges is that which relates
to the immunity of foreigners from taxation. In view of
the great practical importance of the subject, the situation merits some special notice.

In reviewing the origins of the Mixed Courts it has
been explained how the development of the doctrine
that foreigners could only be sued in their Consular
Courts, had led to the remarkable state of affairs that
foreigners were practically immune from the application of the laws of the land.

But even before the inauguration of the Mixed Courts
it had become evident that in at least one field of life exceptions must be made to this privilege. Foreigners
could not be permitted to withhold all contribution to
the Egyptian revenue. Such a privilege would be intolerable and in the end would necessarily react to the
disadvantage of those in whose behalf it might be
claimed. Obviously foreigners could not be accorded the

[20] The Medical Practices Act of October 27, 1928, authorizes the courts,
in the cases of convictions for the illegal practice of medicine, to order the
closing of the offender's office and the confiscation of his professional
equipment.

privilege of holding land without paying a land tax; nor could they expect to become importers without paying customs dues or to engage in manufacture or agriculture without submitting their products to the same dues as their Egyptian competitors. All these matters have been covered by treaty agreements and by usage. The net result is that there are, practically speaking, no taxes imposed in Egypt to which foreigners and Egyptians are not subject alike. Foreign consent has been secured to sufficient categories to, so far, meet national necessities. And the Egyptian Government has been naturally unwilling to impose further taxes on its own nationals which it cannot compel foreigners to pay.

Thus the obligation to pay a land tax was tacitly accepted by foreigners as an incident of the privilege to own land, a privilege that was freely granted the foreigner in Egypt long before it was formally conceded by law in Turkey in 1867. The question of customs duties was covered by an elaborate series of commercial treaties. These, however, cease to be effective in 1930, leaving Egypt free, so it has been commonly assumed, to put into effect her new protective tariff on February 17, 1930, subject to respect for capitulatory rights in matters of administration. A house tax was agreed at a convention held in London in 1885, at which time the so-called six great Powers took occasion formally to recognize "the equity of submitting their subjects in Egypt to the same taxes as natives."[21] Again,

[21] Noradounghian, IV, 354. See Bibliography. Also Milner, chap. iv. While the Egyptian Government insisted that approval of the house tax was requested as a matter of grace and not of obligation, the Court of Appeals has held that the act implied a surrender of any legal *right* to impose a tax on foreigners in such cases without the approval of their governments. It has also held that the general right to tax land includes the right to impose a tax on date palms. The Government has recently sought the approval of the Powers to a watchman or *ghaffir* tax payable jointly by landlord and tenant. This tax was enforced against foreigners

in 1890, an international agreement was reached covering the right of the city of Alexandria to impose municipal taxes.

Beyond these categories of taxation, however, the privileges of the Capitulations rise as a bar, but just exactly where the bar is placed is a question which hardly admits of a precise answer. The difficulty is that the capitulatory privilege in this matter has its basis in various disconnected clauses of early Turkish treaties, which have reference for the most part to situations different from those which exist today. They were aimed primarily at relieving the foreigner from certain vexatious exactions, described by name, and which it is difficult to apply to existing conditions. The difficulty is increased by the fact that there are few precedents, that is, cases where the right of taxation has been contested and a decision has been reached, either in the courts or through diplomatic channels. While it has been often broadly stated that taxes may not be imposed on foreigners in Egypt without the consent of their governments, there have not been wanting vigorous protests against any such claim as being utterly unwarranted either in the text of the Capitulations or in the usage which has developed from them.[22]

under the *régime* of martial law but its payment was subsequently generally refused, as being an unauthorized exaction. Cf. cases cited, Bestawros, *op. cit.*, I, 248.

[22] Thus in 1922 the Government's Legal Advisers (*Comité du Contentieux de l'Etat*) composed of five members, three of whom were English and two Italian, and all of them men of ability and standing, took occasion in a Memorandum presented to the Court of Appeals to record their protest against the current notion that the principle was general exemption. "This Committee has always held the opinion that the common belief that foreigners in capitulatory countries are in general exempt from all taxation (*charges fiscales*) is without foundation. No such general exemption is to be found in any capitulatory agreement, all such agreements being limited to exempting foreigners from the head tax imposed on those of its subjects who have been considered as *rayas* (foreigners) and from certain taxes either considered to be vexatious or con-

Generally speaking, the prohibition extends to all forms of direct taxes, except as specially authorized by the Powers, but does not apply to excises or taxes on the products of local industry.[23]

Examples of such latter forms of taxation are the imposition, in 1901, of a tax of 8 per cent (abolished in 1925) on cotton goods manufactured in Egypt; the imposition in 1920 of a tax on cotton ginned in the country now approximately $1.00 per hundred pounds; and taxes on petroleum products, alcohol and alcoholic liquors, and salt. Nor has it been considered that the Capitulations are opposed to the imposition of *bona fide* inspection fees. Such fees may be imposed either on the occasion of each inspection or as an annual license fee. But if they are taxes in disguise the question becomes more delicate as illustrated by a recent governmental project submitted for approval to the Mixed Courts but subsequently withdrawn, involving the imposition of a substantial tax on automobiles. The same principle applies to professional examination fees. The General Assembly has recently approved a ten-pound fee for the examination required as a condition of the right to practice medicine in Egypt. This decision marks an interesting development. In 1891 the French Government had invoked the text of the Capitulations[24] in opposition to a

trary to the freedom of commerce and industry.'' For Turkish Memoir addressed to the Powers, see Gelat, I, Part I, 497.

[23] Cf. Lord Cromer (*Report*, 1916, p. 13), ''No direct tax can be imposed upon Europeans without the consent of all the Powers.'' Lord Milner (chap. iv), ''. . . exemption from all direct taxes except the land tax.'' In 1879 the Court of Appeals observed (*R.O.*, IV, 341) that while the Government might not impose personal taxes (*impôts personnels*) on foreigners, without the consent of the Powers, it enjoyed the right, under existing commercial treaties, to impose on foreigners ''engaged in commerce or industry'' the payment of the same exactions (*droits*) as in the case of natives. Cf. decisions of same court in 1894 and 1902, *Bulletin*, VI, 272, and XIV, 146. Also cf. Borelli Bey, p. xii and du Rausas, II, 465.

[24] Article LXIII, French Capitulations of 1740. ''Les marchands français et autres défendants de la France pourront voyager avec les

professional tax (two pounds and a pound and a half
respectively) on physicians and pharmacists, and a li-
cense fee (five pounds) on the opening of a pharmacy.
The Egyptian Government while protesting that what
it described as *droits de chancellerie* were entirely outside the scope of the Capitulations, withdrew the objectionable taxes "out of deference to the wishes of the
Government of the Republic,"[25] a phrase which is indeed significant of the moving spirit in the development of capitulatory "usage" in Egypt. The varying
treatment accorded to the same subject in 1891 and 1928
is furthermore suggestive of the lack of all definitive-
ness in the fundamental rights on which the discussion
turns, as well as, perhaps, of an increasing liberalness
of viewpoint on the part of the Powers.

The capitulatory privilege of inviolability of domicile
presents the second of the two capitulatory problems
which currently claim the attention of the judicial
legislator in Egypt.

It has been frequently stated that this privilege prevents any search being made in the home of a foreigner
without the consent of his consul or his representative.[26]
Such a statement is inexact. What is required is merely

passeports qu'ils auront pris sur les attestations des ambassadeurs ou
des consuls de France; et pour leur sûreté et commodité, ils pourront
s'habiller suivant l'usage du pays, et faire leurs affaires dans mes Etats,
sans que ces sortes de voyageurs, se tenant dans les bornes de leur devoir
puissant être inquiétes pour le tribut nomme Kharatch, *ni pour aucun
autre impôt.*" Gelat, II, Pt. I, 691.

25 "Documents Diplomatiques," *Affaires d'Egypte, 1884–1893*, p. 431.

26 Thus Lord Cromer, in his *Report* for 1906 (p. 13), observes that no
such domiciliary visit "can take place in the house of a European without
the consent of his consular representative having been previously obtained." Again in *Modern Egypt*, he states that the Egyptian police "cannot enter the house of a European without such consular consent nor without the presence of a consular representative." To the same effect De
Rausas, I, 135. "If the consul refuses to accompany the officers or to
send his representative, the officers are powerless to enter the home of the
foreigner." Also Scott, p. 156: ". . . the Consul himself, or his dragomen, must be present during the entry."

notice to the consul, who is privileged to attend or to send a representative, usually a native consular messenger or *cawass*. If no representative of the consulate puts in his appearance the search proceeds as if he were present. His attendance is merely for the purpose of seeing that the rights of the foreigner are not abused and of taking note of the facts.[27]

The provisions of the Customs Regulations, as approved by the Powers, are a good example of the protection generally stipulated in the laws, and it is a not uncommon practice to find these provisions incorporated by reference in later laws. They provide that search either of a house or warehouse or other building shall be made only upon order of the local director of customs and in presence of an official of that service and a special representative of the Government. If the search is to be made in a home, a copy of the order must be sent to the consul interested, in order that he or his agent may be present. If, within four hours after service of this notice, the consulate has not been heard from, the search proceeds. If the search is to be made in a building altogether separate from residential quarters it is sufficient if the notice is given to the proprietor or his representative, although in their absence it may be served on the consulate. At one time it was generally assumed that in Egypt this privilege had been extended to cover places of business. Of late years, however, various acts have been approved by the assemblies of the Mixed Courts in

[27] Apart, furthermore, from the general capitulatory privilege as thus outlined, the Charter of the Mixed Courts contains a special proviso forbidding the entry of a home after nightfall without the presence of the consul (or his representative) or in the absence of his authorization, except in the case of *flagrant délit* or where there is a call from within for help. In 1926 an effort was made by the Egyptian Government to secure the consent of the Powers to the abolition of this restriction in the case of offenses against the anti-narcotic laws, but the effort has not yet been successful.

which visits and searches are permitted in business establishments without such notice. Among recent examples of such provisions, which are of interest also as illustrating the character of legislation which is constantly being submitted to the Mixed Courts for their approval, is an important law approved as a police measure by the General Assembly of the Court of Appeals in April, 1926, regulating the use of radio in Egypt and based on the London Radio Convention of 1912 and the Rules of the St. Petersburg Convention as revised in Paris in 1923. The act contains a far-reaching proviso for visit and search both on land and on shipboard.

Owing to the *régime* of martial law (November 2, 1914—July 5, 1923) which, for the time being, supplanted the normal legislative processes of the country,[28] sessions of the Legislative Assembly were at first infrequent. The earliest exercise of the new legislative function was in 1912, and involved an amendment to the Mortgage Law, increasing the security of the mortgagee for accrued interest. A second law, approved in the same year, permitted the inclusion of arbitration clauses in government contracts—a measure the wisdom of which has been put to considerable doubt since its adoption. A third change altered those provisions of the Civil Code, under which the right to carry irrigation water across neighboring lands was limited to the property immediately adjoining but did not extend to properties further removed. Another law revised the procedure in regard to the execution of judgments involving the sale of real estate, and a complementary measure took the form of the Five Feddan (Acre) Law based on similar legislation in other countries (including the homestead laws of the United States). It gave protec-

[28] See chap. iv.

tion to the small cultivator of under five acres against being dispossessed of his land, house, and farming utensils for debt, a protection rendered necessary by the action of an army of usurers, many of them foreigners, and which latter were able, under the cover of the protection granted by the Capitulations, to lend money successfully to the farmers at exorbitant rates, frequently running as high as 30 and 40 per cent.

In 1913 important changes were made in the codes of procedure looking to the expedition of litigation and the wiping out of various devices resorted to by debtors, to delay judgments. In 1916 a single law was approved by the Assembly, regulating the drying out of marshes and pools. In 1917, also, a single law was approved, modifying criminal procedure. In 1918 a law was approved exempting wages and pensions from seizure for debts due the state or government agencies. During the next three years the Legislative Assembly was not convoked, but in 1922 it approved a law which had previously been promulgated under authority of martial law, and which aimed at relieving the evil caused by the shortage of houses. The law limited the rental of unfurnished houses to an increase of 50 per cent over that paid in on August, 1914, and otherwise protected the tenant in his enjoyment of the property. In 1924 this restriction was allowed to lapse.

In 1923 the Assembly approved the extremely important measure, which its members had been largely instrumental in preparing, establishing a new system for recording deeds and mortgages.

Passing to more recent activities of the Assembly, we may note in addition to the examples mentioned earlier in this chapter, a law establishing governmental regulation of the trade in fertilizers with the object of preventing the farmer from being victimized by the sale of worthless substances; a law aimed at discouraging dilatory legal procedure by requiring the preliminary deposit of the amount of certain statutory penalties imposed by the code upon litigants who unsuccessfully invoked certain special proceedings authorized by law; a law opening to the Government the processes of administrative levy for the recovery of a special class of taxes where the obligation to pay the tax was the result of a voluntary acceptance by the taxpayers.

In the year 1928–29 the Legislative Assembly was not convened, but preliminary consideration was given to various important projects, notably a law aimed at the prevention of the mixing of different grades of cotton and two laws touching eminent domain. One of these, which was finally approved in November, 1929, enlarges the Government's right to condemn private property in the carrying out of projects of municipal and village improvement having specially in view sanitary as also aesthetic considerations. It further authorizes resale by the Government of property thus expropriated. The other introduces the principle of the obligation of the benefited and neighboring landowner to make an equitable contribution to the cost of improvement in the form of a proportion of the increased value of his property.

Turning to the other branch of the legislative labors of the Court of Appeals, that involving the approval of police measures, the list of measures which have been approved by this Assembly is a much longer one and is considerably wider in scope. This scope has already been indicated in the review of the criminal jurisdiction of the courts—and a few further illustrations have been given above. To these may be added certain measures approved during the year 1927–28, such as an important Medical Practices Act; a law regulating the conduct of pharmacies and the commerce in poisonous drugs; a law prohibiting the hunting of gazelles; and an elaborate revision, already mentioned, of the Anti-drug Law of 1925. In 1928–29 only three new measures were approved by this Assembly—a law further regulating hotels, cafés, theaters, and other "public establishments"; a law regulating the occupation of dragomen; and one requiring the inoculation of animals against the "coal disease."

The Antidrug Law of 1928 merits special reference. It is characterized chiefly by greatly increased severity in penalties imposed as compared with those imposed by the law of 1925. Thus it embodies a penalty of imprisonment, with labor, for a period of from one to five years, in addition to a fine of from two hundred to a thousand pounds. But, as in the case of the earlier law, these penalties cannot apply to foreigners, whose punishment under this law is necessarily limited to those applicable to police offenses, viz., a week's imprisonment and the fine of a pound, but with the important incidental penalties (which, as we have seen, also exist in the Medical Practices Act) of suspension of the right to pursue a profession, the forfeiture of property and the closing of an office or establishment. It may well be that the punishment of imprisonment, in the form established by the new narcotic law is excessive, even in spite of the gravity of the evil it is designed to suppress. But even if this be so, it only serves to emphasize the glaring disparity of treatment as between foreigners and Egyptians and to call attention to the injustice of a situation which is largely responsible for the appeal which Egypt is making today for the transfer of full criminal jurisdiction to the Mixed Courts.

Such, in brief, is the legislative system governing the enactment of laws applicable to foreigners in Egypt.

324 THE MIXED COURTS OF EGYPT

Evolving slowly from the modest beginning established under Lord Cromer (then Sir Evelyn Baring) in 1889, it has come in large measure to realize, though in a manner quite different from that of the International Legislative Assembly which he sought to create, Lord Cromer's ambition to establish a machinery "for enacting laws generally applicable to the whole of the inhabitants of Egypt."

As already shown, the system is incomplete. A field is still reserved to that process of "legislation by diplomacy" which Lord Cromer so bitterly deplored. The fiscal problem is not covered. All matters touching the structure of the courts are still within the control (and protection) of the Powers. But the scope of the legislative activities of the Mixed Courts is very large; its importance is steadily increasing. Without hesitation it can be said that the legislative system has been a success—that it is not only a complete protection to the interests of foreigners, but is an invaluable contribution to the legislative life in Egypt.

As to the objection that the system violates the principle of the separation of powers, by uniting the legislative and judicial function, the practical answer is that the principle cannot fairly be applied to the case in hand.

There is no liberty [observes the founder of this doctrine], if the judicial function is not separate from the legislative and the executive. If it were joined to the legislative office, there would exist an arbitrary power over the life and liberty of citizens, for the judge would be himself the law-maker; if it were joined to the executive office, the judge might assume the power of an oppressor.[29]

By no stretch of the imagination can any trace of the

[29] Montesquieu, *Spirit of Laws*, Book III, Chap. VI.

evils thus foreshadowed be read into the picture of things as they exist in Egypt. The rights of foreigners in matters of legislation are merely accorded the safeguard of the approval of a body called into being for the purpose of protecting those rights. It is a body equipped above all others to know what those rights are. It does not, except in rare instances, propose the laws, nor does it promulgate them. Officially its rôle is limited to that of a simple veto or approval. Beyond that, its usefulness in the proposal of amendments or in the technical and difficult matter of legal draftsmanship depends entirely upon the spirit of coöperation which exists between it and the Government of the country. So far, this spirit has been excellent, as is witnessed, among other things by the constant practice of informal interviews with representatives of the Government touching possible modifications in the proposed laws.

It is, of course, true that the assemblies are not composed of men of various classes in the communities. By their very internationally cosmopolitan character, however, they are adapted to represent, or are in a position readily to ascertain, the viewpoint of the different foreign communities whose interests may be affected. The responsibility imposed upon them is taken with great seriousness. Careful preliminary study is made of every measure; committee reports and minutes are circulated; the observations of the various public or private organizations who might be interested, are invited; representatives of such bodies are frequently invited to appear before committees to present their observations; memorials are often received from outside sources, and generally speaking the proposed measure is submitted to the most careful inquiry.

The critic unfamiliar with the practical working of the system might be tempted to suggest the possibility of combinations between groups of Powers to adversely affect the interests of other groups. The experience of forty years of judicial coöperation in legislative councils is sufficient basis on which to qualify any such fears as beyond the realm of the most remote possibility. In the first place, even if the six Egyptian members voted *en bloc* for a law, its approval would require the concurrence of the representatives of eight other countries (unless both the British member and the British Procureur-General were among those in its favor, in which case seven others would suffice). The possibility of any such combination being formed at the expense of the remaining Powers is not to be taken seriously. Assuming the possibility that the interests of Egyptian and foreign members might become sharply divided (a situation which so far has not occurred), it is impossible to conceive of laws to which the interests of the foreign Powers would be seriously in conflict. Divisions do not run along national lines. The spirit of international bargaining which too often characterized the older system of legislation by diplomacy, and which on occasion brought in political considerations wholly unrelated to the merit of the particular project under discussion, is nonexistent. The members of the assemblies are not the diplomatic agents of their governments, and are not under instructions from their respective foreign offices. It was precisely to avoid a system where such "instructions" could play a disastrous part that the new system was designed. The legislators hold office for life. While they are, of course, alive to the interests of the country from which they come, it is, above all, the mutual and inseparable interest of Egypt and the strangers within her borders—the general interests of the public—that guide their decisions. It is this spirit and the habit of daily contact and discussion with their Egyptian colleagues that make possible the free and friendly and unembittered discussion that has contributed so largely to the success of the system. Indeed, so successful has the experiment been that it seems quite possible that the system will soon be extended so as to take over such measure of legislative activity as is still reserved to the older diplomatic method. Suggestions to this end have been frequently made by both Egyptian and European spokesmen, and have today assumed a definite diplomatic form. Thus, in the Memorandum presented in 1919 to the Peace Conference at Paris, outlining the Egyptian national claims, and bearing the signatures of many of the principal nationalist leaders of the country, including that of the late Zaghloul Pasha, it is stated that

as regards legislation and taxation, foreigners will find their interests amply secured by making the consent of an existing international organization necessary before any law can be applied to, or any tax be imposed upon, them. This organization is none other than the General Assembly of the Mixed Court of Appeal ordained by the law of 11th November, 1911. By the addition of other elements this organization will perfectly answer the above end.

In a draft note regarding the Capitulations prepared in London in November, 1927, during the course of the negotiations leading to the proposed treaty rejected by Egypt in 1928, it is suggested[30] that the powers of the Legislative Assembly of the Mixed Courts

should cover all Egyptian legislation, with the exception of legislation imposing financial burdens on foreigners and legislation relating to the constitution and jurisdiction of the Mixed Tribunals themselves. The former class should not come into force until the representative of His Britannic Majesty has

[30] *Egypt*, No. 1 (1928), p. 42.

declared himself satisfied that it does not discriminate inequitably against foreigners.

As to the second class it was suggested that fundamental changes in the Mixed Courts system should continue to require the approval of the powers.

The adoption of these proposals would have added little to the powers already exercised by the Legislative Assembly of the Mixed Courts. A much broader view of the situation, however, has been taken in the Anglo-Egyptian proposals of August, 1929. These would extend the powers of the Assembly to cover all cases where foreign assent is now necessary except laws affecting "the constitution or jurisdiction" of the Mixed Courts themselves, and which properly enough should continue to require the assent of the Powers.[31] The note explains that it should be the duty of the Assembly to satisfy itself that the legislation in question

is not inconsistent with the principles generally adopted in modern legislation which is applicable to foreigners, and, with particular relation to legislation of a fiscal character, that it does not inequitably discriminate against foreigners, including foreign companies.[32]

[31] See Appendix K.

[32] Compare the observations on this point of the Egyptian Prime Minister Mahmoud Pasha in the course of a public address, August 24, 1929. "As to the application of Egyptian legislation to foreigners, including the imposing of taxes, Great Britain accepts that the approval of the capitulatory Powers be replaced by the ratification of the General Assembly of the Mixed Tribunals. This ratification, however, should in no manner constitute partnership in the disposing of the general state of affairs, nor should it entail any interference in legislative matters or in the question of taxes. The duty of that General Assembly should only be confined to making sure that foreigners should not suffer any miscarriage of justice or molestation." *Egyptian Gazette*, August 26, 1929. Also declaration of the same in the *Egyptian Green Book*, 1929, p. 18, that the functions of the Mixed Courts "would on the one hand, be enlarged so as to embrace fiscal legislations, and on the other, would be so narrow as to be limited to the mere assurance that fiscal legislations do not inequitably discriminate against foreigners . . ." and that the courts "would not have

The language employed suggests on the one hand a limitation and on the other an extension of the existing legislative powers of the Mixed Courts. At present the approval of the Legislative Assembly is exercised on the basis of completely free discretion. The suggestion is, it should hereafter be limited to an inquiry as to whether a proposed measure meets the generally accepted standards of modern legislation. But as to the new field of fiscal legislation the test is to be still more specific—that of "inequitable discrimination," which recalls the test already applied in the case of police laws, that they must be of common application to all inhabitants of the country.

Whether the consent of the Powers will be forthcoming to this extension of the legislative functions of the Mixed Courts remains to be seen. Primarily a judicial body, the courts would have no reason to welcome such an addition to their responsibilities in the legislative field. Nor would they have any reason to fear it. Their structure is far too solid, their position too well established. The new duty would fall within the limits of a long-established procedure. If it should be considered a step toward the solution of the problem of the Capitulations in Egypt they could afford to assume it without serious concern for the consequences.

the right to interfere, as they do at present, on certain occasions, in the subject (*le fond*) of the legislation or its opportuneness.''

CHAPTER XVIII

REFORMING THE REFORM

THE creation of the Mixed Courts did not completely solve the problem of the Capitulations. To the reformer of the future was left, as we have seen, the abolition of "legislation by diplomacy" and the "closing of the consular courts"—and after these, in the more distant future, the problem of the merging of all the various and complex judicial institutions of the land into a single unified national system.

Throughout the long struggles to achieve these ends the Mixed Courts have always played a conspicuous rôle. Their place in the fight for legislative reform has just been traced; the part they have played in the struggle for judicial reform remains to be set forth.

At this point it is important to insist upon a distinction, too often not made clear by writers on Egyptian affairs, between the Mixed Courts and the Capitulations. It is a distinction vital to the whole problem of reform in Egypt. The Mixed Courts have often been referred to as part of the "capitulatory *régime*." But they form no part of the Capitulations. The term "Capitulation" properly refers to only those special privileges for foreigners, which were inherited by Egypt from Turkey and were allowed by a process of abusive interpretation and acquiescence to develop into the system whose inconveniences gave rise to the founding of the Mixed Courts. These privileges, as already explained, consisted primarily in a complete legislative and judicial immunity for foreigners. To these were added certain other special privileges such as inviolability of

domicile and immunity from search or arrest. To a very
large extent the capitulatory immunities were super-
seded by the Mixed Courts. These courts stand upon an
independent basis of treaty and statute and have today
no organic relation to the Capitulations. In the sense in
which the word is commonly used in the Egyptian press
today, the "Capitulations"—i.e., what is left of them,—
the existing jurisdiction of the Consular Courts, and the
privileges just mentioned, could be abolished tomorrow
and the Mixed Courts would remain unaffected except
in so far as the interested nations might decide to confer
upon them *additional* powers to meet the problem arising out of the abolished consular jurisdiction.

The distinction here insisted upon has been emphasized on many occasions. It is clearly set forth in the latest official proposals for the settlement of the political
differences between Great Britain and Egypt. The draft
proposals for an Anglo-Egyptian Treaty exchanged in
August, 1929, after recognizing that "the capitulatory
régime now existing in Egypt is no longer in accord with
the spirit of the times," declare that his Britannic Majesty "accordingly undertakes to use all his influence
with the Powers possessing capitulatory rights in
Egypt to obtain, in conditions which will safeguard the
legitimate interests of foreigners, the transfer to the
Mixed Tribunals of the jurisdiction of the existing Consular Courts, and the application of Egyptian legislation to foreigners." In other words the Capitulations,
or, rather, their principal remaining expressions—i.e.,
the Consular Courts and legislative immunity—are to
be abolished through a transfer of the exterritorial
privileges which they represent to the protection of a
national Egyptian institution functioning with the aid
of foreign coöperation—the Mixed Courts.

With this preliminary distinction made, let us resume our review of the progress of judicial reform in Egypt.

As an integral part of Lord Cromer's unsuccessful fight for the establishment of an international legislative council, he included a twofold judicial reform. The first of these was the abolition of the Consular Courts; the second was the reorganization of the Mixed Courts themselves.

In the face of the consensus of opinion today that the criminal jurisdiction of the Consular Courts should be transferred to the Mixed Courts, it seems strange to have to record that so wise a statesman as Lord Cromer should have been unwilling to accept this very obvious solution of the problem of consular jurisdiction. He did oppose it, however, and this upon the ground that it represented an extension of the "international principle"—a principle, he declared, against which he had always firmly set his face in all of its various manifestations in Egyptian affairs.[1] He accordingly proposed that the consular jurisdiction be transferred to an entirely new system of criminal courts, to be established by his projected legislative council, but with the proviso that such courts must be composed either of a single foreign judge or of a bench of which three-fifths of the judges should be foreigners.

As for his proposed "reorganization" of the Mixed Courts, Lord Cromer explained that his plan involved

[1] *Annual Report*, pp. 13, 15. See also *Annual Report* (1904), pp. 8-9. "Without in any way contesting the fact that the Mixed Courts have in the past rendered good service to Egypt, or the further fact that their existence is, for the time being, necessary to the welfare of the country, I venture to assert that any extension of the international principle, at all events, in so far as judicial and administrative questions are concerned, is not in the true interests either of the Egyptians or of the Europeans resident in Egypt; and that reform, if it is to be undertaken at all, should move rather in the counter-direction, namely that of gradually freeing Egypt from such international shackles as now exist."

the permanent establishment in Egypt of Law Courts, which
may not be always composed in a manner precisely similar to
the present Mixed Courts, but which must always be of an
essentially international character. Any changes in their composition will depend on the decision of a Legislative Assembly
which will itself be international.

A competent observer, writing in 1907, thus interpreted this latter part of Lord Cromer's program:

The new Court would appear to be the present Native Court
transformed and expanded. The Mixed Courts are to disappear
when the reformed Courts are prepared to take over their
work; and the present Mixed Court Judges ''are to be entitled
to retain their posts, and their services are to be available'' in
the new Courts.[2]

Lord Cromer was careful to insist, however, that as he
viewed it his plan, so far from abolishing the Mixed
Courts, tended rather to perpetuate them.

I cannot say if any one will be disposed to describe this system as one involving the ''abolition of the Mixed Courts.'' To
me it would appear that a more correct definition would be to
say that the proposal invites the perpetuation to all time of the
judicial system generally described as that of the ''Mixed
Courts.''[3]

There is no more brilliant chapter in English diplomatic history than that which records Lord Cromer's
achievements in Egypt. No one can study the long record of his administration and measure the benefits
which it brought to the land in which he labored, without
being lost in admiration for his strength and wisdom

[2] Scott, p. 317. See Lord Cromer: ''I regard it as equally clear that,
under any circumstances which are likely to arise, the British and Egyptian Governments would desire to avail themselves of the services of the
very capable and experienced Magistrates whom those Courts include.''
Annual Report (1904), p. 9.

[3] *Report* (1906), p. 13.

and vision, or without being carried away by the mag-
nanimity and nobility of his personal character. In his
attitude toward the Mixed Courts, however, the historian may be permitted to doubt the soundness of his
conclusions. Lord Cromer was above all an administrator and not a lawyer. He was a despot, even if the most
benevolent of despots. He believed thoroughly in the
centralization of power, and to him the Mixed Courts
which had been established before the British occupation, and were under the protection not of England
alone but of all the Powers alike, represented an *im-
perium in imperio* which was in conflict with that principle.[4] He did not fairly discriminate between the requirements of a strong judicial system and of a strong
civil administration and, it seems fair to say, did not
realize that the genius of the Mixed Courts centered
largely in that very independence which he begrudged
them; that it was above all this ''international'' character that guaranteed them their independence; but that
the justice that they rendered was essentially ''national'' and not an expression of the international principle.

Again we must recall the traditional British conception of the supremacy of legislative power. The Mixed
Courts were not subject to any immediate legislative
control. Their charter was a treaty. It could with diffi-

[4] ''The principal defect of the Mixed Courts,'' complains Lord Cromer
(*Modern Egypt*, II, 318), ''is that the judges are not merely interpreters
of the law; they are also, to a great extent makers of it. They are not
under the effective control of any legislature. If, as is both natural and
occasionally almost unavoidable, they attempt, by a somewhat strained
interpretation of their charter, to usurp functions which do not belong to
them, there is no one to restrain them.'' Similarly Lord Milner deprecated
the ''want of any effective control of criticism'' of the decisions of the
Mixed Courts. ''Imagine the decrees of this Government liable to be set
at naught by courts of its own creation.'' Milner, *England in Egypt*
(13th ed.; London, 1920), p. 225. Read in the light of history these observations are a witness rather to the essential strength, than to any weakness
of the Mixed Court system.

culty be amended. It was necessarily the function of the
supreme judicial organ of the courts to interpret this
charter as well as the unwritten law of the Capitulations. Such interpretation could not be contested by any
authority established in the land. It is easy to realize
that a judicial independence so unique and so absolute
was readily calculated to invite the jealous scrutiny of
an all-powerful civil administrator.

Lord Cromer withdrew from Egypt in 1907, with his
reforms unrealized. In 1911 there was set in motion the
legislative assembly described in the preceding chapter.
From then on until toward the ending of the War, no
projects of reform were presented involving material
changes in the Mixed Courts. As the War drew to a
close, however, it was decided to renew the attack upon
the ancient problem. In 1917 the Egyptian Government
appointed what was heralded as the most important
public body to be named in thirty years—a mixed commission of foreigners and Egyptians to whom was committed the task of elaborating the reforms that would
be rendered necessary by the generally anticipated
abolition of the Capitulations at the end of the War.
Prominent among its members was Sir William Brunyate, the British Judicial Adviser to the Egyptian Government, who gave his name to that portion of the projects of the commission which touched the Mixed Courts.

In March, 1918, a year after its creation, after having
held 134 sessions, the commission issued a public announcement[5] outlining generally a plan of organization
which had been presented for its study and which contemplated a unification of the three jurisdictions of the
Mixed, the Native, and the Consular Courts, with a
Court of Appeals sitting at Cairo. The announcement
covered broadly many reforms in law and procedure.

[5] See *Gazette des Tribunaux Mixtes,* No. 90, April, 1918.

They responded to a movement which had "for its object a fundamental break with traditions and a more or less openly avowed Anglicization of the law and legal institutions of Egypt."[6]

Among other changes, the new plan proposed the adoption of the English system of "registrars" for simplifying and giving greater precision to the questions finally presented to the courts. It proposed also the suppression of the Commercial Code, and its absorption, as far as necessary, into a new Code of Contracts, and in part into a series of new code laws including, as an example, the English Bills of Exchange Act. In general as to those branches of commercial law which had been the subject of recent legislation in England, the commission was of opinion that in view of the special political situation of Egypt, it was to the English law that recourse should be had.

The publication of this announcement was followed by even more disturbing rumors as to the rôle of the French language under the new *régime*. As expressed in the *Report of the Milner Mission* which visited Egypt in the following year,

Although this Commission had issued no report a general impression prevailed that it contemplated the superseding of the Mixed Tribunals by new Courts in which the English language and British legal procedure would predominate—a measure which would entail disabilities on the Native Bar and paralyze the foreign advocates who had hitherto used the French language.[7]

6 Sir William Brunyate, former Judicial Adviser to Egyptian Government. Lecture at Cambridge University, August, 1924. The lecturer adds that he personally strongly deprecated this movement, which he had always opposed during his long term of office, his views on the subject having been shared by both Lord Cromer and Lord Kitchener. See *Egyptian Gazette* (Alexandria), September 13, 1924.

7 *Report of the Milner Mission* (London, 1921), p. 13.

The reception which greeted the announcement of the commission forms one of the liveliest chapters in the history of the Mixed Courts. The bar was deeply aroused, and at once entered the lists in vigorous protest against any attempt to substitute the English language or tradition for those on which the history of the courts had been built. With biting sarcasm the monthly *Bar Magazine* replied to a memorial which had been presented to the commission by an informal committee of ten English lawyers, comprising, alleged the journal, practically the entire British bar in Egypt, and whose practice lay chiefly before the British Consular Courts, as contrasted with the seven hundred non-English members of the bar of the Mixed Courts. This was followed by the publication of an elaborate protest signed by some three hundred members of the Mixed Bar which was adopted by the General Assembly of the bar with a motion authorizing its Council to take the most vigorous measures to defend the interests of the bar.

The protest assumed that this proposed reform contemplated the eventual displacement of French by English as a court language, and denounced the proposal as a practical impossibility.

To plead in a language [declares the protest], is not merely a matter of speaking it with more or less fluency. It requires a fundamental grasp of the language; an ability to speak and write it with complete facility; a habit of thinking and feeling in it; above all it requires that one shall have received through its medium, that legal "formation" which is based not only upon legal experience but upon one's general education. In this country the basis of intellectual thought and the judicial life is essentially Latin.

The principal sponsor of the reforms was not slow in coming to their defense. In a letter to the editor of the *Bar Gazette,* Sir William Brunyate expressed his regret at the erroneous fear "that at an early date French may disappear as a judicial language," explaining that, in the tentative draft, the English and French languages were placed upon an equal footing. He added:

It appears to be recognized that at some date in the more or less remote future English is destined to replace French as the *lingua franca* of the foreign communities in Egypt. . . . It is, on the other hand, indubitable that the slowest progress has been made in non-Egyptian legal circles. I should venture to hope that this is nowise due to the fact that French legal principles cannot be conveniently formulated in a language other than the French language, because such a proposition would appear to me to throw grave doubts on the general validity of the principles in question. The more simple explanation is that hitherto no steps have been taken to render possible the hearing of cases in the English language. It is obvious that measures in that sense must be taken in the near future.

This reply added fuel to the fire. Retorts were plentiful. The fundamental differences between the Latin and the Anglo-Saxon systems were eloquently developed and the demonstration was undertaken that any attempt to reproduce the principles of Latin law in the English tongue would be not merely difficult but impracticable.

The result of the controversy was to abundantly demonstrate the strength of French legal traditions in Egypt and the hopelessness of any attempt to break with them. Broader political developments led to the permanent suspension of the work of the commission. The project to modify materially the use of the French language as the working language of the Mixed Courts was never heard of again.[8]

8 See the observations of a leading British authority: "The Anglo-Egyptian proposals on this point were fiercely and unjustly attacked, as designed primarily to secure the substitution of English for French law, or to favor the English Bar at the expense of the foreign. The foreign community became convinced that their rights were being bartered and

A second and more auspicious effort at reform, but which also involved the error of attempting to change the essential structure of the Mixed Courts, was developed as a result of the labors of the Milner Mission which was dispatched to Egypt late in 1919

to report on the existing situation in the country and the form of the constitution which, under the Protectorate, will be best calculated to promote its peace and prosperity, the progressive development of self-governing institutions, and the protection of foreign interests.

While the mission was still in Egypt a careful project for the reformation of the Mixed Courts had been undertaken under the leadership of Sir Cecil Hurst, a member of the mission.[9] Under it the Mixed Courts were to be reorganized, and to them was to be committed full criminal jurisdiction over foreigners, as well as jurisdiction in all civil cases involving foreigners of the same nationality, including cases of *personal status*. This, of course, meant the closing of the Consular Courts, after agreements to that effect had been entered into between Great Britain and the capitulatory powers. Judges of the Mixed Courts were to be appointed and promoted by decree "on the proposal of

Egyptians murmured that England was seizing every institution in the country. . . . No Commission was ever assembled in Cairo better equipped for its task: no Commission failed more lamentably to reap the reward of patient effort" (Lieutenant Colonel Elgood, *Egypt and the Army*, pp. 292–293).

[9] The project was presented for public discussion under a series of *Draft Laws for the Reconstituting the Mixed Courts* (Cairo Government Press, 1920. French and English). These were prefaced by a brief "Explanatory Memorandum" and included the following: "Draft Judicature Law (No. 1), 1920. Reconstituting the Mixed Courts on a New Basis with Extended Jurisdiction" (74 articles); "Draft Judicature Law (No. 2) 1920. Prescribing the Legislation to be applied by the Reconstituted Mixed Courts" (57 articles); "Draft Judicature Law (No. 3) 1920. Staff, Internal Organization, etc." (136 articles). In the important matter of criminal procedure, and pending the promulgation of a new code, it was proposed to follow the procedure of the Native Courts.

the Minister of Justice and with the approval of the High Commissioner.'' ''Judges of the existing Mixed Courts who may be appointed to the bench of the reconstituted Courts'' were to be entitled to benefit by various specified special conditions relating to pension and retirement. As to new legislation affecting foreigners, wherever such legislation had theretofore required the approval of the Powers, or of one or other of the two assemblies of the courts, ''the counter signature of the High Commissioner'' was thereafter to be necessary.

The starting point of this project was a surrender by the Powers of their capitulatory rights to Great Britain, as trustee for foreign interests in Egypt. In order to secure this transfer Great Britain opened the necessary diplomatic negotiations. Some of the smaller Powers gave their consent, and treaties were actually negotiated with Greece, Sweden, Denmark, Norway, and Portugal. But the acceptance of the larger Powers was not forthcoming. Among others, the United States demurred. ''The suggestion with respect to the exercise of capitulatory rights in Egypt through a third power does not appeal to my Government as one that could well have practical application,'' wrote the American Ambassador in London in his reply to the British Government, and while the American Government at the same time invited the furnishing of further explanations, the reply gave little reason to suppose that the fundamental conception of the plan would receive American support.[10]

10 The draft of a convention for the renunciation of capitulatory rights in favor of Great Britain was submitted to the United States on June 29, 1920. In a recent magazine article (''Trustees for the Sphinx,'' *North American Review*, March, 1928) Judge Crabités refers to this proposal as having ''been predicated upon the hypothesis that Great Britain would become the Trustee for all of the capitulatory rights then enjoyed by the ten European Powers and the United States,'' and adds: ''It conferred, in its last analysis, upon another nation the right to protect our nationals

JASPER Y. BRINTON
(UNITED STATES)
JUSTICE OF THE COURT OF APPEALS

In the meantime negotiations covering the general political situation and looking to the conclusion of a treaty between England and Egypt continued. In November, 1921, in a memorandum of clauses covering the proposed agreement handed by Lord Curzon to the Egyptian representative, it was stated that Great Britain would continue to conduct with the Powers the negotiations for the abolition of the Capitulations. To this statement the Egyptian delegation replied that it had been led to suppose that, the problem of the Capitulations having been postponed, "there ought to be no further question of it in the agreement, and that it would be dealt with later by Egypt, the party chiefly interested, with the diplomatic cooperation of her ally."

The political wheel continued to revolve. A few months later appeared the British Declaration of February 28, 1922 (proclaimed by Egypt on March 15, which is thus observed as a national holiday), abolishing the protectorate and declaring Egypt "to be an independent sovereign state," but reserving absolutely "to the discretion of His Majesty's Government until such time as it may be possible by free and friendly discussion and friendly accommodation on both sides to conclude agreements in regard thereto between His Majesty's Government and the Government of Egypt," the four questions of security of empire communications, the defense of Egypt, the Sudan and "the protec-

in their relation with a third Power. This ran counter to the genius of our institutions. It, therefore, precluded the possibility of our falling in line with what others had done. This decision of Washington probably surprised many a well informed statesman. But it had about it the ring of finality." The late Judge Herreros (*Livre d'Or*, p. 300) was of the opinion that the principal obstacle to the project was the opposition of the Mixed Courts themselves to a proviso which contemplated that the final Court of Appeal should be the British Privy Council. For text of the Greek, Swedish, Danish, and Portuguese treaties, see *British Treaty Series* (1921), No. 5, 14, 15, and 23. For text of Portuguese treaty see Beer, p. 562.

tion of foreign interests in Egypt and the protection of minorities.'' Needless to say this latter reservation involved no interference with the *régime* of the Mixed Courts.[11]

On April 19, 1923, the new Egyptian Constitution was formally proclaimed. This document contained no reference to the Mixed Courts, but their continued existence is impliedly recognized by a clause providing that the constitution shall not be construed so as to impair the obligations of Egypt toward foreign states or the rights of foreigners, acquired by virtue of law or custom.[12] The few general declarations of right touching the administration of justice as, for instance, the independence of the judiciary, the right of the accused to the services of an attorney in his defense and the principle of public hearings, are already, for the most part, covered by the charter and statutes of the Mixed Courts themselves.

For the next few years the question of reform remained in abeyance, but on December 25, 1927, the Egyptian Government handed to the capitulatory Powers a circular note accompanied by a series of six definite projects of reform touching the Mixed Courts. The most important of these involved the extension of the jurisdiction of the Mixed Courts to several new categories of criminal offenses. These six proposals were the follow-

[11] In referring to this reservation, the late Sir William Hayter, formerly legal adviser to the Egyptian Government, observes: ''One of these, the protection of minorities, has probably ceased to be of any importance, since the Copts have very wisely decided to throw in their lot with their Moslem fellow-countrymen. Foreigners, again, are for the most part amply protected by the Capitulations; and the Powers are, generally speaking, perfectly able to safeguard the interests of their own nationals in Egypt, if they should require to be safeguarded.'' *Recent Constitutional Developments in Egypt*, Lectures prepared for the Local Lectures Summer Meeting (Cambridge, 1924).

[12] ''The application of this Constitution shall not be allowed to impair the obligations which Egypt owes to foreign states, nor the rights which foreigners shall have acquired in Egypt by virtue of laws, treaties and accepted usages.'' Article 154.

ing: (1) Modification of the present legislative system by abolishing the three months period allowed to the Powers in which to request a reconsideration of a law approved by the legislative assembly of the Court of Appeals (see chap. xvii); (2) Extension of the criminal jurisdiction of the Mixed Courts to various new categories of offenses, including violations of the antinarcotic, white slave, and pure food and drug laws, and the laws against gambling and the circulation of obscene literature (see chaps. xii and xvii); (3) Abolition of the institution of assessors (or associate lay judges) in the trial of misdemeanors (see chap. xii); (4) Creation of a new chamber of three justices (in addition to the existing chambers of five) in the Court of Appeals with jurisdiction over special classes of appeals (see chap. viii), and the according of discretion to the Egyptian Government to remove the seat of the Court of Appeals to Cairo (see chap. v); (5) Abolition of the present requirement that the presidents and vice-presidents of the several courts should be foreigners, and providing that in every case one of these two offices be held by an Egyptian (see chap. viii); (6) Repeal of existing prohibition against the bestowal on the judges by the Egyptian Government, of titles and decorations (see chap. v).

In presenting these specific proposals to the Powers, the Egyptian Government observed that it had had for a long time under consideration plans for an early general revision of the capitulatory *régime* of a character which, while affording the necessary protection to the interests of foreigners, would be more compatible with the sovereignty and interests of the country and its progress and evolution.

This reference to a larger program of reform may be read in connection with the contemporary, but in large measure independent, discussions which accompanied the negotiations carried on between Great Britain and Egypt between July, 1927 and March, 1928, with a view to the signing of a treaty of alliance, but which were not made public until the rupture of negotiations in March.

By Article 9 of the Draft Treaty, the British Government undertook "to use all its influence with the Powers possessing capitulatory rights in Egypt to obtain the modification of the capitulatory *régime* now existing in Egypt so as to make it conform more closely with the spirit of the times and with the present state of Egypt."

In a draft note which accompanied Sir Austen Chamberlain's letter of November 24, 1927, addressed to Lord Lloyd, and which, it is declared, was prepared after a discussion (in London) between Sir Cecil Hurst (the principal sponsor of the plan of 1920) and Sarwat Pasha, the Egyptian Prime Minister, there is a declaration of willingness "to agree to the utilization of those draft laws (of 1920) as the basis of the proposed reform of the capitulatory régime if the foreign Powers are willing to transfer to the Mixed Tribunals the jurisdiction of their consular courts." No reference, however, is made to the original proposal of structural changes in the Mixed Courts or to a British trusteeship for foreign interests which lay at the foundation of the Hurst proposals. The note of 1927 recognized that "on points of detail many changes will no doubt be required," and particular reference is made to the probable difficulty of securing the agreement of some of the Powers to transfer to the Mixed Courts suits relating to the *status personnel* of their nationals. It is therefore suggested that transfer in these matters should be made optional, although, declares the note, it is anticipated that Great Britain itself would "agree to the Mixed Tribunals exercising jurisdiction in these matters in cases where British subjects are concerned." Other suggestions were that Egyptians charged with political offenses against foreigners should be tried in the Mixed Courts and that the royal prerogative of pardon should be exercised on the advice of a committee to consist of the Minister of Justice, the Judicial Adviser, and a third person.

The suggestions thus presented in November, 1927, necessarily succumbed to the fate of the treaty negotiations which were terminated in March by the rejection of the proposed treaty by the Egyptian Government. This, however, did not necessarily involve the fate of the six specific proposals put forward by Egypt in December, 1927. But response to the Government's project had been somewhat disappointing. The note had suggested that if the proposals were not accepted before January 31, 1928, an international commission should be convened in Cairo in February to examine the viewpoints of the several Powers. Obviously the time allowed was too short to permit the proper preliminary study of the question. The fall of the ministry of Sarwat Pasha, by whom the project had been presented, and the *coup d'état* of June, 1928, suspending the Parliament, naturally had their effect on the diplomatic machinery. Replies were slow in coming in and in October, 1928, the Egyptian Government again called the matter to the attention of the Powers. Unanimous agreement of all the Powers upon all the six proposals in the form proposed was not to be expected. Some, at least, of the proposals were frankly undesirable. But the alternative suggestion that the Powers should agree to the convening of an international commission was met by a disposition on the part of some of them to insist on a greater elaboration of the Government's projects and, more particularly, on a detailed statement as to certain special measures of guarantee, as a preliminary condition to the acceptance of the proposal to convene the commission. In the meantime, as is commonly the case, personal and national interests entered into the discussions. It was generally conceded that the creation of a new chamber in the Court of Appeals to consist of three justices, with a special jurisdiction, would be less desirable than the plan which had been advocated by the Court of Appeals itself, of adding a new chamber of five to the three chambers already existing. But in such an event, from which Powers would the new judges be selected? This question assumed an importance in diplomatic discussions that had no proper relation to the essential merits of the reforms. It finally became generally known that a group of continental Powers had elaborated a proposal for the creation of two new chambers of five each in the Court of Appeals, thus increasing the court from sixteen to twenty-six members, and calling for the nomination of six new foreign justices—a plan which at least could boast the diplomatic virtue of allowing all national aspirations to be fully taken care of. This proposal came as a surprise to the Court of Appeals and contributed to a decision on the part of the Egyptian Government to supplant the very limited projects of reform, the execution of which promised to be so costly, by a larger program. Work was accordingly pressed forward on the reform of the Code of Criminal Procedure, as being the most important preliminary step toward inducing the Powers to accept the criminal jurisdiction of the Mixed Courts in exchange for the consular jurisdiction. The direction of this reform has already been reviewed.[13]

13 See chap. xii. At the same time steps were taken to bring about

At this stage the program of judicial reform again became involved in larger political negotiations. As already mentioned the Anglo-Egyptian draft treaty of August, 1929, included the problem of the Capitulations. This portion of the proposals followed closely the suggestions of the proposals of 1927 for the transfer of consular jurisdiction to the Mixed Courts, and were in fact largely couched in identical language. Apart, however, from the proposals touching legislative powers, and those touching the reform of criminal jurisdiction already discussed there are a few significant changes in plan. The suggestion that all Egyptians charged with the commission of political offenses against foreigners should be tried by the Mixed Courts is omitted. In the matter of the pardoning power, touching sentences imposed on foreigners, which under the proposals of 1927 was committed to the "advice of a committee composed of the Minister of Justice, the Judicial Adviser and a third person," it is proposed under the new plan that the Minister of Justice "will consult the Judicial Adviser, so long as that official is retained, before tendering his advice to the King."[14]

It will be observed that the proposed transfer of consular jurisdiction to the Mixed Courts is general in its terms and thus would include not only full criminal ju-

needed reforms in civil and commercial procedure by the appointment of a strong commission to revise, and so far as possible, to unify the existing codes of procedure of the Mixed and Native Courts. The members of this commission include, President, Mohamed Bey Moustapha, a former President of the Native Courts; Mr. Holmes, Procureur-General; Justice Van Ackere of the Mixed Court of Appeal; Justices Soudan and Berzi Bey, of the Native Court of Appeals; Judges Ricol and Bechmann of the District Courts of Alexandria and Cairo; Mr. de Bellefonds and Mr. l'Abbaté, Royal Counselors; Mr. Besly, Secretary to the Judicial Adviser, as Secretary to the Commission; and two members of the bar, Mr. Boulad, the Bâtonnier of the Mixed Courts Bar, and Mr. Kamel Bey Sidki, who is also a member of the Egyptian Senate.

[14] For text of portions of proposals dealing with these topics, see Appendix K.

risdiction over foreigners, but all cases of civil and
commercial litigation between foreigners of the same
nationality. As to questions involving *personal status,*
however, this note also observes that as "it may be difficult" for some Powers to agree to such transfer it
should remain optional, although, it likewise adds, it is
anticipated that an agreement can be reached that the
Mixed Courts "should exercise jurisdiction in these
matters in cases where British subjects are concerned."

The problem of the transfer of criminal jurisdiction
has been long anticipated and, as pointed out, prepara-
tions are well under way to make its achievement possible. The transfer of the civil and commercial jurisdiction of the consuls should not present serious difficulties. The transfer of jurisdiction in the case of personal
status, however, raises questions of a delicate character
which, so far, have not been thoroughly examined. As a
whole the program is a large one. It will demand the
best efforts of the most competent authorities to carry
it to completion.[15] But with coöperation between Great
Britain and Egypt assured through the adoption of a
solid political accord, there is reason to hope that the
approaching negotiations, whether they be carried on
through diplomatic correspondence or through the summoning of an international commission, will be fruitful
in results and will not only crown the long struggles of
a generation of reformers, but will bring to their completion the monumental labors of the founders of the
Mixed Courts.

15 "In that judicial Tower of Babel, with its firmly rooted legal preju-
dices and its polyglot traditions, the men responsible for reform find
themselves confronted with a task which will tax their ability to the utmost—one, indeed, which I venture to think is as complicated and delicate
as any which have perplexed the minds of international jurists and legal
administrators in any other country" (Sir Malcolm McIlwraith. See
Egyptian Gazette, December 9, 1918).

CONCLUSION

EGYPT is the despair of prophets. It is the Land of Paradox where "grapes do grow from thorns and figs from thistles" and where "only the provisional endures." It would be rash indeed to attempt to predict the future that lies in store for the Mixed Courts. But it may not be out of place to summarize in a few concluding paragraphs some of the principal factors which seem most likely to affect the working out of their ultimate destiny.

To many foreign observers the most striking fact in connection with the Mixed Courts would perhaps be this, that in spite of their capitulatory origin, and in a day when the Capitulations are decidedly out of fashion, the courts have so far won favor in Egyptian eyes that, instead of their abolition being demanded, a plan which involves the extension of their powers is generally conceded by Egyptians themselves to be in the interests of the country.

The explanation of this state of affairs lies in the remarkable success with which the protection of foreign interests has been reconciled with the claims of Egyptian nationality. It was an Egyptian statesman, supported by an Egyptian ruler, who called them into being. They form an integral part of the Egyptian judicial system. They are maintained by the national treasury. Their writs run in the name of the Egyptian Sovereign. It is he who appoints their judges. While a majority of these judges must be selected from among foreign nations they are none the less officials of the Egyptian State. The little army of employees who serve the courts are in the main composed of Egyptian subjects. The

courts are indeed Egyptian Courts and a national
Egyptian institution.

The country, moreover, appreciates the contribution
which the courts have made to its national prosperity.
They have solved a problem which lay at the very
foundations of its commercial and industrial life. This
was the problem of guaranteeing security to the foreign
capital and enterprise upon which the modern development of the country has so largely depended. It is a
problem which has involved the intermingling of many
races, languages, and religions and the interplay of
many foreign laws and institutions against the background of a highly organized commercial life. It is no
reflection on Egypt, but is of the essence of the problem
itself, that "the coöperation of the foreign specialist"
as Nubar Pasha phrased it, has been resorted to for its
solution.

Another element which has had its influence in the
past is the fact that the Mixed Courts, founded as they
were before the British Occupation of Egypt, have enjoyed international protection and, as such, have been
outside the sphere of influence, administratively speaking, of the occupying power. This stability, this guarantee of continued and unchanged existence throughout
periods of political uncertainties and transition, have
been regarded by Egyptians as a claim to national
favor.

But there is another factor of much greater importance in commending the Mixed Courts to the good will
of Egypt. They represent the surest and quickest road
of escape from the extraterritorial infringement of
sovereignty embodied in the Consular Courts and in the
still remaining diplomatic control over legislation affecting foreigners. It is easy to present arguments, both
practical and theoretical, against these infringements,

but only through utilizing the services and enlarging the functions of the Mixed Courts have feasible plans for their suppression been forthcoming. Such plans have today reached a stage of detailed discussion. There is reason to hope that they can be carried into execution.

Assuming, then, that the powers of the Mixed Courts are to be materially enlarged in the near future, what of the more distant day? It is hard to answer. Whether the Mixed Courts will eventually merge with the Native Courts as was at one time generally assumed, who can say? While such a modification may be the strictly logical solution of the problem, there are practical reasons making against it. "In one form or another the principle of the Mixed Courts will endure in Egypt," observes an authority of long experience and high distinction.[1] Even were the present system of foreign representation to be gradually modified so as to eliminate, little by little, the foreign judges (as has been the case in the Native Courts), the practical needs of a cosmopolitan business community and the existence of a well-developed jurisprudence and legal tradition, and of a French speaking bar, might well suggest the indefinite continuance of the Mixed Courts long after its magistracy had lost its present international complexion. And here would enter into play another element which in the past has had decisive weight in determining the lot of reforms in Egypt, namely, the great technical difficulty of the problems presented. The whole machinery of justice in Egypt is so complicated and so delicate, the interests to be considered so varied, that the task of carrying through any substantial modification requires the most expert knowledge and the utmost patience and skill. So long as the existing system can be made to re-

[1] Francis Laloë, President of the Court of Appeals, 1920–22.

spond to existing conditions, modifications, however desirable in theory, will be slow in coming.

The net result of these observations may perhaps be summarized by saying that the Mixed Courts enjoy the respect of Egypt because they have rendered service without offense, and that as far as can be seen a long period of enlarged usefulness lies before them. How long that period will be, and when and through what transformations it will come to an end, it would be rash to predict. Will the Mixed Courts indeed celebrate their Centennial as they have already celebrated their Semi-Centennial? It seems not improbable. But whatever the answer, one thing is certain. The future is a matter of no importance to those who are now bending their efforts to maintain the fine traditions of a great judicial institution. Come what may, if today's work be well done, it will not be lost to the Egypt of tomorrow.

APPENDIX A

BIBLIOGRAPHY

THE bibliography of the Mixed Courts is extensive. In the course of the sixty years which have elapsed since the plan of the courts was first definitely presented to the Powers, practically every feature of the organization and every phase in the history of the institution has lent itself to some form or other of printed discussion. Probably no judicial system of equal age has given rise to a more varied or more polyglot accumulation of legal literature. Much of this literature is relatively inaccessible. It includes a large number of monographs, pamphlets, and articles, mostly now of purely historic interest and published on the continent, usually in France or Italy. Of these documents there exists no complete collection, and it would be a useless task to attempt to list them in the present bibliography. Many of them will be found listed in the printed catalogue of the Library of the Court of Appeals, as also in an excellent bibliography of modern Egypt, published in 1918. (*Bibliographie Economique, Juridique et Sociale de l'Egypte Moderne, 1789–1916,* par René Maunier, Directeur de la Statistique au Ministère de la Justice. Le Caire. Institut Français d'Archéologie Orientale.) All that will be here attempted is to present, under a few convenient classifications, the principal sources of authority readily available to the legal historian, together with references to a few monographs of special interest. Libraries or students desiring to secure special works or collections of documents touching the Mixed Courts may count on the coöperation of the Librarian of the Court of Appeals, or that of the American representative upon its bench. Volumes hereafter noted, which have been published in Egypt, may be secured from the *"Librairie Judiciaire 'Au Bon Livre,' Ibrahimieh, Alexandria,"* which will also handle subscriptions to the law journals.

I

ORGANIC LAWS, CODES, STATUTES, AND DECISIONS
OFFICIAL PUBLICATIONS

As indicated in the preface, among the principal sources of authority for the statements of fact appearing in this work, are the various offi-

cial or semiofficial volumes covering the Charter and Codes of the
Mixed Courts, as adopted at the time of their institution and since
amended; the Statutory Law of Egypt, outside of the Mixed Codes;
and the reported Decisions of the courts themselves.

The standard collection of the *Codes and Statutes* is a two-volume
work under the title *Codes Egyptiens et Lois Usuelles en vigueur en
Egypte,* compiled by J. A. Wathelet, Royal Counselor to the Egyptian Ministry of Finance and R. G. Brunton, former controller in the
Ministry of Justice, and published in Brussels by the firm of Veuve
Ferdinand Larcier, 26–28 rue des Minimes. Volume I contains the
codes, both for the Mixed Courts and the Native Courts. Volume II
contains the remaining statute laws (*Lois Usuelles*). Volume I, 3d
edition, is dated 1925, but has been supplemented by loose-leaf ad-
denda. Volume II, 2d edition, comprises the statute law to August
15, 1927. This volume also contains the *Charter* of the Mixed Courts
(*Règlement d'Organisation Judiciaire pour les Procès Mixtes en
Egypte*) and the General Statute of the Courts (*Règlement Général
Judiciaire*). A translation of the former document also appears in
Foreign Relations, U.S. 1873, and in the English edition of the codes
mentioned below. The charter is also printed in Hertzlet, XII, 303,
British and Foreign State Papers, LXVI, 593. A translation is given
hereafter in Appendix E.

There is also a widely used edition of *Mixed Codes* published by the
Egyptian Government in 1917. An English translation of the *Codes*
was published in London in 1892. (*The Egyptian Codes,* Wm. Clowes
and Sons.) In the same year there was published in Cairo under the
title *La Législation Egyptienne Annotée,* an annotated edition of the
codes together with a collection of diplomatic documents relating to
the Mixed Courts. This volume is commonly referred to by the name
of its editor, Borelli Bey. It has long since been out of print.

The official reports of the *Decisions* of the Court of Appeals, so
far as they are marked for publication by the several presidents of
chambers, appear in the monthly *Bulletin de Législation et de Jurisprudence Egyptiennes* founded in 1889, a publication privately
owned, but under the patronage of the Court of Appeals, from which
it receives an annual appropriation. Up to the present time four
decennial index volumes have appeared. The judicial year 1929–30
comprises the forty-second volume. These reports also publish all laws
and decrees affecting the Mixed Courts as well as the more important
measures of general interest. Prior to the founding of the *Bulletin* the
decisions of the Court of Appeals were published in the *Recueil*

Officiel des Arrêts de la Cour d'Appel Mixte (R.O.). There is also a two-volume digest of the jurisprudence of the Mixed Courts, Lantz, *Repertoire,* covering the years 1894–1905.

A second and wholly separate legal enterprise is the monthly *Gazette des Tribunaux Mixtes d'Egypte,* now in its twentieth year, together with its supplementary publication, the triweekly *Journal des Tribunaux Mixtes,* published under the same editorial management by a small group of lawyers. These publications enjoy the patronage of the courts, and the *Journal* has been designated as one of the official newspapers for the publication of legal notices and advertisements.

The *Gazette* publishes legal articles, book reviews, and a digest of current decisions with head notes and annotations by the staff. It is a storehouse of legal discussion covering all important matters touching the recent history of the Mixed Courts. It ordinarily includes some thirty pages of reading matter. The reading matter includes editorials, signed articles on legal problems, a report of events of current legal interest, and a carefully prepared digest of current decisions, including those of the District Courts which are not otherwise published in printed form except so far as they occasionally appear in the European legal journals, notably the French *Revue de Droit Maritime,* in the case of important maritime decisions. The *Journal,* though similar in form to its sister publication (ten inches by twelve), contains usually some half a dozen pages of reading matter, supplemented ordinarily by twenty or thirty pages of legal notices. The *Journal* is distinguished by a lighter treatment of current legal topics. Its "imaginary conversations" are often both subtle and humorous, and its reports of leading decisions are frequently admirable both in legal analysis and literary skill. To complete the list of periodical literature, reference should be made to *L'Egypte Contemporaine,* a monthly review of twenty years standing, published by the Royal Society of Political Economy, Statistics, and Legislation. Almost every number of this review contains one or more articles of a legal character affecting the Mixed Courts. Most of the articles are in French, but articles in English appear occasionally. Subscription to the *Bulletin* (foreign) is two pounds sterling; to the *Gazette,* P.T. 150 ($7.50); with *Journal,* P.T. 250 ($12.50).

Among the many other official documents touching the Mixed Courts, mention may be specially made of the *Annual Reports* of the Judicial Advisers, a series of documents of the greatest interest which unfortunately was discontinued during the War. Many of these are still obtainable. See *Catalogue of Publications in Stores* (Government Press: Cairo, 1925), which gives list of reports available. The same catalogue, which may be obtained upon application to the Government Publications office, contains a list of many other available documents touching more or less directly the Mixed Courts as, for instance, certain of Lord Cromer's reports, the Government Budgets, various official compilations of laws, etc. The various public documents, blue-books, white-books, etc., of the several capitulatory Powers are a mine of historical interest. There is also published an annual report of the Procureur-Generals of the Mixed Courts, which contains statistical information regarding the work of the courts. Mention should be made also of the elaborate annual folio volume of some five hundred pages containing the budget of the Egyptian state, and of which extracts (1929–30) have been printed as an appendix to this volume. In 1914 the Department of Justice published an *Annuaire* reviewing, *inter alia*, the organization of the Mixed Courts.

II

COLLECTION OF TREATIES COVERING CAPITULATORY RIGHTS, ETC.

ARISTARCHI BEY: Législation Ottomane (Constantinople, 1874), 7 vols. A standard compilation of Turkish laws which contains a number of documents touching the capitulatory *régime* in Egypt.

EGYPT: Ministère des Affaires Etrangères. Recueil des Conventions et Protocoles relatifs à la Réforme Judiciaire (Cairo, 1891). A Government pamphlet of sixty-five pages containing the principal diplomatic documents exchanged with each of the several foreign powers relative to their acceptance of the *régime* of the Mixed Courts.

GATTESCHI: Manuale di Diritto Pubblico e Privato Ottomano, compilato dal Dotor Domenico Gatteschi (Alexandria, 1865). Contains the texts of the principal capitulations also of the decrees relating to the Mixed Commercial Tribunals which preceded the formation of the Mixed Courts.

PH. GELAT BEY: Répertoire Général Annoté de la Législation et de l'Administration Egyptienne (Alexandria, 1906). An extensive work devoted solely to Egypt and containing the French (and in some instances the English) text of the various Turkish Capitulations.

HERTSLET: Treaties in Force, by Sir Edward Hertslet (London). In this standard British compilation will be found (Volume II) the

English text of the British Capitulations as also (Volume XIV) the treaties and other engagements under which Great Britain accepted the *régime* of the Mixed Courts.

MOLLOY: Treaties, Conventions, International Acts, Protocols and Agreements between the United States and other Powers, compiled by William M. Molloy (Washington: Government Printing Office, Vols. I and II, 1910; Vol. III, 1913. This standard American compilation contains, under the title Ottoman Empire, pages 1318 *et seq.*, the Turkish Treaty of 1830, comprising American capitulatory rights in the Ottoman Empire (including Egypt) as well as subsequent treaties of closely related interest.

MOORE: International Law Digest (Washington: Government Printing Office). In Volume II, Chapter VII, of this great work, under the title "Exemptions from Territorial Jurisdiction," may be found (paragraph 286) a valuable compilation of official documents and diplomatic correspondence relating to the Mixed Courts in Egypt.

NORADOUNGHIAN: Actes Internationaux de l'Empire Ottoman, by Gabriel Effendi Noradounghian, Conseiller légiste à la Porte Ottomane (Paris, 1897). This excellent and elaborate compilation in four volumes contains the French text of all the more important Capitulations.

SUDAN: Ordinance promulgated by the Governor-General of the Sudan (Cairo, 1907). Contains the Anglo-Egyptian Agreement of 1889, for the administration of the Sudan, Article VIII of which excludes the jurisdiction of the Mixed Courts from that territory.

UNITED STATES FOREIGN RELATIONS: Papers Relating to the Foreign Relations of the United States (Washington: Government Printing Office). This series contains many documents touching the relations of the United States to the Mixed Courts at various stages of their history. It is particularly valuable in connection with the founding of the courts. See volumes covering period 1869–75. In Volume II, 1873, Part I, pages 1112 *et seq.*, will be found a translation of the Charter of the Mixed Courts.

UNITED STATES: Messages and Papers of the Presidents, 1789–1897, by Richardson. In Volume VII, pages 390–391 (edition of 1897), will be found the Presidential Proclamation of March 27, 1876, accepting the *régime* of the Mixed Courts, and suspending, *pro tanto,* the consular jurisdiction exercised in Egypt under the Act of June 22, 1860. (See Appendix H, *infra.*)

YOUNG: Corps de Droit Ottoman, par George Young, 2me Secrétaire de l'Ambassade d'Angleterre (Oxford: Clarendon Press, 1905),

7 vols. in French, Preface in English. This admirable compilation long since out of print, is a monument to British scholarship. Each chapter is prefaced by an important historical survey, and the whole is enriched by excellent annotations. In Volume I will be found a compilation of the laws touching judicial reform in Turkey and the gradual development of the Turkish Mixed Courts.

III

MISCELLANEOUS WORKS IN ENGLISH

BEER: African Questions at the Paris Peace Conference, by George Louis Beer, Chief of the Colonial Division of the American Delegation to Negotiate Peace (New York: Macmillan & Co., 1923). This carefully documented work published after the author's death is a model of thorough scholarship and a fitting memorial to the author's distinguished diplomatic service. Part IV, "Egyptian Problems," pages 287–409, contains an excellent short review of modern Egyptian history and a survey of the capitulatory system.

CHIROL: The Egyptian Problem, by Sir Valentine Chirol (Macmillan, 1921). This is one of the ablest of the many recent volumes on this general topic. While not discussing particularly the problems of justice, it contains many references to the Mixed Courts and gives an excellent historic background of the international situation.

COLVIN: The Making of Modern Egypt, by Sir Auckland Colvin, K.C.St., K.C.M.G., C.I.E., British Comptroller-General in Egypt (London, 1906). This volume contains, Chapter XVIII, a brief discussion of the abuses connected with the workings of the Consular Courts.

CROMER: Modern Egypt, by the Earl of Cromer (Macmillan & Co., 1908), 2 vols. This masterly work stands *facile princeps* among all works on Modern Egypt. Its chapters on "The Judicial System" (XLII), "European Privilege" (LII), and "Justice" (LVIII) review the capitulatory problem as it presented itself to England's great pro-consul.

DE LEON: The Khedives of Egypt, by Edwin de Leon, ex-American Agent and Consul-General in Egypt (London: Sampson Low, 1877). This readable volume contains a practically contemporary account of the early efforts at reform which preceded the inauguration of the Mixed Courts.

DICEY: The Egypt of the Future, by Edward Dicey, C.B. (Heinemann, 1907). This volume contains some interesting first-hand material relating to the Khedive Ismail and the founding of the Mixed Courts

ELGOOD: Egypt and the Army, by Lieut. Col. P. G. Elgood (Oxford University Press, 1924). A good survey of war-time Egypt. It discloses, better than any other authority, the causes which led to the consolidating of the nationalist spirit.

——: The Transit of Egypt (London: Edward Arnold & Co., 1928). A most important work. Contains an admirable survey of Egyptian history from the Persian conquest to the present day. Dispassionate and well written.

FARMAN: Egypt and Its Betrayal. An account of the country during the Periods of Ismail and Tewfik Pashas, and of How England Acquired a New Empire, by Hon. Elbert E. Farman, LL.D., Judge of the Alexandria District Court, formerly U.S. Consul-General, Cairo (New York: Grafton Press, 1908). Includes a short review of the organization of the Mixed Courts.

HALTON: An Elementary Treatise of the Egyptian Civil Codes, 1904 and 1911, by H. W. Halton, LL.D., Judge in the Native Court of Appeal, Cairo (Cairo: Imprimerie Nationale), 2 vols. An excellent survey of Egyptian civil law.

HARRISON: The Homely Diary of a Diplomat in the East, by Thos. Skelton Harrison, former American Diplomatic Agent, Cairo (Boston: Little, Brown & Co.). Contains many references to the Mixed Courts.

HINCKLEY: American Consular Jurisdiction in the Orient, by Frank E. Hinckley. Lowdermilk & Co., Washington, 1906. On pages 153–158 of this most useful volume will be found a short review of the Mixed Courts.

HOWELL: Egypt's Past, Present, and Future, by Hon. J. Morton Howell, M.D., LL.D., former Minister of the United States to Egypt (Dayton, Ohio: Service Publishing Co., 1929). This lively account of the author's six years diplomatic service in Egypt contains some interesting references to the Mixed Courts.

LOW: Egypt in Transition, by Sidney Low, with an introduction by Lord Cromer (Macmillan, 1914). This book contains several references, not always well founded, to the Mixed Courts.

MCCOAN: Egypt under Ismail, by J. Carlile McCoan (London: Chapman & Hall, 1889). See Chapter VIII for a brief reference to the early history of the Mixed Courts.

MILNER: England in Egypt, by Viscount Milner, G.C.B. (1892).

This classic work on Egypt (which had reached its thirteenth edition in 1920) is second only to that of Lord Cromer.

PENFIELD: Present Day Egypt, by Frederic Courtland Penfield, formerly United States Diplomatic Agent and Consul-General to Egypt (The Century Co., 1903). Illustrated. An excellent popular work which has passed through several editions.

SCOTT: The Law Affecting Foreigners in Egypt, by James Harry Scott, B.A., LL.M., Lecturer at the Khedivial School of Law, Cairo (Edinburgh: Wm. Green & Sons, 1907). A scholarly work of very special value in its review of the early development of the capitulatory system in Egypt.

TRAILL: England, Egypt, and the Sudan, by H. D. Traill, D.C.L. (E. P. Dutton & Co.). Contains a review of the founding of the Native Courts with some references to the Mixed Courts.

———: Lord Cromer. A Biography, by H. D. Traill (London: Bliss Sands & Co., 1897). Includes an interesting criticism of the decision of the Mixed Courts in the case of the Sudan Expedition, referred to in Chapter XIII hereof.

VAN DYCK: Report on the Capitulations of the Ottoman Empire, by Edward A. Van Dyck, Consular Clerk at Cairo (1881), 2 parts. Senate Executive Document No. 3, Forty-sixth Congress, special session; Senate Executive Document No. 87, Forty-seventh Congress, first session. A valuable document containing material not otherwise accessible.

WALTON: The Egyptian Law of Obligations, by Frederick Parker Walton, K.C. (Quebec), B.A. (Oxon.), LL.B. (Edin.), LL.D. (Aberdeen and McGill), Director of the Sultania School of Law, Cairo. Formerly Dean of the Law Faculty, McGill University, Montreal (London: Stevens & Sons, 1920), 2 vols. A scholarly and highly interesting survey of the Egyptian Law of Contracts, with special reference to its relation to French and English Law. Now in its second edition.

IV

MISCELLANEOUS WORKS TOUCHING THE MIXED
COURTS AND THE DEVELOPMENT OF THE
CAPITULATORY SYSTEM

ABD EL-FATTAH EL-SAYED BEY et MARC DESSERTEAUX: Traité Théorique et Pratique de Procédure Civile et Commerciale Egyptienne Spécialement devant les Tribunaux Mixtes (Dijon, 1926).

The first-named author is a member of the Court of Appeals. His French collaborator is a Professor of Civil Law at the University of Dijon. An excellent practical treatise on procedure before the Mixed Courts, with interesting comparisons with French law.

——: Traité Théorique et Pratique des Effets de Commerce (Dijon, 1928). A careful short review (pp. 210) of the law of commercial paper in Egypt.

Abou Haif: La Procédure Civile et Commerciale et l'Organisation Judiciaire en Egypte (Cairo, 1915).

Antoine Aziz: Le dossier égyptien (Alexandria, 1929). The most complete up-to-date collection of documents touching the political and capitulatory régime in Egypt (announced).

Artin Bey: La Propriété Foncière en Egypte, par Yacoub Artin Bey (Le Caire, 1883). A review of the land system in 1883.

Barakat Bey: Des Privilèges et Immunités dont jouissent les Etrangers en Egypte vis-à-vis des Autorités Locales, by M. Bahi-ed-Dine Barakat (Paris, 1912), p. 320. This work was a doctorial thesis presented to the Law School of the University of Montpellier by a jurist who now occupies a seat on the native Court of Appeals, and who was formerly a member of the Court of Appeals of the Mixed Courts. It contains one of the best surveys that exists of the development of the Capitulations in Egypt, and is enriched by an extensive bibliography.

Barkouky: Les Rapports du Pouvoir Judiciaire et du Pouvoir Exécutif en Egypte. Influence des Principes du Droit Français sur les Idées Orientales en Matière de Droit Public (2ᵐᵉ éd.; Paris: Dalloz, 1925) p. 171. An interesting survey of the relations between the judiciary and the executive in the Egyptian system.

Batcheller: Selected cases decided by George S. Batcheller in Summary Court, Cairo, 1898–1901. With introductory note in English (Cairo, 1902).

Benoit: Etude sur les Capitulations entre l'Empire Ottoman et la France et sur la Réforme Judiciaire en Egypte, par Auguste Benoit (Paris, 1890), p. 156. Contains a good brief review of the system as it existed in 1890.

Bestawros: Code Civil Egyptien Mixte Annoté, by Gabriel Bestawros, Avocat à la Cour. Vol. I, Articles 1–65 (Paris, Lib. Gen. de Droit et de Jurisprudence, 1929), p. 567. The first volume of a four-volume digest of decisions on the Civil Code. An admirable and much-needed work.

Blanchard: La théorie de l'acte de souveraineté et de l'acte d'administration en droit mixte égyptien (Bruxelles: Revue Droit International, 1908).

FARAG: Le Rôle des Tribunaux Mixtes et Indigènes d'Egypte en matière de Statut Personnel, by Wadie M. Farag, Docteur en Droit (Paris, 1926), p. 266. An excellent up-to-date review of the question of personal status in Egypt (Le Caire: Caraites et Rabinites, 1918).

FÉRAUD-GIRAUD: De la Juridiction Française dans les Echelles du Levant, by D. Féraud-Giraud (Paris, 1866), 2 vols. This book contains documents not to be found elsewhere, including copies of Rules for the Commercial Courts at Alexandria and Cairo, promulgated September 3, 1861, by Cherif-Pacha, President of the Egyptian Grand Council (p. 309), and the Rules of Procedure for the courts (p. 464).

GAVILLOT: Essai sur les Droits des Européens en Turquie et en Egypte, by J. C. Aristide Gavillot, Juge au Tribunal Mixte de Commerce du Caire (Paris, 1875).

GEORGE: La Responsabilité de l'Etat Egyptien à raison de l'exercise de la Puissance Publique, par Henri George Lyon (Paris: Paul Guenther, 1914), 2 vols.

GRANDMOULIN: Traité élémentaire de Droit Civil Egyptien, Indigène et Mixte, comparé avec le droit français, by Grandmoulin, 2 vols. Avocat du Gouvernement à la Cour d'Appel Mixte d'Alexandrie. Rennes, Libraire Thanoux, Rue Nationale, £2. A good general treatise on Egyptian Civil Law by a competent authority.

——: Droit Pénal Egyptien Indigène (Cairo, 1908), 2 vols., £2.

——: La Procédure Pénale Egyptienne (Cairo, 1910), £2.

HAZAN, A.: La banqueroute et son instruction (1929). Librairie Au Bon Livre, Ibrahimieh, Alexandrie. P.T. 65.

HERREROS: Les Tribunaux Mixtes d'Egypte, by Enrique Garcia de Herreros (Paris, 1914). A concise review of the Mixed Courts system as it existed in 1914, with many interesting commentaries. The author, at the time of the publication of the volume, was Judge in the District Courts and was later promoted to the bench of the Court of Appeals.

HEYLIGERS: L'Organisation des Tribunaux Mixtes d'Egypte, by Adrien Theodore-Louis-Allard Heyligers, Judge of the Alexandria District Court. Recueil des cours de l'Académie de Droit International, 1927. Librairie Hachette (Paris, 1928), II, 5–107. Six lectures delivered by one of the Dutch judges of the Alexandria District Court before the Academy of International Law at The Hague. The

lecturer enjoys a reputation as a spirited and graceful writer.
These lectures form the best extant short survey of the Mixed
Courts system.

HULTS: Eléments d'un Répertoire Alphabétique de Droit Civil
Egyptien. A digest of civil law, in both the Mixed and Native
Courts, by E. de Hults, Conseiller à la Cour d'Appel Indigène du
Caire (2d ed., 1926), I; (1927), II. Price P.T. 100 each.

JEHAY: De la Situation Légale des Sujets Ottomans non Mussulmans,
par le Comte F. Van den Steen de Jehay (Brussels, 1906). A good
review of the status of the religious communities in Turkey before
the War. On pages 220 *et seq.*, will be found the English text of the
charter accorded to the Protestant community in Turkey in 1850.

LAMBA: Droit Public et Administratif de l'Egypte, by Henri Lamba,
Professeur de Droit Administratif et de Législation Financière à
l'Ecole Khédiviale de Droit (Cairo, 1909). Contains a good summary of the Egyptian judicial machinery with some valuable notes
on the taxation of foreigners, etc.

——: De l'Evolution de la Condition Juridique des Européens en
Egypte (Paris, 1896).

——: Le Régime des Capitulations (Paris, 1898).

LIVRE D'OR: Memorial volume published on occasion of semicenten-
nial anniversary of the Mixed Courts (Alexandria, 1926). An invaluable compendium of material relating to the Mixed Courts,
profusely illustrated. £1.10.0.

MAAKAD, ADIB BEY, and CHARLES RUELENS: Notions Générales sur
les Juriditions Mixtes d'Egypte (2d ed.; Alexandria, 1925). A
valuable, practical compendium of the laws, rules, and orders touching the organization of the Mixed Courts and their procedure.
£1.10.0.

MANDLESTAM: La Justice Ottomane dans ses rapports avec les Puissances Etrangères, par André Mandlestam (Paris, 1908). An excellent work by a Russian Jurist of high authority in this field.

MASSAOUDA: Contribution à l'Etude du Wakf en Droit Egyptien, by
Abbas Yaphet Massaouda, Thèse pour le Doctorat, Université de
Paris (1925).

HASSAN MOHARREM: Modes de l'Acquisition de la Nationalité Egyptienne, Thèse pour le Doctorat, Université de Paris (1926).

MESSINA: Traité de Droit Civil Egyptien Mixte, par Salvatore Messina, Juge au Tribunal Mixte d'Alexandrie (1927), I; (1928), II;
(1930), III. The most exhaustive and scholarly volumes yet published on the law of the Mixed Courts. They form part of a pro-

jected eight-volume treatise, and include the substance of a series of admirable monographs on special topics which the author has published during the past four or five years. Price P.T. 150 each.

——: La Juridiction Administrative des Tribunaux Mixtes. A valuable monograph on the legal status of the Government in litigation before the Mixed Courts. Price P.T. 125 each.

PALAGI: La Loi Mixte sur la Procédure Civile et Commerciale, by Dario Palagi, former Bâtonnier of the Mixed Courts (Alexandria, 1924–1926), 3 vols. These volumes form part of a series of admirable annotated digests of the statute law and decisions of the Mixed Courts, of which others are noted below. Price for the series P.T. 280.

——: La Loi Mixte sur la Saisie Immobilière (Alexandria, 1930). Price P.T. 100.

——: La Loi Mixte sur les Procédures d'Exécution, sauf la Saisie Immobilière (Alexandria, 1924). Price P.T. 100.

——: Exposé Méthodique du système de la loi Egyptienne en Matière de Faillite, Concordat Préventif et Banqueroute (2me éd.; Alexandrie, 1928). Price P.T. 100.

——: Le Code de commerce mixte annoté, avec appendice (1929). Price P.T. 100.

——: Le Code de commerce maritime mixte annoté (1929). Price P.T. 100.

——: Quelques Observations en Matière de Compte-Courant. Price P.T. 20.

RAUSAS: Le Régime des Capitulations dans l'Empire Ottoman, by Pelissié du Rausas (Paris, 1902). (Out of print.) This standard work on the Capitulations, by the venerable director of the French Law School at Cairo, is the most frequently cited volume on problems of capitulatory law in Egypt.

SAYOUR HOMÈRE: Répertoire de la jurisprudence des appels sommaires (Alexandria, 1916). A digest of decisions in summary court cases. £1.5.0.

SIDAROUSS: Des Patriarcats dans l'Empire Ottoman et Spécialement en Egypte, by Sesostris Sidarouss (Paris, 1907). An excellent review of the legal status of the Non-Moslem Communities in Egypt, with valuable appendices.

SOUCAIL: Manuel de Droit Commercial Egyptien (2d ed.; Alexandria, 1922). An excellent small handbook of Egyptian Commercial Law as administered in the Mixed Courts.

VERCAMER: La Juridiction Mixte Egyptienne et ses Attributions Législatives, by Em. Vercamer, Conseiller à la Cour Mixte d'Alexandrie (Brussels, 1911). A carefully documented and authoritative review of the development of the legislative powers of the Mixed Courts up to the reform of 1911.

VROONEN : Traité Pratique de Droit Pénal et d'Instruction Criminelle, by Eugène Vroonen, Vice-President of the District Court, Mansourah (Alexandria, 1929). An excellent and complete up-to-date review of the criminal law and procedure of the Mixed Courts by a judge who has had extensive experience with the criminal courts. Price P.T. 150.

WATHELET: Problèmes politiques et législatifs de l'heure présente en Egypte, by Jules Wathelet, former legal adviser to the Egyptian Government. Revue de l'Université de Bruxelles (1929), No. 4. The best recent short review of the legislative problem in Egypt.

DE WEE: La Compétence des Juridictions Mixtes d'Egypte, by Maurice de Wee, Juge aux Tribunaux Mixtes (Brussels, 1926). £1.

ZOHNY: L'Article 11 du Règlement d'Organisation Judiciaire pour les Procès Mixtes en Egypte, by Abd-el-Salam Zohny, Avocat à la Cour, Docteur en Droit, Thèse pour le Doctorat, Université de Lyon, 1914 (Impr. A. Mulcey).

V

ARTICLES AND ADDRESSES IN ENGLISH RELATING TO THE MIXED COURTS OR TOUCHING VARIOUS PHASES OF THE CAPITULATORY PROBLEM IN EGYPT

BATCHELLER: "The International Law Courts of Egypt," by Hon. G. S. Batcheller, Judge of the District Court, Cairo, Albany Law Journal, I (1879), 289.

BRINTON: "The Mixed Courts of Egypt," by Jasper Y. Brinton, American Journal of International Law, Volume XX, No. 4, October, 1926.

BROWN : "The Capitulations," by Prof. Philip Marshall Brown, Foreign Affairs, June, 1923.

CRABITÉS: "The Courts of Egypt," by Pierre Crabités, Judge of the Cairo District Court, American Bar Association Journal, August, 1925.

——: "The Omnipotent Bar of Islam," American Bar Association Journal, December, 1927.

——: "Trustees for the Sphinx," North American Review, March, 1928.

——: "The Fiftieth Anniversary of the Mixed Tribunals of Egypt," Nineteenth Century and After, March, 1926.

——: "An American Discusses the Egyptian Problem," National Review, October, 1929.

CROMER: "The Capitulations in Egypt," by the Earl of Cromer, Nineteenth Century, July, 1913. Also published in Political and Literary Essays (1st series; London: Macmillan, 1913).

——: Introduction to Sidney Low's "Egypt in Transition" published in Political and Literary Essays (2d series, 1914).

——: "The Situation in Egypt," Address before the Eighty Club, December 15, 1908 (London: Macmillan, 1909).

HAYTER: "Recent Constitutional Developments in Egypt," by the late Sir William Hayter, K.B.E., formerly Legal Adviser to the Egyptian Government. Two lectures prepared for the Local Lectures Summer Meeting (Cambridge, 1924).

McILWRAITH: "The Mohammedan Law Courts of Egypt," by Sir Malcolm McIlwraith, K.C.N.G., late Judicial Adviser to the Egyptian Government, Nineteenth Century, October, 1916.

——: "Egypt in War Time," Fortnightly Review, August, 1917.

——: "The Declaration of a Protectorate in Egypt and Its Legal Effects," Journal of Comparative Legislation and International Law, XXXIX (1917), 238.

——: "The Egyptian Government and the Caisse de la Dette," ditto, I (O.S.), 386.

MORGAN: "The International Tribunals of Egypt," by Philip Hicky Morgan, Judge of the Alexandria District Court, Appleton's Journal, XXIV (1880), 242, 308.

RAVNDAL: "The Origin of the Capitulations and of the Consular Institution," by G. Bie Ravndal, Senate Document No. 348, Sixty-seventh Congress, first session. This is a most useful compilation and discussion of historical material relating to the capitulations by an authority on capitulatory law who was for many years America's Consul-General at Constantinople.

SILLEY: "The Egyptian Law Courts." Lecture, by Mr. Reginald Silley, a prominent member of the British bar in Egypt, Egyptian Gazette, March 10, 13, and 14, 1925.

——: "Law Reform in Egypt," ibid., November 24, 25, 26, 1925.

THAYER: "The Capitulations of the Ottoman Empire and the Question of Their Abrogation as It Affects the United States," by Lucius Ellsworth Thayer, American Journal of International Law, April, 1923.

B

JUSTICES OF THE COURT OF APPEALS
(April 1, 1930)

Date of commission

PRESIDENT

MICHAEL HANSSON	(Norway)	April	13, 1915

VICE-PRESIDENT

RALPH P. B. CATOR	(Great Britain)	November	7, 1916

ASSOCIATE JUSTICES (in the order of their seniority)

SOUBHI BEY GHALI	(Egypt)	April	27, 1914
MOUSTAPHA BEYRAM BEY	(Egypt)	June	19, 1919
RICHARD A. VAUX	(Great Britain)	December	15, 1920
ALEXANDER COCKBURN McBARNET	(Great Britain)	December	16, 1920
JASPER YEATES BRINTON	(United States)	October	31, 1921
GIOVANNI BAVIERA	(Italy)	March	6, 1922
BERNARD FAVENC	(France)	November	15, 1922
CONSTANT VAN ACKERE	(Belgium)	November	1, 1924
YUSSOUF ZULFICAR BEY	(Egypt)	December	14, 1926
CONSTANTIN VRYAKOS	(Greece)	November	1, 1927
MOHAMED CHOUCRI BEY	(Egypt)	December	3, 1927
RAOUL HOURIET	(Switzerland)	October	15, 1929
COUNT DE ANDINÓ	(Spain)	October	29, 1929
ABDEL FATTAH EL SAYED BEY	(Egypt)	November	16, 1929
ISKANDAR AZER BEY	(Egypt)	March	17, 1930

C

JUDGES OF THE DISTRICT COURTS
(April 1, 1930)

ALEXANDRIA
FOREIGN JUDGES

PRESIDENT

ERLING QVALE	(Norway)	October	16, 1913

VICE-PRESIDENT

MANOEL MONTEIRO	(Portugal)	October	5, 1916

Date of commission

ASSOCIATE JUDGES

PAUL BENEDUCCI	(Russia)	November	9, 1918
W. H. H. THORNE	(Great Britain)	February	1, 1919
SALVATORE MESSINA	(Italy)	March	13, 1920
JONKHEER VAN ASCH VAN WYCK	(Holland)	April	30, 1921
TH. HEYLIGERS	(Holland)	April	30, 1921
S. A. VLACHOS	(Greece)	May	30, 1921
A. C. M. VILLELA	(Portugal)	May	8, 1922
ROBERT L. HENRY	(United States)	November	10, 1924
EUGENE VROONEN	(Belgium)	May	1, 1926
NIELS DAHL	(Norway)	October	8, 1926
JOSEPH RICOL	(France)	March	10, 1929

NATIVE JUDGES

KELDANY ANTOINE BEY	December	16, 1920
MOHAMED TEWFIK ZAHER BEY	April	16, 1923
MOHAMED ALY ZAKI BEY	February	26, 1924
AHMED MAZLOUM BEY	October	2, 1924
MAHMOUD SADEK BEY	May	19, 1926
MAHMOUD BEY SAÏD	December	30, 1927

CAIRO
FOREIGN JUDGES

PRESIDENT

FRANCIS J. PETER	(Switzerland)	October	1, 1912

VICE-PRESIDENT

GEORGES MOLOSTVOFF	(Russia)	April	17, 1910

ASSOCIATE JUDGES

PIERRE CRABITÉS	(United States)	June	8, 1911
VINCENZO FALQUI-CAO	(Italy)	March	28, 1916
FRANCO GAUTERO	(Italy)	March	14, 1920
HANGS BECHMANN	(Denmark)	October	5, 1922
MAURICE DE WEE	(Belgium)	April	22, 1924
JOSÉ FESSER Y REINA	(Spain)	May	3, 1925
ARTHUR PRESTON	(Great Britain)	May	19, 1925
LEON BASSARD	(France)	November	14, 1925
JOHN BLAKE-REED	(Great Britain)	May	30, 1926

Date of commission

TORSTEN SALEN	(Sweden)	October	21, 1926
WALTHER UPPENKAMP	(Germany)	December	14, 1926
CHARLES PUECH	(France)	March	31, 1927
MURRAY GRAHAM	(Great Britain)	December	5, 1929
JULIAN M. WRIGHT	(United States)	January	15, 1930

NATIVE JUDGES

ZAKI GHALI BEY	March	9, 1922
MOUSTAPHA NEGUIB BEY	September	6, 1923
MOHAMED NEGUIB CHOUCRI	November	8, 1923
HASSAN KAMEL BEY	December	15, 1924
MOHAMED FOUAD HOSNI BEY	May	19, 1925
MOHAMED ONSY	December	19, 1926
YOUAKIM MIKHAIL BEY	December	3, 1927
MAHMOUD HASSAN BEY	February	10, 1929

MANSOURAH
FOREIGN JUDGES

PRESIDENT

ANTONIO PENNETTA	(Italy)	December	2, 1924

VICE-PRESIDENT

HUGO WICKSTROM	(Sweden)	December	1, 1926

ASSOCIATE JUDGES

DEMETRE SARSENTIS	(Greece)	November	1, 1927
ANDRÉ MAVRIS	(Greece)	April	25, 1929
JACQUES ACHILLE EEMAN	(Belgium)	April	25, 1929
CARL SEIDEUN LARSEN	(Denmark)	January	21, 1930

NATIVE JUDGES

SOLIMAN YOUSRI	May	13, 1929
MOUSTAPHA MOHARRAM MOUKHTAR BEY	August	27, 1929
AHMED SAROIT	March	18, 1930

(Appointment of a Spanish judge shortly expected)

D

FOREIGN PRESIDENTS OF THE COURT OF APPEALS

DR. ALOYSE LAPENNA	(Austria)	1875–1881
GIOVANNI GIACCONE	(Italy)	1881–1894
MAURICE BELLET	(France)	1894–1902
ANTOINE DE KORIZMICS	(Austria)	1902–1909
GUISEPPE MORIONDO	(Italy)	1909–1911
CHARLES GESCHER	(Germany)	1911–1914
LIONEL SANDARS	(England)	1914–1916
ALBERT DE SOUZA-LARCHER	(Portugal)	1916–1920
FRANCIS LALOË	(France)	1920–1922
ERNEST EEMAN	(Belgium)	1922–1924
NICOLAS CAMBAS	(Greece)	1924–1927
MICHAEL HANSSON	(Norway)	1927–

E

CHARTER OF THE MIXED COURTS

(RÈGLEMENT D'ORGANISATION JUDICIAIRE POUR LES PROCÈS MIXTES
EN ÉGYPTE)

(*Dates in parentheses are those at which articles have been amended*)

TITLE I

Jurisdiction in civil and commercial matters

CHAPTER I

Courts of First Instance and the Court of Appeals

I. Institution and composition

ARTICLE 1. There shall be established three District Courts of first instance, at Alexandria, Cairo and Mansourah. (1887.)

ART. 2. Each of these Courts shall be composed of seven judges, four foreigners and three natives. Judgments shall be given by three judges, of whom two shall be foreigners and one a native.

One of the foreign judges shall preside, with the title of Vice President. He shall be selected by a majority vote of the foreign and native members of the Court of Appeals, from an alphabetical list

APPENDICES   371

presented by the General Assembly of each District Court, and which
shall include five candidates in the case each of Alexandria and Cairo
and three candidates in the case of Mansourah. (1911, 1915.)

In commercial affairs the District Court shall add to its number
two merchants, one a native and one a foreigner, who shall enjoy the
right to vote, and who shall be chosen by election.

ART. 3. There shall be at Alexandria a Court of Appeals composed
of eleven justices, four natives and seven foreigners.

One of the foreign justices shall preside, with the title of Vice President.
He shall be designated by an absolute majority of both the
foreign and native members of the Court.

The opinions of the Court of Appeals shall be rendered by five
justices, of whom three shall be foreigners and two shall be natives.
(1911, 1915.)

ART. 4. The number of the judges of the Court of Appeals and of
the District Courts may be increased if, in the opinion of the Court
of Appeals, the necessity of the service requires it, but always without
altering the proportion established between the native and the
foreign judges.

In the meantime, in case of absence or disqualification at any one
time of two or more members of the Court of Appeals, or of the
District Courts, the President of the Court of Appeals may cause the
deficiency to be supplied, in the case of foreign judges, by their colleagues
from other District Courts or by the foreign justices of the
Court of Appeals. Whenever a justice of the Court of Appeals shall
be thus delegated to take part in the sessions of one of the District
Courts he shall preside over the Court.

ART. 5. The nomination and the choice of judges shall belong to
the Egyptian Government; but in order that it may be assured as to
the guarantees presented by the persons whom it may select, it shall
address itself unofficially to the Ministers of Justice abroad, and will
engage only persons who have received the approval and authorization
of their own Government.

ART. 6. There shall be in the Court of Appeals and in every District
Court a chief clerk and several sworn assistant clerks, who may act in
the chief clerk's place.

ART. 7. There shall also be in the Court of Appeals and in every
District Court, a sufficient number of sworn interpreters, as also the
necessary body of bailiffs, who shall be assigned to the hearings of
the Courts and who shall have charge of the service of writs and of
the execution of judgments.

Art. 8. The clerks, bailiffs and interpreters shall be in the first instance nominated by the Government, and in the case of the clerks they shall be chosen for the first time abroad, among ministerial officers who have performed, or among persons able to perform, the same functions abroad. The clerks, bailiffs and interpreters may be dismissed by the Court to which they are attached.

II. Jurisdiction

Art. 9. These Courts shall have exclusive jurisdiction over all litigation in civil and commercial matters between natives and foreigners and between foreigners of different nationalities, outside of the law of personal status.

They shall have jurisdiction over real estate actions between natives and foreigners or between foreigners of the same nationality or of different nationalities.

The Municipality of Alexandria, in its relations with natives, shall not be subject to the jurisdiction of the Mixed Courts. (1900.)

Art. 10. The Government, the Administrations, and the estates of His Highness the Khedive, and the members of his family, shall be subject to the jurisdiction of these Courts in litigation with foreigners.

Art. 11. The Courts may not give decisions affecting the ownership of the public domain.

They may not entertain jurisdiction over acts of sovereignty nor over measures taken by the Government in the execution of and in conformity with the laws and regulations of the public administration.

However, without being permitted to interpret an act of administration or to interfere with its execution, they shall have jurisdiction over all cases involving an infringement arising from such act of the vested rights of any foreigner, as recognized either by treaties, by laws or by contract. (1900.)

Art. 12. There shall not be submitted to these Courts any suits of foreigners against religious establishments, which shall involve the recovery of the possession of real estate actually in the possession of such establishments, but the Courts shall have jurisdiction over claims involving the question of legal ownership, no matter who the claimant or the defendant may be.

Art. 13. The sole fact that real estate has been mortgaged as security for debt to a foreigner shall render these Courts competent to decide on the validity of the mortgage and all its consequences so far as, and including, the forced sale of the property and the distribution of the proceeds.

ART. 14. The District Courts shall delegate one of their judges, who, acting as a justice of the peace, shall endeavor to conciliate parties and shall render judgment in cases where the amount involved does not exceed a figure to be fixed by the Code of Procedure.

III. Hearings

ART. 15. Hearings shall be public except in cases in which the Court, by a decision accompanied by a statement of reasons, shall order the clearing of the Court in the interests of morality and public order. The right of defense shall be free.

ART. 16. The judicial languages employed in the pleadings and in the preparation of documents and decisions are: Arabic, English, French and Italian. (1905.)

ART. 17. Only persons possessing a legal diploma shall be admitted to represent and defend persons before the Court of Appeals.

IV. Execution of judgments

ART. 18. The execution of judgments shall take place independently of any administrative, consular or other action, and upon the direct order of the Court. Execution shall be effected by the bailiffs of the Court with the assistance of the local authorities, if this assistance shall become necessary, but always without any administrative interference. However, the official charged with the execution of sentence by the Court shall be obliged to inform the consul of the day and the hour of the execution, and this under penalty of rendering the execution null and of rendering himself liable to damages. The consul so informed shall have the privilege of being present at the execution, but in case of his absence the execution will proceed.

V. Irremovability of judges. Promotion. Discipline

ART. 19. The judges who compose the Court of Appeals and the District Courts shall be irremovable. This irremovability shall last only during the five-year period. It shall become definitely established only after the completion of this trial period.

ART. 20. Judicial promotion and the transfer of judges from one Court to another shall take place only by their consent and on the vote of the Court of Appeals, after receiving advices from the other Courts who may be interested.

ART. 21. The holding of the office of judge, clerk, chief clerk, interpreter and bailiff shall be incompatible with the holding of any other salaried office and with the business of a merchant.

ART. 22. Judges shall receive no honorary or material distinctions from the Egyptian Government.

ART. 23. All the judges of the same category shall receive the same salary. The acceptance of any remuneration besides their salary or of an increase of salary or of valuable gifts, or of any other material advantages, shall involve for the judge concerned a forfeiture of his post and of his salary, without right to indemnity.

ART. 24. Discipline of the judges, officers of justice and of lawyers is reserved to the Court of Appeals. The disciplinary penalty to be applied in the case of judges for acts compromising their judicial honor or the independence of their vote, shall be their dismissal from office and the loss of salary, without right to indemnity.

The penalty applicable to lawyers for acts which compromise their honor shall be disbarment.

Decisions shall be rendered by the Court of Appeals in General Assembly by a majority of three-fourths of the justices present.

ART. 25. Any complaint presented to the Government by a member of the consular corps against the judges involving any matter of discipline, shall be referred to the Court of Appeals, which shall be required to examine the complaint.

CHAPTER II

The Parquet

ART. 26. A Parquet shall be established, at the head of which shall be a Procureur General.

ART. 27. The Procureur General shall have under his direction at the Court of Appeals and at the District Courts, a sufficient number of assistants for the conduct of trials and for the policing of the judicial sessions.

In the cases provided for in Chapter 9, Title 3, of the Penal Code, prosecution against a foreigner must first be authorized by a member of the Parquet of foreign nationality, or by a foreign judge who shall have been delegated for this duty by the Court of Appeals. (1906.)

ART. 28. The Procureur General may occupy his seat at the sessions of all the chambers of the Court of Appeals and of the Courts of First Instance, at all criminal sessions and at all General Assemblies of the Court of Appeals and of the District Courts.

ART. 29. The magistrates of the Parquet shall be removable from office and shall be appointed by His Highness the Khedive.

CHAPTER III

Special and Transitory Provisions

ART. 30. The right of peremptory challenge of judges, interpreters and of written translations shall be reserved to all the parties.

ART. 31. There shall be in every record office of the District Courts an employee of the Mehkemeh (Native Court), who will assist the clerk in respect of deeds of real estate, and of deeds establishing rights affecting real estate, and who shall make thereof a copy which he shall transmit to the Mehkemeh.

ART. 32. There shall also be at the Mehkemeh, clerks delegated by the clerk of the District Court, who shall transmit to him, in order to be recorded in the office of the recorder of mortgages, all acts of conveyance of real property, and acts creating mortgages upon real estate. These transmissions shall be made under the liability for the payment of damages and of disciplinary prosecution, but the failure of transmission shall not involve nullity of the deed.

ART. 33. Agreements, acts of gift and deeds constituting mortgages or conveyances of real property, when received by the clerk of the District Court, shall be considered as authenticated documents and their original shall be deposited in the clerical archives.

ART. 34. The new Courts in the exercise of their jurisdiction in civil and commercial matters, and within the limits of the jurisdiction conferred upon them in penal matters, shall apply the codes presented by Egypt to the Powers, and in case of silence, insufficiency, and obscurity of the law, the judge shall follow the principles of natural law and equity.

ART. 35. One month before the assembling of the new Courts, the Government will cause the codes to be published, and a copy of the same, in each of the judicial languages, shall be kept on deposit, until the beginning of the functioning of the Courts, in each moudirieh, at every consulate, and at each record office of the Court of Appeals and of the District Courts, which shall at all times preserve on record a copy of the same.

ART. 36. The Government will also publish the laws relating to the personal status of natives, a schedule of judicial fees, and the ordinances affecting the regime of lands, dykes and canals.

ART. 37. The Court of Appeals shall prepare the General Rules of

Court covering the policing of the trials, the discipline of the courts, officers of justice and of the bar, the duties of the attorneys representing the parties at the trials, the admission of indigent persons to the privilege of free legal aid, the exercise of the right of peremptory challenge and the procedure to be followed in case of equal division of votes touching a decision of the Court of Appeals. The project thus prepared shall be transmitted to the District Courts for their observations, and after a new deliberation of the Court of Appeals, which shall be final, shall be put in execution by decree of the Minister of Justice.

ART. 38. The various Courts in civil and commercial matters shall not assume jurisdiction over mixed litigation until one month after their establishment.

ART. 39. Cases already commenced before the consuls at the time of the inauguration of the Courts, shall be carried to final judgment in their original forum. Nevertheless, at the request of the parties litigant, and with the consent of all the interested parties, such cases may be referred to the new Courts.

ART. 40. The new laws and the new judicial organization shall have no retroactive effect.

TITLE II

Jurisdiction in penal matters (1900)

CHAPTER I

Police Courts, Misdemeanor Courts and the Court of Assizes

I. Composition of Courts

ARTICLE 1. The judge for the trial of police offenses in the case of foreigners shall be one of the foreign members of the District Court.

ART. 2. The Council Chamber, both for the case of misdemeanors and of felonies, shall be composed of three judges of the District Court, of whom one shall be a native and two shall be foreigners. (1900.)

ART. 3. The Misdemeanor Court shall be composed of three judges of the District Court, including one native and two foreigners, and of four foreign assessors, if the accused shall be a foreigner.

If, however, the accused shall be a native, or if the prosecution shall include both foreigners and natives, all the assessors shall be native. (1906.)

Art. 4. The Court of Assizes shall be composed of three justices of the Court of Appeals, including one native and two foreigners.

The twelve jurors shall be foreigners, if the accused is a foreigner. If the accused is a native, or if the prosecution is directed against foreigners and natives, half of the jury shall be native.

Half of the assessors and jurors shall belong to the nationality of the accused, if he shall make such request. In the event that the list of jurors or assessors of the nationality of the accused shall be insufficient, the latter shall designate the nationality from which shall be chosen the jurors necessary to complete the required number. (1906.)

Art. 5. When there are several accused, each one shall have the right to demand an equal number of assessors or of jurors of his nationality without, however, increasing the total number, and subject to an appeal to lot to determine which of the accused, by reason of the limit in number, will be deprived of exercising this right.

II. Jurisdiction

Art. 6. There shall be submitted to the jurisdiction of the Mixed Courts:

1. Prosecutions for police offenses committed by foreigners.

2. Prosecutions against principals or accomplices in the case of misdemeanors specified in Chapter 9, Title 3, of the Penal Code, covering mixed bankruptcies.

3. Prosecutions against the principals and accomplices in case of the felonies and misdemeanors hereafter specified. (1900.)

Art. 7. Felonies and offenses committed directly against the judges, the jury and the officers of justice, in the performance of or on the occasion of the performance of their duties, viz.:

a. Contempts by gestures, words or threats.

b. Slanders and abuse, whether committed in the presence of the judge, the jury, or of an officer of justice, or whether committed within the judicial precincts or published by placards, writings, prints, engravings, or emblems.

c. Acts of violence against their person, including blows, wounds and homicide, with or without premeditation.

d. Acts of violence performed against them, or threats made against them in order to secure the performance of an unjust or illegal act, or the abstaining from a just and legal one.

e. Abuse by a public functionary of his authority against them committed with the same purpose.

f. Attempts at corruption exercised directly against them.

g. Recommendations made to a judge by a public functionary in favor of one of the parties.

ART. 8. Felonies and offenses aimed directly at the execution of the judgments and decrees of justice, viz.:

a. Attacks and resistance with violence or assault against the judges while in the performance of their duties, or against officers of justice while preparing documents or lawfully aiding in the execution of the judgments or decrees of justice, or against depositaries or the agents of the police force charged with rendering assistance in such execution.

b. Abuse of authority by a public functionary in order to prevent such execution.

c. Larceny of judicial documents with the same object.

d. Breaking of seals affixed by judicial authority; destroying goods seized by virtue of an ordinance or a judgment.

e. Escape of prisoners detained by virtue of a decree or a judgment, and all acts which directly procured such escape.

f. Concealment of prisoners who have escaped, in the cases mentioned.

ART. 9. Felonies and offenses chargeable against judges, jurors and officers of justice, when they shall be accused of having committed them while in the performance of their duties, or through an abuse of their powers, viz.:

In addition to the ordinary felonies and offenses which may be imputed to them in those circumstances, the special crimes and offenses are:

a. Unjust judgment given by favor or enmity. b. Corruption. c. Concealing attempts at corruption. d. Denial of justice. e. Violence exercised against private individuals. f. Violation of residence without the legal formalities. g. Extortions. h. Embezzlement of the public funds. i. Illegal arrests. j. Forgery of judgments and decrees.

ART. 10. The preceding provisions shall include, under the designation of officers of justice, the clerks, the sworn assistant clerks, the interpreters attached to the Courts and the titulary tipstaffs, but not the persons who may happen to have been incidentally and specially designated, by delegation of the Court, for the service of a document or of a bailiff's writ.

CHAPTER II

Provisions Derogating from the Code of Criminal Procedure (1906)

I. Prosecution

ART. 11. When a member of the consular corps shall make complaint of any unlawful act committed by a judge or an officer of justice, the government shall give the necessary orders to the Public Ministry, which shall be required to follow up the complaint.

ART. 12. All prosecutions for crimes and misdemeanors shall form the subject of an investigation, the results of which shall be submitted to the Council Chamber.

ART. 13. The consul of the accused shall, without delay, be informed of any prosecution for crimes and offenses commenced against such national.

II. The Preliminary Investigation

ART. 14. The preliminary investigation, as well as the arguments, shall be conducted in that one of the judicial languages with which the accused is acquainted.

ART. 15. Every preliminary investigation against a foreigner, as well as the direction of the arguments at the trial, shall be conducted by a foreign judge both in police cases as well as in cases of misdemeanors and felonies.

ART. 16. If the person accused of a crime or misdemeanor has no lawyer, one shall be appointed by the Court at the opening of the investigation, and this under penalty of nullity of the proceedings.

ART. 17. Until it is ascertained that there exist in Egypt adequate places of detention, accused persons under arrest shall be delivered to the consul immediately after the examination and within twenty-four hours after the arrest, unless the consul authorizes detention in the government prison.

ART. 18. The witness who shall refuse to testify, either before the examining judge or before a Court, shall be subject to imprisonment of from one week to one month in cases of misdemeanors, and not exceeding three months in cases of felony and in any case to a fine of from 100 to 4000 Egyptian piastres. These penalties shall be pronounced, as the case may require, either by the District Court or by the Court of Appeals.

ART. 19. The only witnesses who may be challenged are those in direct line of ascent and descent, and the brothers and sisters of the accused, or his kindred persons connected with him by marriage to the same degrees, and his or her husband or wife, even if divorced, provided that the hearing of the testimony of such persons shall not involve the nullity of the proceedings, if neither the prosecuting officer nor the civil prosecutor nor the accused shall have challenged them.

ART. 20. When, in the course of an investigation, it shall be found necessary to make a domiciliary visit, the consul of the accused shall be informed. A procès-verbal shall be drawn up covering the notice given to the consul. Copy of this procès-verbal shall be left at the consulate at the time of the notice.

ART. 21. Except in the case of flagrant délit or a call for help from within, no domicile may be entered during the night except in the presence of the consul or of his delegate, provided that the consul has not authorized such visit without his presence.

III. Settlement of questions of jurisdiction in cases of conflict

ART. 22. Three days before the meeting of the Council Chamber communication of the record of the investigation shall be made to the consul or to his delegate.

Copies of documents demanded by the consul must be delivered to him, under penalty of nullity.

ART. 23. If, upon receiving communication of the documents, the consul contends that the affair belongs to his jurisdiction and that it should be referred to his Consular Court, the question of jurisdiction, if contested by the Mixed Court, shall be submitted to the arbitration of a board composed of two judges of the District Courts or of the Court of Appeals, selected by the President of the Court of Appeals, and of two consuls chosen by the consul of the accused.

ART. 24. When the examining judge and the consul shall conduct at the same time an investigation into the same case, if one or the other of them does not think proper to concede his lack of jurisdiction, a Council of Arbitration shall be convened in order to settle the difference, on the demand of one of the parties.

It shall be understood that such conflict can never be raised by the examining judge in the case of an ordinary felony or misdemeanor; moreover the felony or the misdemeanor which he shall allege to have been committed, shall be described in the indictment before him in conformity with the aforesaid categories of criminal acts, jurisdiction over which has been conferred upon the new Courts. Finally, if the judge or officer of justice injured has made his original charge before the Consular Court, such Court shall pass upon the charge and no question of conflict shall be allowed.

ART. 25. The Court which, after the aforesaid formalities have been complied with, shall remain in charge of the affair, shall have final jurisdiction in the case and may not thereafter be declared incompetent.

IV. *Trial before the Court of Assizes*

ART. 26. Before the Court of Assizes, when the pleadings shall be closed and the questions to be presented to the jury shall be determined, the President shall sum up the case and review the principal evidence for or against the accused.

V. *Of Appeal and of Review of Sentences on Questions of Law*

ART. 27. Appeals from convictions, when allowed in cases of simple police, will be brought before the Court of Misdemeanors.

ART. 28. A review on the law, in case it is authorized by the code of criminal procedure against convictions in penal matters, shall be brought before the Court of Appeals composed as in the case of civil matters. Justices of the Court of Appeals who shall have sat in the Court of Assizes, may not hear appeals from the decision of the Court.

VI. *Selection of jurors and choice of assessors*

ART. 29. The list of the jurors of foreign nationality will be drawn up annually by the consular corps.

To that effect every consul will furnish the Dean of the consular body a list of his countrymen fulfilling the conditions required for jurors. Jurors must be thirty years of age and must have resided at least one year in Egypt.

ART. 30. The final list will be made by the consular corps from the aforesaid several lists, after a process of elimination, until the total required number is obtained, not exceeding two hundred and fifty.

ART. 31. The maximum number of jurors of each nationality shall be thirty and the minimum eighteen, provided in the latter case that the composition of the particular national colony makes this possible.

ART. 32. The assessors, in cases of misdemeanors, shall be chosen by the consular body from the jury list.

ART. 33. The minimum number of assessors shall be six and the maximum twelve.

ART. 34. When a misdemeanor is to be tried in a town where there is not a sufficient number of foreign assessors, the Court of Appeals will designate the assessors from the neighboring District Court, who shall be required to serve.

ART. 35. Assessors and jurors who refuse to appear to perform their duties, shall be sentenced by the District Court or by the Court of Appeals, as the case may be, to a fine of from 200 to 4000 Egyptian piastres, unless they shall show lawful excuse for their absence.

VII. Execution of sentences

ART. 36. Until it is ascertained that an adequate supply of places of detention actually exists in Egypt, persons condemned to imprisonment shall be detained in the consular prison if the consul so request.

ART. 37. The consul whose subject undergoes his punishment in the establishments of the Egyptian Government shall have the right to visit the jails and satisfy himself as to their condition.

ART. 38. In case of conviction of capital punishment, the representatives of the Powers will have the right to assume custody of their subject. To that effect a sufficient delay must intervene between the sentence and its execution in order to give to the representatives time to express their intentions in the case.

TITLE III

I. Special Disposition

ART. 39. There will be established at the new Courts a sufficient number of agents, chosen by the Courts themselves, to assist, as need may be, the judges and the officers of justice in their duties, reserving always to the Courts and to the officers of justice the right to invoke the aid of any agent of the police force in case of flagrant délit or where there is immediate danger in delay.

II. Final Disposition

ART. 40. During the five year period no change shall take place in the system adopted. After this period, if experience has not confirmed the practical usefulness of the judicial reform, the Powers shall have the right either to return to the old order of things, or to negotiate other arrangements with the Egyptian Government.

F

DECREE OF JANUARY 31, 1889, CONFERRING LEGISLA-
TIVE POWERS ON GENERAL ASSEMBLY
NOUS, KHEDIVE D'EGYPTE

Vu Notre Décret, en date de ce jour, portant prorogation des Tribunaux Egyptiens Mixtes;

Sur la proposition de Nos Ministres de l'Intérieur et de la Justice et l'avis conformé de Notre Conseil des Ministres;

Avec l'assentiment des Puissances mentionnées dans Notre Décret susvisé;

DÉCRETONS:
Art. 1.

A partir du 1 février 1889, et sauf la disposition contenue dans l'art. 2 de Notre Décret susvisé, les Tribunaux Egyptiens Mixtes appliqueront les ordonnances actuellement en vigueur ou qui seront édictées à l'avenir par Notre Gouvernement, concernant le régime des terres, digues et canaux; la conservation des antiquités; la voirie (Tanzim); l'hygiène et la salubrité publiques; la police des établissements publics, tels que: hôtels, cafés, maisons meublées, cabarets, maisons de tolérance, etc.; l'introduction, la vente et le port d'armes et de matières explosibles ou dangereuses; le droit de chasse; le règlement des voitures et autres moyens de transport; la police des ports de navigations et des ponts; la mendicité, le vagabondage, le colportage, etc.; les éstablissements incommodes, insalubres et dangereux et, en général, tous règlements permanents et généraux de police et de sûreté publique.

Art. 2.

Les ordonnances à édicter en ces matières seront promulguées à la suite d'une délibération de l'Assemblée Générale de la Cour qui se bornera à s'assurer:

1) que les lois et règlements proposés sont communs à tous les habitants du territoire sans distinction;
2) qu'ils ne contiennent aucune disposition contraire au texte des Traités et Conventions et, enfin, que dans leurs dispositions ils ne contiennent aucune peine supérieure aux peines de simple police.

Art. 3.

Nos Ministres de l'Intérieur et de la Justice sont chargés de l'exécution du présent Décret.

G

LAW OF NOVEMBER 11, 1911 (AMENDING ART. 12 CIVIL CODE) CREATING EXISTING LEGISLATIVE ASSEMBLY OF COURT OF APPEALS

Les additions et modifications à la législation mixte seront édictées sur l'initiative du Ministère de la Justice, à la suite et en conformité d'une délibération de l'Assemblée Générale de la Cour d'Appel Mixte à laquelle sera appelé le juge le plus ancien de chaque nationalité dont le Gouvernement a adhéré à la Réforme Judiciaire de 1875, et qui n'est pas représentée par un conseiller à la Cour.

L'Assemblée ne sera valablement constituée que par la présence d'au moins quinze de ses membres.

Tout conseiller à la Cour dont l'absence ou l'empêchement est constaté en vertu d'un règlement intérieur à élaborer par l'Assemblée Générale de la Cour en séance ordinaire, sera remplacé par le juge le plus ancien de la même nationalité. Le juge le plus ancien absent ou empêché dans les mêmes conditions sera remplacé par le juge subséquent de la même nationalité.

La délibération devra avoir été prise à la majorité des deux tiers des membres présents.

Les projets de loi ainsi approuvés ne peuvent être promulgués que trois mois après leur approbation.

A la demande d'une ou de plusieurs Puissances, formulée au cours de ce délai, ils seront à l'expiration dudit délai, soumis à une nouvelle délibération. A la suite de cette nouvelle délibération, le projet de loi qui aura réuni la majorité des voix requise pourra être promulgué sans autre formalité ni délai.

L'Assemblée Générale de la Cour en séance ordinaire pourra saisir le Ministre de la Justice de propositions de réformes en matière de législation mixte.

Toutefois, il ne pourra être apporté en vertu de cet article aucune modification ni addition au Règlement d'Organisation Judiciaire.

Les lois ainsi préparées entreront en vigueur par la simple publication au "Journal Officiel."

A défaut de publication dans un délai de trois mois à partir du moment où cette publication peut avoir lieu, le projet de loi sera considéré comme abandonné et ne pourra être repris qu'en se conformant à nouveau aux dispositions du présent article.

H

THE UNITED STATES AND THE MIXED COURTS

It has sufficiently appeared, from our story of the founding of the courts, that the long and complicated negotiations which preceded their formation were carried on not so much with a group as with a large number of individual Powers. Each Power had to be separately convinced and with each there were conducted independent *pourparlers* covering every phase of the long struggle. The history of the campaign is thus recorded in some fourteen separate collections of diplomatic correspondence, much of it now inaccessible. Many important documents remained in the archives at Constantinople—and many others doubtless have long since disappeared. In some cases, however, it is still possible to follow in official documents the story of the individual negotiations and among these is the case of the United States, which from the outset gave its support to the new project. The record of these negotiations holds some added interest through the fact that during much of this period the United States was represented at the Ottoman Porte by one of that small but distinguished group of author-diplomats which has shed so much lustre on American diplomatic history.

By the irony of fate the first knowledge of the projected judicial reform in Egypt received by the American Government was in the form of an appeal to the United States to lend its influence to prevent the realization of the project. According to a letter addressed on December 22, 1867, to the American Secretary of State, the Government of Greece was of opinion "that so important a modification, and one touching so nearly the rights of foreigners in Egypt, seemed to be premature, and that too much ignorance, too much fanaticism, and abuses too inveterate, obtained as yet in the indigenous element for it to be called to exercise high judiciary functions." The problem as to the language to be used, also troubled the Greek Government: "Another question is, what language is to be preferred in these Tribunals. The Arabic is not understood by the Christians and there is no reason for one of the European idioms to be favored more than another."

The reply of the United States to this protest was noncommittal. "The questions which it discusses will receive due attention at my hands should they hereafter come to the attention of this Department," was the laconic response of the Secretary of State. A week later, however, in writing to the consul-general at Alexandria, the Secretary gave an intimation as to the future attitude of the United States toward the project. Replying to a dispatch from the consul advising him of the existence of Nubar Pasha's project, as developed during the summer of 1867, he writes:

The United States, owing to their remoteness from Egypt have less direct interest in the question than the European Christian Powers. They have also, perhaps, more confidence in the safety and success of government reform, even in those countries which have not been completely administered within the range of international law and established by Christian nations.

The Secretary, therefore, directs the Consul-General to keep him fully informed as to any propositions presented by the Egyptian Government "together with your own opinions concerning the probable operation and results of such a change as the Egyptian Government desires."

At about this time there was communicated to the United States Government the copy of a letter addressed by Lord Stanley, the British Minister, to the British Consul-General in Egypt, and supporting in general terms the idea of the reform. One phrase of this letter recalls concisely a notable tradition of British diplomacy: "You will say, however, that Her Majesty's Government consider that practical results, even though they may fall short of theoretical perfection, are principally to be aimed at. . . ."

A few months later, however, it appears that Lord Stanley was somewhat less enthusiastic as to the outcome of the new project. Reporting a conversation with him in London, in May, 1868, the United States Ambassador advises the Secretary of State that "his Lordship expressed great doubt whether anything was likely to come of the matter. Neither was he disposed to think the evils of the present system so serious as they had been represented."

The request of the Secretary of State to be kept advised by our consul-general of all developments was not neglected. On February 29, 1868, the consul makes an exhaustive and favorable report to our Government, forwarding at the same time translations of the celebrated report of Nubar Pasha to the Egyptian Viceroy, which was the starting point of the reforms. This had been communicated to him by order of the Viceroy, who had personally expressed the hope that the United States would be represented in any conference which might possibly be held to consider the problem. The consul's letter contains an interesting reference to the opposition generally shown to the scheme, by foreigners in Egypt, and only serves to emphasize the credit due to those who carried it through to success in the face of the most formidable obstacles:

Mr. Rangabé has told you of the dislike with which the scheme was received by the Greek community here, and it is proper that I should state that the same feeling of dislike was general among Europeans. The English newspapers were invited by correspondents resident in Egypt to oppose the plan, and to criticize what was supposed to be Lord Stanley's support of it; but this feeling of opposition, although almost universal, would no doubt be considerably mitigated if the scheme were better understood.

Analyzing the plan presented by Nubar Pasha, the consul put his finger on the central point of the problem—the execution of judgments. He points out the grave defect in the working of the existing "commercial courts" due to the fact that when judgments are given against natives there is no sure means of securing judgment, and adds these misgivings:

On the other hand, I doubt whether the large European communities would willingly accept at present a measure which should arm any tribunal of the Egyptian Government, however composed, with power to touch the persons or property of Europeans otherwise than through their respective Consulates.

As it happened, this subject proved to be the storm center of the subsequent deliberations, though fortunately the difficulty proved not to be insurmountable. Fearing, however, that the obstacle might prove fatal to the plan, the consul carefully developed, for the consideration of his own government, an alternative plan looking to the immediate creation by the Egyptian Government, without further consultation with other governments, of a special court of five judges, of whom two or three should be Europeans, and who should be assured of appointments for at least a certain term of years.

Let this tribunal [he suggested] have jurisdiction over all cases brought by foreigners against the Egyptian Government or against native subjects. Let its decisions be promptly and fully executed by the Egyptian Government. If this is fairly done, the tribunal would at once become among Franks (foreigners), the most popular institution in Egypt. But give also to this tribunal jurisdiction over cases between subjects of different nationalities when the parties so consented. Its jurisdiction would be eagerly accepted, and in process of time it could be made compulsory.

In another letter sent at the same time, Mr. Hale observes:

I have reason to believe that it would be agreeable to the English if we proposed something like what I have ventured to suggest for your consideration, and you will see by the paper enclosed that it does not differ widely from the French conclusions. I am sorry I cannot tell you by this post how the Viceroy would like it. I suspect, however, he would prefer almost anything to a total failure of his plan.

His government's reply to Mr. Hale's proposal was friendly but reserved: "The suggestions which you have made," writes the Secretary of State in April, 1868, "seem to be judicious, but I am not able at present to give you any definite instructions upon the subject."

In due course the assembling of a commission was determined upon and Mr. Hale was appointed as the representative of the United States, and as such took an active part in the discussions. An interesting reference to his work is to be found in a letter written from Constantinople in 1873 by the United States Minister, urging our government to give its immediate adherence to the final project. This letter uses as an argument for such action—"the warmth with which the gentleman who was then United States Consul General in Egypt (Mr. Hale) entered into the original scheme, almost shaping by his counsels the work of the first Commission."

This high appreciation finds confirmation in the skilful arguments with which Mr. Hale accompanied the final report of the commission, when forwarding it to Washington. One or two of his observations are worth referring to.

After explaining that two questions still remained to be decided, viz., whether the jurisdiction of the new courts should extend to foreigners of different nationality and whether it should include criminal cases, Mr. Hale leaves his own convictions in no doubt: "My opinion is in favor of the more extended jurisdiction in both cases."

Upon the second of these questions Mr. Hale's letter furthermore furnishes an eloquent denunciation of the existing system of the Consular Courts as a medium of enforcing criminal justice in Egypt: "The condition of justice in the Consular Courts in all affairs between local subjects and foreigners would be laughable if it were not shameful."

That portion of Mr. Hale's observations which refer to the immediate interest of Americans in Egypt is equally true today:

We have in Egypt but a small permanent colony of resident Americans, and a considerable number of visitors. Our colony is naturally almost exclusively composed of honest and law-abiding persons. To such persons it makes very little difference by what Court, being an honest Court, they may be tried, in the unlikely case of an allegation of their wrongdoing; but it is of course of great consequence to them that they shall be assured that persons of whatever nationality who may attempt to wrong them, shall not go unpunished.

The letter concludes with a direct plea for American support:

If therefore you should decide to support the plan of the Government as now modified,—I think that you will not affect injuriously the interests of citizens of the United States resident or travelling in Egypt, while you will afford a welcome encouragment of the Khedive in his efforts to effect a desirable reform in a matter of admitted abuse.

That the consul's advocacy of the reform was not in vain is evidenced from the following passage from the reply which he promptly received from Washington, the substance of the reply having indeed been communicated to him by telegraph:

The views expressed by you have the general approbation of this Department. It has great satisfaction in recognizing in the propositions of the Egyptian Government an earnest and intelligent effort to put the administration of Justice within its territory upon a basis beneficial and satisfactory as well to foreign residents as to its own subjects.

Shortly subsequent to this, Mr. Hale's place as consul-general was taken by a Mr. Beardsley, who continued to fight for the adoption of the reform with the same interest as his predecessor. Writing to Washington in 1873, he pleaded: "The speedy acceptance of the Judiciary Reform now under consideration by all the Powers would be an act of mercy to Egypt."

Nor is his picture of the evils of the existing system of consular justice less eloquent than that of his predecessor.

I do not think it is a very serious reflection on the Consular Corps of Egypt to say that as a rule Justice is not administered in their Courts. Legal attainments are not always made a test of appointment to these positions and even the best legal minds might be confused with sixteen different Codes to deal with. Besides, several of the Consuls-General in Egypt are not natives of the countries they represent and have a very imperfect knowledge of their law. From this state of things results legal chaos and the consular tribunals are choked with thousands of cases which, owing to disputed jurisdiction, unjust decisions, lack of executive power, etc., can never be settled until some reform is introduced.

At this point in the history of the reform, the change of the scene of negotiations to Constantinople resulted in transferring to the American Minister at Constantinople the responsibility for presenting the case of the reform to his home government. This important office was at that time held by the talented diplomat to whom reference has already been made, Mr. George H. Boker of Philadelphia. Mr. Boker proceeded to handle the situation with vigor and skill, and to his gifted pen we owe some of the most interesting commentaries on the events of this crowded period. Previously even to this juncture of affairs he had expressed himself in no uncertain terms as to "The Reform."

It seems to be unjust [writes the Minister on October 1, 1872] that there should be any hesitation to permit the Egyptians to take that first step towards self-government which will be the result of an independent judiciary—an institution which forms the basis of human freedom in all civilized countries, and which assures to the citizens liberty and equality in precise proportion to the perfection of their legal systems. . . .

My own opinion is that sooner or later all the great Powers will agree to permit the Egyptian Government to put its legal project into practice, to the great future benefit of a thriving and friendly country, which has so long been restrained in its just political aspirations by the irresistible pressure of foreign nations. Egypt is in a way to be coddled to death, or to lose everything like national character by the over-solicitous nursing of her too affectionate friends. The Suez Canal has become another bond of closer union and increased care, and the great Powers vie with one another, and amicably wrangle over their protégé, in order to induce her to adopt every policy that may be imposed, rather than one which she may evolve from her own consciousness of her political and her domestic needs.

It should be a source of sincere satisfaction to us if the Government of the United States may be the first to recognize the justice of the Egyptian project, and to sanction so far as we may, the trial of the system on the terms laid down in the enclosed protocol. Our example would have great influence in bringing about a successful issue to the negotiations with the other great Powers. As the matter now stands, it is promised that Italy will shortly agree to the proposition; England is favorable but awaits the action of the other Powers; Russia will give in her adhesion as soon as she is satisfied as to what the others will do; Germany and Austria will follow the lead of Russia; France will probably hang back until the last; and as to the opinions and actions of the smaller Powers, they are of no importance, as the system will go into operation as soon as the consent of the great Powers can be settled. . . . I therefore recommend that the Government of the United States should be the first to do simple justice toward our ancient ally.

In the following April (1873) Mr. Boker reports again on the project, analyzing carefully its relation to existing treaty rights and presenting a practical suggestion as to the kind of constitutional action most desirable in order to enable the United States to adhere to the reform without permanently abandoning her treaty rights. He concludes with this final argument in favor of the plan:

There seems to be little real danger in conceding to the Egyptians the privilege of trying their system since, as they well know, should it prove a failure in practice, the strong hand of the Great Powers will be laid upon it, and the old order of things will be reestablished, long before the probational five years, or any considerable part of them, shall have elapsed.

Another letter of about the same date contains these interesting observations: "The Khedive has had hard and up-hill work with his darling project. . . . Among despotic governments he has met with the opposition which he expected."

On May 29, 1873, Mr. Boker communicated to Washington a copy of a letter addressed by the British Ambassador, Sir Henry Elliott, to the Egyptian Minister of Foreign Affairs formally accepting on the part of Great Britain the plan of the proposed judicial reform, subject, however, to the condition "of avoiding giving any preponderance to one nationality over another in the selection of the judges, either in constituting the tribunal or in supplying the vacancies that may from time to time occur."[1]

In August Mr. Boker again urges the project, this time calling particular attention to absence of any serious risk to foreign interests if the reform were accepted.

"Bound as the Khedive now is, by restraining agreements, there can be but little danger in permitting him to act as he can in his fettered condition, for the whole future of the question of judicial reform is safely lodged in other hands."

The Minister concludes his appeal with a telling reference to the liberal traditions of his country in its dealings with small powers,

[1] See chap. v, *supra.*

adding that the failure of the United States to be the *first* to join the reform had been a source of astonishment and chagrin to the Khedive which was more to be regretted than to be wondered at "considering the proverbial liberality of our Government towards all nations, particularly towards the weak and oppressed, and the alacrity with which we have conceded to communities of men the right of self-government, and all the minor rights which necessarily spring from that great principle."

The delay of which Mr. Boker complained, however, was not due to any indifference on the part of his home government, but merely to the necessity, under our constitutional system, of invoking the aid of Congress to bring about the necessary suspension of consular jurisdiction, which had been, if not established, at least definitely confirmed and defined, by an act of Congress and whose partial suspension it was believed should be effected under the same authority. In his Annual Message in December, 1873, President Grant urged Congress to give the matter its early attention.[2] That body lost no time in acting and the necessary law was adopted March 23, 1874, authorizing the President to suspend the operations of the law of 1860 relating to consular jurisdiction, as soon as he had received satisfactory information of the organization of the new tribunals on a basis likely to secure to Americans in Egypt "the same impartial justice" which they had enjoyed under the Consular Courts. The adoption of this law was of course immediately communicated to the Egyptian Government and effectively guaranteed the participation of the United States in the new *régime*.

The remaining step was a mere official formality which was necessarily compelled to await the actual organization of the courts. On being advised by the Vice-Deputy Consul-General of the United States that the new courts were officially installed on January 1, 1876, and had begun to hear cases regularly on February 27, the President, on March 27, 1876, issued a Presidential Proclamation formally suspending consular jurisdiction in Egypt, "during the pleasure of the President" in so far as the new jurisdiction covered the same matters.[3]

[2] "As Congress, however, has by law provided for the discharge of judicial functions by consuls of the United States in that quarter under the Treaty of 1830, I have not felt at liberty formally to accept the proposed change without the assent of Congress." See *Messages and Papers of the Presidents* (ed. 1898), VII, 238.

[3] For copy of this proclamation see *infra*, Appendix K. In the event of a diplomatic agreement being reached to transfer to the Mixed Courts the existing criminal jurisdiction of the Consular Courts (or a portion of it),

In the meantime the judges representing the United States had been
appointed and had entered upon their duties.

During the early negotiations for the establishment of the Mixed
Courts, it appeared doubtful whether the United States would contribute judges to the new judiciary. Such a doubt was expressed by
the government in 1870, but was coupled with the reservation that it
would desire in any event to remain within "the range of choice of the
Egyptian Government and stand upon an equal footing in this respect with the other Christian powers." In 1873 we find Nubar Pasha
asking the American representative, "Why should our country be
deprived of the luminaries which your country can bring us?" A year
later the French Consul-General, in a letter to his Minister of Foreign Affairs, observed that "certain of the Powers, notably England,
the United States and Russia, appear to be renouncing, for the present, their right to send judges to the lower courts. General Stanton
tells me that the salaries of English judges throughout the three king-
doms are so high that they would reluctantly consent to expatriate
themselves. And as for the Americans and Russians, their colonies
are composed of a few protégés, but very few nationals."

These hesitations, however, were as already indicated dispelled before the opening of the courts, and the United States has been continuously represented in both the upper and lower bodies.[4]

In the Court of Appeals its first representative was Judge Victor
Barringer, formerly attorney-general of North Carolina, who was
named to the Court of Appeals on its inauguration in 1875 and remained on the bench until his resignation in 1894. His three immediate
successors on the upper court were Judge Anthony M. Keiley of
Virginia (1894–1902), Judge George Sherman Batcheller of New
York (1902–08), and Judge Somerville Pinkney Tuck (1908–20).
Each of these three judges had previously served in the District Courts
—their total lengths of service in the Mixed Courts being twenty-one
years for Judge Batcheller and sixteen years each in the case of his
two colleagues.

Judge Batcheller had been named to the District Court at Cairo on
its opening in 1875 and resigned in 1885 to enter politics in New York.
After serving in the New York legislature and as Assistant Secretary

the question may arise as to whether the authorization of the act of 1874
can be said to cover the new conditions presented a half century later;
or whether a new congressional authority will not be required.

[4] With the exception of the period of a year, 1920–21, in the Court of
Appeals, due to difficulty encountered in the choice and approval of a
nominee.

of the Treasury and as Minister to Portugal, he returned to the Mixed Courts in 1897, and after five years in the District Court at Cairo was named to the Court of Appeals.

The other American judges, who served only in the District Courts, have been Judge Philip Hicky Morgan (Louisiana) (1877–80); Judge Elbert E. Farman (1885–89); Judge Ernest H. Crosby (1889–94); Judge Walker Fearn (Alabama) (1894–97); Judge William Grant Van Horne (Utah) (1902–24); Judge Walter van Rensselaer Berry (New York) (1908–11).

The four present American representatives on the courts are Judge M. Pierre Crabités of Louisiana, appointed in 1911 to the District Court at Cairo, Judge Robert L. Henry (D.C.L., Oxford) of Illinois, appointed to the Alexandria District Court in 1924, Judge Julian Wright, for several years a resident of Paris, appointed to the Cairo District Court in January, 1930, and the author of the present volume, appointed to the Court of Appeals in 1921, one year after the retirement of Judge Tuck, whose happy memory is still green in judicial circles in Egypt.

I

BY THE PRESIDENT OF THE UNITED STATES OF AMERICA:

A PROCLAMATION:

WHEREAS by the first section of an act entitled "An act to authorize the President to accept for citizens of the United States the jurisdiction of certain tribunals in the Ottoman dominions and Egypt, established or to be established under the authority of the Sublime Porte and of the Government of Egypt," approved March 23, 1874, it was enacted as follows:

That whenever the President of the United States shall receive satisfactory information that the Ottoman Government or that of Egypt has organized other tribunals on a basis likely to secure to citizens of the United States in their domains the same impartial justice which they now enjoy there under the judicial functions exercised by the minister, consuls, and other functionaries of the United States pursuant to the act of Congress approved the 22d of June, 1860, entitled "An act to carry into effect provisions of the treaties between the United States, China, Persia, and other countries giving certain judicial powers to ministers and consuls or other functionaries of the United States in those countries, and for other purposes,'' he is hereby authorized to suspend the operations of said acts as to the dominions in which such tribunals may be organized so far as the jurisdiction of said tribunals may embrace matters now cognizable by the minister, consuls, or other functionaries of the United States in said dominions, and to notify the Government of the Sublime Porte, or that of Egypt, or either of them, that the United States during such suspension will, as aforesaid, accept for their citizens the jurisdiction of the tribunals aforesaid over citizens of the United States which has heretofore been exercised by the minister, consuls, or other functionaries of the United States.

And whereas satisfactory information has been received by me that the Government of Egypt has organized other tribunals on a basis likely to secure to citizens of the United States in the dominions subject to such Government the impartial justice which they now enjoy there under the judicial functions exercised by the minister, consul, or other functionaries of the United States pursuant to the said act of Congress approved June 22, 1860:

Now, therefore, I, Ulysses S. Grant, President of the United States of America, by virtue of the power and authority conferred upon me by the said act approved March 23, 1874, do hereby suspend during the pleasure of the President the operation of the said act approved June 22, 1860, as to the said dominions subject to the Government of Egypt in which such tribunals have been organized, so far as the jurisdiction of said tribunals may embrace matters now cognizable by the minister, consuls, or other functionaries of the United States in said dominions, except as to cases actually commenced before the date hereof.

In witness whereof I have hereunto set my hand and caused the seal of the United States to be affixed.

       Done at the city of Washington, *this 27th day of March,* (SEAL.) *A.D. 1876,* and of the Independence of the United States of America the one hundredth.

U. S. GRANT.

By the President:
  HAMILTON FISH,
    Secretary of State.[5]

  [5] *Messages and Papers of the Presidents* (Government Printing Office), VII, 390.

J

EXTRACTS FROM THE EGYPTIAN NATIONAL BUDGET

FOR THE FISCAL YEAR 1929–1930 AS AFFECTING THE MIXED COURTS

(*Figures indicate Egyptian pounds. The value of an Egyptian pound is five dollars.*)

Egyptian Pounds (L.E.)

Receipts   1,325,000
Expenditures   426,809
_____
Net Revenue   898,191

RECEIPTS—DETAIL

JUDICIAL FEES:

Civil and Commercial Section

Drafting and copying fees   185,000
Reimbursement of travelling expenses . . .   70,000
Stamp duty   45,000
Ad valorem fees:
  On judgments   55,000
  On adjudications   40,000

Criminal Section

Drafting and copying fees   2,000
Fines and confiscations   2,000

REGISTRATION AND NOTARIAL FEES:
Drafting and copying fees   90,000
Conservation fees   30,000
Stamp duty   5,000
Special paper and photographic reproductions   26,000
Ad valorem fees:
  On transfer of property   675,000
  On mortgages and judgment charges . . .   30,000
  On other deeds   70,000

EXPENDITURES—DETAIL

JUDICIAL EXPENSES
SALARIES, WAGES, AND ALLOWANCES

	Salary Scale	Amount 1929–30 L.E.
JUDGES:		
Court of Appeals:		
Foreign (10)	1,800–2,200	21,650
Native (6)	1,200–1,600	9,050
Tribunals of First Instance:		
Foreign (36)	1,400–1,800	59,850
Native (17)	800–1,200	19,150
PARQUET:		
Procureur-General	1,800–2,200	2,200
Chief of Parquet	1,000–1,400	1,400
Chiefs of Parquet (2)	800–1,200	1,800
Chief of Parquet	800–1,000	850
Substitutes (5)	540– 780	3,120
Assistant substitutes (4)	240– 600	1,014
ADMINISTRATIVE:		
Chief Registrar and Inspector (2) .	900–1,140	2,260
Chief Registrars (3)	720– 960	2,952
Secretary to Parquet		780
Registrars (2)		1,596
Secretary Court of Appeals . . .		840
Chief Interpreter		648
Chief Bailiff	540– 840	840
Sub-inspectors (2)		1,560
Chief Accountant		840
Registrar Accountants (2) . . .		1,560
Registrars (9)		5,334
Assistant Registrars (5)		2,742
Interpreters (2)	240– 600	966
Secretaries (2)		972
Chief Bailiffs (3)		1,656
Interpreters (7)	240– 516	3,414

	Salary Scale	Amount 1929–30 L.E.
Bailiffs (26)		8,490
Secretary		378
Assistant Secretary	180– 468	336
Assistant Accountant		264
Aide Controleur, taxes		294
Interpreters, 2d class		3,549

CLERICAL:

Employees Grade A (83)	240– 516	32,694
Employees Grade B (188) . . .	120– 336	44,474
Employees Grade C (239) . . .	72– 216	30,672
Special increases		252

NON-CIVIL SERVICE CLERICAL POSTS:

Chief Ushers (5)	710
Assistant Chief Usher	137
Ushers (32)	3,097
Messengers, Farrashes, etc. (103) .	6,810

ALLOWANCES:

Secretary Mixed Courts Legislative Assembly	70
Delegate Cashier	120

TRANSPORT, TRANSFER, AND TRAVELING ALLOWANCES	50,700

UNIFORMS AND CLOTHING	1,027

RENTS:

Office of Cairo delegation	624
Office of Alexandria delegation . .	144
Office of Mansourah delegation . .	459
Annex to Alexandria Court . . .	1,560

LAND REGISTRATION EXPENSES

ADMINISTRATIVE:

Registrars of mortgages (3) . . .	540– 840	2,310
Sub-inspector	540– 840	672
Registrars (3)	240– 600	1,584
Interpreter, 1st class	240– 516	486

	Salary Scale	Amount 1929–30 L.E.
Interpreters, 2d class (4)	180– 468	1,158
Employees (19)	180– 468	4,004

CLERICAL:

Employees Grade A (24)	240– 516	8,742
Employees Grade B (80)	120– 336	18,680
Employees Grade C (145) . . .	72– 216	20,493
Special increases		132

NON-CIVIL SERVICE:
Posts of various categories (52) . .   2,674

UNIFORMS AND CLOTHING   195

MISCELLANEOUS CHARGES

Carried in Budgets of Other Departments than Ministry of Justice

MINISTRY OF PUBLIC WORKS:
On account of construction new courthouse, Cairo, estimated total cost L.E. 160,000 50,000

MINISTRY OF INTERIOR (Police) 617

MINISTRY OF COMMUNICATIONS (Post Office) 3,842

PENSIONS (Judicial Section alone) 39,453

K

CAPITULATIONS
British Note
"Your Excellency.

Paragraph II of the proposals provides as follows:

'His Britannic Majesty recognizes that the capitulatory regime now existing in Egypt is no longer in accordance with the spirit of the times and with the present state of Egypt.'

'His Britannic Majesty accordingly undertakes to use all his influence with the Powers possessing capitulatory rights in Egypt to obtain, in conditions which will safeguard the legitimate interests of foreigners, the transfer to the Mixed Tribunals of the jurisdiction of the existing Consular Court, and the application of Egyptian legislation to foreigners.'

"It will be useful if I explain to Your Excellency the lines on which I think this reform of the capitulatory regime might well proceed, as I shall be prepared to support the efforts of the Egyptian Government to conclude arrangements with the Powers on these lines when a treaty based on the proposals comes into force.

"It was hoped in 1920, when negotiations were in progress between the British and Egyptian Governments, that arrangements might be made for the closing by foreign Powers of their Consular Courts in Egypt. Draft Laws were accordingly prepared in that year extending the existing jurisdiction of the Mixed Tribunals, and enabling them to exercise all the jurisdiction now exercised by the Consular Courts.

"I shall be prepared to agree to the utilisation of those draft Laws as the basis of the reform of the capitulatory regime if foreign Powers are willing to transfer to the Mixed Tribunals the jurisdiction of their Consular Courts.

"On points of detail many changes will no doubt be required.

"These must be discussed by experts.

"There are, however, certain modifications which will, I think, be necessary in any event, and which I desire to take this opportunity of pointing out to Your Excellency.

"It may be difficult for some Powers to agree to the transfer to the Mixed Tribunals of all suits relating to the "Status Personnel" of their nationals.

"Transfer in the case of these questions should be facultative.

"Jurisdiction in such matters should remain with the consular authorities unless an agreement is made between the Egyptian Government and the foreign government concerned for its transfer to the Mixed Tribunals.

"I anticipate agreement that the Mixed Tribunals should exercise jurisdiction in these matters in cases where British subjects are concerned.

"In the case of pardons or remissions of sentences imposed on foreigners, and also in connection with the execution of capital sentences imposed on foreigners, the Minister of Justice will consult the Judicial Adviser, so long as that official is retained, before tendering his advice to the King.

"I recognise that the conditions in which the Capitulations are at present applied as regards the power of the Egyptian Government to legislate for or to impose taxation on Foreigners are no longer consistent with modern conditions.

"I should be prepared to agree that in future any assent which is necessary before Egyptian legislation, including fiscal legislation, is applied to foreigners shall be given by the General Assembly of the Mixed Tribunals, except in the case of legislation relating to the constitution or jurisdiction of the Mixed Tribunals themselves, which should not come into force until it has been approved by the Powers.

"It should be the duty of the General Assembly of the Mixed Tribunals to satisfy itself that the legislation in question is not inconsistent with the principles generally adopted in modern legislation which is applicable to foreigners, and, with particular relation to legislation of a fiscal character, that it does not inequitably discriminate against foreigners including foreign companies.

"An extension of the criminal jurisdiction of the Mixed Tribunals will necessitate the preparation and promulgation of a new Code of Criminal Procedure.

"The draft laws prepared in 1920 contain certain provisions of importance on this subject of criminal procedure (Articles 10–27 of Law 11, draft of the 18th April, 1920), and Your Excellency will no doubt agree that the new Criminal Code should not diverge from the principles laid down in these articles.

"There are certain matters as to which it will be necessary for agreement to be reached between the Egyptian Government and His Britannic Majesty's Government in the United Kingdom, but I do not think it necessary to do more at the moment than mention these subjects.

"The first is the definition of the word 'Foreigner' for the purposes of the proposed extension of the jurisdiction of the Mixed Tribunals.

"I understand from Your Excellency that the Codes now enforced by the Native Courts in Egypt, subject to the Native Courts all persons in Egypt other than those who by Law, usage or treaty are withdrawn from their jurisdiction.

"I am content to accept this principle provided that it is understood that all foreigners who have enjoyed the benefit of the capitulatory regime in the past will fall under the jurisdiction of the Mixed Tribunals irrespective of changes of sovereignty effected after the War of 1914–18.

"The second is the increase in the personnel of the Mixed Tribunals which will be necessitated by the proposed extension of their jurisdiction, and, as part of this question, the new functions of the Procureur General of the Mixed Tribunals and the Staff which will be necessary to enable him to discharge those functions satisfactorily.

"The Judicial Adviser will, so long as that official is retained, be consulted with regard to the appointment of foreign judges in the Mixed Tribunals and of foreign members of the Parquet, if any."

INDEX

About, Edmond, 30
Accusatory system, 209
Acquittal, 209
Act de gestion, 231
Administration, act of, 227, 231, 232
Advisers, legal, 316 n.
Affectation hypothécaire, 171
Agrégés, 272
Ahmed le Fellah, 30
Aid, free legal, 266; system of, 267–268
Alexandria, bombardment of, 52; Municipality of, 108, 246; riots of 1921, 69
Alexandria Tramway Case, 113, 231–232
Alimony, 296
America, 28, 220, 238; Government of, 340; *see also United States*
Amos, M. Sheldon, 55 n.; quoted, 155 n.
Analogy, principle of, 153
Anglo-Egyptian Proposals, of 1927, 345; of 1929, 211, 328; extracts from, 399
Anglo-Egyptian Treaties, 100, 331, 341
Anglo-French accord, 57
Anglo-French Agreement of 1874, 80
Antidrug Act of 1925, 313; of 1928, 313, 323; revision of, 323
Antiquities, preservation of, 231
Antiquities Service, 230
Appeal, 122, 171; cross-, 168 n.; from consular jurisdiction, 9; on points of law, 206, 209; right of, 199, 255, 268–269
Appeals, Court of, 12, 45, 71; dis-

tribution of judges in, 82; justices of, 72; legislative actions of, 302 n., 323; plenary sessions of, 123–124; position of, 300; proposed changes, 71; special commissions of, 52; vacancies in, 77; *see also* Appellate Court
Appellate Court, duties and responsibilities of its President, 135; plenary sessions of, 131; powers of, 308; size of chambers, 124; *see also* Court of Appeals
Appels incident, 168 n.
Apprenticeship, legal, 121, 253–254
Arguments, oral, 144
Aristotle, 159
Armenians, 11; orthodox, 285
Assessors, 12, 125, 204, 205, 343; commercial, 205; election of, 125; foreign, 125, 214; institution of, 126; judge-, 194; list of, 205; nationality of, 205; rights of, 205; service of, 126
Assizes, Courts of, 220; reform in, 217
Astreints, 170
Attachments, property, 108, 169; execution of, 169; and garnishment, 168; Mixed Courts in, 109
Attorney, District, 201
Austria, 9, 26, 28, 37, 40, 69, 78, 94, 100, 102, 105, 120, 224; surrender of capitulatory rights, 40, 70; Consular Courts of, 65; representation of in Mixed Courts, 70; treaty with Egypt in 1929, 103
Avoué, office of, 163, 164, 247

Badges, official, 133

from Mixed Courts, 331; exterritorial privileges, 331; infringement of sovereignty, 350; jurisdiction of, 36, 44, 101, 239, 280, 288–289; organization of, 289; proposals for reform of, 294; suppression of criminal jurisdiction of, 289
Courts of Wards, 283–285; reforms in, 284
Crabités, Judge, 80 n.; quoted, 340 n.
Credit, commercial in Egypt, 108
Crédit Lyonnais, 52
Creditors, foreign, 174; union of, 178
Crimes, categories of, 195
Cromer, Lord, 27, 41 n., 47, 63 n., 82 n., 276, 283, 304, 317 n., 324, 336 n.; achievements of, 333; plans for reform, 305, 332, 333; quoted, 301, 302, 303, 307, 334 n.
Cross-examination, right of, 206, 262; limitations of, 187
Curzon, Lord, 62 n., 341
Custodian, public, 64
Customs, 315; administration of, 108; regulations, 319
Czechoslovakia, 100

Date, certification of, 248
Death, penalty of, 175
Debtors, property of, 168
Decisions, deliberation in, 140; postponement of, 140; rapidity of, 140; reports and publications of, 158; sur le champ, 140
Decorations, honorary, of judges, 343
Decree, 173; of 1889, 314, 383
Deeds, recording of, 248, 321; registered, 250; unregistered, 251
Default, sentence by, 198
Defense, "vexatious," 174
Délégations, 250

Denmark, 28, 40, 81, 222, 340
Digest, legal system of, 156
Disciplinary Commission, 244
Dispositif, 143
Distribution of Proceeds, Courts for, 252
District Courts, 71, 120; admission to, 256; in bankruptcy, 176; judges of, 72, 204, 367–369; jurisdiction of, 237; selection of its Presidents, 134; size of chambers, 124; special chamber of, 51
Dockets, court, 138 n.
Documents, admissibility of, 192; examination of, 192; filing of, 141; language of, 141; verifications of, 191
Domestic relations, 98, 149, 277, 288, 289
Domicile, inviolability of, 318, 331
Dossier, 117, 137–140, 202; object of system, 141
Double dégré, 119
Draft Treaty, 344
Dragomen, 103, 323; native consular, 105
Droits de chancellerie, 318
Duguit, Leon, 235 n.; quoted, 234

Écoles de Cadi, 283
Education, legal, 253, 270, 272, 273
Egypt, absorption of legislation, 58; administration of in 1914, 64 n.; Capitulations of, 3; Constitution of, 233, 234, 342; cosmopolitanism of, 276; the Government, 238; judicial institutions of, 63; national prosperity, 349; obligations to the Mixed Courts, 54, 240, 350; political status of, 62; a Protectorate, 62; reciprocal rights of, 245; self-government of, 33
Egyptian Civil Code, divisions of, 149

Imprisonment, 200; for bankruptcy, 181

Inchcape, Lord, 237

Incompatibility, of professions, 266

Indemnity, equitable, 233; law of 1923, 69, 245

Indictments, 203, 205

Industrial development in Egypt, 117

Instruction, 201

Interest, legal rate of, 128

International Commission, of 1869, 26; of 1880, 74; of 1903, 306; of 1917 and its plan, 335; on the Public Debt, 224; *see also* Commissions

Interpreters, court, 141

Interrogatories, 187

Inventions, protection of native, 161

Irrigation, legislation affecting, 151, 320; service of, 227

Ismail Pasha, deposition of, 48–49

Italians, 28, 55, 60, 94, 220, 224, 257, 275, 316 n.

Italy, 26, 37, 40, 44, 78, 81, 120, 126, 222, 237 n.; code of, 159 n.; consular courts of, 211; delay of renewal of adhesion to Powers, 43; and Nubar Pasha, 30; as protector of Swiss, 104

Japan, 40 n., 101

Jeopardy, double, 206

Jews, 11, 257, 285; *see also* Rabbis

Judges, appointments of in Mixed Courts, 349; apportionment of, 73, 79–80, 82, 136; apprenticeship of, 83; -assessors, 194; commissioning of, 43; compensation and salaries of, 45, 83; consular, 291, 294; costume, 133; discipline and impeachment of, 86; Egyptian, 201; honors and decorations of, 87; independence of, 88, 157–158; foreign, 15, 80, 214, 239; lay-, 204, 218; legal experience of in Egypt, 77; naming of, 43, 73, 75; numbers of, 120; in political and diplomatic life, 88; promotions of, 77, 94; qualifications of, 75–76; recruitment of, 77 n.; religious, 284; rotation of, 136; referee and bankruptcy, 177, 252; as reporters, 76; responsibility, 159; retirement age of, 86; schools for, 283; status of, 43; tenure of office, 86; *see also* Justices

Judgments, classes of, 170; by default, 170–171; execution of, 169; invalidation of, 173

Judicial Adviser, 77; appointment of, 56; British, 55, 278; position of, 57; services of, 55

Judicial Sales, courts for, 252

Judiciary, system of organization, 119; discipline of, 173; independence of, 15, 87, 342; function of separate from legislature, 324

Juge, 72

Juge d'Instruction, 200–202, 213; authority of, 202

Jurisdiction, 112; appeals from, 203; categories of, 247, 297; civil, 45; commercial, 45, 127; conflicts of, 294; *contentieuse*, 247; criminal, 45, 195, 342; criminal and the Mixed Courts, 323, 346; extrajudicial, 168; extraterritorial, 294; *gracieuse*, 168, 247; plan for unification of, 335

Jurisprudence, comparative, 282; *constante*, 158; Egyptian, 147

Jury, 16, 196, 291; charge to, 208; common-law, 205; criminal, in Egypt, 220; Grand, 203, 213; impaneling of, 207; lay element

in, 218–220; nationality of, 208; system, 194, 207; verdict of, 209
Justice, denial of, 173; international, 51; obstruction of, 199; system of in Egypt, 351
Justices, British, 309; of Court of Appeals, 367; foreign, 312; rotation of, 207; *see also* Judges

Kâït Bey, capitulations of, 5
Khedive, deposition of, 62; suits against, 46, 47
Kings, Valley of the, 230
Kitchener, Lord, 336 n.; quoted, 186
Koran, law of, 6, 281, 283; changes in, 282

"La Coutume," as a source of law, 152
Laloë, Francis, 54 n., 351 n.
Land system, 116, 249; proposed reform of, 249
Landlords, 68
Landowners, 315; protection of foreign, 248
Language, Arabic, 132, 133, 141, 245, 271, 273, 278; of the Courts, 132; English, 217, 273, 336, 337, 338; French, 54, 75, 76, 132, 141, 146, 187, 273, 278, 336, 338; Greek, 141, 187; Italian, 132, 133; judicial, 141; official, 132
Lausanne, Treaty of, 7
Laws, accessibility of, 114; administration of, 145; Admiralty, 117; Anglicization of, 336; bankruptcy, 196; constitutional, 233; common, 148, 153, 158, 192, 203, 237; consular, 294; corporate, 106, 117; family, 284; foreign patent, 161; international, 117, 296; interpretation of, 153; maritime, 117; "mixed," 307; native, 297; national, 65; re-

forms in, 306, 335; natural, 154, 160; secularization of, 283; source of in Egypt, 151, 159; statute, 150, 297; substantive, 148; testamentary, 117; written, 154, 158, 272
Lawyers, foreign, 256; in journalism, 264; restriction of activities, 262; professional life of, 263; rights and liberties of, 264; visiting, 256
Legal systems, as source of law of Mixed Courts, 148, 297; American, 177, 233, 235 n., 272; Anglo-Saxon, 90, 138, 156, 165, 183, 198, 200, 210, 222, 223, 236, 247, 338; Austrian, 258; of Egypt, 167, 183, 255; English, 156, 217, 256, 290, 336; of France, 90, 116 n., 122, 128, 140, 150, 152, 153, 156, 163, 183, 185, 194, 198, 200, 207, 220, 222, 226, 236, 247, 248, 255, 258, 262, 338; German, 217; Italian, 258; Latin, 166, 183, 207, 269, 278, 338; Mohammedan, 116 n., 148, 274, 282; Mussulman, 172, 282 n.; penal, 195; Roman, 116 n., 119, 147, 148, 153, 266, 282; Turkish, 287
Legislation, by diplomacy, 59, 197, 221, 301, 303, 330; Egyptian, 331; fiscal, 329; internal, 150; judicial, 151, 154–155; *mixte*, 307; need for, 162; separation from judicial function, 324; social object of, 153; during the War, 67
Legislative Assembly, creation of in Mixed Courts, 306; composition of, 308; procedure, 309–312, 320; foreign interests in, 312
Leon, Edwin de, 10 n., 48 n.
Lesseps, Ferdinand de, 24, 35
Levantines, 275
Liability, governmental, 226, 234;

principles of, 229; theory of, 223

Liberum veto, right of, 301

Library, 258, 353; of Alexandria, 353; *Judiciaire*, 357

Licence en droit, 271

Lien, property, 170

Limitations, statutes of, 209; in commercial courts, 128

Liquidation, compulsory, 179; judicial, 175

Litigants, nationality of, 136

Litigation, civil, 110, 120, 348; commercial, 110, 115, 120, 125, 348; current, 112–113; expedition of, 321; land, 115; real estate, 120; public interest in, 115; tax on, 259

Livre d'Or, 21 n., 58 n., 278 n., 341 n.; *see also* Golden Book

Lloyd, Lord, 60, 136 n., 344

Low, Sidney, 234 n.

Luxor, 230

McIlwraith, Sir Malcolm, 55 n., 63 n., 305 n.; quoted, 70 n., 156 n.

Magistrate, examining, 200

Magistrature, assise, 91; *debout*, 91

Malfeasance, judicial, 172

Manoury, M., 145 n.

Marriage and divorce, laws pertaining to, 280, 284, 285, 288, 296; secularization of, 288

Martial law, 62, 64, 65, 67, 81; abolition of, 102, 245; *régime* of, 104 n., 320; post-war application of, 67; suspension of, 69

Medical Practices Act, 314 n., 322, 323

Medicine, right to practice, 317

Meglis El Hasby, 283, 287

Merchant, definition of, 180

Millerand, President, 265 n.

Milner, Lord, quoted, 39; Mission, 245, 336, 339

Ministère Public, 90

Ministry of justice, 55, 94; attitude to Mixed Courts, 56 n.; Egyptian, 278

Misdemeanors, 195, 199; Court of, 199, 203, 204; composition of, 217; reform in, 217; trial in, 205

Mixed Courts, *see separate heading*

Mixed Courts, Anglicization of, 336–337; annual term of, 132; as arbiter, 296; in bankruptcy, 174, 181, 182, 215; Bar of, 256, 337; budget, 239; by-laws of, 267; and Capitulations, 63 n., 330, 331; and Consular courts, 104, 295, 330–331; contact with people, 121; control of, 241; diplomacy in, 58; and Egypt, 105, 342, 352; extension of, 45, 329; expense and maintenance, 239, 240, 349; foreigners in, 351; and foreign states, 236; functions of, 247; future of, 332, 349, 352; contact with Egyptian Government, 65, 69, 232; growth of, 251; guarantees of, 213, 222; history of, 1, 4, 16, 58, 105, 221, 330, 349; impartiality of, 80, 82, 136; independence of, 238; jails of, 211; judicial powers and output, 252, 300;

  jurisdiction of, 44, 97, 100, 107, 110, 149, 210, 223, 230, 232
  administrative, 213, 230, 236
  civil, 15, 97
  commercial, 15, 97
  criminal, 15, 90–97, 105, 122–123, 150, 181, 195, 216, 218 ff., 313, 342, 343, 347; limitations of, 211; proposed transfer of to Consular Courts, 331–333
  Governmental, 69, 145, 224, 225

121; judges, 121; jurisdiction of, 130; sessions of, 132

Sweden, 28, 81, 340

Switzerland, 22, 28, 78, 79, 81, 309; civil code of, 159; Judges, 309; peoples as protégés, 103

Syndics, 177; duties of, 177; official, 176; selection of, 177

Synod of the Nile, 286

Syrians, 99, 245, 257, 282, 285

Talmud, the, 285

Tarbouche, 133

Tariff, protective, 315

Taxation, 308; of foreigners, 314; right of, 316

Taxes, authorized by Powers, 317; automobile, 317; on date-palms, 315 n.; for foreigners and natives, 315; *ghaffir*, 315 n.; house, 315; income, 106; land, 315 n.; land registration, 250; on local products, 317; municipal, 316; professional, 318; registry, 251

Tenants, protection of, 68, 321

Testimony, oral, 183, 184, 187; importance of, 188; right to, 184

Tierce opposition, 171

Titles, honorary, 343

Tobacco Monopoly, 237

Torrens System, 249

Torts, 117

Trade, regulation of during War, 64

Trademarks, 117, 160; registration of, 161; violation of, 162

Trader, bankrupt, 174

Tribunals, 72; administrative, 276; *des Contraventions*, 198; international, 116; Mixed, 9, 331; native, 296

Triple Alliance, 58

Trust, religious, 296

Trustees, official, 176

Turkey, 99, 237, 285, 315, 330; and

Capitulations, 5, 7; capitulatory privileges guaranteed, 6; codes of, 147; concessions of, 34, 229; in Egypt, 5, 33, 62, 227; termination of sovereignty, 63; treaties with, 316

Turkish Tribute Bonds, 95

Turkish Tribute Case, 228

Tutankhamen, 230

United States, 26, 37, 40, 42, 78, 81, 340; and capitulatory agreements, 5; Consular Courts of, 291–293; delay of renewal of adherence to Mixed Courts, 43; and Mixed Courts, 385–395; responsibilities of consular officers, 293; *see also* America

University of Egypt, 270

University of El Azhar, 274, 283

Usage, law of, 152

Van Ackere, Judge, quoted, 155 n.

Verdicts, correction of, 207; criminal, 206

Versailles, Treaty of, 40, 102

Veto, right of, 301

Wakfs, 116, 282 n., 296

Walton, Professor, 273

War, and Mixed Courts, 69, 286; effects of, 62, 69, 229, 273; legislation during, 67; litigation during, 70; political changes of, 99

War, Franco-Prussian, 21, 33

"Watching brief," 167

Wekil, 287

Witnesses, attendance of, 185; challenge of, 185; examination of, 184, 186, 187; oath of, 186, 187; privileges of, 185; testimony of, 185, 186, 206

Women, as bar members, 257; as stagiaires, 257

Zaghloul Pasha, 283, 327